PICKETT'S
CHARGE
IN
HISTORY
AND
MEMORY

CIVIL WAR AMERICA

Gary W. Gallagher, editor

The University of North Carolina Press

Chapel Hill and London

CAROL REARDON

PICKETT'S CHARGE

IN HISTORY AND MEMORY

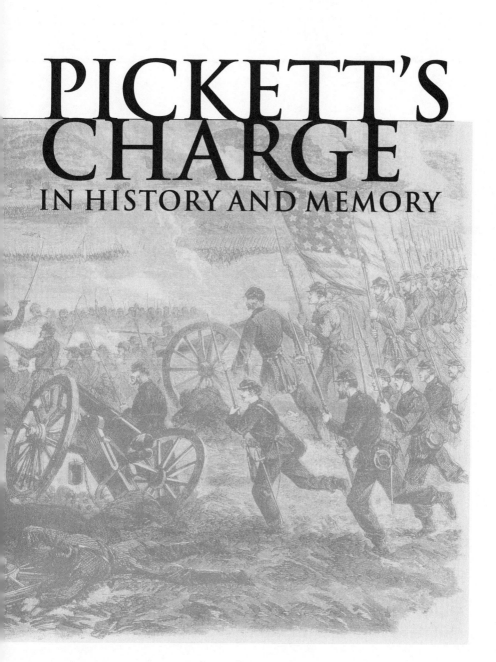

© 1997

The University of North Carolina Press

All rights reserved

Manufactured in the United States of America

The paper in this book meets the guidelines for
permanence and durability of the Committee on
Production Guidelines for Book Longevity of the
Council on Library Resources.

Library of Congress Cataloging-in-Publication Data

Reardon, Carol.

Pickett's charge in history and memory / Carol Reardon.

p. cm. — (Civil War America)

Includes bibliographical references (p.   ) and index.

ISBN 0-8078-2379-1 (cloth: alk. paper)

1. Gettysburg (Pa.), Battle of, 1863.   2. Gettysburg (Pa.),
Battle of, 1863—Historiography.   3. Pickett, George E.
(George Edward), 1825–1875.   I. Title.   II. Series.

E475.53.R33   1998

973.7'349—dc21   97-10965

CIP

01 00 99 98 97   5 4 3 2 1

For Seminar 13,

U.S. Army War College

Class of 1994

CONTENTS

Acknowledgments *ix*

Prologue. History, Memory, and Pickett's Charge *1*

Chapter 1. Disconnected Threads *11*

Chapter 2. Scarcely Anybody Can Give a Correct Account *39*

Chapter 3. History as It Ought to Have Been *62*

Chapter 4. Binding the Wounds of War *84*

Chapter 5. Monuments to Memory *108*

Chapter 6. Southern Dissenters Speak Out *131*

Chapter 7. Virginia Victorious *154*

Chapter 8. Hand-Grips at the Sacred Wall *176*

Epilogue. The Old Bright Way of the Tales *199*

Notes *215*

Bibliography *255*

Index *275*

ILLUSTRATIONS

Map of the deployment of Union and Confederate commands 7

Lt. Frank Aretas Haskell *14*

Colonel Hall's map *22*

Maj. Gen. George E. Pickett *33*

The first visual image of the July 3 charge based on fact
   to appear in the Northern press *45*

Maj. Gen. Winfield S. Hancock *47*

Manuscript map of Gen. A. R. Wright's and Pickett's attacks *58*

James Walker's depiction of the events of July 3 at Gettysburg *71*

Peter F. Rothermel's canvas of the events of July 3 *72*

Woodcut of Robert E. Lee meeting Pickett's men after the
   July 3 charge *74*

Lt. Gen. James Longstreet *86*

LaSalle Corbell Pickett *100*

Pickett's division memorial in Hollywood Cemetery, Richmond *106*

The field of Pickett's Charge in the 1880s *111*

Veterans of the 13th, 14th, and 16th Vermont remembered
   their flank attack this way *117*

A perspective of the July 3 charge that focuses on the
   fight near Ziegler's Grove and the Bryan barn *123*

Brig. Gen. James Johnston Pettigrew *134*

Judge Walter Clark *148*

Map offered in defense of North Carolina's claim to have
   advanced farther on July 3 than any other command *151*

Kirkwood Otey *156*

Capt. W. Stuart Symington *161*

Union veterans return to the high water mark on
   November 19, 1885 *178*

Virginia and Pennsylvania fly their flags at the stone wall, July 1913 *193*

Pickett's Virginians and Webb's Pennsylvanians at
   the stone wall, July 1913 *194*

ACKNOWLEDGMENTS

Pickett and his men have been a part of my life for almost fifteen years. While I cannot possibly share Sallie Pickett's degree of idolatry for them—that cannot be duplicated—I do take inspiration from them. At times, the prospects for living through a frontal assault against Cemetery Ridge or surviving the pressures of "publish or perish" seemed remarkably similar.

The research for this study had been stored away for more than a decade when Professor Gary W. Gallagher convinced me to disinter it. His ever-so-gentle prodding makes him the godfather of this book, and I am grateful for his encouragement.

Over the years, many institutions have been generous with their time and resources, notably the Museum of the Confederacy, the Virginia State Library, and the Virginia Historical Society in Richmond; the Virginia Military Institute; the Perkins Library at Duke University; and the Southern Historical Collection at Chapel Hill. Members of the Association of Licensed Battlefield Guides and the staff at Gettysburg National Military Park have provided numerous useful insights. The high-quality assistance rendered by the very able historians at the U.S. Army Military History Institute remains in a class by itself. I also thank Louise Hartman for her ability and willingness to ferret out key research material inaccessible north of the Mason-Dixon line.

Throughout the project, my parents, and Skip, Molly, and Taylor provided unstinting and unqualified support of all kinds.

This book is dedicated to the very special group of true professionals who made my year as the Gen. Harold Keith Johnson Visiting Professor of Military History at the Military History Institute an unforgettable one: Seminar 13, U.S. Army War College Class of 1994. The stalwarts of "Los Gatos" include: COL Steven P. Ankley, USA; COL Luis Barbosa, Colombian Army; COL Jack Castonguay, USA; COL Edward A. Cerutti, USA; COL Vladimir S. Chugunov, Russian Army; COL Stephen B. Curran, USA; BG J. Russ Groves, now Adjutant General of the Commonwealth of Kentucky; COL David L. Hartman, USA; COL Ancil L. Hicks, USA; COL George A. Higgins, USA; BG Geoffrey C. Lambert, USA; COL Emil F. Meis, III, USA; COL Michael D. Rochelle, USA; Col. J. R. Rosa, USAF; COL Jeffrey A. Sorenson, USA; and Ms. Tina Street, U.S. Army Corps of Engineers. Thanks, too, to the rest of my faculty team: COL Fred E. Bryant, USA; CDR David Birdwell, USN; and especially Col. Mark A. Williams, USAF. The members of Seminar 13 and their families made this civilian visitor a welcome part of their lives, let me rattle on interminably about history's importance, and, in a most special moment, crossed over the stone wall at the Angle with me on 18 September 1993.

Carol Reardon

State College, Pennsylvania

July 1996

PROLOGUE

HISTORY, MEMORY, AND PICKETT'S CHARGE

Lieutenant Frank A. Haskell, who probably saw and then wrote more about the last great Southern assault on Cemetery Ridge at Gettysburg than any other eyewitness on that field, begrudgingly admitted that even his own powers of observation had limitations. After describing to his brother in voluminous detail and colorful prose all he could recall of the stirring events of July 3, 1863, he concluded that "a full account of *the battle as it was* will never, can never be made. Who could sketch the changes, the constant shifting of the bloody panorama? It is not possible." He feared that the great battle's "history, just, comprehensive, complete will never be written." With resignation, he concluded that "by-and-by, out of the chaos of trash and falsehood that the news papers hold, out of the disjointed mass of reports, out of the traditions and tales that come down from the field, some eye that never saw the battle will select, and some pen will write what will be named *the history*."[1]

A perceptive pessimist, Haskell understood that two powerful forces frame the way we recall past events: the objectivity of history—the search for "truth"—and the subjectivity of memory, which shapes perceptions of that "truth." He also realized that the tension between those two forces likely foredoomed to failure the efforts of even the most disinterested chronicler intent on recording for posterity what happened on July 3 at

Gettysburg. Historians indeed would try to reconstruct what happened that day from snippets of description culled from official reports and hundreds of personal testimonies and weave together from these fragments of individual experience what they hoped would be an accurate and coherent narrative. Even the best scholar, however, could not tell the whole story. The selectivity of the soldiers' memories had made this impossible. Years after the war, a Michigan veteran challenged his comrades to "recall, if you can, any engagement of the war and positively state, of your own knowledge, that you passed through some particular field (a wheat field, for instance) when you were ordered forward to charge the enemy's position." He knew that if they remembered crossing through a field at all, they likely would not recall its size, shape, or crop cover because, in battle, "your horizon range was limited" and "many little incidents occurred in your immediate vicinity of which you were not cognizant."[2] Any history of the events of July 3 at Gettysburg, then, must begin with an acknowledgment that traditional research materials for battle studies should be accepted less as objective truth and more, as historian David Thelen suggests, as memories that were "authentic for the person at the moment of construction."[3] Much of the popular appeal the great charge still holds today results from the triumph of the forces of memory over history.

These memories offer valuable insights of their own. Even if they could not comprehend all they saw or did on July 3, soldiers tried for years to explain it to themselves, their families and friends, and even future generations. To celebrate personal survival or to find greater purpose, solace, or inspiration in what they witnessed, they gave in to the seductive, subjective, even self-indulgent pull of memory, preserving only those moments and events that held special meaning to them. The evocative nature of many of these memories easily captured the uncritical eye of chroniclers who neatly imposed a sense of order upon them and, as Haskell predicted, called it "history." He indeed had hit the mark squarely when he suggested that the "eye that never saw the battle" exercised great power in choosing the memories deemed worthy of perpetuation. As a consequence, we know less about what really happened on July 3 at Gettysburg than history purports to tell us.

Nonetheless, that great discriminating "eye" anointed this one single event—the great Confederate charge of July 3—as the pivotal episode of the three-day fight. So much changed, or seemed to change, with the repulse of that assault. Victory finally visited the Army of the Potomac, and the Army of Northern Virginia bore the unaccustomed weight of defeat. As time passed and even greater meaning adhered to the repulse of the attack, the charge and its repulse took on a new role as the line of demarcation that ended all doubts about the resolution of the conflict and presaged the fall of the Confederacy, the end of the war, the continuation of the republic. Thus, this one special episode earned unique names that set it apart from every other military maneuver on that bloody field: "Pickett's Charge" and, for some, "the high water mark of the Rebellion."

Pickett's Charge holds a secure place in our national imagination, but it rests on the double foundation of both history and memory. The two forces have blended together so seamlessly over the years that we cannot separate them now. Over the years, partisan chroniclers, poets, artists, novelists, visitors, even entrepreneurs, have found special inspiration in the events of July 3 at Gettysburg, often in ways the soldiers themselves could not have foreseen. "Memory begins when something in the present stimulates an association," one scholar has suggested.[4] A certain irony attends the fact that, in a nation that loves a winner, we remember the élan of the defeated Southerners before we recall the gallantry of the victorious Union defenders. The endurance in the nation's historical consciousness of Pickett's Charge suggests that it inspired—and still inspires—reflections and emotions that spring from a source far removed from respect for historical "truth."

Indeed, as historian James H. McRandle has argued, when "popular history sings of events and makes them great, it transcends the realm of record and enters that of myth."[5] Over the years, Pickett's Charge has roamed restlessly through both the world of history and the world of myth. It finds an entirely comfortable place in neither realm. We demand much of our past. The most enduring moments that claim places in American public memory—the images that best capture and hold longest the popular interest—possess the ability to bridge past and present. In ever-changing and often contentious ways, these episodes touch on basic values, honored traditions, deep-seated fears, unfulfilled hopes, and unrighted wrongs.[6]

From the time the battle smoke cleared, Pickett's Charge took on this kind of chameleonlike aspect and, through a variety of carefully constructed nuances, adjusted superbly to satisfy the changing needs of Northerners, Southerners, and, finally, the entire nation. In the immediate postwar years, the gallantry and sacrifice of the Confederate infantry on July 3 gave Southerners some much needed heroes to help ease the pangs of defeat and, in some ways, to validate and represent all that was right about the Lost Cause. As times changed, memories of Pickett's Charge proved sufficiently flexible to provide the setting for one of the first visible tests of Northern and Southern readiness to bury forever sectional ill will. Northern forces of reaction against quick reconciliation found in Pickett's Charge a useful emotional touchstone for voicing deep resentment over what they perceived to be the South's successful efforts to rewrite the war's history. Veterans from both armies, including many who had not fought at Gettysburg at all, endowed the events of July 3 with great symbolic meaning that celebrated their contributions to the civic life of their nation and raised concerns about rapid postwar social, political, and economic changes that could destroy what they had fought so hard for. Southern veterans' efforts to secure in the national memory a variety of specific memories of the great charge spawned a particularly vicious literary war that pitted Virginia against North Carolina, Alabama, Mississippi, Florida, and Tennessee in ways that revealed that state pride ran far more deeply than did any commitment to preserving "the truth" of history. Virginia won that war and did so decisively by seamlessly blending appeals to history's objectivity with timeless values of gallantry, heroism, and noble sacrifice that struck chords in the entire nation's historical imagination. Our current memories of an event called "Pickett's Charge" emerge from all these contexts and more, lending credence to a modern scholar's assertion that "the curious refusal of popular history to take cognizance of established facts" results less from sheer ignorance than from "purposes different from professional historical accounts."[7]

Over the years and in many ways the story of Pickett's Charge indeed has found itself suspended precariously between the two realms of history and memory. Certainly the golden anniversary ceremonies at Gettysburg in 1913 demanded little adherence to historical fact. As old men in blue shook hands with old men in gray at a weedy stone wall near a clump of trees, most Americans "knew" in their hearts, if not in their heads, all they needed to "know" about Pickett's Charge.

A few days after he survived Pickett's Charge, Pvt. William H. Jones of the 19th Virginia summed up his entire experience in the "awful Battle at gettysburg" with the very succinct comment that "it was the most awful Battle that I ever have Bin [in] yet."[8] Nearly a century later, chronicler George Stewart began his story of the day's events with a far more effusive statement: "If we grant—as many would be ready to do—that the Civil War furnishes the great dramatic episode of the history of the United States, and that Gettysburg provides the climax of the war, then the climax of the climax, the central moment of American history, must be Pickett's Charge."[9] Between "the most awful Battle" and "the central moment in American history" rests strong testimony to the power of memory.

The historical event called "Pickett's Charge" rests on a foundation of a few "knowns" and a few more credible assumptions. The following is the cast of characters—and their *generally accepted* historical roles—in the military action between Seminary and Cemetery Ridges at Gettysburg on July 3, 1863.[10]

Gen. Robert E. Lee's Confederate Army of Northern Virginia attacked Maj. Gen. George G. Meade's Army of the Potomac on July 1, 1863. After two days of bloody fighting and heavy losses, neither army showed any sign of disengaging.

About midnight on July 3, Meade called together his corps commanders for a council of war. After much discussion, he asked three questions: Should we stay or leave the field? If we stay, do we attack or await attack? If we await attack, how long? One by one, the tired officers recorded their votes to stay, await attack, and wait at least one day. As the meeting broke up, Meade told Brig. Gen. John Gibbon that if Lee attacked on July 3, it would be along his front on Cemetery Ridge.[11]

Lee's own plans, if he had gotten his way, would have made a liar of Meade. He wanted to launch a coordinated assault against both Union flanks. Lt. Gen. Richard Ewell's Second Corps would renew its efforts against the Union right on Culp's Hill, and Lt. Gen. James Longstreet's First Corps would step off from the area around the Peach Orchard against the Union left.[12] That plan quickly fell apart, however, when at 4:30 A.M. the Union XII Corps opened the day's fighting with an effort to recapture their lost trenches at the base of Culp's Hill.

Lee then revisited his options. He deemed disengagement unacceptable. Waiting passively for Meade to move offered no great appeal either. Longstreet urged a move around the Union left to place the Southern army in a solid defensive position between the Union army and Washington.[13] But Lee's comment as he looked out at Cemetery Ridge—"the enemy is there and I am going to strike him"—reveals both his continuing offensive-mindedness and his understanding of prevailing military theory, which taught that a defensive posture did not win decisive battles. As fierce fighting continued on Culp's Hill, Lee discarded his initial plan as unworkable. He chose as the new focal point for his efforts on July 3 just where Meade had predicted, the center of the Northern line atop the gentle slope of Cemetery Ridge. Some of Lee's men—the 1,500-man Georgia brigade under Brig. Gen. Ambrose R. Wright—briefly had pierced that portion of the Union line the evening before.[14] A similar attack in greater strength might succeed, and Lee believed his men could do this.

Many chroniclers have tried to describe the great Southern charge and the impressive Northern defense of July 3. Still, despite the recollections of thousands of eyewitnesses, many of its most important details remain open to conjecture.

The Confederate attack on Cemetery Ridge began with an artillery bombardment to soften the Union line. This much we know. Command arrangements and coordination of the artillery on both sides, the number of Southern guns involved, the number of Northern guns that returned fire, the duration of the cannonade, and the effectiveness of the gunnery all remain points of contention, however.

The size of the attacking force cannot be stated with absolute authority, either. For a few decades after the war, veterans on both sides tended to cite numbers ranging between 17,000 and 20,000. For many more years after that, Longstreet set the standard with his comment that no 15,000 troops ever arrayed for battle could take Cemetery Ridge. Modern histories of the attack have reduced the number to a range somewhere between 10,500 and 13,000.[15] No one "knows" the number. Likewise, contemporary sources reached no consensus on what formation the attacking Southerners employed, what efforts were made to coordinate Pettigrew's and Pickett's separate columns, or what was the exact number of Union troops who deserved credit for participating in the repulse.

When it comes right down to it, tables of organization provide some of the few "knowns" of this day's effort. Lee gave Longstreet tactical command of the attack, but he already had made many key decisions. He had selected the attacking force, for instance, committing two entire divisions and elements of two others. From Longstreet's First Corps came the fresh division commanded by Maj. Gen. George E. Pickett, whose command included three brigades, each comprised of five veteran Virginia infantry regiments. All three of Pickett's brigade commanders at Gettysburg had seen combat before. Brig. Gen. James L. Kemper, a Virginia politician, commanded the 1st, 3rd, 7th, 11th, and 24th Virginia. Brig. Gen. Lewis A. Armistead, a veteran of the antebellum U.S. Army, led the 9th, 14th, 38th, 53rd, and 57th Virginia. A newcomer to the division, West Point-educated Brig. Gen. Richard B. Garnett, led the 8th, 18th, 19th, 28th, and 56th Virginia. With two of the division's brigades left in Virginia to defend Richmond, the strength of Pickett's small division ranged anywhere from a staff officer's assessment of 4,700 to a more modern study that sets the number at closer to 6,100.[16] In the late morning of July 3, Garnett and Kemper deployed their men in the low, open fields of the Spangler farm east of the treeline on Seminary Ridge, Garnett's men stretching north from the farm buildings and Kemper's lining up south of them. A slight

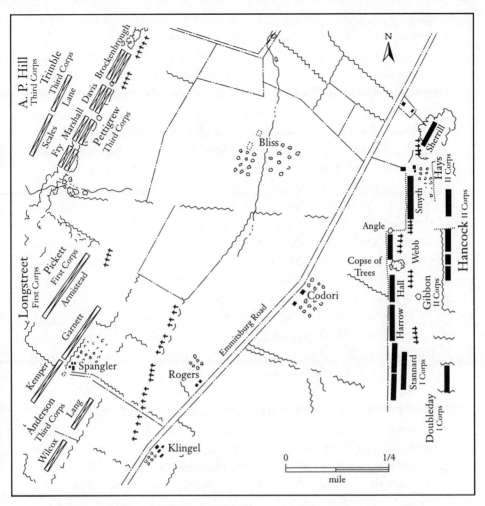

Deployment of Union and Confederate commands, 1 P.M., July 3, 1863

rise just west of the Emmitsburg Road protected them for the time being. In line more or less behind Garnett, Armistead's men remained in the shade of the trees on the ridge until the order came to advance.

The second division assigned to the assault, Brig. Gen. Henry Heth's men of Lt. Gen. A. P. Hill's Third Corps, had opened the battle on July 1. Heth had been wounded that day, and on July 3, Brig. Gen. James Johnston Pettigrew entered on only his second day as acting division commander. He led four brigades. Brig. Gen. James J. Archer's 1st, 7th, and 14th Tennessee, along with the 13th Alabama and 5th Alabama battalion, had opened the battle against Buford's Union cavalry. When Archer became a prisoner later that day, Alabama Col. Burkett D. Fry had replaced him. The 2nd and 42nd Mississippi and the 55th North Carolina of the brigade of Brig. Gen. Joseph R. Davis—nephew of Jefferson Davis—had fought around the Railroad Cut on July 1; the welcome arrival of the 11th Mississippi helped to make good some of their heavy losses. Pettigrew's own brigade, the 11th, 26th, 47th, and 52nd North Carolina now under Col. James K. Marshall of the 52nd, had inflicted horrible casualties on the Iron Brigade in Herbst's Woods on July 1 and absorbed great losses as well. Col. John M. Brockenbrough's small brigade, the 40th, 47th, and 55th Virginia and 22nd Virginia battalion, fought near the McPherson barn on July 1. Pettigrew's men deployed on the reverse slope of Seminary Ridge, behind the McMillan farm. As Lee, Longstreet, and Hill all make clear in postbattle reports, Pettigrew's division was an integral part of the attacking force, not a support element.[17] Since Pickett and Pettigrew would march forth on different axes of advance, cooperation was essential to success, but history is relatively silent on measures taken by any senior leader to assure that troops from two different corps could coordinate their actions in the heat of battle.

To strengthen the striking power of the two divisions, Lee assigned additional troops to the assaulting force. To support Pettigrew, Lee selected two brigades of Maj. Gen. W. Dorsey Pender's division of the Third Corps, that of Brig. Gen. James H. Lane, a Virginian, who led the 7th, 18th, 28th, 33rd, and 37th North Carolina, and that of wounded Brig. Gen. Alfred M. Scales, whose 13th, 16th, 22nd, 34th, and 38th North Carolina now marched under Col. W. Lee Lowrance. Maj. Gen. Isaac R. Trimble held temporary command of these two brigades.

To support Pickett's right flank, Lee chose two more Third Corps brigades from the division of Maj. Gen. Richard H. Anderson. Brig. Gen. Cadmus M. Wilcox's 8th, 9th, 10th, 11th, and 14th Alabama and Col. David Lang's 2nd, 5th, and 8th Florida all had suffered serious losses the previous afternoon.

While Lee's men deployed and prepared for the day's grand assault, across the valley on Cemetery Ridge waited two divisions of Maj. Gen. Winfield S. Hancock's II Corps.[18] This was Hancock's first battle in corps command, but both he and his veteran troops had fought in many earlier battles, the most recent of which occurred just the day before when they blunted Wilcox, Lang, and Wright's advances on their front. Gibbon's division, as Meade had pointed out the night before, held the center of the ridge near a clump of trees that the Southern gunners used as their aiming point.[19] At the stone wall just down the slope from the trees lay the 69th and 71st Pennsylvania of Brig. Gen. Alexander S. Webb's brigade of Philadelphia regiments; the 72nd Pennsylvania and elements of the detached 106th Pennsylvania formed a second line on the crest of the ridge.

Deployed south of Webb, also in two lines, lay Col. Norman J. Hall's brigade: the 59th New York, 7th Michigan, and 20th Massachusetts, running north to south in front; the 19th Massachusetts and 42nd New York lay in support. Brig. Gen. William Harrow's brigade—the 82nd New York, the 19th Maine, what was left of the famous 1st Minnesota, and the 15th Massachusetts, north to south—extended the line south from Hall's position.

North of Gibbon's three brigades, Brig. Gen. Alexander Hays deployed two of his three brigades.[20] Hays's and Gibbon's men did not form a single continuous line. The north-south stone wall in Webb's front formed the soon-to-be-famous Angle by making a ninety-degree turn to the east for about eighty yards before it angled back to the north; this geographical eccentricity forced Hays's men to deploy behind its shelter higher up the slope, disconnected from Gibbon's front line. On nearly the same line as Webb's supporting units near the crest of the ridge lay most of Col. Thomas A. Smyth's brigade: 14th Connecticut, 1st Delaware, 12th New Jersey, and 108th New York. On Smyth's right, four New York regiments—the 39th, 111th, 125th, and 126th—now served under Col. Eliakim Sherrill, a replacement for Col. George L. Willard, who had been killed on July 2. The 8th Ohio of Col. Samuel S. Carroll's brigade in Hays's division remained on Cemetery Ridge, where it had stayed on the II Corps picket line facing west along the Emmitsburg Road when the rest of the command redeployed to Cemetery Hill on the evening of 2 July.

Hancock's II Corps artillery bolstered the Cemetery Ridge line. The six guns of Lt. Alonzo H. Cushing's Battery A, 4th U.S. Artillery, deployed just north of the copse of trees, within the Angle. Capt. T. Fred Brown's Battery B, 1st Rhode Island Artillery, and Capt. James McK. Rorty's Battery B, 1st New York Artillery, reinforced Gibbon's line just south of the trees. Capt. William A. Arnold's Battery A, 1st Rhode Island Artillery, held the knuckle of the stone wall just where it headed north again after forming the Angle. Lt. George A. Woodruff's Battery I, 1st U.S. Artillery, deployed near Sherrill's New Yorkers among the trees of Ziegler's Grove.[21]

Union soldiers from Maj. Gen. Abner Doubleday's division of the I Corps lay just to the south of Hancock's men and shared responsibility for the defense of Cemetery Ridge.[22] Col. Theodore Gates, with his own 80th New York and the 151st Pennsylvania, had fought hard on McPherson's Ridge on July 1; the right of Gates's self-styled "demi-brigade" rested near the left flank of Harrow's brigade. Survivors of Col. Roy Stone's 143rd, 149th, and 150th Pennsylvania regiments, hard fighters near McPherson's barn on July 1, deployed within rifle shot of the front line as well. Three regiments from Brig. Gen. George J. Stannard's brigade—the 13th, 14th, and 16th Vermont—completed the I Corps presence in the front line. The Vermonters, nine-month men recruited the previous autumn, were within weeks of their discharge. They had tasted battle for the first time only the previous afternoon.

South of the I Corps line, well within range of the field over which Confederate troops must advance toward the clump of trees, the Army of the Potomac's chief of artillery, Brig. Gen. Henry J. Hunt, had massed batteries the evening before to repel any further advance of McLaws's and Anderson's divisions. Drawing upon the Artillery Reserve, he had placed this line of cannons to extend the II Corps gunline and to complement the massed guns on the XI Corps front on Cemetery Hill that easily could sweep the fields west of the clump of trees.

Of these organizational matters, we can be certain. But from the moment the Washington Artillery fired the first signal shot to open the cannonade, the historical record clouds considerably. Indeed, accounts of the fate of that first shot, as eyewitnesses record it, provide a foretaste of the fog of war that invests all that follows. Depending on whom one chooses to believe, that projectile nearly cut in two Lt. S. S. Robinson of the 19th Massachusetts; or it sailed harmlessly over an officer of that same regiment who lay wounded in a hospital way behind the front lines; or it exploded behind the Vermont brigade; or it was a dud that hit near the lines of the 12th New Jersey; or it exploded on a rock in the 12th New Jersey's line, scattering gravel all over nearby soldiers.[23]

As these individual memories of one small episode reveal, much of what history tells us is "true" about Pickett's Charge may not rest on a strong foundation of fact. From the very start, in its efforts to answer questions about the formation of the attacking column, the number of lines, who broke first, who advanced farthest, who stayed the longest, and who fell back fighting, history has competed with, been obscured by, even attacked by, memory. Every narrative of Pickett's Charge we read today includes this subtle subtext, and the student of history must be wary of memory's introduction of the fog of war. Myth and history intertwine freely on these fields, and some of their tendrils always will defy untangling.

1

DISCONNECTED
THREADS

Fifty years after Pickett's Charge, survivor D. B. Easley of the 14th Virginia finally admitted he had not seen very much of his regiment's most famous assault. He had become "so engrossed with his part of a fight" that he recalled "very little else." In apologizing for the haziness of his memory, he conceded an even more telling point: in the heat of battle, a soldier "fails to note all he does see."[1] Offering an equally important caveat, a Pennsylvania captain explained that many soldiers could not describe the chaos of combat, so they filled their letters, diaries, and official reports with exaggerations, fabrications, generalizations, or laconic dispassion. He feared that despite the efforts of conscientious historians "to weave a symmetrical whole from such disconnected threads," they really preserved only a few bits of any military action, even one so dramatic as the great charge at Gettysburg on July 3, 1863.[2]

A battlefield, according to military historian S. L. A. Marshall, is indeed "the lonesomest place which men share together."[3] Each soldier's perceptions of what he saw or did in combat—or what he thought he saw or did—became individualized sets of memories. Moreover, such personal recollections are very selective. No soldier recalls every action he takes or every observation he makes in battle, argues historian Richard Holmes, because "the process of memory tends to emphasize the peaks and troughs of experience at the expense of the great grey level plain."[4] Those peaks and troughs provide the disconnected threads of experience the Pennsylvania captain described. Only the most exceptional events, even on this momentous day in American military history, were likely to leave lasting marks in the soldiers' memories.

What did the survivors of that day tell us? Immediate postbattle musings offer glimpses of the horrific clash of arms. Collectively, however, they represent only a set of remarkable moments. These fragments of memory, as historian C. Vann Woodward has asserted, provide "the twilight zone between living memory and written history" that becomes the "breeding ground of mythology."[5] All too often, however, this mythology wears the mantle of "history," and it is the perpetuation of this kind of record—written by the "eye who never saw the battle"—that Lieutenant Haskell dreaded.

What do those fragments tell us about what happened between Seminary Ridge and Cemetery Ridge at Gettysburg on the afternoon of July 3, 1863? They tell us many important things, and not all of them are obvious to the best scholars. Historians often miss one particularly important point about that day: thousands of soldiers marched away from Gettysburg with no lasting memory at all of the great charge of July 3. Pvt. Samuel A. Firebaugh of the 10th Virginia recalled his own tough fight on Culp's Hill early that same morning as "the hardest contested battle of the war, lasting 6 hours" but dismissed the assault that afternoon with "Hill attacked on the right."[6] Col. Moses B. Lakeman of the 3rd Maine, after a hard fight at the Peach Orchard on July 2, summed up the next day with a few unspectacular observations: "Went to support of Second corps; no casualties. Rained at night. Enemy completely repulsed in our front all day. Commanding brigade."[7] The grand assault left no mark at all in the memories of the thousands of Gettysburg's survivors who played no part in the attack or its repulse.

More interesting, of course, are the memories of soldiers who did participate in the event. Honest soldiers, such as Sergeant Easley, realized that they just did not see enough of the fighting on July 3 to explain very much about it. As a Pennsylvania soldier suggested, "None but the actors of the field can tell the story" of a battle, and even then, "each one can tell of his own knowledge but an infinitisimal part."[8] This truth behind these veterans' observations compels both explanation and appreciation.

First, both the linear formations the armies used and the sheer numbers of soldiers involved in the fight on each side that day limited each combatant's field of vision. One of Davis's Mississippians best described the problem to his general a few years later: "I was very much like the

French Soldier of whom you sometimes told us, who never saw anything while the battle was going on except the rump of his fat file leader."[9]

In addition, the irregular terrain on the field of the great charge also limited what each soldier could see of the day's action. The physical conformation of the July 3 battlefield was—and still is—deceiving. Then, as now, trees, patches of underbrush, and rock outcroppings dotted the fields and slopes. The front of Webb's brigade stretched only several hundred yards, yet one man of the 72nd Pennsylvania later wrote that "those of us who were with the rest of the brigade knew nothing of the Sixty-Ninth [Pennsylvania], except as we heard their cheers and the crack of their rifles" because they were "partly concealed from view by the clump of trees."[10] The land between Seminary and Cemetery Ridges rolls gently, often dipping low enough to hide and shelter advancing soldiers. A low finger of ground jutting westward from the area around the Angle and the clump of trees toward the Emmitsburg Road, a subtly significant terrain feature largely unnoticed in 1863 and seldom noted today, effectively cut the battlefield in two. This subtle ripple cut the lines of sight along the lines of command responsibility: Pettigrew and Trimble fought Hays north of it, Pickett fought Gibbon south of it. Only a few soldiers saw much of both clashes. Smoke and the sheer number of horses and men on the field also made it difficult for any single individual to see much that day.

While limitations in visual contact circumscribed what any one man actually saw of Pickett's Charge, Easley's assertion that a soldier in the heat of combat "fails to note all he does see" deserves even more explanation. If a soldier set in memory only certain peak experiences and left the troughs unrecorded, what factors determined what would be remembered?

Most soldiers who took part in the fight on July 3 had seen combat before, and those experiences shaped perceptions now. North Carolina artilleryman Joseph Graham watched Southern infantrymen look out over the valley and heard them say: " 'That is worse than Malvern Hill.' "[11] After the fight ended, Pvt. J. L. Bechtel of the 59th New York wrote: "Antietam was nothing compared to it."[12] The battle at Fredericksburg the previous December supplied many soldiers with the most obvious point of comparison. Capt. Henry L. Abbott watched the advancing Confederates and knew his men "would give them Fredericksburg."[13] Sgt. Alex McNeil of the 14th Connecticut bragged that his regiment "paid the Rebels back with *Interest*, for our defeat at Fredericksburg."[14] On the day after the great charge, Capt. J. J. Young of the 26th North Carolina wrote that "it was a second Fredericksburg affair, only the wrong way."[15]

Some veterans knew that they lost more than physical vigor when the

Lt. Frank Aretas Haskell, General Gibbon's aide, who understood that his long narrative of the events of July 3 was just one man's story, not history (Massachusetts Commandery, MOLLUS, USAMHI)

adrenaline rush of battle waned. They could forget much of what they saw or did. In times of extreme stress such as that induced by combat, argues Richard Holmes, the human brain only "records clips of experience, often in erratic sequence."[16] Lieutenant Haskell clearly understood something about the process of memory when he warned his brother not to expect to learn much about the fight from the postbattle accounts of senior officers: "The official reports may give results as to losses, with statements of attacks and repulses; they may also note the means by which results were attained, which is a statement of the number and kind of forces employed, but the connection between means and results, the mode, the battle proper, these reports touch lightly." Even Haskell did not claim to write anything more than "simply *my account* of the battle."[17] Veterans admitted that in official reports—and in histories based on them—"much of the planning and more of the doing has been omitted."[18]

Historians have been slow to appreciate what Haskell and other veterans understood. The letters and diaries of veteran soldiers, far from providing concrete evidence of "the doing," reveal that much of "the doing" had become routine. Thus, they tell very little about the fighting that scholars seek to describe. By 1863, veteran Pvt. William Hatchett of the 22nd Virginia Battalion could sum up the great charge at Gettysburg in a single sentence: "The last day which was the 3d we charged across an open field about a mile while they played on us with grape and cannister very heavy."[19] Even many longer accounts, such as that of the 34th North Carolina's Lt. Burwell T. Cotton, reveal few more specifics about "the doing" than the official reports of which Haskell complained: "[We] charged them through an open field 1½ miles to their breast works. They threw shells, grape and canister as thick as hail. When we got in two hundred yards of them the infantry opened on us but onward we pressed until more than two thirds of the troops had been killed, wounded and straggled. Our lines were broken and we commenced retreating. A good many surrendered rather than risk getting out. They captured four flags in our brigade leaving only one. We lost four killed dead on the field and some six or seven wounded."[20]

Doubtless Cotton and many others who survived July 3 agreed with a Vermont veteran who wrote, "Much history was made on this charge that can never be known, and much, though seen and realized that can never be adequately described!"[21] Their reticence sprang from several sources, and a tendency to ignore the routine is only one of them. As Paul Fussell argues, the English language contains substantial numbers of words with sufficient power to convey images of destruction, violence, and death. Civil War soldiers simply did not use them very much, in part, it seems, from a concern about propriety and gentility.[22] They apparently appreciated the truth behind Fussell's rhetorical question: "What listener wants to be torn and shaken when he doesn't have to be?"[23]

More to the point, however, many veteran soldiers had tired of trying to explain combat to those who could not comprehend its horrors. "Every war begins as one war and becomes two, that watched by civilians and that fought by soldiers," historian Gerald Linderman has argued.[24] Just before the battle, Union general Alpheus S. Williams explained the difference to family at home: "No man can give any idea of a battle by description nor by painting." In graphic prose, he commented on the crashing roll of muskets, the thud of cannon balls as they thud through columns of human bodies, and "the 'phiz' of the Minie ball." He advised that "if you can hear and see all this in a vivid fancy, you may have some faint idea of a battle," but you still had to "stand in the midst and feel the elevation which few can fail to feel, even amidst its horrors, before you have the faintest notion of a scene so terrible and yet so grand."[25] Thus, just after July 3, a soldier from Maine could describe graphically the valley just south of the main thrust of Pickett's Charge and still warn his correspondent that even "after what I have written you have no idea of the s[c]ene. . . . You look at it on too small a scale."[26] When veteran survivors of Pickett's Charge sat down to write about July 3, then, they recorded highly selective impressions framed largely by previous experiences and personal notions of what their audiences either wanted to hear or could comprehend.

In any case, no matter what kind of language they employed—the unadorned, unemotional prose of Lieutenant Cotton or the more emotionally charged narrative of Lieutenant Haskell—soldiers wasted little time reflecting on the troughs of their experience. They recalled little of what they perceived to be routine, ordinary, or unexceptional, and although their contemporaries on the homefront (and subsequent historians) have not always understood this fact, most of what the combatants did before, during, and after the great charge at Gettysburg fit into these categories. What was expected of them on July 3 differed little from what had been required of them on previous battlefields.[27] In the end, only four elements of this day's work truly impressed the survivors as exceptional and worthy of special notice: the preassault cannonade, a few specific elements of the Confederate advance, the desperation and chaos at the Angle, and the high cost of such decisive results. About "the doing" of the rest of the charge, they told us remarkably little; yet most narratives of July 3 are built on these disconnected threads.

What did the soldiers recall of these four peak experiences? To begin, most soldiers, except for those directly caught up in the firefights near

Culp's Hill and Spangler's Spring, began their written accounts of July 3 with the great artillery bombardment. At that moment, they all seemed to shake free of the routine of eating, marching, deploying, and resting. Individual perspective then dictated what each soldier found most fascinating.

Artillerymen found the bombardment a marvelous opportunity to consider technical aspects of their craft. With professional, nearly clinical, detachment they reported on ranges, rounds fired, and their effectiveness. Entirely occupied with their mission, they found only a single perception worth further mention: they never had seen the long arm employed on such a scale before. Captain Graham with the Charlotte Artillery described it as "the heaviest Artillery duel of the war, (and said to have been heavier than the cannonade at Balaklava)."[28] Across the valley, where the converging fire of the Southern guns made Cemetery Ridge a particularly dangerous position, Capt. C. A. Phillips of the 5th Massachusetts broke from the formalities of official language in his professional assessment with colorful prose that suggests he witnessed something exceptional, if not particularly effective: "Viewed as a display of fireworks, the rebel practice was entirely successful, but as a military demonstration, it was the biggest humbug of the season."[29]

Union infantrymen lying passively on the slopes of Cemetery Ridge with no duties to distract them, however, had plenty of time to reflect on the hell they endured. Memories of the hail of shot and shell—however long it lasted—left its mark. "When a man imagines that every moment is his next to last," Fussell noted, "he observes and treasures up sensory details purely for their own sake."[30] The sheer violence of the bombardment stunned Northern infantrymen. Lt. Henry P. Clare of the 83rd New York, posted well in reserve, believed that "heaven had opened its gates and poured forth . . . their murderous messengers of death with the determination of annihilating our entire army."[31] Sgt. John Plummer of the 1st Minnesota admitted that he and his comrades usually did not mind cannon fire, but this day they hugged the ground to avoid "the hissing, screaming, bursting missiles, and all of them really seemed to be directed at us."[32] A private in the 108th New York must have believed the Southern gunners aimed at him personally, especially after "five different cannon-balls struck a large oak tree three feet in diameter, which stood not five feet from where I lay."[33]

Even if in a technical sense the Confederate artillerymen mostly over-shot their mark, each round that found a target—each hit filling only the briefest moment in time—left lasting impressions. The bombardment's most riveting moment for Private Bechtel came when one shell passed "through our brestwork killing 1 and wounding six of our company including my self."[34] Nearby, William B. Hoitt of the 19th Massachusetts, bruised by a fragment while shells "rained over and down upon us like hail stones," found himself astonished "that I 'still lived.'"[35] Col. Norman J. Hall explained in his official report that "the terrible grandeur of that rain of missiles and that chaos of strange and terror-spreading sounds, unexampled, perhaps, in history, must ever remain undescribed, but can never be forgotten by those who survived it."[36]

Perhaps those who best appreciated what the Union infantry endured that day lay in the Southern ranks across the valley. General Davis downplayed his loss to Union counterfire as small: two men killed and twenty-one wounded.[37] The small numbers probably meant little to Lt. William Peel of the 11th Mississippi, who watched "the most appaling [sic] scene that perhaps ever greeted the human eye" when a shell that struck the ground near the head of Lt. Daniel Featherstone ricocheted and "entered his breast, exploding about the same time & knocking him at least ten feet high, & not less than twenty feet from where he was lying."[38] In the lines of the 19th Virginia of Garnett's brigade, Maj. Charles S. Peyton watched in horror as Lt. Col. John T. Ellis raised his head during the heat of the firing and took a solid shot full in the face.[39] Pvt. Granville Belcher of the 57th Virginia, who was on detached duty in the rear during the cannonade, sympathized with the plight of his friends on the front line: "I was six miles from the battle field & wanted to get further."[40]

The unprecedented violence of the bombardment: soldiers remembered this, above all else. The fine details—the starting and ending times, its duration, the number of cannons involved on either side—interested soldiers chiefly as evidence of the extreme danger of the moment. That perspective helps explain, even as it does not resolve, some glaring time discrepancies that plague studies of the fight. The very busy Maj. Benjamin Eshelman of the Washington Artillery noticed Southern infantry advancing a mere thirty minutes after one of his batteries fired the first signal shot. In sharp contrast, Col. James Mallon of the 42nd New York, hunkered down under "a destructive artillery fire, which will ever be remembered by those subjected to its fury," estimated that his men endured it for four hours.[41] While senior Union commanders such as Hunt and Hancock might equivocate in their professional estimation that the II Corps line had been the target of 100 to 125 Southern cannons, Private Bechtel seemed absolutely confident in his conclusion that he had endured the fire of exactly "113 guns for one hour and a half."[42]

When the cannons fell silent, even the dullest private in the ranks knew what would happen next. The Confederate infantry must advance.

Southern soldiers wrote little about deploying for their charge. Pettigrew's and Trimble's men had done this before, only two days earlier. Senior Confederate officers employed the traditional terminology of the tactics manuals to describe routine movements; just a few quickly corrected misalignments warranted further comment. Only the exceptional won special notice. The heat of the day drew the attention of Lt. W. B. Taylor of the 11th North Carolina to men "fainting all along the [line] before [we] started on the charge."[43] Artilleryman Graham recalled the usually stalwart infantrymen's "want of resolution," made all too obvious when he heard one of them say, "'I don't hardly think that position can be carried.'"[44]

The second memorable moment of July 3 began when Pettigrew's Confederate infantry emerged from the woods on Seminary Ridge. This formation, in plain sight of thousands of Northern soldiers from the moment it broke out of the treeline, followed a straight line of march toward the Union line. Since survivors recalled few details about the routine movement, except for the stout post-and-rail fences that disrupted their forward progress, the passive observers on Cemetery Ridge left the most dramatic accounts of the Southern advance.[45]

Passive anticipation of battle often causes more stress and focuses the senses more sharply than does actual combat. Union veterans of many firefights in the wooded Virginia countryside seldom had seen so many soldiers at any one time as they now saw marching across that open field. Moreover, they had about twenty minutes to appraise the threat they faced and to prepare both physically and psychologically to deal with it.[46] While Hancock admired their "precision and steadiness that extorted the admiration of the witnesses of that memorable scene," Hays watched them march as "steady as if impelled by machinery."[47] A private in the 108th New York marveled that "they looked in the distance like statues. On they came, steady, firm, moving like so many automatons."[48] Down by the Angle in the stone wall, a Pennsylvania private enjoyed the panoramic view: "It was a grand sight and worth a mans while to see it."[49]

Impressions of power overrode attention to technical details of military formations. Many Union soldiers described a standard two-rank battle line. Others saw something more, but they rarely agreed on just what they observed. Hancock saw two-rank lines "supported at different points by small columns of infantry." Maj. Theodore Ellis, with the 14th Connecticut north of the Angle, noted two battle lines "re-enforced on the right and left by a third line." Lt. Col. Franklin Sawyer of the 8th Ohio saw columns, not lines.[50]

Soldiers became so entirely focused on the majesty and power of Pettigrew's advance out of the trees and down the slope of Seminary Ridge across their immediate front that only a few Union troops—mostly Stannard's Vermonters and others considerably south of the copse of trees—really saw the first appearance of Pickett's division as it came up over the rise of ground near the Spangler barn. They, too, described its formation generally as a two-rank line, with a variety of incongruities. A Vermont lieutenant saw "a column, and a very wide and deep one. General Stannard also insists that it was a column and its depth was almost equal to the length of the line of battle of the 13th and 16th Vt. Regiment."[51]

The rolling terrain apparently limited the number of Union soldiers who could see or appreciate the threat presented by the approach of two distinct assaulting forces, however. Lt. John Dent of the 1st Delaware, likely writing the first battle critique of his military career, stood nearly alone in noting that the strength of "the Pickett column moving on us in an oblique direction from the left, the Pender [sic; Pettigrew] column moving on us in an oblique direction from the right, both columns converging in our immediate front."[52]

Fear and awe left stronger impressions in Northerners' memories than did such routine matters as assault formations or preparations to repel the attackers. On the afternoon of July 3, a Pennsylvania private confided to his diary that if the South succeeded now, it would be "all up with the USA."[53] That night, Pvt. Charles Belknap of the 125th New York wrote that he and his comrades had "waited in almost breathless suspense for the enemy who was moving on toward us like an avalanche."[54] The 12th New Jersey's Cpl. Christopher Mead thanked the "God of our nation we had more in reserve" after Union skirmishers ran "like so many frightened sheep."[55] It had worried the 14th Connecticut's Alex McNeil that "we had only one line of troops to contend with three lines of the enemy."[56] Even Colonel Hall thought the Southerners "gave the appearance of being fearfully irresistible."[57]

When the Union artillery opened on those parade-ground ranks, the disconnected threads representing thousands of individual perceptions of Pickett's Charge multiplied in profusion. As a soldier makes contact with his enemy, a kind of tunnel vision overcomes him. When the battle ends, individual memories of the battle fix "upon those moments of terror and excitement when it seemed to the soldier that his life was in extreme peril."[58] Perspective still shaped those recollections, however.

After he watched his men advance under Union artillery fire, Maj. Charles Peyton of the 19th Virginia remembered "as many as 10 men being killed or wounded by the bursting of a single shell."[59] Pvt. William H. Jones of that regiment wrote home that "I never though[t] I would come owt. we had to advance wright in front of the Batteries which were fireing every second Loded with grape and canister."[60] In reality, the steady march of the great gray wave substantiated Hancock's criticism of the Union gunners' "feeble fire" and artillery chief Hunt's admission that "the enemy advanced magnificently, unshaken by the shot and shell which tore through his ranks from his front and from our left."[61] But to the Southerner breasting that fire, even a single well-placed burst—such as the odd round from Little Round Top that could rake Pickett's line—could leave singular memories.

To a veteran, one firefight seems much like any other; to a rookie, each sensation in battle is new. As the Virginia advance met its first resistance ahead of the main Union line, the green 13th and 14th Vermont recalled very colorfully the first brush with Garnett and Kemper. They boasted of a volley that leveled the Virginians' front rank, which forced them "to slacken and nearly halt," and Stannard expressed pleasure that the enemy did not "escape the warm reception prepared" for them.[62] In contrast, a veteran Virginia major recalled only brushing away some pesky skirmishers, and from the still-quiet copse of trees, Lieutenant Haskell observed the firing and noted only that "the gray lines do not halt or reply, but withdrawing a little from that extreme, they still move on."[63]

Both Union soldiers south of the copse of trees and Pickett's survivors commented on the unusual indirect approach march that the Virginians employed. "We moved alternately by the front & by the left flank under a most deadly fire of infantry & artillery," explained Capt. William W. Bentley of the 24th Virginia.[64] The Vermonters, and then other Union commanders just north of them, gave their own hot fire the credit for the Virginians' continued sideling movement toward the Angle in the stone wall. This action confused Northern observers. Despite a stout resistance, the Southerners did not retreat, they did not immediately return fire, and they seemed to march on purposefully and with stalwart determination, first east, then north, then east again. This unnerved Union commanders, and Colonel Gates, for one, remembered that when the Southerners finally opened fire, the fighting became "especially obstinate." He believed "for a considerable time the chances of success appeared to favor first one side and then the other."[65] The uniqueness of the Virginia advance intrigued Colonel Hall so much that he illustrated it on a map submitted with his postbattle report.[66] As they executed their unusual approach march, even under the hot fire of Gates, then Harrow, then Hall, the Virginians' apparently deliberate concentration for a final rush against the Union line at the clump of trees held the close attention of every Northern soldier on Gibbon's front.

No such sense of crisis swept through Hays's men, and their immedi-

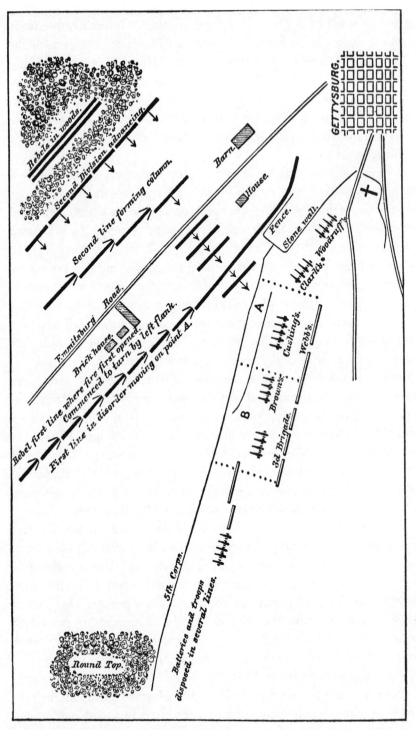

Colonel Hall's map, illustrating the unusual nature of the advance of Pickett's men against his position on July 3, 1863 (OR 27 [1]:438)

ate recollections reflected a greater sense of confidence. As they prepared to meet Pettigrew and Trimble's Alabamians, North Carolinians, Mississippians, and Tennesseans, most of Hays's men could not see much of the crisis building on Gibbon's front. As one of Hays's men admitted, "Pettigrew commanded the column nearest our position," and as it approached the II Corps front, "it was about all that we could see of the line."[67] The Southern battle line approached to within 200 yards (or less), and then the textbook offensive move met a textbook defensive response.

Although briefly hot and unquestionably costly, the clash on Hays's front possessed little that the soldiers deemed overly dramatic or exceptional. As Capt. George Bowen of the 12th New Jersey summed it up, "They fell like wheat before the garner, but still on they came until they were within a dozen feet of us when those that were left threw down their guns and surrendered."[68] A comrade noted only that "the whole line became engaged in repulsing an attack made in force by the enemy, completely routing him."[69] Colonel Smyth described the work of his brigade briefly: "So effective and incessant was the fire from my line that the advancing enemy was staggered, thrown into confusion, and finally fled from the field, throwing away their arms in their flight."[70] Lt. Col. James Bull of the 126th New York wrote only that "the enemy, advancing in four lines across the flat, were subjected to a murderous fire of musketry and artillery, and were driven back in confusion, after an engagement of about an hour," a report so sparse that he even omitted recording the capture of three sets of Confederate colors.[71]

Unquestionably, many personal dramas played out on Hays's front, but no great moment of crisis compelled the survivors to preserve many of them. Captain Bowen saw a few Southerners to his left get "over the fence and to the battery" of "steel rifled cannon," probably those belonging to Arnold's Rhode Islanders, and watched "one confederate jump on one of the guns, wave his flag and give a cheer," before a gunner felled him.[72] Some of Davis's men—Lieutenant Peel among them—made it to the Bryan barn, but Hays's men held, and they no longer felt the sense of urgency that compelled their attention to the Southerners' advance. One unimpressed New York private downplayed the scene: "When within musket range the infantry rose up and gave them a withering shower and the gray lines melted away."[73] Hays, never a subtle man, summarized his division's fight by noting that "in less time than it takes to record it," the Southerners "were throwing away their arms and appealing most pitiously for mercy."[74]

The only Union unit on Hays's front to win special attention in later years did so because it performed in an unusual way. The 8th Ohio, redeployed from the west-facing picket line to face south, took Pettigrew's and Trimble's men in flank and, in combination with "the fire from the front, together with the concentrated fire from our batteries," destroyed Davis's ranks.[75] Some of Lane's men apparently obliqued to strengthen that flank, but many other Southerners, shaken out of ranks at first contact, only kept up a desultory fire from the Emmitsburg Road. Still others may have drifted southward away from the threatened flank and joined in—without formal organization—with Pickett's men.[76] The success of Hays's men in preventing the Confederates from breaking their line, ironically enough, helped to relegate them to the role of bit players, preserved the fiction of an all-Virginia Pickett's Charge at the expense of Pettigrew's and Trimble's men, and marked the "high tide of the Rebellion" at the copse of trees in Gibbon's line.

In contrast to the unexceptional nature of the fight on Hays's front, several factors made the fight at the Angle entirely memorable. First, the contest concentrated great numbers of soldiers into a fairly small space, more dramatic in its visual impact and far more chaotic in imagination than a general firefight along a division front.[77] The soldiers here fought at extremely close range—measured in feet, not yards—even before the final penetration. And, of course, the odd maneuvers of Pickett's men had telegraphed their intentions. Every soldier on that part of the field knew where the issue would be decided. Anticipation did not inspire dispassion.

Perceptions of what happened at the Angle and around the copse of trees in the next half hour—no more—provide the contest's most numerous and vivid disconnected threads. The survivors' recollections both compress and expand time, rendering impossible efforts to reconstruct a reliable sequence of events. They seldom relate formal tactical movements; they care little for the deploying or countermarching of regiments and brigades. Mostly they offer a stunning array of moments marked by violence and confusion.

The Virginians' final approach to the wall transfixed the Union defenders. Capt. William Davis of the 69th Pennsylvania felt "as if no power could hold them in check."[78] Although Garnett went down only twenty-five paces from the wall and Kemper fell seriously wounded, the Confederates did not waver. Webb watched as the Virginians advanced "in four solid lines right up to my works and fences, and shot my men with their muskets touching their breasts."[79] Haskell thought odds favored the Virginians. Counting "more than a dozen flags to Webb's three," he feared that before too much longer "there will be none alive for the enemy to overpower."[80]

For many Union soldiers, the moment of direst crisis had come. Webb watched Armistead and "perhaps 100 men of his command and with several battle-flags" pierce his line.[81] Captain Davis saw them cross over the wall to his right and "literally came right on top of our men."[82] Webb "stood but thirty-nine paces from them," and "their officers pointed me out, but God preserved me." When Pickett's men "came over the fences, the army of the Potomac was nearer being whipped than it was at any time of the battle," he admitted. When some of his Pennsylvanians fell back, abandoning several guns of Cushing's battery at the wall, Webb admitted that he felt so angry, "I almost wished to get killed. I was almost disgraced."[83] To Haskell, "the fate of Gettysburg hung upon a spider's single thread!"[84]

Desperate times called for desperate measures. In hundreds of acts of personal heroism, entirely independent of each other, Union men responded. Many could not remember or explain what they did in the next few minutes, but few forgot how they felt.

Despite the deaths of their senior officers, the men of the 69th Pennsylvania refused their right flank and kept fighting, "for new ardor seemed to inspire our men to greater exertions."[85] Haskell drew his sword to rally other scattered Pennsylvanians: "Was not that a fit occasion, and these fugitives the men on whom to try the temper of the Solinzen steel?"[86] Just when Pvt. William Burns thought "it was all up with us," Webb "went right in front of us and led us when we gave a yell and charged on them and drove them back with great slaughter."[87]

Troops that moved to Webb's aid recalled similar feelings. When Col. Arthur Devereux brought his 19th Massachusetts to the clump of trees, he found "considerable confusion here."[88] Orders went unheard; only part of the 7th Michigan followed Lt. Col. Amos Steele toward the trees, and they fell into disorder when he took a bullet through the head. The officers of the 20th Massachusetts waved their swords to try to control a fight that had become "very confused, every man fighting on his own hook, different regiments being mixed together, and half a dozen colors in a bunch."[89] Hall noted that his men tended to fall back a pace or two each time they reloaded, giving the line "a retiring direction," so he roamed up and down his line to force his men to keep their places.[90] In all that confusion, Colonel Devereux still thought the fight "seemed to hang in the balance whether we should drive the enemy out of our works, which they had entered, or they succeed in carrying the position."[91]

Some of Harrow's men now came to help Hall and Webb. "The fighting here was desperate for a time," understated Capt. Henry Coates of the 1st Minnesota of their clash at the copse.[92] Perhaps that battered regiment—so badly bloodied on July 2—had a special reason to remember this fight. Sgt. John Plummer wrote that his comrades "took revenge for what they had done to our poor fellows the day before. . . . Most of us fired twenty rounds, and at close range enough to do splendid execution; and if we didn't kill some Secesh in that battle we never did, and I fear never will during the war."[93] Still, most of Harrow's men apparently reached the trees after the contest had been decided. Probably because each one of these regiments suffered more losses on July 2 than they did this day, their commanders remarked little about their part in repulsing Pickett's Charge.[94] Col. Francis E. Heath of the 19th Maine noted simply, "When the enemy advanced, I was ordered with the rest of the brigade to the support of the Second Brigade."[95] Lt. Col. George C. Joslin of the 82nd New York recalled only that when Pickett's men pierced the Angle, "we moved by the right flank a short distance and became hotly engaged. After about an hour's fighting, the enemy were repulsed."[96]

The end came quickly, dramatically, and, contrary to most formal histories, more from a contest of wills than by the force of any controlling hand. The comingled commands of Harrow, Hall, and Webb, supported by fresh artillery, closed on the Southerners for one final clash in the Angle and at several spots along the wall. Angered by the death of their color bearer, the 72nd Pennsylvania crowded forward as a "maddened load, men, arms, smoke, fire, a fighting mass. It rolls to the wall—flash meets flash, the wall is crossed—a moment ensues of thrusts, yells, blows, shots, and undistinguishable conflict." It took only a few minutes of hand-to-hand fighting to repulse "the crowd—for such had become that part of the enemy's column that had passed the fence."[97] The Union defenders looked much like a mob, too, Sergeant Plummer noting that "in the last charge nearly all the flags of the division were together in a corner where the rebels got a hold."[98] Hancock could not find formal language to explain what he observed; he simply described the situation as "peculiar" and blamed the "ambition of individual commanders to promptly cover the point penetrated by the enemy, the smoke of battle, and the intensity of the close engagement" for the confusion.[99]

Fewer Southern postbattle accounts of the fight at the wall survive, but just as Haskell described the Union counterattack as a "new battle, deadlier, stormier than before," Capt. A. N. Jones of the 7th Virginia likewise noted its "redoubled violence."[100] General Armistead had gone down. The fighting took place at such close quarters that Webb told his wife that the Confederate general "was killed within 40 feet of me & in my rear."[101] The most important thing on the minds of Virginians—beyond survival itself—was the need for help. "At this critical juncture when seconds seemed more precious than hours of any former time, many an anxious eye was cast back to the hill from which we came in the hope of seeing supports near at hand," wrote Colonel Mayo in an eloquent after-action report, "and more than once I heard the [desperate?] exclamation, 'why don't they come!' But no help came."[102] Major Peyton "hoped for a support on the left (which had started simultaneously with ourselves), but hoped in vain."[103]

Within a few minutes, the Southern line began to pull back to Seminary Ridge. Impending victory changed impressions in Northern accounts from fear to boastful confidence. When six New Yorkers finally subdued a Southern officer who refused to give up his flag, they recalled that his entire command "came over the fence like a flock of sheep."[104] Stannard's Vermonters, who helped to open the fight on this sector of the field, now got to close it. The 13th and 16th Vermont had redeployed facing north-ward, advanced on the Virginians' right flank, and opened "one of the most withering fires" its colonel ever saw. Although the 11th and 24th Virginia turned to face the threat, they stood only briefly "before the larger portion of them surrendered and marched in—not as conquerors, but as captives."[105] Confederate survivors retreated westward to the sanctuary of Seminary Ridge.

Few but the participants themselves noted the belated advance of Wilcox's Alabamians and Lang's Floridians. Smoke and terrain obscured them from view of both lines. Union artillery hammered them, and then, just as the Floridians came to a skirt of woods at the foot of Cemetery Ridge, the 14th and 16th Vermont faced south and attacked their left. Badly battered the day before, they quickly retired. From the thinned ranks of the 2nd Florida, David Maxwell, with magnificent understatement, summed up the day's action: "The fighting was terrible and with the exception of a few positions gained by us, things remained as they were the night before."[106]

Despite all he wrote about the great charge, Lieutenant Haskell knew that neither he nor his comrades in arms could ever do it justice: "Many things cannot be described by pen or pencil—such a fight is one. Some hints and incidents may be given, but a description or picture never. From what is told the imagination may for itself construct the scene; otherwise he who never saw can have no adequate idea of what such a battle is."[107]

The chaos of battle quickly gave way to what Richard Holmes describes as "an overwhelming human desire to lend form and meaning to a bewildering series of random experiences."[108] After the charge, soldiers used the final exceptional element of the events of July 3—the personal and military cost of its results—to do just that.

The Union victors did not appreciate just how much they had accomplished. While "a great relief seemed to rest on the minds of everyone," they were not sure that the battle was over.[109] Each man in the 71st Pennsylvania at the Angle slept that night and the next with three loaded muskets by his side.[110] Even in victory, the final stage of battle ritual—cleaning up the field of carnage—muted their joy and sealed lasting memories.

Veterans of the Army of the Potomac seldom saw the aftermath of battle like they did now. The profusion of dead and wounded enemy in their front fascinated them. They buried fallen Southern officers together with some degree of decorum, but they stripped dead Confederate enlisted men of food and valuables, tossed them into shallow trench graves, and made no effort to identify individual remains.[111] Indeed, some perceived the Confederate dead as almost inhuman. The 148th Pennsylvania's Sgt. Thomas Meyer, who served on a burial detail near the Angle, recalled with revulsion their "faces black as charcoal and bloated out of all human semblance; eyes, cheeks, forehead and nose all one general level of putrid swelling, twice the normal size, with here and there great blisters of putrid water, some the size of a man's fist on face, neck and wrists." [112]

The dead Southerners seemed less fearsome now. "It was a horrible sight to see those poor fellows lying there who a few hours before were in the full bloom of manhood," wrote Pvt. Loren Goodrich of the 14th Connecticut.[113] A Michigan soldier who walked "over a portion of the ground where Pickets great charge terminated" often stepped in pools of clotted blood, noting, however, that "it was Rebel Blood so it did not seam so bad." [114] Fate held special horrors for Pvt. Garrett Deacon of the 12th New Jersey, who drew picket duty on the Emmitsburg Road that night. At first horrified by the sight of the dead and the sounds of the wounded, he awoke from a nap to find himself next to a dead body. Only the memory of a wounded Southern woman who "was hoolern all nite the ofel that I ever hurd in my life" left a deeper mark.[115]

Just as the great masses of enemy slain awed them, Union survivors realized as well that not all the dead wore gray. Indeed, as survivors of the Philadelphia Brigade later recalled, "The moment the attack was repulsed and the excitement of the battle was over, the mournful inquiry passed from one to another, Who of our comrades have fallen?" [116] The exultation of victory that allowed a Massachusetts officer to repress acknowledgment of his unit's casualties drained away quickly, leaving him with "a great weight at my heart." [117]

Battle ritual demands special handling of those who die in a victorious cause. More than comradeship alone dictated that Northern survivors bury their own dead with a show of respect far greater than that accorded to slain Confederates. Capt. Charles E. Nash of the 19th Maine watched his men "perform the last sad rites. Our own dead were buried in groups, the name and regiment of each placed at the end of the little mounds." Only then did they proceed to dig trench graves for the enemy dead.[118]

Additionally, survivors felt the need to make heroes of their dead comrades. Through their courage in combat, they might continue to "strengthen the cause of the living by giving example of the bravery needed on the battlefield, and all the dead are remembered as brave."[119] The 1st Delaware mourned the loss of Lt. William Smith, who fell as the regiment charged the retreating foe and lay in death with "his sword . . . in one hand and a captured rebel flag in the other."[120] Colonel Mallon of the 42nd New York saluted Sgt. Michael Cuddy, who, after falling mortally wounded, "rose by a convulsive effort, and triumphantly waved in the faces of the rebels, not 10 yards distant, that flag he loved so dearly, of which he was so proud, and for which his valuable life, without a murmur, was freely given up."[121]

But pain mixed freely with pride. The decimation of veteran Union regiments could hurt unit cohesion and identity as deeply as personal losses might affect individuals. Private Hoitt expressed great delight that the 19th Massachusetts had helped to give "the Johnnies Hail Columbia," but he mourned that the unit was "pretty well played out." With its ten companies consolidated into four, Hoitt figured, "I don't think my services will be required any longer, as there is no longer a Co. I in the regiment."[122] Captain Nash realized just how much "our ranks in the field are now weak and thinned. There is many an absentee at roll call. We need more men."[123]

Only victory lightened the burden of mourning. Captured Southern battle flags offered the most tangible evidence of Union success. The rookies of the 16th Vermont fawned over the 2nd Florida's inscribed flag.[124] The 14th Connecticut picked up five sets of colors, but Major Ellis took special pride in those of the 1st and 14th Tennessee and the 16th North Carolina, each of which bore the names of at least twelve earlier battles.[125] Several high-ranking Northern officers took banners away from their rightful captors to give them to their own units. A witness who understood the special distinction attached to the capture of enemy flags swore with righteous indignation that "death is too light a punishment for such a dastardly offense."[126]

Individual Union soldiers reacted to the reality of the victory in many ways. Some gave in to boasting. Pvt. Albert Emmell of the 12th New Jersey wrote home that the Confederates "came trying to strike terror into Yankee hearts by unnatural shrieks and yells. But it was a no go. The old Second [Corps] is not to be frightened by a little noise coming from Rebel throats."[127] Officers became uncommonly generous with praise. Colonel

Hall freely shared his men's battle honors with "those who assisted them" at "the turning point of the battle" at the Angle. After all, "the decision of the rebel commander was upon that point, the concentration of artillery fire was upon that point; the din of battle developed in a column of attack upon that point; the greatest effort and greatest carnage was at that point; and the victory was at that point."[128] General Harrow, whose men Hall had just saluted, celebrated a "common struggle and a common success, as the gallant dead and wounded of each of the brigades of the division there fallen amply testify."[129]

Indeed, the decisive victory so clearly belonged to the entire Union that only a few individuals came away from July 3 as living heroes. Lieutenant Haskell won Gibbon's praise for "his conspicuous coolness and bravery," Colonel Hall's thanks for finding reinforcements and "innerving the troops to their work by word and fearless example," Colonel Devereux's accolades for his extraordinary efforts to close the breach in Webb's line, and Harrow's official notice of his "constant exertion in the most exposed places."[130] General Webb, who later would receive the Medal of Honor for his conduct on July 3, explained simply that "had Pickett broken through my lines this army would have been routed." He had just taken command of his brigade, and "my men did not know me. It was necessary to establish myself. They were to be made to feel that I ordered no man to go when I would not go myself."[131] Only Hancock won more admiration. As one of his staff officers crowed, "Our General, I mean Gen. Hancock, was the hero of the fight. Oh, but he is a gallant man!"[132] Private Hoitt, one of Hancock's men, likely agreed, warning his sister not to "place too much faith in Meade. The different Corps Generals fought and won the battle of Gettysburg."[133]

All these things—the capture of flags, the honors rendered to dead warriors, and the praise for living heroes—meant so much to so many primarily because they evoked memories of victory, not merely of battle. "Now, the simple state of facts is just this," wrote a Connecticut survivor, "we repulsed the attacks of the enemy, repulsed them tremendously and effectually; and in this was our victory."[134] Victory provided the context for consolation and inspiration.

Success had come so suddenly on July 3 that a Northern artilleryman explained, "How great our victory had been, or what loss we had inflicted on the enemy we had little idea of."[135] For now, few dared to look beyond the tactical victory they had won that day. It took time for Capt. Samuel Fiske of the 14th Connecticut—the famous "Dunn Browne" whose humorous essays on military affairs appeared in many Northern newspapers —to realize that he finally found his "desired opportunity of seeing a battle in which there was real fighting; hard, persistent, desperate fighting; fighting worthy of a noble cause and the confidence of a gallant people" that gave "the dear old, brave, unfortunate Army of the Potomac" a chance to cover itself with glory.[136]

Charles C. Coffin, the Boston *Journal*'s correspondent at Gettysburg, produced one of the most frequently quoted sentiments about the outcome of the fighting of July 3: "The invasion of the North is over,— the power of the Confederacy broken. There at that sunset hour I could discern the future; no longer an overcast sky, but the clear, unclouded starlight,—a country redeemed, saved, baptized, consecrated anew to the coming ages."[137] But these words did not reflect the mood of the army. Wild celebrations quickly quieted as survivors savored their victory and mourned their dead.

As the North celebrated its victory of July 3, Lee's army had to cope with a costly and unaccustomed reverse. "Our army was bo[u]yant and full of life and the repulse [was] wholly unexpected by men and officers," mourned Lt. Col. A. S. VandeGraff of the 5th Alabama Battalion.[138] As they sought explanations for their defeat and for their huge losses, the unsuccessful assault of July 3 that forced Lee's decision to return to Virginia drew Southern soldiers' close scrutiny.

For a while, many Southern soldiers refused to concede defeat.[139] David Maxwell of the 2nd Florida gave little credence to Northerners who boasted about the "*disorder* and *confusion* attending our *precipitate retreat*" on July 3 and insisted, "Their right to claim a victory I will dispute."[140] Even as late as July 16, Private Belcher of the 57th Virginia wrote home that "bothe sides was whip[p]ed" at Gettysburg and believed that "the yanks commence[d] fawling back five hours before Lee did."[141]

Many Southerners begrudgingly admitted defeat, of course, but in that first rush of indignation and surprise, they blamed the reverse on cowardly Union troops who had refused to fight fair. The events of July 3 most clearly made their point. A few days after the battle, North Carolinian W. H. Proffitt explained that "the enemy secured an elevated position and fortified it well which saved them from their usual fate."[142] Edgeworth Bird of Georgia recalled the Northern position as "rock walls built on mountain sides and tops" where Southern troops "performed heroic deeds, and died heroic deaths."[143] Even several weeks later, Mississippian John S. Lewis admitted that he was still too angry to write about the July 3 fight: "The whole army charged and was driven back, though the cowards would not charge our shattered lines in turn—the lion they knew was hurt but not killed."[144] Virginian Charles Minor Blackford understood only that while "our men made a charge which will be the theme of the poet, painter and historian of all ages, they could not maintain the enemy's lines much less capture them." [145]

Unlike their Northern opponents, Southern soldiers refought their battle in fine detail. On July 3, Sgt. Robert A. Moore of the 18th Mississippi had entered into his diary: "General Pickett's division captured the enemy's works but were forced to abandon them. Our loss has been heavy & we have accomplished nothing." [146] Now such generalization satisfied few.

Army rumor quickly shifted blame away from cowardly Yankees to culprits who could be found within their own ranks. As South Carolina cavalryman Stephens C. Smith wrote home, "Pickets Division at one time charged a 32 Gun Battery of the Enemy and took it, but not being supported in time, were compelled to fall back, in doing which it was terribly cut up." [147] Virginian H. T. Holladay wrote pointedly that "Pickett's division was ordered to charge—& did so—most gallantly & gained the works, but not *being supported* had again to fall back. . . . Our loss was terrible— Pickett's Division was almost annihilated." [148]

Very soon, specific scapegoats emerged. Jedediah Hotchkiss, the noted Southern cartographer, wrote in his diary that "we drove the enemy from their works, but our supports were not near enough and the enemy rallied & regained them. Pickett's div. took the hill on the right, but Pettigrew failed to sustain him." [149] Sgt. James Kirkpatrick of the 16th Mississippi watched Pettigrew's division advance after the bombardment and noted that "they make a very feeble effort & accomplish nothing. The troops in the movement were mostly North Carolinians." Distance, lack of shelter, and the sun's heat were "the only excuse[s] that can be plead in their behalf." [150] Lt. William Calder of the 2nd North Carolina, for one, wrote his mother that the last day's attack was "the finest charge of the war and had Pickett's division been supported we could have held the field but Heth's division failing to come up as it should have done they were forced to retire." [151] As the army retreated back to Virginia, allegations of blame lodged against Pettigrew's troops for the failure of the July 3 charge clearly had won credence throughout the army.

It was no surprise that Pickett's Virginians very much wanted to know —and make sure others knew—who deserved blame for what happened to them. First, they simply deflected any possible discredit from themselves. William H. Cocke of the 9th Virginia knew his comrades had done their best, but their supports had run "like sheep—thanks to Gracious they were NOT Va. troops." [152] James J. Phillips of the same unit concurred in his assessment of the "cool deliberate gallantry" displayed by "our Division by our Brigade and by our regt." Their dead "raised for themselves

Maj. Gen. George E. Pickett (Francis Trevelyan Miller, comp., Photographic History of the Civil War *[New York: Review of Reviews, 1911], 9:215)*

and for our dear Old Va. a monument of fame which shall be gazed upon as long as brave deeds live in history & in song." [153]

Then Pickett's men and many of their comrades in the First Corps fixed on various Third Corps commands as the troops that failed to do their duty on July 3. Artilleryman James Dearing wrote his mother, "Well! we took those heights but could not hold them. Pickett's little division of 4000 Virginians took them by themselves unsupported and unassisted. Gen'l Heth's Division started on his left but never reached their works. . . .

From the fact of not being able to hold the heights Pickett took we were disappointed in the fruits of our Campaign."[154] Artilleryman E. Porter Alexander agreed: "Pickett's Divn was to make the charge—unsupported it afterwards appeared in the rear, & Pettigrew's Divn of A. P. Hill's Corps was to go on his left," but "when Pettigrew's Divn. on Pickett's left broke & fell back under the fire," the gallant assault failed.[155]

This finger-pointing in no way represented an orchestrated effort by Pickett's survivors to protect their own reputations at the expense of any other troops. For now, the Virginians' search for answers demonstrated only one way of coping with trauma. Although all fifteen of Pickett's regiments had seen combat before July 3, they had not fought together as a division in any serious action before that day. Then, in short order, almost 10 percent lay dead or mortally wounded.[156] Many hundreds more suffered serious wounds, and still more spent the rest of the war in prison camps. No other division in the Army of Northern Virginia consisted of troops from only a single state, and Charles Minor Blackford knew that both the army and the Old Dominion would feel the concentrated losses deeply. "I grieve deeply over Pickett's division, in which I had so many friends," he wrote home. "Poor Virginia bleeds again at every pore. There will be few firesides in her midst where the voice of mourning will not be heard when the blacklettered list of losses is published."[157]

Never before bloodied the way they were on July 3, Pickett's survivors found themselves overwhelmed by a profound sense of loss. Surgeon Charles E. Lippett of the 57th Virginia tried to record dispassionately in his diary the fate of Armistead's brigade: "Every field officer in our Brigade was either killed or wounded. . . . Every officer commanding a co[mpany] in the 57th Va was killed, wounded or taken prisoner." The division hospital was "filled to overflowing." But emotion finally slipped through: "The Div covered itself with glory but alas at such a cost."[158] Private Jones of the 19th Virginia mourned the loss of nearly all his leaders: "Col Ellis was kilt Col Gant was wounded we have now [sic; no] CO [commanding officer] at this time."[159] Captain Griggs of the 38th Virginia knew only that "all my Lieuts are wounded 20 of my Co are wounded & 17 missing I do not know who is living. I carried 49 muskets into the fight." He prayed that God would "comfort those who lay wounded from to-day's work & soon restore them to health[,] go to the many distressed families & enable them to bear their losses without Complaint."[160]

Since the Southern army had surrendered possession of the battlefield to the victorious Northerners, many survivors carried back to Virginia pressing personal questions for which they could find no answers. Private Hatchett could not search for his uncle, "who went into the fight at

Gatersburg and was killed or taken prisoner. He had not been heard from since."[161] As late as August 2, Private R. P. White of Armistead's brigade still could learn nothing about the fate of two cousins who went into the July 3 charge with him. He knew one had been wounded in the hand but knew nothing about the fate of the other. He did not know yet that both Privates William Daniel Ross and James Eastin Ross were dead.[162] William Cocke worried about "poor [John] Jenkins—no one knows what has become of him. . . . I'm afraid he was killed—he has told me several times that he wouldn't be taken a prisoner." With his friend missing, Cocke felt "perfectly lost."[163] Capt. Henry T. Owen of the 18th Virginia noted that "everyone has lost friends and comrades and did not fully appreciate the misfortunes" until they were back in Virginia.[164]

It hurt survivors to relay word of defeat and death to folks back home. On July 11, William Fitzgerald of the 18th Virginia wrote to the wife of Lt. George W. Jones, who was wounded in the charge: "George received a flesh wound in the leg. He bled a good deal & seemed considerably exhausted. When I left him he was doing very well." He added as a hopeful note, "The Yankees got them and no doubt will treat them well." Jones survived, although he would not be paroled from Johnson's Island until 1865.[165] But not all the stories had happy endings. All through July, the family of Col. J. B. Magruder of the 57th Virginia heard rumors that their kinsman had been captured and cared for by "a Yankee captain belong[ing] to the Epsilon Alpha society." In August, another family member finally dashed their hopes, telling them that the colonel "now sleeps, among those gallant spirits, who that day bore our banner so nobly against the ramparts of the enemy, on the battle field in a foreign land." He offered a bit of consolation: "He died with his laurels thick around him."[166]

Pickett's men were not the only survivors of that charge who needed to pick up the pieces of their shattered lives, of course. On July 9, Capt. B. F. Little of the 52nd North Carolina in Pettigrew's brigade, who lost an arm in the charge, still worried because "I do not know what became of my lieuts." Two weeks later he still marveled at his own survival: "How favored not to have lost my life in the terrible charge. . . . The Col & Major were both killed & Lt Col shot down near me, but he was only shot through the thigh."[167] Lt. W. B. Taylor of the 11th North Carolina expressed relief that he had survived unscathed, with only holes in his clothes and a dent in his scabbard. He knew he had been luckier than most: "Our company went into the fight the third day with 30 men rank and file. . . . Our company came out with 8 men."[168] W. F. Fulton of the 5th Alabama Battalion in Archer's brigade wrote that "Co A is all right and in excellent spirits, I mean those that are left."[169]

Somehow, however, the sense of loss among Pettigrew's and Trimble's survivors seemed different than that which swept through Pickett's division. These units already knew from many previous battles what hard combat could cost them; Lane's North Carolina brigade, for instance, had absorbed more casualties at Chancellorsville a few months previously than any equivalent Confederate command had. The events of July 3 did not present them with an experience they had not faced before. Moreover, the pain of loss diffused itself across units from several states and did not concentrate the burden on one. Additionally, Pettigrew's and Trimble's survivors lost heavily on two days at Gettysburg, on July 1 as well as July 3. They did not leave Gettysburg obsessed about what happened to them between the two ridges south of town.

Survivors of Wilcox's and Lang's command on Pickett's right flank shared the same kind of diffused sensibilities after losing heavily on both July 2 and 3. An Alabama captain explained that they charged the Union works for two days "to no effect only the loss of men." As a result, "there is not many of our neighborhood boys left in the company now. My self and Hamilton is all that is here. Oh! how lonely I feel." [170] Raymond J. Reid of the 2nd Florida wrote to a friend that after fighting on July 2 and 3, "but few of our little band came out. . . . It is sad indeed to compare our little band now with what it was." [171] Lt. Isaac Barrineau of the 8th Florida wrote that he and three messmates came safely through their fight on July 2, but on July 3, he took a bullet in the arm, another was wounded, and a third was unhurt. Of the fourth messmate, Barrineau knew nothing: "Blan poor fellow is missing I dont know wether he was killed wounded or taken prisoner." Nearly a month later, guessing his friend had died, he urged his sister not to be "discouraged when our friends fall in battle for it is impossible for us to gain our independence without losing some of our brave Boys." [172]

The most profound sense of loss seemed to take hold only after Lee's army arrived safely south of the Potomac. [173] There, in relative security, they could begin to comprehend the full dimensions of what had happened to them. By late July, one of E. Porter Alexander's staff officers lost his earlier optimism: "Every one feels how disastrous to us our defeat at Gettesburg was and every body had found out by this time how badly we where [sic] repulsed to use the most moderate term for our reverses there." [174] In August, Lt. William A. Miller of the 18th Virginia was glad that "all of my boy's are well what few are left"; but he still thought about "many of those noble faces that I have been accustomed to See" who "are sleeping their last-Sleep on the blood Stained field of Gettysburg." [175]

No one in either army knew just what July 3 meant yet. As Douglas Southall Freeman wrote later of Southern perceptions after the battle,

"Every emotion there was of vain and costly assault, every one except a consciousness that more than a battle had been lost; the enemy had beaten them back; they could do no more. The rest of it—war's decision, America's destiny, the doom of the Confederacy—all this was read afterward into the story of their return." [176] Nor did Union survivors yet realize that they would have to reweave the disconnected threads of their July 3 memories in the years ahead. For now, the war dragged on. Appomattox lay nearly two years in the future.

Still, especially for some in the ranks of Pickett's three battered brigades, deeply disturbing memories of Gettysburg lingered. Even as he looked out on refilled ranks just before Christmas in 1863, Capt. Henry T. Owen described for his wife a recurring dream in which troops stretched out to his right and left as far as the eye could see, the whole line buffeted by enemy artillery and musket fire:

> Far away to the front, I saw the dim outlines of lofty hills, broken rocks and frightful precipices which resembled Gettysburg. As we advanced further I found we were fighting that great battle over again and I saw something before me like a thin shaddow which I tried to get around an[d] go by but it kept in front of me and whichever way I turned it still appeared between me and the enemy. Nobody else seemed to see or notice the shaddow which looked as thin as smoke, and did not prevent my seeing the enemy distinctly thru' it. I felt troubled and oppressed but still the shaddow went on before me. I pushed forward in the thickest of the fray trying to loose sight of it and went all through the Battle of Gettysburg again with the shadow forever before me and between me and the enemy and when I came out beyond the danger of shot it spoke and said "I am the angel that protected you. I will never leave nor forsake you." The surprise was so great that I awoke and burst into tears. What had I done that should entitle me to such favour beyond the hundreds of brave and reputed good men who had fallen on that day leaving widowed mothers and widowed wives, orphan children and disconsolate familes to mourn their fates.[177]

For so many Virginians, Gettysburg left even deeper scars.

Survivors of Gettysburg took away different sets of memories. Northerners gloried in victory, which sanctified their dead and gave new life to their cause. Just how these grand results had been accomplished mattered comparatively little; as Abraham Lincoln would say over the graves of the slain warriors, there was enough glory at Gettysburg to go around. Southerners, by contrast, felt deeply the sting of defeat. What happened at Gettysburg—in its smallest details—mattered to them very much. Both celebrating Northerners and mourning Southerners, however, shared a common need: a context for their sacrifice. Army gossip and camp rumor could fulfill only so much of this need; the disconnected threads of others did not flesh out a picture all survivors could understand. For that, the soldiers—and their friends and family at home—turned to the newspaper.

2

SCARCELY ANYBODY CAN GIVE A CORRECT ACCOUNT

"It's queer that scarcely anybody can give a correct account of a battle," wrote a Connecticut survivor of July 3, adding "I have seen all sorts of incorrect statements of it in the papers every day since."[1] Despite his skepticism, however, he and his fellow soldiers in both armies relied heavily upon the public press to tell them about great battles in which they played small parts. They also counted on newspapers to keep their families and friends informed. The soldiers might send home tidbits of army gossip, odd vignettes, and tidings of joy and sorrow, but many, such as North Carolina captain Benjamin F. Little, encouraged folks at home to read the paper, so that "you will get more correct news of the fights than I can give you."[2]

To cover the great charge of July 3 or any other Civil War battle well, the journalistic community faced two tough jobs. Field correspondents had to gather and then try to weave together disconnected threads of personal testimony and camp rumor into coherent narratives. By doing so in ways that informed readers without confusing or repulsing them, they greatly influenced the way history later recorded that very conventional infantry attack.[3] After all, newspapermen were the first to call this assault "Pickett's Charge."

The reporters' second obligation limited their ability to fulfill the first.

They had to file stories quickly. With an information-starved populace demanding news and company profits standing to benefit from increased readership, timely reporting often mattered more than detailed or accurate accounting. This priority also helped to carve out a special niche for Pickett's Charge in history and popular memory.

By July 3, 1863, the journalistic communities in both the North and the South understood their dual obligations.[4] As news from Gettysburg arrived in New York City, a reporter watched as "crowds collected around the bulletin boards of the newspaper office." He, and no doubt many others, had come to appreciate the high demand for war news as fast as it could be sent "to all the cities and hamlets within reach of the telegraph wires and the railroads."[5]

About forty-five war correspondents traveled with the two armies to Gettysburg.[6] Most, but not all, at this point in the war knew enough about the military art to explain the basics about campaign strategy, troop movements, tactically important terrain features, and military administration. But combat reporting still confounded them. "I am a poor hand to describe battles I do not see," admitted Whitelaw Reid of the Cincinnati *Gazette*.[7] He might well have added that fights he did witness proved no easier to explain. Still, such honesty did not stop him and his colleagues from attempting to describe the chaos of combat for readers who could not begin to comprehend it. The correspondents' inability to portray the horrors of battle did not seem to bother them much. They compensated for gaps in information and inadequacies of perspective with literary artistry, the real soul of this journalistic era's craft.

As long as their colorful and impressionistic stories reached their editors on time, reporters believed they had discharged their obligations. As Reid explained, none of his colleagues could "undertake a minute detail of the operations on all parts of the field." He himself dared to write only "the merest outline of its leading features—then off for Cincinnati by the speediest routes."[8] Southern journalists felt time's pressure even more; each had to decide whether to stay with the army in Pennsylvania or to rush back to telegraph offices in Shepherdstown, Martinsburg, or Winchester to file incomplete stories that might scoop competitors nonetheless.

Editors in New York and Richmond set the standards for war reporting for their respective sides. Well before the Civil War, editors throughout the entire nation routinely "clipped"—copied verbatim, with attribution—articles from New York newspapers, and even in 1863, such items from Northern sources still found their way into Southern dailies. Able reporters from the major New York dailies, the *Tribune*, *Herald*, and

Times, traveled with the Union armies, and the cooperative efforts of these men—along with talented writers for major newspapers in Philadelphia, Baltimore, Boston, and elsewhere—covered the entire North's need for war news. By contrast, Richmond editors possessed much less experience, and really not much interest, in serving the entire Confederacy. While their reporters covered as many of the major armies as they could, Virginia's press corps often found its credibility and its partisanship attacked by a host of critics throughout the South. Still, Richmond's influence as the Confederacy's journalistic heart in 1863 cannot be controverted.

Northern and Southern coverage of Pickett's Charge fit into a pattern for battle reporting that had evolved over the first two years of the war. Editors took seriously their obligation to provide comprehensive coverage of the entire conflict, not just the major battles. In July 1863, the siege at Vicksburg, an abortive Union advance on Richmond, and military activities around Charleston all commanded considerable ink even while dramatic events took place in Pennsylvania. Political news from Washington and Richmond, local affairs, business information, even international items always required space, too. By the time the armies met at Gettysburg, therefore, newspapermen developed a fairly concise format for handling news from the front.

Large-type headlines and timely telegraphic reports first drew an audience. These snippets explained little and often teemed with inaccuracies, but editors used them to whet readers' appetites for the hard news to come. Then, to aid comprehension, editors frequently provided a fairly general map of the battle site. Finally, within a few days of the fighting's end, major papers might include one or more general overviews, fleshed out with letters from soldiers, telegraphic exchanges between senior commanders, and, of course, long casualty lists. And this was the extent of typical battle reporting. Correspondents followed the armies into new campaigns, and editors found new stories to tell. One short week after Gettysburg, New York newspapers carried only casualty lists, the only bit of "old news" the draft riots did not push off the front page.

Northern coverage of July 3 fits this pattern especially well. For major papers, the edition of Monday, July 6, carried the first word about the great charge of the previous Friday, for the most part in telegraphic dispatches from the field. While sorrow muted the joy of the victorious Northern soldiers, readers saw mostly bold headlines that carried glorious news. "Splendid Triumph of the Army of the Potomac," proclaimed a headline in the *New York Times*.[9] A far more excited *Harrisburg Daily Telegraph* editor announced: "The Rebellion Receives Its Death Stroke."[10] In large letters, the *Philadelphia Inquirer* printed "VICTORY!!" over a figure of the Stars and Stripes and included appropriate heroic verses with the ecstatic notation: "Waterloo Eclipsed!!"[11]

Below such glad tidings came other important news about the battle. Here, army gossip, which promised even more spectacular success or foretold greater calamities, blended inseparably with truth. Within a single column of such promises, a Harrisburg newspaper asserted that "Rebel Generals Longstreet and Hill Wounded and in Our Possession," "Rebel General Longstreet Mortally Wounded and Since Dead," and "The Rebel General A. P. Hill Killed."[12] Wishful thinking ran wild. The *New York Times* reported "The Rebel Retreat Cut Off" and hinted at impending annihilation: "The Rebel Pontoon Bridge at Williamsport Destroyed."[13] Such claims reveal the single most compelling point of interest to Northern editors: decisive victory.

Victory, of course, followed the repulse of the July 3 charge. Just as that action drew superlatives from soldiers, its awesome aspects inspired correspondents, too: "The sun of Austerlitz is not more memorable than that which is just flinging its dying rays over the field of this third day of successful battle," a reporter wired his editor just hours after the fighting ended. "The battles of Wednesday and yesterday were sufficiently terrible, but in that which has raged today the fighting done, not only by our troops, but by those of Lee's army, will rank in heroism, in perseverance, and in savage energy, with that of Waterloo."[14]

Many of the same elements that impressed soldiers about the great assault also touched the correspondents' imagination. The ferocity of the artillery bombardment challenged the descriptive powers of the reporters—most of whom observed it far from harm's way—just as it had amazed the soldiers who endured it. "The cannonading of Chancellorsville, Malvern and Manassas were pastimes compared with this," *New York Times* correspondent Samuel Wilkeson wrote.[15] Reid described the air along the Taneytown Road near Meade's headquarters as "alive with all mysterious sounds, and death in every one of them." He heard " 'muffled howls' that seemed in rage because their missile missed you, the angry buzz of the familiar Minie, the *spit* of the common musketball, hisses, and the great whirring rushes of shells."[16] The reporters appreciated that it had not been a one-sided exchange. "Our batteries returned the compliment with interest," wrote an observer, who noted that *the air seemed literally thick with iron*, and for more than an hour it seemed impossible that man or beast could live through it."[17]

As passive observers, reporters might have noted details about the cannonade that eluded soldiers on the front line, but they did not. Newspaper accounts set the beginning and the duration of the artillery preparation no more consistently than had the soldiers, nor did reporters speculate much on the number of guns involved. The soldiers had been impressed mostly by the shelling's intensity, and reporters conveyed this notion to their readers. One reporter used the human cost as his bottom line: "I have only to state that Captain Rorty, Lieut. Cushing and Lieut. Woodruff, commanders of batteries, were killed, and that scarcely more than one officer remains uninjured in command of any of the batteries engaged" in an artillery duel that "kept up without cessation for nearly three hours."[18]

A silence finally fell over the field, and the breeze carried away some of the powder smoke. Veteran soldiers had known that the hush would be short-lived, and experienced reporters understood that, too. Reid watched the attacking force advance "sooner, indeed, and wider than was expected."[19] And just as Northern soldiers found different ways to describe the formation the Southerners employed, correspondents wrote of two lines, "three lines, with twenty thousand men," columns, or simply "masses."[20] According to L. L. Crounse of the *New York Times*, Longstreet's whole corps was "hurled upon our position by column in mass, and also in lines of battle."[21]

Northern accounts of the actual clash of arms included few details about the day's military action. Individual brigades and regiments did not march across the page. Unless they died in combat, all but the most senior commanders remained unnamed. Troop strengths and dispositions, except in most general terms, did not appear. Reporters described the ebb and flow of battle in colorful prose, but they did not explain or analyze the reasons for the inevitable advances and retreats that marked the day's action. They simply provided evocative vignettes that set the stage for a most desirable conclusion: victory.

Results mattered. Even as they explained little about the conduct of the battle itself, reporters took great care to remind readers just how much had been at stake on July 3. A writer for the *Baltimore American* explained: "Never was there a more vigorous and deadly assault than that made on our centre by Longstreet."[22] If that attack on "the key to the whole position" succeeded, "they would have forced us into retreat, and the whole battle would have been lost." General Lee "threw his best brigades against it. Wave after wave of living valor rolled up that slope, only to roll back again under the deadly fire of our artillery and infantry."[23]

Recording the sheer drama unfolding before them held their complete attention. Whitelaw Reid had watched as the Confederates came on, "the flower of their army to the front, victory staked upon the issue." For a time, success for Southern arms seemed assured. "In some places they literally lifted up and pushed back our lines." The Union line appeared so weak that "it had not weight enough to oppose to this momentum." Indeed, making a singular episode appear as general experience, the report continued: The Confederates "were upon the guns, were bayoneting the gunners, were waving their flags above our pieces."[24] The stalwart Union line held! Northern reporters celebrated that while Southern soldiers had "penetrated to the fatal point," their ranks then dissolved under a stout Union resistance. Then they retreated in a panic "unparalleled in any battle in which the Army of the Potomac has ever been engaged. The enemy quailed like ewes before a tempest," one correspondent reported.[25]

When the soldiers could not explain to reporters the details of just how they had triggered that rout, Northern writers filled the gap in interesting, occasionally contradictory, ways. Some boasted about the Northerners' fighting prowess. The Southerners "marched up the hill and speedily marched down again, sadly worsted" by their encounter "with earnest men and frowning batteries, dealing death and destruction without stint." Their officers had crowded them forward, but "meeting the inevitable storm of bullets and canister that had so fearfully thinned their ranks during the day they were not to be held under it."[26]

Other Northern reporters endowed the enemy with superhuman qualities to enhance the reputation of the Union soldiers who had sent them reeling. Lt. Henry Clare wrote his brother that "their determination was to effect a storm or die in the attempt, — for such were their orders as were afterward confirmed by prisoners, officers now in our hands."[27] Conversations with Confederate prisoners supplied one reporter with the insight that "this charge was led by Lee in person," and his "name and his presence could certainly not have added to its power or enthusiasm." All the more reason, the writer noted, to celebrate the fact that Union forces still managed to throw back the charge "as a girl hurls the shuttlecock."[28] Another writer learned from prisoners that Lee had threatened to use artillery against his own infantry if it appeared they might fail.[29]

Samuel Wilkeson, the skilled correspondent for the *New York Times*, penned the most widely clipped Northern account of the July 3 charge, and even today it continues to inform histories, novels, poems, and other renderings of the event. Wilkeson's narrative illustrates both the good and bad in Northern reporting about the day's events. Imprecise on specifics, inaccurate in spots, his reports nonetheless brought together for his civilian audience a series of colorful images that conveyed the ferocity and scope of the battle and especially the importance of its results for the Union war effort.

With a professional journalist's eye for interesting stories, Wilkeson's first recollection of the cannonade began with a bird in a peach tree near

*The first visual image of the July 3 charge based on eyewitness sketches to appear in the Northern press (*Harper's Weekly, *August 8, 1863)*

Meade's headquarters interrupted in midsong when a shell screamed over his perch. The air filled with "every size and form of shell known to British and American gunnery," with as "many as six in a second, constantly two in a second" falling all around. He saw an ambulance roll by, pulled by a three-legged horse, its back limb removed by a shell. In the Taneytown Road, Union soldiers "died with the peculiar yells that blend the extorted cry of pain with horror and despair." But of the bombardment's effectiveness, its duration, or its impact on the waiting infantry, he said nothing.

Wilkeson's impressionistic style continued into his account of the assault itself. When the artillery stopped, the Southern troops advanced, and "splendidly they did this work—the highest and severest test of the stuff that soldiers are made of." He noticed—as did the soldiers—that Pettigrew's men of "HILL's division, in line of battle, came first on the double quick. Their muskets at the 'right-shoulder-shift.'" Then, to explain the appearance of Pickett's men farther south, he decided that "LONGSTREET's came as the support, at the usual distance, with war cries and a savage insolence as yet untutored by defeat."

Hill's men disappeared from Wilkeson's narrative as his vision narrowed to exclude all but the critical fight at the Angle. But if Hill's men departed, key actors in the fight near the copse of trees did not appear in their stead. Webb, Harrow, and Hall's names are missing. Indeed, the few tactical details Wilkeson employed might explain nearly any combat action during the war. "The rebels were over our defences." They killed the horses and cannoneers around one cannon and tried to turn it on the defenders until, simply, "the bayonet drove them back." With the help of their artillery, outnumbered Union soldiers undertook first "to beat back LONGSTREET, and then to charge upon him, and take a great number of his men and himself prisoner." He could exaggerate to make a point. The Union fire grew so hot that all of "ARMSTEAD's brigade . . . dropped their muskets and crawled on their hands and knees underneath the stream of shot," crushed by "men who were their equals in spirit, and their superiors in tenacity. There never was better fighting since Thermopylae than was done yesterday by our infantry and artillery." [30] Wilkeson—and many of the best war reporters—excelled at painting these vivid, yet somehow bloodless, images of battle.

When the battle was over, Northern soldiers' "shouts of victory could be heard for many miles when the enemy retreated"; but they still had to deal with the grisly aftermath of battle and a deep sense of personal loss.[31] Civilian reporters, usually not similarly burdened, understood that their readers did not really want to hear about the indescribable horrors they had seen and instead launched a national victory celebration.

On July 6, the *New York Herald* proclaimed that the victory at Gettysburg "has, we verily believe, settled the fate of the rebellion. The issue accepted in the campaign by the rebel General Lee was Washington or Richmond, and he has lost the game." [32] After two years of frustrating defeats, the Union army had found the capable leader it deserved: "It is a 'big thing' for a major general to take command of an army on Sunday and flog the enemy before the end of the week. But it could not have been done with any other than the Army of the Potomac." [33] On July 3, Meade and his army had won a battle greater than Waterloo: "Lee victorious, Baltimore, Washington and Philadelphia would have fallen before him. The rebel flag would have floated over the national capitol." No bit of hyperbole seemed excessive. "The nations of Europe would no longer withhold the recognition [for which] the rebel leaders have for so many months been asking. The way would have been opened for a peace which should embrace the downfall of our government." But that could no longer happen after July 3: "The long suspense is over." [34]

Victory crowned the entire army's brow. Thus only a few of its individual soldiers won national prominence. After a brief flurry of undeserved accolades for Maj. Gen. O. O. Howard (many reporters had watched the charge from good vantage points near his XI Corps headquarters), Maj. Gen. Winfield S. Hancock's II Corps became the darlings of the press. "It was on the Second corps that the flower of the rebel

Maj. Gen. Winfield S. Hancock, commander of the II Corps of the Army of the Potomac. The Northern press made him a hero. (Francis Trevelyan Miller, comp., Photographic History of the Civil War *[New York: Review of Reviews, 1911], 10:179)*

army was concentrated; it was there that the heaviest shock beat upon and shook and even sometimes crumbled our line," Reid wrote.[35] One reporter noted that Hancock was "handsome, with shaven face and wide shirt collar turned down—an absolute American,"[36] and a Baltimore paper proclaimed him "the great hero of Friday's battle."[37] When he fell wounded, his men determined to fight harder, and "when they learned that their wounded commander was still watching them and directing their movements, they fought like demons, and drove back the enemy."[38] A few of Hancock's men still appear in the historical record today; others do not. We recall artilleryman Alonzo Cushing, whom Wilkeson saluted, but we forget Corporal Hayden of the 1st Minnesota, who, the Northern public learned, made ten Rebels surrender.[39]

In addition to celebrating only a few individual heroes, most reporters also underappreciated the contributions of units other than those of the II Corps. One New York correspondent noted that while "Gen. HANCOCK, with the noble old Second Army corps," held the Union center, he was only "aided by Gen. Doubleday's division of the First corps."[40] Specific mention of the Vermont Brigade's attack on Pickett's right flank did not appear at all in some early accounts. A Philadelphia paper extended credit to the III and V Corps, which took no part in the repulse.[41]

Those same Philadelphia newspapers offered the exception to the profusion of generalities that typically described the events of July 3. With pardonable pride, their reporters gave special attention to a local interest story. They bragged about the accomplishments of Webb's Philadelphia Brigade at the Angle: "The doings of this body, attached to the Second Corps, should not be allowed to go unnoticed," and "their unwavering behavior under the most galling fire and the most desperate bayonet charges . . . have made them conspicuous for unexampled daring and bravery."[42]

Although the correspondents waxed eloquent as they praised the victory, they noted its horrendous cost to both sides. Even if most could not share the sense of personal loss the soldiers themselves felt, they still felt compelled to let their readers know that Gettysburg did "not equal in duration the seven days' fight on the Chickahominy, but outstrips it in severity. Indeed, in point of reckless prodigality of human life and desperate valor it will rank with the most celebrated battles of the world."[43] As Wilkeson looked around, he saw ground "red with blood and covered with mangled bodies." In a small space in front of Gibbon's division, he counted seven dead Southerners, three of whom were piled on top of one another. Nearby, fifteen more, "the adventurous spirits who, in the face of the horrible stream of canister, shell and musketry, scaled the fence wall in their attempt upon our batteries" lay stiff in death.[44]

Great, if contradictory, interest in the fate of senior Confederate officers—exclusive of Longstreet and Hill—further confirmed the severity of the fighting. Wilkeson reported Confederate general Richard B. Garnett's death.[45] Another reported that "Gen. Dick Garnett himself was wounded and barely made his escape."[46] Another noted that while most of Garnett's survivors surrendered, the general himself "by the aid of two of his men, succeeded, though wounded, in making his escape."[47] Reports on the mortally wounded Gen. Lewis Armistead cited him as "Olmstead, of Georgia," "Armstead," and in one case, a writer noted the death of the "rebel General Arnold."[48] When Armistead was captured, Wilkeson reported wrongly that he "asked immediately for General Meade, who was his classmate at West Point."[49] Another paper misidentified the captured Col. Birkett D. Fry of the 13th Alabama of Archer's brigade as the Fry who had assassinated a Union general in Tennessee the previous August.[50]

Union casualties deserved better than this kind of morbid interest. A New York reporter wrote that "while the pen turns with avidity to the description of triumphs, I prefer, in this last, greatest, grandest struggle to act the honorable part of the victor, and . . . to tell you of our sufferings."[51] The mortal wounding of Wilkeson's own son on July 1 set the tone for his report, which concluded: "Oh, you dead, who at Gettysburg have baptized with your blood the second birth of Freedom in America, how you are to be envied! I rise from a grave whose wet clay I have passionately kissed, and I look up and see Christ spanning this battle-field with his feet and reaching fraternally and lovingly up to heaven."[52]

The powerful blending of victory and death inspired reporters to seek a deeper meaning in the devastation. Whitelaw Reid noticed some wilted flowers on an old grave in the Gettysburg cemetery: "Human blood watered the roots—patriot blood, that made them doubly sacred." He plucked a few as "my only trophy from that glorious field."[53] T. M. Cook mourned the "terrible sacrifice of noble blood" but took satisfaction in knowing that the "loyal sons of the North have not shrunk to lay down their lives by thousands and tens of thousands to drive back the impudent invader off sacred soil, and their sacrifice has been signally favorable and acceptable."[54] In this way, the Union dead of July 3 became only one part of that necessary sacrifice.

These things, and little more, interested Northern reporters and their audiences. They did not provide the grist for future historical controversy or the enshrinement of a great moment in American military history called "Pickett's Charge." Indeed, when Whitelaw Reid placed "Pickett's splendid division of Longstreet's corps" in the forefront of the assault with "the best of A. P. Hill's veterans in support," he became the only prominent Northern journalist to mention by name the general whose greatest fame attaches to July 3, 1863.[55] S. J. Rea, a special correspondent for the *Philadelphia Inquirer*, learned from some wounded Virginians at a Chambersburg hospital that Pickett's men "were among the troops most relied upon by LEE" and that the division "suffered more than any other division in their whole army." Beyond Reid's brief mention and Rea's sidebar that the division commander "is reported to have been captured, but to have subsequently contrived to escape," Northern press coverage barely mentioned the name of George Edward Pickett.[56]

Northern press accounts, then, contribute vivid images and the glorification of decisive victory to the popular memory of July 3. The Southern press, however, deserves the credit for providing the foundation of facts and fancy for legend building and myth making. Without the attention devoted to the specifics of the July 3 charge contained in the Confederacy's newspapers, American history would know little about it. Moreover, it most likely would not be called "Pickett's Charge."

The Gettysburg campaign had ended in unaccustomed defeat for Lee's army, of course, and the newspapers waded into the public apportioning of blame. Just as the thrill of victory quieted open criticism of Union generalship at Gettysburg, defeat spawned considerable debate in the Southern press. Where controversy arose, no detail faded to unimportance.

Soldiers spent the first week or so after the battle trying to figure out what went wrong, but Southern civilians were not even aware of just how badly their army had fared in Pennsylvania. Editors needed timely news, and until their correspondents could reestablish telegraphic contact, they sought out other sources of information.

The first reliable news available to Southern readers came, ironically enough, from the North. Avid readers scanned pirated copies of Washington, New York, Baltimore, and Philadelphia newspapers in Richmond's Confederate Reading Room. They found much to cheer in accounts of the first two days' fight. Even as late as July 7, North Carolinian Joseph A. Graham, stationed outside Richmond with the 27th North Carolina, wrote home that "the news from our army everwhere is very encouraging. Judging from the Yankee accounts, which are all we can get now, I think that Gen. Lee has given the Yanks a sound thrashing at Gettysburg, Pa." [57]

Still, Richmond editors could not pretend they knew the current fate of Lee's army. On July 7, the *Daily Dispatch* reported that "if the decisive battle has yet been fought, it must have been on the 4th, 5th, or 6th of July," all entirely appropriate for a great Southern victory since "these three days are all honorable in the history of mankind." The importance of July 4 needed no further comment, of course, but the editor of the *Daily Dispatch* felt compelled to note that on July 5 Winfield Scott had won at Chippewa during the War of 1812 and that on July 6 Napoleon had fought his grand battle at Wagram in 1809. The editor confidently wondered: "What will the Yankees do next if this army shall have been annihilated? That is a question which it behooves Mr. Lincoln to think of very seriously." [58]

Wishful thinking buttressed by fragments of news from the North and a solid record of previous battlefield victories permitted such optimism for a while. By July 8, however, the same editor had grown a bit more circumspect: "We feel as well assured that General Lee, if he has met the enemy in a pitched battle, has inflicted a terrible defeat upon them, as we do that we are living, breathing, sentient beings." [59]

Farther south, where people found timely news even harder to get, high hopes lasted even longer. As late as July 13, a South Carolina editor still boasted that "the Yankees MAY report Lee defeated and retreating, and his army demoralized, but we don't believe it. They have no general who can out-maneuver or out-general Lee." [60] A few days later, another newspaper dismissed celebratory articles from Northern papers as "so warped and distorted that the groundwork of truth is scarcely discoverable beneath the mass of pigment and varnish with which it is overlaid." [61]

Despite such bravado, however, the unbroken official silence raised concern. On July 7, the *Daily Dispatch* printed a telegram from a correspondent at Martinsburg proclaiming that "General Lee defeated the enemy in the battle of Friday last" but admitted a loss of 4,000 prisoners.[62] Rumors of over 60,000 Southern casualties arrived in Richmond that same day, but the editor soon reminded readers against reading too much into information from "telegraphic correspondents," who "with the best intentions are often led astray. They are obliged in the absence of official intelligence, to depend on the evidence of persons from the scene of action, who are often but imperfectly informed themselves, and sometimes on mere rumor." Unwilling to concede anything less than complete victory, the editor remained sure that if Lee had fought a decisive battle, he "utterly destroyed the only obstacle that stood between him and Baltimore" and could be expected to take that city in a few days.[63]

Northern dailies of July 6, the first to carry hard news about the bloody charge of July 3 and the ultimate victory of Union arms, reached Richmond by July 8. Richmond editors who just a few days earlier had reprinted Northern claims of Confederate success now asserted that those same sources printed nothing but lies. They continued to claim unprecedented success for Southern arms. A writer for the *New York Times* concluded that "such systematic and direct lying has not heretofore been known in this war, and to equal it we have to go back to the military bulletins of the English when they are engaged in war."[64]

By Friday, July 10, however, while hopes for victory still flickered, unqualified success seemed less and less likely. The confident tone of the Richmond papers wavered. News about July 3 in particular began to swing wildly back and forth between claims of great victory to portents of equally great disaster. An early Southern account of the events of July 3 read: "We *drove the enemy back five miles* to the heights, which he had fortified" and "broke through two of their lines of battle formed to meet the onset of our troops" before being repulsed.[65] Another early account noted that in the fight of July 3, "Hill's corps and Heth's division [were] principally engaged. They reached the entrenchments, as did also the division of General Pickett."[66] Pickett's Virginians never took second place to Hill's troops in the Richmond press again.

About one week after the great charge, the story finally began to unfold, first slowly and then in a great profusion of painful detail. Initial reports from correspondents with Lee's army arrived only as fragments, not the complete stories that Northern readers enjoyed. A reporter's brief conversation with two wounded Virginians who left Gettysburg on July 4 confirmed that Pickett's men had taken part in heavy fighting on July 3, and the reporter noted—without further explanation—that "the loss in the division [was] very heavy."[67] Such tidbits of news deepened all Southerners' concern, but for Richmond residents in particular, hints about Pickett's losses increased their worry. Their fears could not have been lightened when the *Baltimore American* claimed that Longstreet's attack on the Union center cost Lee's men "a loss of life unparalleled by any previous battle in which they had come in conflict with the grand old Army of the Potomac."[68]

Finally, on July 12, the Richmond papers dispelled nearly all remaining doubts about the fortunes of Lee's army and the fate of Pickett's division. The *Richmond Whig* used a familiar comparison: "The disadvantage of our position at Gettysburg may be understood by saying it was decidedly more than the positions of the hostile forces at the late battle of Fredericksburg reversed."[69] No doubt, family and friends of Pickett's men hoped that this report, too, exaggerated the event.

By July 13, nearly every Richmond paper had begun to address the growing certainty that the Southern army had met defeat at Gettysburg. No editor wanted to attach any great shame to the reverse. It had not been a rout. While on July 3 "our troops stormed the first line of the enemy and carried his works," retreat was not shameful since further high losses were not "justified by the results to be obtained," and the retirement of the army "was effected in most admirable order."[70]

By now, however, the long trains of wounded arriving at Richmond hospitals told the story better than the newspapers could. Readers had lost patience. A Confederate officer posted outside Richmond wondered how the first promises of victory could become portents of a "worse than Antietatum [*sic*] or Sharpsburg defeat in Pa." so quickly. He concluded that the early reports had been "fabricated by despatchers, from men who did not know, or care what news was sent, perhaps was sent to deceive us."[71] At least they did not face the uncertainty of knowing nothing at all. As late as July 17, an Alabamian wrote to a Virginia friend, "The news is so scarce here concerning the A.N.V. that I do not know whether Gen Lee was whipped at Gettysburg or not. Write me the result of the battle and what our army is now doing."[72]

Seldom had Richmond editors faced such a daunting task. Even worse, they found themselves caught between conflicting priorities. They had agreed to carry great numbers of official and unofficial government pronouncements important to all Southern citizens that might be "clipped" and reprinted throughout the Confederacy. As Virginians, though, they felt a strong responsibility to give first attention to local readers who had family and friends in Pickett's fifteen regiments.

Virginia readers did not see any such quandary. For them, local concerns came first. The *Daily Dispatch*'s editor understood that "much interest is felt by the public in the fate of the 1st Virginia regiment, which was organized in this city" and took quick steps to discover the truth behind rumors that the unit had been " 'cut all to pieces.' " He then reconstructed the events of July 3 from the stories of recently arrived wounded. Perhaps hearing of the Virginians' first brush against the Vermonters, he told of the several hundred Union soldiers defending the stone wall who "threw down their arms and ran towards our men, giving themselves up as prisoners," regretting only that a "good many of them were killed in running forward to surrender, our men not understanding the meaning of the maneuver." [73]

Such tales of glory did not tell hundreds of Virginia families what they most wanted to know, however. It really mattered little that "seven Confederate flags were planted on the stone fence," when another part of that same sentence read: "Nearly all of our severely wounded were left in the hands of the enemy." It unsettled waiting relatives to read the report of a wounded officer of the 1st Virginia, who described how that unit marched "solemnly and steadily" toward "heavy and compact columns of the enemy" fronted by "a double line of skirmishers to oppose our single line." [74] They really did not want to read that the Union forces were "posted behind a strong stone wall, and had parallels beyond this, so that when one line was taken, another and another remained. These places are not improperly called by the men 'slaughter pens.' " [75]

One by one, each of Richmond's five main newspapers gave in to their local readership and devoted considerable attention to the fate of the Virginia division. Slowly, painfully, twin themes emerged: great loss and great heroism. General Kemper, "shot in the side and groin by a minie ball," had been captured but then rescued by a sergeant of the 1st Virginia, the hero later identified as Leigh M. Blanton of Amelia County. [76] Armistead was depicted as falling mortally wounded "while standing on the enemy's entrenchments with his hat hoisted on this sword, cheering his men on in the charge." General Pickett led a charmed life that day. Uninjured himself, he was "deeply affected by the loss of so many of his gallant officers, and it is said that he wept bitterly over the mutilation of his noble division." [77] Indeed, even as the tragedy that befell his division became more and more apparent, Pickett's personal reputation shone brighter and brighter. Maj. Kirkwood Otey sent one paper the 11th Virginia's casualty report and could not resist avowing that his division commander "showed himself fully worthy of the occasion and of the men he commanded. He and his staff were, happily, unhurt." The lightly wounded Otey freely asserted that "the celebrated 'charge of the 600' at Balaklava was not more daring and is not less entitled to live in history than that of the five thousand Virginians who stormed the heights at Gettysburg."[78]

The collective picture of Pickett's division as it evolved in the pages of Richmond papers creates a stirring image of the gallant Southern man-in-arms and the best blood of Virginia. For drama and pathos, Virginians' portrayals of the division's attack far outstripped what could be found in Northern accounts.

"T. P." wrote how Pickett's men deployed "as coolly and deliberately as if forming for dress parade." Led by Pickett himself, the division always fought well, "but the crowning glory of those patriot heroes was achieved in the assault upon the iron-clad crest of Gettysburg. The list of casualties tells, in terms of truer eloquence, the bravery and patriotism of that blood-stained and scar-honored division, than can any figures of rhetoric or poetry."[79]

Correspondent "Unus" lamented the great sacrifice the attack demanded of the Old Dominion. "How sad to think that after brave men have done all that man could possibly do by their valor, won for themselves an immortal name, that some mismanagement should rob them and their country of the fruit of their heroic deeds." He mourned for "the gallant dead! What pen can do them justice, can express in language sufficiently warm a nation's gratitude, or in strains sufficiently mournful the agony and grief that now broods around many a hearthstone in Virginia." He concluded with a stern demand: "There is fault to be attached to some-one—let our high officers, the proper ones, say to whom."[80]

No official inquiry followed, of course. But the press would not wait for such proceedings in any case. On July 23, a long and detailed article in the *Richmond Enquirer* addressed many of the battle's most important moments with such authority that it very much colored the way the great assault would be handed down to posterity. Seasoned army correspondent Jonathan Albertson, who signed himself only "A," wrote so eloquently about the events of July 3 that many postwar chroniclers and historians have accepted his account as entirely factual.[81]

Albertson's account won considerable credibility in part because he painstakingly explained that he witnessed the advance personally. After the artillery bombardment, during which the "hills and rocks seemed to reel like a drunken man," Albertson observed the formation of the attacking column. Pickett's division deployed "in advance, supported on the right by Wilcox's brigade, and on the left by Heth's division, commanded by Pettigrew." Since he had seen Ambrose Wright's Georgians charge over that same ground the day before, Albertson now watched Pickett's men "prepare for the same bloody trial, and already felt that their efforts would be vain unless their supports should be true as steel and brave as lions."

In the next few weeks, editors throughout the South would clip Albertson's description of the charge itself:

I have never seen since the war began (and I have been in all the great fights of this army) troops enter a fight in such splendid order as did this splendid division of Pickett's. Now Pettigrew's command emerge from the woods upon Pickett's left, and sweep down the slope of the hill to the valley beneath, and some two or three hundred yards in rear of Pickett. I saw by the wavering of this line as they entered the conflict that they wanted the firmness of nerve and steadiness of tread which so characterized Pickett's men, and I felt that these men would not, could not stand the tremendous ordeal to which they would soon be subjected. These were mostly raw troops, which had been recently brought from the South, and who had, perhaps, never been under fire — who certainly had never been in any very severe fight — and I trembled for their conduct. Just as Pickett was getting well under the enemy's fire our batteries ceased firing. This was a fearful moment for Pickett and his brave command. Why do not our guns reopen their fire? is the inquiry that rises upon every lip. Still our batteries are silent as death! But on presses Pickett's brave Virginians, and now the enemy open upon them, from more than fifty guns, a terrible fire of grape, shell and canister. On, on they move in unbroken line, delivering a deadly fire as they advance. Now they have reached the Emmetsburg [sic] road, and here they meet a severe fire from heavy masses of the enemy's infantry, posted behind the stone fence, while their artillery, now free from the annoyance of our artillery, turn their whole fire upon this devoted band. Still they remain firm. Now again they advance; they storm the stone fence; the Yankees fly; the enemy's batteries are, one by one, silenced in quick succession as Pickett's men deliver their fire at the gunners and drive them from their pieces. I see Kemper and Armistead plant their banner in the enemy's works; I hear their glad shout of victory!

Let us now look after Pettigrew's division. Where are they now? While the victorious shout of the gallant Virginians is still ringing in my ears, I turn my eyes to the left, and there all over the plain, in utmost confusion, is scattered this strong division. Their line is broken; they are flying, apparently panic stricken, to the rear. The gallant Pettigrew is wounded, but he still retains command, and is vainly trying striving to rally his men. Still the moving mass rushes pell mell to the rear, and

Pickett is left alone to contend with the hordes of the enemy now pouring in upon him on every side. Garnett falls, killed by a minnie ball; and Kemper, the brave and chivalrous, reels under a mortal wound and is taken to the rear. Now the enemy move around strong flanking bodies of infantry, and are rapidly gaining Pickett's rear. The order is given to fall back, and our men commence the movement, doggedly contending for every inch of ground. The enemy press heavily our retreating line, and many noble spirits who had passed safely through the fiery ordeal of the advance and charge, now fall on the right and on the left. Armistead is wounded and left in the enemy's hands. At this critical moment the shattered remnant of Wright's Georgia brigade is moved forward to cover the retreat, and the fight closes here.[82]

Albertson's piece quickly became a lightning rod for those Southerners who complained about the bias and parochialism of the Richmond press. At the same time, Virginians found in his account authoritative validation of army gossip that already had identified the culprits responsible for the great defeat and Pickett's steep losses. Albertson made many accusations that Virginia readers largely ignored. For instance, he told how Southern batteries had ceased firing because "they had *exhausted all their ammunition,*" and this, he asserted, "would seem to demand investigation." Albertson pointed out that "*twice* we took McPherson's Ridge [actually Cemetery Ridge] — the real key to the enemy's whole position — *once by a single brigade* [Wright's] on Thursday [July 2], and again by a single division on Friday [July 3], and that in both instances we lost it by the failure of proper supports to the attacking parties." He did not assign blame for the failure to support Wright on July 2, but for the loss on July 3 he wrote, "The most careless reader will be at no loss to discover the responsible party." Clearly, Pettigrew's men and Wilcox and Lang from Anderson's division were responsible for the destruction of Pickett's division.[83]

Adjoining columns of the same issue of the *Enquirer* carried a second lengthy article on Pickett's division prepared by a reporter identified only as "T." It reinforced Albertson's vivid commentary entirely. "From the time men first met men in deadly strife, no more unflinching courage was ever displayed by the veteran troops of the most martial people than the battle of Gettysburg witnessed in the determined valor of Pickett's division." They endured the massive artillery bombardment without complaint but not without loss: "See that shattered arm; that leg shot off; that headless body, and here the mangled form of a young and gallant Lieutenant, who had braved the perils of many battles." When Pickett gave the order to advance, "that flag which waved amid the wild tempest of battle at Gaines' Mill, Frazer's Farm, and Manassas, never rose more proudly." When it fell, "see! how quickly it again mounts upward, borne by some gallant man, who feels keenly the honor of his old commonwealth." Pickett had advanced with his men "as if courting death by his own daring intrepidity." The list of known dead and seriously wounded seemed endless, the reporter noted, yet more to be mourned were the unknown dead who found "few opportunities of realizing any distinction, which ambition might covet." He knew "many a Virginia home will mourn the loss of some noble spirit, yet, at the name of Pickett's division, and the battle of Gettysburg, how the eye will glisten, and the blood course quicker, and the heart beat warm, as among its noble dead is recalled the name of some cherished one. They bore themselves worthy of their lineage and their State. Who would recall them from their bed of glory?—each sleeps in a hero's grave."[84]

Accounts of the heroism of Pickett's men appeared in papers throughout the Confederacy, and not all came from clipped Richmond stories. Readers of the Augusta *Daily Constitutionalist* learned from brigade commander Ambrose Wright that Pickett and Pettigrew both began the advance in fine order. But then, "Generals, Colonels, Captains, Lieutenants, privates, as thick as autumn leaves they strew the plain." Pickett's Virginians pushed on, but "on the left Pettigrew's line wavers—it pauses—all is lost—it falls back—it runs. . . . Helter-skelter, pell-mell, here they come. But one thought seems to actuate them all, and that is to gain a safe place in the rear."[85] Pickett's men fell back fighting.

Peter W. Alexander, a correspondent for the *Savannah Republican* and *Mobile Daily Advertiser and Register* wrote the most factual Southern newspaper report on the Gettysburg campaign. Less dramatic and less scathing in tone than Albertson's more frequently cited article, he tried to address the most pressing controversies. He handled the confusing action of July 1 and July 2 with remarkable clarity, but his account of July 3 suffered from a straightforward writing style that some readers found dry. Still, the report shows clearly that, even when stripped of emotional pull, most of the war correspondents who marched with Lee's army had reached a consensus. Alexander recorded that Pickett's order to advance on Cemetery Ridge "was executed in gallant style, and some of the batteries on the Hill were carried" at high cost. Unfortunately, the "want of proper support" (he did not name a scapegoat), "the movement of the enemy upon his exposed and bleeding flanks, and the terrible cross and oblique fire concentrated on him" forced Pickett to fall back with heavy loss.[86] While less exciting than many contemporary accounts of the great charge, its sentiments were sufficiently consistent with those expressed in Richmond to

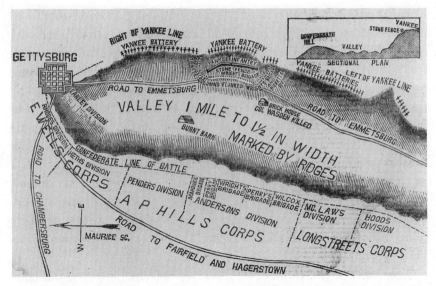

Manuscript map prepared for the Augusta, Ga., Daily Constitutionalist. *Note that only the July 2 attack of Gen. A. R. Wright's Georgia brigade and the attack of Pickett's Virginia division on July 3, both near the copse of trees, win special notice here. (University of Georgia Library, Athens, Ga.)*

reverse the usual practice; Virginia editors clipped extracts of Alexander's article for their own papers.

For nearly a month, the literary outpourings continued. In early August, the *Southern Illustrated News* featured a handsome front-page woodcut of General George E. Pickett. In the accompanying story, after an examination of the general's military career from West Point to San Juan Island, the fortunes of the Virginia division at Gettysburg took center stage. Quoting freely from Albertson's *Enquirer* article and other press accounts, the author reminded readers yet again that "Major General Pickett has well earned and will no doubt receive the meed of his country's praise" and "it is, indeed, a high honor to have belonged to Pickett's Division and to have fought under that gallant commander."[87]

All this coverage was well calculated to ease the heavy hearts of so many bereaved Virginians. But since the coverage contained inaccuracies and hyperbole of all kinds, dissenters demanding redress of both real and perceived grievances stepped forward in great numbers. From their camp near Culpeper, the survivors of Archer's Tennessee brigade took aim at Albertson. Although the correspondent had not mentioned them by name or state, "Deo Vindice" called attention to his "highly derogatory" comments "so grossly untrue that we cannot allow them to pass uncorrected." If Albertson believed that Pettigrew's division was "*sup-*

porting Gen Pickett's division in the fight of the 3d July, and that it failed to do its duty," he was guilty of "an error which only could have been committed by one far in the rear." The critic suggested that "for copper-distilled, unadulterated facts, one must be in closer proximity, though, perhaps, less consistent with personal safety." The Tennesseans, the writer argued, were "in the first line, *supporting* no one." They advanced "as far and as gallantly" as Pickett's men and "were repulsed simultanously with the whole line." The Tennessee critic also admitted that while some elements of Pettigrew's North Carolina brigade had seen less action than the rest of the division, "if Davis' Mississippians, Brockenbrough's Virginians and Archer's Tennesseans—who have participated in every engagement from Williamsburg to Gettysburg—are raw," as Albertson had charged, "then the whole Army of Northern Virginia is in a deplorably crude condition." He concluded that Virginians had never appreciated the efforts of the Tennessee brigade, even though it had "placed many noble souls beneath the green soil of the valley in defence of Virginia's sacred soil." [88]

Similarly, a member of the 13th Alabama, also in Archer's brigade, wrote that "no mere looker on" could know that after taking heavy losses in the opening battle on July 1, the entire brigade "lost over fifty per cent of the remainder on the 3d in that great and glorious charge on the heights." They had gone "to the enemy's guns and took possession, but could not hold them against the strong lines of the enemy" that day. "The bones of many of our comrades tell but too mournfully where we were on that memorable occasion," so he and his comrades found it hard "to have their reputation tarnished by an anonymous letter writer or newspaper correspondent." [89]

Wilcox's Alabamians and Lang's Floridians assigned to the protection of Pickett's right flank also felt the sting of blame for leaving the Virginians to their destruction. Colonel Lang especially criticized Albertson's story, which, he argued, "(unintentionally of course), glaringly misrepresented the part taken by" his brigade on July 3. It also bothered Lang that Peter Alexander's piece mentioned only Wilcox's men and ignored the Florida brigade that "moved side by side with Wilcox's during the entire day, losing nearly two-thirds of the entire number taken into action." It was easy to see why he resented the omission of any reference to Florida troops: "They fight, not for vain dreams of glory, nor yet for newspaper fame, or notoriety; but they are unwilling to stand by in silence and see their deeds so misrepresented to posterity, as to cause their children to blush for shame when they read of them in days to come. All we ask of those who record history, while we make it, is simply justice." [90]

"A Private" of the 2nd Florida warned the Richmond *Sentinel* that "when our good names were foully assailed, and slander, with her busy tongues, falsely coupled the words cowards and Florida brigade together, at the fatal field of Gettysburg, wonder not that we turn like the trodden and tortured worm, and deny the foul calumny, and claim justice." The Floridians had left the field only after everyone else had retreated, he asserted. He invited "the skeptic to visit our camps, and after seeing our decimated ranks, he will no longer doubt the credit we are entitled to." [91]

North Carolina felt the insult most keenly of all. In the *Raleigh Register*, a North Carolinian complained of the "grossest injustice to Gen. Pettigrew's brigade" contained in Albertson's article and cited in refutation the "letter—the last he ever wrote—from General Pettigrew to Gov. Vance—[which] speaks favorably of the conduct of this brigade, telling their 'friends to be proud of them as they deserve it.' " [92] The casualty lists of the 11th, 26th, and 47th North Carolina regiments of that brigade showed how hard they had fought at Gettysburg. He doubted that "the Enquirer's correspondent, by his own admission, although standing upon 'an eminence,' " could have seen as much of the brigade's conduct through the smoke of the battlefield as had the general himself. They, too, resented that their "reputation should be tarnished by an anonymous newspaper correspondent." [93]

North Carolinians had a particularly long-lasting distrust of Virginia, and the press controversy revealed only one more side of a longstanding interstate rivalry going back to colonial times. But that mattered little to Carolinians now. During the Seven Days campaign and again after Chancellorsville, when North Carolina casualties were the highest in the army, they felt the Virginia press ignored their efforts. [94] Gettysburg represented only the most recent instance of biased reporting. By late July, the situation worsened dramatically. North Carolina's commitment to the Southern cause itself seemed to come under the fire of the Richmond press. While Gettysburg casualty lists still rolled in, Richmond papers also carried the proceedings of meetings held in numerous North Carolina regiments to reject the stand of state "conservatives" such as W. W. Holden who worked against the war effort. After surviving the July 3 charge, the men of the 34th North Carolina, among others, felt compelled to adopt public resolutions that condemned Holden and "all who sympathize with . . . those who seek our destruction." [95] Coming on the heels of their substantial losses at Gettysburg, these further burdens proved too heavy to bear silently. As one Tar Heel living in Richmond told a friend at home about the Richmond press's coverage of political news, "Lying is contagious as well as smallpox, & our editors have caught the disease." [96] North Carolina would never forget July 1863.

The wartime Richmond press coverage of the events of July 3 left the kind of lasting images most first impressions imprint. Most enduring of all, of course, would be its tendency to play up the sacrifice of Pickett's division. Virginia editors put the priorities of their local readers first. They tried hard to weave together the sad story, and they tried to get it to worried readers as quickly as they could. Local concerns proved to be of such paramount importance that they really never addressed the legitimate criticisms of those Southerners who resented the way units not of Pickett's command were portrayed.

The passage of time rendered that final point moot, for now at least. On August 1, the editor of the Richmond *Examiner* wrote that "the military situation has no longer that degree of interest which it possessed during the past 3 months." [97] The Northern press had moved on two weeks earlier.

As the war dragged on, new heroes pushed both Pickett's men and Hancock's II Corps out of the headlines. New scapegoats moved Pettigrew's men out of the public eye, too. In later years, the Northern press's celebration of a great victory and the Southern search for a scapegoat to bear the burden of blame for Virginia's dead would prove irresistible to chroniclers of the event. These sentiments would help win for Gettysburg and the July 3 charge the special designation of the turning point of the rebellion. But no such realization had swept through the armies or the nation in the summer of 1863. True, the great charge of July 3 may have left the arena of current events by August 1. Far more important, however, it now stood poised in the entryway of Clio's gates.

3

HISTORY AS
IT OUGHT TO
HAVE BEEN

Soon after witnessing the great events of July 3, a reporter guessed that in time Gettysburg would fascinate both North and South alike. Even though he realized that "our better feelings are antagonistic to war," he knew that battle would "stir us as thunderbolts." The great charge could not fail to inspire poets who "stirred out fancy" about the martial bearing of soldiers marching into battle or those who "recite in melody attuned to sympathy, the history of the wounded drummer boy or the dying volunteer." And these were only two ways in which the nation might preserve popular "heroic and melancholy" wartime memories.[1]

This correspondent understood that the past served peoples and nations in many ways. Indeed, as historian Michael Kammen has argued, societies "reconstruct their pasts rather than faithfully record them," and "they do so with the needs of contemporary culture clearly in mind."[2] Even before the war ended, Northerners and Southerners had begun to look back at the events of July 3 with just such selectivity of purpose.

Pickett's Charge found a place in two of the conflict's first and most enduring memories. First, a cataclysm on the scale of the Civil War seemed to demand a point of demarcation, a specific moment when no doubt remained about its ultimate end. By 1870, that clump of trees on Cemetery Ridge where Northern defenders stopped Southern attackers and seemed to put the two armies on the road to Appomattox had won unique designation as "the high water mark of the Rebellion." Certainly the war saw many other valiant charges. Some, such as the Union's frontal assault at Missionary Ridge and the Confederate attack at Gaines' Mill, had succeeded. The North's bloody frontal assaults at Fredericksburg and the South's slaughter at Franklin had failed. Nearly all had exacted heavy cost, just as had the July 3 charge, but somehow these bloodlettings never held anything more than tactical importance. Pickett's Charge meant something more. The seductiveness of the notion that somehow this one moment marked the war's turning point quickly blurred the historical reality that very few soldiers who survived the charge and its repulse actually had felt that way.

Pickett's Charge also helped to forge a second lasting image in the immediate postwar years, one that set aside a place of honor for all soldiers who played a part in the war's pivotal moment. Virginians embraced that idea first, and that made a big difference in the way July 3 would find its way into the national imagination. Burdened by military defeat, massive political and economic disruption, and a deep sense of personal and community loss, they enshrined Pickett's men as heroes of the Lost Cause and, without calculation, found evidence for the rightness of their stand in their soldiers' courage that day. Early on, the Virginians who lost at Gettysburg won a special place in memory.

The emergence of these two images in the immediate postwar years made Pickett's Charge an emotional touchstone for both North and South. Historical accuracy mattered less than the versatility of these two images and their ability to serve both sections. This irony reflects the validity of historian Marc Bloch's observation that "by curious paradox, through the very fact of their respect for the past, people came to reconstruct it as they considered it ought to have been."[3]

The first step in this transformation required that stirring impressions of the events of July 3 be preserved in more enduring literary forms than ephemeral newspaper coverage. Books and magazines picked up the story well before Appomattox.

Before the middle of 1864, Lt. Col. Arthur James Lyon Fremantle of Her Majesty's Coldstream Guards and unofficial military observer with Longstreet's Corps, praised the special sacrifices of Virginia troops in the July 3 fight in *Blackwood's Magazine* and in Northern and Southern editions of his diary.[4] He conceded that the Virginians had advanced "together with Heth and Pettigrew in Hill's corps," but he saved his greatest praise for Pickett's men alone. He admired their discipline as the wounded passed him "in numbers as great as the crowd in Oxford-street in the middle of the day." When Pettigrew's men retreated and left Pickett's troops to fight on alone, Lee had told Fremantle, "This has been a sad day for us, Colonel—a sad day; but we can't expect always to gain victories." Then the observer marveled as the general calmed Pickett's men: "*All this has been MY fault*—it is *I* that have lost this fight, and you must help me out of it in the best way you can." Lee's conduct was "perfectly sublime."[5]

Edward A. Pollard, noted author and editor of the *Richmond Examiner*, also celebrated well before the war ended the special bravery of Pickett's men. In his polemical *The Second Year of the War*, he described as the "most glorious incident of Gettysburg, and the one upon which the eye of history will beam" the "steady movement of Pickett's men into the tempest of fire and steel, against a mountain bristling with guns." Nothing would "exceed it in sublimity on any of the battle-fields of the revolution." The impact of the July press coverage clearly showed. Pickett's men carried the position, but "Pettigrew's division had faltered, and that gallant commander in vain strove to rally the raw troops." While commemorating in detail the losses of Pickett's division, he ignored those of Pettigrew and omitted all reference to Wilcox, Lang, or Trimble.[6] Pollard even retold the story in his summary of the Confederate war effort's third year.[7]

Through literary efforts like these, the North Carolina, Mississippi, Alabama, and Florida survivors of the July 3 charge who fought on in the ranks of the Army of Northern Virginia began to recede into the shadows of history. In late 1863, when Maj. W. J. Baker of Pettigrew's North Carolina brigade read Pollard's book, he worried that "these injurious accounts [might] go to the world uncontradicted" or might "be incorporated into the history of the war without protest."[8] In the spring of 1864, Capt. Louis G. Young of Pettigrew's staff tried to convince readers of the *Richmond Enquirer* that Tennesseans, Alabamians, and North Carolinians reached the wall and retreated alongside Pickett's men.[9] If changing the accepted story was his goal, it would seem that he wasted his time.

Northerners had much to say about Gettysburg well before Appomattox, too. Indeed, as the importance of its results took on sharper relief, Northerners quickly began to point to it as "a"—if not yet quite "the"—decisive turning point in the war.

A wide variety of literary genres told Northerners the story of July 3. For Pennsylvanians especially, the repulse of the great charge ended the enemy's threat to their home state, and eyewitness accounts from local civilians froze those most thrilling moments. Gettysburg College professor Michael Jacobs watched "two long, dark, massive lines" of "Virginians" (although they more likely were Pettigrew's men) emerge from the woods just south of the McMillan orchard. Never correcting his order of battle, he placed Pettigrew's *brigade*—not division—on Pickett's left and Wilcox's Alabamians with Ambrose Wright's Georgians—not Lang's Floridians—on Pickett's right. A bit of army gossip from July 1 now became part of the July 3 story as well: the attacking Southerners so completely believed they faced only Pennsylvania militia that they contemplated their bloody repulse "with evident amazement." [10] The factual inaccuracies bothered few Northerners. Mostly, they shared Jacobs's heartfelt emotion.

Wartime audiences also read with interest the inspirational tales of Pennsylvania hospital workers. Volunteer nurses from Lancaster "gazed with overpowering awe" upon scenes that would draw reverent travelers as those who "now visit Austerlitz, Wagram, Marengo, or Waterloo." [11] One harried doctor recalled the remark of one visitor to his hospital: " 'It is awful to see what slaughter has been wrought, and the misery that has followed.' " But a legless Union soldier responded: " 'Yes, it is awful, but then the *result* is glorious.' " [12]

A few regimental histories published during the war years reinforced the importance of the battle's results. While they glossed over tactical details, survivors expressed deep satisfaction that "the nation's honor is being vindicated, and the fate of America is to be decided." [13] One of Stannard's Vermonters offered few specifics about his comrades' flank attack on Pickett's men but recalled "the thousand displays of the bravery of nameless common soldiers; the thousands of bright hopes extinguished; the thousands of noble intellects destroyed . . . and the sickening, frightful carnage" they had borne without complaint to advance a righteous cause.[14]

Travel narratives, a favorite antebellum story-telling device, also illustrated the wave of euphoria that swept through the North with the repulse of Lee. Visitors came to Gettysburg in "an impulsive outburst of almost irrepressible joy" to express "their gratitude to God for a most signal deliverance enkindled anew." [15] Well before Appomattox, one Northerner who viewed the battlefield suggested an inscription for a monument to the Union dead there: "Pilgrim! go and proclaim at the Capitol and all abroad that we, soldiers of the Republic, fell here in defense of its laws, its liberties, and its life." [16]

To inform the many visitors who came to Gettysburg, printed guides to the battlefield appeared almost overnight. Celebration took precedence over accuracy. Theodore Ditterline left out Pettigrew's and Trimble's commands entirely in describing how Pickett's three brigades made the attack with only "several brigades from Anderson's Division" in support.[17] "Pickett's charge, numbering some 20,000 men" displayed "the extraordinary spectacle of ten thousand men playing at 'leap-frog!' " wrote George J. Gross, who included the inactive brigades of Wright, Posey, and Mahone in the charge and left out Pettigrew and Trimble.[18] Another early account made clear that the stakes on July 3 had been so high that Union soldiers found a wounded Confederate carrying "an order from Lee commanding him to carry the position if it cost him every man in his command."[19]

The emotion and inspiration in these wartime narratives played well in the North. No objective accounting of the events of July 3 seemed necessary now. Indeed, a Northern visitor to the battlefield in early 1864 believed that "of this daring and foolhardy charge of the enemy . . . the country is already sufficiently informed."[20] To those who asked, " 'What other than SOUTHERN troops would have made that charge?' " one Union man knew the only answer that mattered: "Northern endurance and pluck were more than a match for Southern impetuosity and dash. . . . It was the turning point of the grand drama, and, with the sun, on that 3d day of July, went down *the sun of the 'Confederacy' forever!*"[21]

In the first flush of victory after Appomattox, Northern writers quickly secured Gettysburg's claim to the central place in the war's history and in the nation's memory. In impressively large, ornately bound, comprehensive popular chronicles of the entire conflict, they saluted their soldiers' finest hours. Readers of these self-styled "histories" demanded little analysis or critical evaluation. Mostly, they wanted a good story. Thus, when Northern authors had to offer rich description of the stirring events of July 3, they had to turn to the detail and drama that had filled the pages of the wartime Richmond press.

In their detailed accounts of Pickett's Charge, then, Northern authors plagiarized freely, questioned little, and validated flawed, yet familiar, Virginia images as national "history." In William Parker Snow's account, Pickett's men advanced bravely, while Pettigrew's "mostly raw soldiers" broke and flew "panic-stricken to the rear," leaving the Virginians to contend as best they could against fearful odds.[22] In his *History of the Great Rebellion*, Thomas P. Kettell's imagination ran wild: "Pickett, with his long, flowing hair, affecting the recklessness of a Murat, sprang to the head of his column, which rent the air with a hideous yell, as the troops advance." When Pettigrew's men buckled, the Union troops overlapped Pickett, "who is thus forced to let go his hold and retire with what luck he may."[23]

Horace Greeley's two-volume *American Conflict* typified the postwar style of historical pseudoresearch. Not satisfied merely to incorporate Richmond press images of July 3 into his own narrative, he simply printed lengthy extracts of Albertson's newspaper account. Sharp readers might spot a small note: "It is simple justice to brave foes to note that this imputation on Pettigrew's brigade has been proved unjust." Most, however, could easily continue on undistracted to read Northerner Whitelaw Reid's 1863 assessment of the battle's results: "It was not a rout, it *was* a bitter, crushing defeat. For once the Army of the Potomac had won a clean, honest, acknowledged victory."[24]

Images of the titanic struggle on Cemetery Ridge had never left the memory of Charles Carlton Coffin, the *Boston Journal* correspondent at Gettysburg. In the postwar years, he wrote volumes replete with images of the "thin blue ribbon" of II Corps defenders. The Southern soldiers "move upon the run,—up to the breastwork of rails,—bearing Hancock's line to the top of the ridge,—so powerful their momentum." But he also accepted the Richmond version of specific events. Pickett's men fought until their supports were "gone,—fleeing over the field, broken, shattered, thrown into confusion." Coffin wrote from the field in 1863 that he could foresee the war's end, but now he recalled it all far more emotionally: "How inspiring the moment! How thrilling the hour! It is the high water mark of the Rebellion,—a turning-point of history and of human destiny!"[25]

William Swinton, perhaps even more than Coffin, helped to secure in popular memory the specific image of the fight at the copse of trees as the high water mark of the war. Unlike most of his contemporaries, Swinton believed in the importance of original research, and he talked to senior commanders on both sides to flesh out his narratives. Where Coffin wrote evocatively of a "thin blue ribbon" of Union defenders, Swinton provided numerical evidence to demonstrate that only two incomplete II Corps divisions, about 6,000 troops, deployed to meet perhaps 15,000 Confederates. But even Swinton could be lured into using colorful Southern press accounts. His Confederate infantry stepped off the pages of the Richmond papers. Union musketry revealed "the unequal metal of the assaulting mass, and proved what of it was iron and what clay." When Pettigrew's "comparatively green" troops fled, "Pickett's division remained alone a solid lance-head of Virginia troops, tempered in the fire of battle." It alone crested Cemetery Ridge. Union defenders finally pushed them back, but Swinton conceded to the Confederate soldier the respect due his effort: "Whatsoever valor could do to wrest victory from the jaws of hell, that it must be conceded the troops of Pickett had done."[26] Although Swinton had more to say about the Union defenders than did most Northern writers of the immediate postwar years, his descriptions of Southern troops never strayed far from Richmond newspaper images. The Virginians' "disciplined *steadiness*" helped Gettysburg earn its place among the "first-class battles of history."[27]

By 1870, Gettysburg's place as the Confederate high tide seemed secure.

The perspective gained by the passage of just a few years made clear that the attack on July 3 was "the crisis of the war—the salvation of the North." Its repulse ended the last serious threat of invasion. Too much of "the very flower and *elite* of that incomparable Southern infantry, which, tempered by two years of battle" had been killed, wounded, or captured in Pennsylvania for the Confederacy to try it again. Gettysburg took first place among the Federal successes in the summer of 1863: The "clamor of Titanic war" in Pennsylvania "was echoed back from the borders of the Mississippi and the Alpine heights of the Cumberland Mountains."[28]

History issued no strong challenge at this time to these interpretations of the recent past. The silence was deafening. If no one questioned these conceptions while the events that inspired them remained fresh in memory, however, they likely would prove resistant to doubt in the future. As a people, Americans have evinced little interest in military affairs once wars have ended. Armies demobilize and soldiers return to farm, factory, or classroom. All things martial lose their attraction as veterans and their families put the past behind them, seek stability in day-to-day endeavors, and work for the future. This pattern held true after the Civil War, too. The enthusiasm that greeted the flurry of postwar celebratory volumes quickly faded, and as Michael Kammen rightly asserts, "the more we read about memory, the more we are also reminded about amnesia."[29]

The quiet time gave both North and South a chance to mourn and to begin healing. Even in the victorious North, the war and this battle brought lasting sorrow. The historical record did not always provide the most appropriate forum for deep emotions, however, so other more evocative forms of expression won popular favor. Early postwar poetry about Gettysburg blended the twin themes of triumph and tragedy:

> Full many a dark-eyed Southern girl shall weep her lover dead;
> But with a price the fight was ours—we too have tears to shed!
> The bells that peal our triumph forth, anon shall toll the brave,
> Above whose heads the cross must stand—the hillside grasses wave![30]

In time, the funereal qualities of Northern poetry gave way to far more positive expressions of accomplishment and glory, as in Pennsylvania veteran John C. Kensil's "Battle-field of Gettysburg, After Twenty Years":

> Then, charging all along our lines, beneath that July sun,
> The back-bone of Rebellion broke, and Gettysburg was won.
> And when the smoke had rolled away, 'twas a sickening sight indeed,
> For Pickett's line was swept away by the smoking guns of Meade.
> 'Twas a gallant charge—a forlorn hope—and well may history say:

"No grander charge the world had seen than Pickett's charge that
    day!" [31]

Emotion, selective memory, and the euphoria of triumph reshaped rec-
ollected events of July 3 in a variety of ways. The first burst of Northern
regimental histories to appear after the war continued to surrender factual accuracy to dramatic retelling of danger and sacrifice. According to
the historian of the 1st Massachusetts, Pettigrew had led the charge of
"Pickett's, Anderson's, Heth's, and Pettigrew's divisions," with Pickett as
his second-in-command.[32] A man in the 17th Maine—who probably saw
none of the assault—described "the most magnificent charge that had been
attempted during the war" in which Pickett's division "formed in seven
lines, *en masse*."[33] Color Sgt. Daniel G. Crotty of the 3rd Michigan wrote
of two Southern charges that day. The first forced a gap in the Union line
that closed when they heard that McClellan was coming up with 40,000
men. Eleven thousand under General Pickett made the second charge, but
"only one thousand got back safe."[34]

Ironically, the selective memory that exaggerated events could work
equally well in reverse to eradicate entirely all mention of Pickett's
Charge. In a slim volume of poetry and literary ramblings, Miss E.
Latimer described a tremendous artillery duel after which the Louisiana
Tigers charged the Union line. A bit later, an afterthought "associated
with" this advance, came another attack by the "flower of southern chivalry, without figure of speech,—young men, and brave" that "combined
the weight of the phalanx with the swiftness of the legion." Fortunately for
the Union, it failed.[35] Pettigrew and Trimble were ignored, as they often
were, but Hancock and his II Corps and even Pickett and his Virginians
had disappeared, too.

The drama of the moment also appealed to those who chose paint
and canvas over prose and printer's ink. Artists produced a great variety
of visual representations of the charge in this overwhelmingly Northern
form of tribute.

John B. Bachelder, who arrived at Gettysburg shortly after the end of
the fight and quickly became known as the unofficial "government historian" of the fight, also produced the first commercially successful graphic
rendition of the battlefield. Based on eighty-four days of interviews with
wounded soldiers of both armies and bearing the validating signatures of
the senior commanders of the Army of the Potomac, Bachelder's "isometric drawing" went on sale in early 1864.[36] Impressed by Bachelder's
effort, Col. David T. Jenkins of the 146th New York hinted to him, "I have
often thought I would give anything for an oil painting by a good artist

of that scene which I will never forget while life lasts."[37] Jenkins died at the Wilderness a few months later, but Bachelder remembered his suggestion and soon after the war convinced James Walker, a noted painter of historical scenes, to cooperate on a massive canvas based on the isometric map to be called "The Repulse of Longstreet's Assault."

To produce as close to "a literal rendition of the subject" as possible, Bachelder permitted Walker no artistic license. He prepared a descriptive key to accompany the painting, its focal point at the Angle demonstrating the early pervasiveness of high water mark imagery. He included in his booklet part of his conversation with Longstreet. "I have called your assault the 'tidal wave' and the copse of trees in the center of the picture the 'high water mark' of the Confederacy," he told the general. Longstreet replied, "You said rightly. We were successful until then. From that point we retreated and continued to recede, and never again made successful headway."[38]

If he accepted the high water mark concept, Bachelder still maintained remarkable freedom of mind in other matters. In 1870, he stood almost alone in rejecting several key elements of the Richmond version of Pickett's Charge. He believed Pickett and Pettigrew advanced simultaneously and that Pettigrew's men played more than supporting roles. He emphasized that Virginians alone enjoyed the protection offered by high ground east of the Spangler barn until they had advanced almost to the Emmitsburg Road. Rather than criticize Pettigrew's men for breaking too early, he considered it a "great wonder" that "they succeeded in advancing as far as they did." At the very least, he made certain Walker gave no Southern state's troops "undue prominence."[39]

Those who viewed the painting at exhibitions throughout the North did not come for a history lesson, however. While a Bostonian admired the scene for showing that "battles have less romance than reality, and that a modern fight . . . is an affair entirely different from the duels which make up the battles of the painters," most found their emotions—not their intellects—more deeply stirred. General Webb felt that "if any person desires to witness an American battle, he can sit down and imagine himself in the midst of this scene." Veterans showed their children where they had "rescued liberty from the grasp of invasion." An artilleryman viewed the painting thirty-two times, noting each time black-clad mothers who came to see where a son "had offered up his young life, a sacrifice to the cause of liberty."[40] Bachelder later commissioned a steel engraving of the painting, each artist's proof commanding a pricey $100.[41]

Other paintings proved equally effective in fixing in the popular mind Pickett's Charge as the Confederacy's high water mark. Among the most

*James Walker's depiction of the events of July 3 at Gettysburg
(Massachusetts Commandery, MOLLUS, USAMHI)*

memorable, Peter F. Rothermel's massive 32-by-16¾-foot canvas of the fight at the Angle, the largest of six scenes commissioned by the Pennsylvania legislature, still hangs in the state museum.[42] A more romantic painter than Walker, Rothermel permitted bits of artistic license; he painted General Meade into his scene, for instance, even after Meade himself insisted that he was not on the field at the moment depicted. To the audience present in Philadelphia for the painting's unveiling in December 1870, however, such minor concerns mattered little. Meade, William T. Sherman, and even old John Burns heard speaker Joseph Harrison explain that "our country is not prolific in war art, and it is well it is so, as it proves us to be a peaceful nation." Nonetheless, he continued, Gettysburg "appeals to us more strongly for remembrance than any other" battle in American history. Col. William McMichael then appealed to the crowd's emotions, not their sense of history, as he spoke of the 18,000 battle-tested Confederates, with only Pickett's men singled out as "a titanic war bolt—shaft of adamant, edges of steel." They might "seem too brave to kill," but "those are not men, they are furies, maddened with treason, frenzied with hate." And who stopped them? "Hall to the rescue!—Seventy-second, down on them like tigers! Flank them, Stannard! Crush them, Gibbon! Mash them, Webb!"[43]

Over the years, a few sharp-eyed critics spotted elements of all three days' battles compressed into the scene. A rival artist pointed out that Armistead appeared twice—once with his hat on his sword fifty yards in front of a battery and again with his hand on one of those same guns.[44] Most viewers, however, cared only that the painting appropriately saluted the nation's greatest battle, for "its results shaped the nation's life; its glory is the nation's property."[45]

Peter F. Rothermel's canvas of the events of July 3 at Gettysburg still hangs in the Pennsylvania State Museum. (Massachusetts Commandery, MOLLUS, USAMHI)

Artistic outpouring continued into the 1880s. Frenchman Paul Phillip-poteaux's famous cyclorama, still on display at Gettysburg, resulted from the efforts of a team of artists. After visiting the site of the charge, Phillippoteaux composed a representation of the fight for Cemetery Ridge that stunned in both scope and detail. European-style haystacks, some white-trousered soldiers, and a mounted officer representing Armistead revealed some factual flaws, but American viewers loved it anyway. It portrayed "the valor, patriotism and courage of the American soldier, and in a manner to show what it cost to preserve this Union and put down treason and rebellion," one admirer gushed.[46] A Boston reporter, reacting to the painting, wrote that the repulse of Pickett's "men of iron" lowered the curtain "on the master act of the great confederate general."[47]

All these impressionistic, derivative, and factually fuzzy Northern exultations of the turning point of the war helped Virginia preserve unchallenged its glowing images of Pickett's men as well. Indeed, many Virginians readily accepted Northern constructions of the high water mark. They further ennobled the sacrifice of Pickett's brave men who tried so hard to break that Union line. Their effort and experience seemed somehow to embody the course of the Lost Cause itself. All loyal Southern soldiers gave all they had, absorbed horrendous losses, and continued to fight even when no hope of success remained. The Virginians retreated on July 3 from no fault of their own, just as Lee surrendered at Appomattox when no other options remained.

Southerners knew they had to protect these images, too. A quick review of eleven American history texts published right after the war brought "emotions of inexpressable sadness" to one Southerner, especially when he noted that all these books argued "that the people of the North alone are fit to rule, while the people of the South deserve only to be ruled by them." He knew defeat had not broken the South's spirit nor disproved the rightness of its cause. Indeed, he argued, "we of the South would not, at this moment, change places with our victorious and triumphant enemies of the North," for "it is better to be the victims than the authors of oppression."[48] Southerners like this man still needed heroes to bear high the Lost Cause's colors, and Pickett's men qualified for just such a role.

Just as Northerners indulged in a postwar frenzy of literary celebration, Southerners took up their pens in defense of the Confederacy's course. Some, such as former vice president Alexander Stephens, argued at length in turgid prose about the legal foundations of the doctrine of secession. Others, like their Northern counterparts, turned out lengthy polemical "histories" of the Lost Cause. And just as Northerners found other genres of expression to commemorate victory, Southerners found a variety of outlets that allowed them to give vent to their feelings about the trials of defeat and Reconstruction.

Biography served this purpose very well, and no single figure provided as much moral leadership for Southerners as did Robert E. Lee.[49] In his own life, Lee combined strong character with positive accomplishment that sustained his faith in his cause and in himself during the war and allowed him to accept defeat and uncertainty with dignity. Nowhere did Lee's strength in adversity so clearly reveal itself as it did on July 3, 1863. If that day at Gettysburg was the crisis of the Union, it was also the crisis of the Confederacy. Lee's first biographers, many of them Virginians, drew heavily upon the Richmond press's version of events and placed Pickett's men side by side with their great leader at the very center of the day's action. Even as bit players, Pickett's men successfully held on to—even enhanced—the special distinction they had won that day.

Early on, the image of Pickett's men in Lee biographies took on a reliable sameness. James Dabney McCabe wrote that Pickett's division "was composed of the flower of the Virginia infantry, and was an object of pride to the whole army."[50] Edward A. Pollard continued to assert that the "Virginia Division will live as long as there is a pen to transcribe deeds of glory and living hearts to treasure the proud and tender memories of the past." This "solid lance-head of Virginia troops tempered in the fire of battle" included "much of the best and most cultivated manhood in the State," all "worthy of the blood which coursed in their veins."[51] Lee's sublime composure while rallying the survivors of the charge explained why

This popular woodcut of Robert E. Lee meeting Pickett's men after the July 3 charge appeared in Cooke's A Life of Gen. Robert E. Lee *and other early biographies that stressed the general's strength of character. (Massachusetts Commandery, MOLLUS, USAMHI)*

even wounded Virginians "returned to their places with cheers for their beloved commander." [52]

Such men deserved a commander worthy of them, and George Pickett filled the place admirably. He was, after all, "the product and representative of the best school of the Virginia gentleman." After the great bombardment of July 3, the Virginia division, "led by their heroic commander, with his long hair waving in the breeze, and his sword pointing straight on to the enemy," never wavered, "for they were fighting for the honor of the Old Dominion." Pickett and his men never failed Lee. Even at Five Forks on April 1, 1865, when the division's collapse hastened the dissolution of the Petersburg defenses, a postwar Virginia author generously claimed that Pickett's command "bore the brunt, and gave way only when the force of the enemy became overwhelming." [53] No wonder the destruction of such troops at Gettysburg elicited Lee's admission of guilt—"It is all my fault"—and his greatest lamentation: "Too bad! Oh, too bad!" [54]

Biography offered one way to secure the Southern version of the late war, but it was not the only literary avenue open to them. This was fortunate, since in the aftermath of defeat, Southerners, like Northerners, shied away from serious discussion of military affairs. An escape into the world of light fiction offered wonderful diversion, and here, in the writings of some of the South's most prominent novelists, Confederate heroes and Virginia's glories on the battlefield held sway. Until the late 1870s at least, much Southern fiction echoed the unrepentant tone of Lost Cause apologists and historians, and Southern novelists penned some delightful stories designed to assuage the tortured souls of their countrymen.

John Esten Cooke, a noted antebellum author, took up his literary skills again in the postwar years after service in the Confederate cavalry. His *Wearing of the Gray* briefly saluted Pickett's men, who, while Jeb Stuart's horsemen fought east of Gettysburg, "were making their 'wild charge'" and "advancing into that gulf of fire from which so few were to return."[55] Fiction drew the greater part of Cooke's postwar attention, however. Cooke's fictional Colonel Surry provided a welcome heroic figure, who, even in defeat, did not regret that the South "bore the blood-red battle-flag aloft in so many glorious encounters, amid foes so swarming and so powerful—that she would not yield." Finding the battles of July 1 and July 2 difficult enough to reflect upon, Cooke's fictional characters found it much gloomier to consider the July 3 charge, a scene "which Lee's old soldiers approach with repugnance. That thunder of the guns which comes back to memory seems to issue, hollow and lugubrious from a thousand tombs." Hammered by artillery and musketry, "all but a handful of Pickett's Virginians pass into eternity." Who could doubt the rightness of a cause that inspired such sacrifice? No wonder Cooke believed that "there are spots on the earth's surface, over which the Angel of Death seems to hover. One of these is the town of Gettysburg, in Pennsylvania," where "the most precious blood of the South poured out like water." This was "the real end of the great struggle, not at Appomattox."[56]

Virginians like Cooke played an influential role in early postbellum Southern literature of all sorts. George W. Bagby took Richmond by storm in the winter of 1865–66 with "Bacon and Greens," his tribute to the traditional "native Virginian" coping with the changes brought by war and emancipation. He mourned with the old man left alone in a cold cabin when his wife could not survive the "shock of war," his daughters fled to nearby towns for safety, and his three sons lay "under the sod at Manassas, at Gettysburg, at Chickamauga." Even through a mostly comical narrative, few readers missed Bagby's main point. Reconstruction brought many uncertainties, but the Virginian "nevertheless objects to dying while there is anything left to live for; and there is something to live for."[57] He doubtless concurred in spirit with Cooke's assertion that "Virginia is not poor and bare, as some suppose her. She is rich beyond royal or imperial dreams—for she has that charge" to her credit.[58]

Windy political discourses, biographies, novels, and short stories helped to keep alive in the South a flicker of interest in recent military affairs. A number of undersubscribed, financially strapped (and occasionally misnamed) scientific, literary, and historical journals also sprang up throughout the South to offer farming tips, spin tall tales, and teach history lessons in the spirit of the Lost Cause. Few lasted more than a year or two, but these multipurpose literary outlets provided an avenue for Southerners who still wanted to argue about the war.

Gettysburg proved especially difficult to deal with. The Lost Cause's high water mark held many bitter memories and recriminations, but for now, at least, few wrote or spoke publicly about them. Lee himself seemed to be the greatest obstacle to reopening discussion about that battle. He had observed in 1868 that "the time is not come for impartial history. If the truth were told just now it would not be credited."[59] Since he had come to be regarded so highly, one Southerner later wrote, "So long as General R. E. Lee remained alive, no utterance in public fell from any Confederate officer's lips concerning the loss of the field of Gettysburg."[60]

Not surprisingly, then, the few Southern authors who chose to address the Gettysburg issue in the immediate postwar years stuck to the well-marked trails blazed by the wartime Richmond press. Although Albert Bledsoe rejected the notion that Gettysburg had been a decisive defeat— certainly no high water mark—and dismissed earlier works on the battle as irreparably marred by "passion, prejudice and ignorance," one part of his story remained unchanged. "Steadily and grandly did these Virginians cross the valley of death"; as Pettigrew's men "wavered and broke under the terrible fire" they faced, "Pickett went on."[61]

North Carolinians used regional journals to continue to strike out against the Richmond version of Pickett's Charge. In *The Land We Love*, editor and former Confederate general Daniel H. Hill proffered an olive branch at first: "We scorn that narrow sectionalism which will not admit that Virginia displayed a grand heroism and fortitude under misfortune."[62] When Virginia's hold on the images of July 3 remained unchanged, however, Hill asserted that each North Carolina corporal could "write a more *truthful* history than any yet put forth" and "he could tell what actually occurred, without drawing upon the fancy and the imagination." He despised "misstatements prejudicial to the honor and character" of Pettigrew's brigade at Gettysburg. Virginians "are given to bragging too much!" Hill insisted. Hill admired "this State pride, this disposition to stand by her own sons. It is one grand reason for Virginia's greatness." He wished "we had some of the same spirit in North Carolina!"[63]

Unless and until Southern critics figured out how to counter the Virginia version of the events of July 3, Pickett's men could retain their special mystique. In 1870, Walter Harrison, a Fredericksburg attorney and a member of Pickett's wartime staff, helped preserve that image with a small, laudatory book entitled *Pickett's Men, A Fragment of War History*. As one of the first Southern unit histories worthy of the name, its publication by a prominent New York publishing house guaranteed it would attract the attention of not just the South but the entire nation.

Harrison wrote his book for three reasons. First, Pickett's men unquestionably deserved such a tribute. He inscribed in his preface Robert E. Lee's comment about the division's efforts in the 1864 defense of Richmond: "We tried very hard to stop Pickett's men from capturing the breastworks of the enemy, but couldn't do it."[64] Second, during the war, the Virginia state government had directed all its military units to compile a record of services and a roll of honor to be preserved in the state archives. Many of those records had burned during the evacuation of the capital, however, and Harrison had decided to reconstruct the history of Pickett's division while the memories of the survivors remained fresh. Third, and less graciously, Harrison also admitted that his work was intended "to correct many misapprehensions and errors" in those first Northern pseudohistories of the war concerning the conduct of Pickett's men at Five Forks. Harrison assured readers that the book was "not designed for the vain-glorification of any man or set of men." He hoped only to salute the division's dead and honor "the fortunate few" who survived.[65]

Showing remarkable restraint in dealing with the division's most memorable experience, Harrison devoted only three of his twenty-five chapters to Gettysburg and only one specifically to the charge. He played down the division's strength, asserting that Pickett sent only 4,481 muskets (4,700, if officers are included as well) into action on July 3, making any advance seem "like a truly 'forlorn hope' on an extensive scale." He recalled an uncommonly strong Union line of "two tiers of artillery, and two lines of infantry supports," but the "well-proved metal of these veterans" doubtless convinced Lee that " 'Pickett's Men' could and would 'carry anything they are put against.' "

Embracing the image of Gettysburg as "high tide," Harrison believed that both men and officers knew that "the great question of the campaign, perhaps of the whole war, was hanging on the next few hours." They fought not for "love of fighting," a notion he found "poetical, but fabulous," but simply to do what had to be done. As Harrison recalled, the Virginians spearheaded the attack; Pettigrew and Trimble moved "simultaneously in support" in a second and third line. Pickett's men penetrated the Union line and "stretched out a hand to grasp a victory at that moment; but, alas! the blood-red hand was not sufficiently strong." He asked, of course, "Where then were their supports? where were those two lines that were to follow up this glorious burst of valor? Another, alas!—the SECOND and THIRD places had been too hot for them," and they had fallen back. Thus ended "this day's fight, so brilliantly begun for the Confederates, so important in the history of the war, so crushing in its effects to the whole army of Northern Virginia."

Harrison diplomatically stated that he neither intended to censure the troops that failed to support Pickett's men nor to glorify the Virginia division at the expense of other troops. He merely intended to record "the final discomfiture of Pickett's men at Gettysburg." He resented Lee's decision to assign the division's survivors to provost guard duty—"doubtless a post of honor we had merited from being so badly mauled"—but he recalled with pride Lee's special commendation: "No one grieves more than I do at the loss suffered by your noble division in the recent conflict, or honors it more for its bravery and gallantry."[66]

Even if Harrison said he had not intended to build a monument to his comrades, he nonetheless did just that. The Stonewall Brigade still commanded honor. The boy cadets of the Virginia Military Institute still remained justifiably famous for their fight at New Market. But neither could match the pride and pathos increasingly attached to Pickett's men alone. In 1868, noting that only six of the original eighty recruits in one company of the 19th Virginia still remained alive, a Virginia clergyman thanked God that those few special survivors "still live to grace the private walks of life with their social virtues, as they were an ornament to the ranks as brave and intrepid soldiers."[67]

Each soul given over to the Lost Cause deserved Virginia's devotion, but none earned it more than those who died in the war's most desperate moment. Eulogy for the wartime dead remained a useful literary form in the postbellum South well into the 1870s and helped to preserve the memory of many of Pickett's men. The lamented Capt. George H. Geiger, Kemper's aide-de-camp, "cannot fail to win admiration wherever the great qualities of man are truly appreciated." The immortality of his name, won in the charge of July 3, 1863, "belongs alike to all the Virginians whose heroism made it a great deed." Who could forget the inspiring last words of Capt. Thomas G. Pollock, another of Kemper's aides: "Boys, I trust you will all behave like Southern soldiers." William Fauntleroy Cocke, who claimed kinsmen in many of Virginia's oldest families, had enlisted as a private when he could have had a commission for the asking. A lieutenant at Gettysburg, "ready for that terrible onset which was to send a wail of agony through the entire land," Cocke advanced to about seventy or eighty yards from the wall, when he "heard the Voice which said 'COME UP HITHER.' " Could men such as these die for anything less than a sacred cause?[68]

Richmond did not stage an elaborate postwar celebration of the Fourth of July until 1871. Another commemorative occasion, Memorial Day, pulled at their hearts even more. Public sentiment grew especially gloomy in 1872, when the bodies of Virginia's dead at Gettysburg were disinterred from their trench graves for reburial at Hollywood Cemetery. Pickett's men finally came home.

Although Walter Harrison did not live to see the ceremonies, he already had sensed the mood of such an occasion: "Our cup of bitterness was filled to the overflowing, and . . . our resources were so crippled, that we never — no, never — recovered from the blow."[69] On June 20, 1872, crowds watched in respectful silence as wagons draped in black and white and covered with flowers and Confederate flags bore to Hollywood the first 708 of 2,601 sets of remains that would be reinterred in that cemetery. At least 325 of those first 708, in boxes marked "P" for "Pickett's command," came from the Codori farm. City police and a military band led a parade of city officials. With George E. Pickett himself the chief marshal, a procession of over 1,000 Confederate veterans, including former generals John D. Imboden, James H. Lane, and Patrick T. Moore, escorted the remains.[70] The previous evening the survivors had swapped stories of the Pennsylvania campaign and fallen friends. Now, in the funereal grandeur of the procession, Pickett felt that "from their eternal silence, those who marched heroically to death looked down upon us." He had been "greeted with the words — 'My husband was killed at Gettysburg' — 'My son is lying there among the dead' — 'My brother was with you there' — so many crushed hearts filling my heart with grief." So many, that he concluded: "If the cry of my soul had been voiced it would have been the echo of that at Gethsemane!"[71]

A Virginia writer recorded in a heartbreaking short story his vivid impressions of the occasion. As "old soldiers with the scars of Gettysburg upon them guard the relics of their comrades," they blessed the memory of the fallen. Not all could cope with the emotion of the day. A child asks her older brother to tell her about Gettysburg. He tells her first of their other brother, a young lieutenant, one of Pickett's men so full of the "spirit of command so often found in connection with great powers and great energies." After the cannonade, Pickett had spoken to his men simply, saying "nothing dramatically high-wrought, effective, or telling. Eminently brave nations have very different ways of doing these things. This was the Virginia way." Inspired by his general's words, the young lieutenant in Pickett's division advanced close to the wall and fell with a bullet through the heart. Time had not softened the loss, for the surviving brother says, "I cannot dwell upon it—let others if they can, who feel it less, at all events less bitterly and personally than I," adding, "In justice this must be done in time to come." And it would happen. "As long as the name of Virginia lasts, so long will the recollection of the charge at Gettysburg survive" and swell the hearts of "true Virginians" who "recall the deeds of their countrymen on that immortal day." [72]

Similar ceremonies, considerably more understated, took place at Raleigh, Charleston, and Savannah, as the Gettysburg dead came home. From the "thirsty soil of Gettysburg" that "drank in some of the best blood of North Carolina," 103 sets of remains came home.[73] But neither in size nor in emphasis on any one part of the battle did these other Gettysburg memorials match Virginia's outpouring of public sorrow. Five years after the reinterments, a veteran of the 18th Virginia admitted that it still saddened him to know that while some of the honored dead rested in Southern cemeteries, others had turned to dust under the soil where they fell, "which now the plow-boy, whistling as he plows, turns over as common earth, unconscious that his plowshare is stirring sod hallowed by the blood of as brave men as the Continent has ever known." [74]

But it was the funeral of one, not the mourning of many, that showed the nation just how much the effort of Pickett's men at the Confederacy's high tide had established them as one of the chief symbolic banner-bearers of the Lost Cause. On July 30, 1875, on a business trip to Norfolk, George Pickett died of "an abscess on the liver." Because of the heat of the summer, Pickett's remains were placed in a vault for temporary interment the next day. Former generals Henry Heth and William Mahone attended hastily arranged ceremonies. Colonels Walter Taylor and James Corley represented Robert E. Lee's staff. The general was interred with solemn Episcopal rites and choral accompaniment. The presiding clergyman praised Pickett's "heroic struggles, stern adherence to duty, and the firm determination with which he pursued a line of action he deemed right," all traits that "have made him immortal, and they are the secret of his brilliant career." [75]

The outpouring of public grief at Pickett's passing spread throughout Virginia and the South. On the day of his funeral in Norfolk, Richmond flags flew at half-mast.[76] Newspaper eulogies cast Pickett in heroic mold. "Another of Virginia's great generals passed from earth when the spirit of George E. Pickett took its flight," wrote the editor of the *Atlanta Constitution*, adding that "Virginia mourns him as she does her Lee, her Jackson, her Garrett [sic; Garnett], her Armstead." [77] A Richmond editor praised Pickett's military career as "indeed brilliant. He had the fortune, which gallant soldiers call good, to be where the hottest fighting was; and he always won glory whenever the opportunity occurred."[78] The most fitting eulogy for a dead soldier, one Virginian wrote, "is that his men and officers 'believed' in him and followed him wherever he led." Glossed over for now was all memory that he had graduated last in his class at West Point; now, gracious editors wrote simply that at "the end of his curriculum he was duly graduated." He bore no blame for the collapse of the Confederate line on April 1, 1865; instead, "he beat the enemy in the first day's fighting at Five Forks." Although Lee had removed him from command, eulogists wrote only that he "delivered his final battle on the 6th of April, 1865, at Sailor's Creek, when the glorious battle flags of the Lost Cause were waving almost for the last time."[79]

Even Northerners mourned. According to a Philadelphia editor, Pickett's greatest service and "that for which he will mainly be remembered," was his role at Gettysburg. Writing as if no other troops took part in the charge, the journalist noted that "the assault of his division of five thousand men on the Federal lines . . . on the 3d of July, was one of the most heroic deeds of arms of which the Southern army can boast."[80]

Heavy rains kept down the numbers at a public meeting called to honor the general's memory at Richmond on August 3. The effusive sentiments of those who attended flowed freely, however. James Kemper, now the governor of Virginia, could not trust himself to speak of his general: "The heart feels most when the lips move not. Through a series of fierce and bloody ordeals he was my commander, my comrade, and my friend." The assemblage approved a set of resolutions that mourned a hero "whose name and fame are indissolubly linked with and illustrate the name and fame of the historic Army of Northern Virginia." The lamented general deserved a place among the Commonwealth's most stalwart defenders. As Capt. George D. Wise avowed: "Virginia has a right to be proud of her dead, of her Lees, her Jacksons, her Hills, her Stuarts, and her Picketts."[81]

No doubt, as the eulogies continued, the events of July 3, 1863, linked Pickett inseparably to his men and to posterity. July 3 would always be the memorable day that "covered Pickett and Pickett's men with imperishable glory, and linked their name with the noblest and the saddest story of Confederate achievement." One Virginian claimed that "no grander sight ever fascinated the gaze of military men than that of those noble heroes charging in steady and unbroken lines of battle through smoke, and fire, and death, up that fatal hill."[82] One clergyman asserted that "in Pickett and Pickett's men the glory of Virginia is best illustrated." And another noted that in Pickett's Charge "the name of Virginia was baptized in fire and will illuminate forever the temple of history." Former artilleryman

Robert Stiles praised Pickett's great modesty and the appropriateness of his leadership of "a division that deserved 'to rank with the Terribles of Marshal Victor or the Tenth Legion of Caesar.'"[83]

As important as it was to remember Pickett as a soldier, it was just as essential to commemorate Pickett as a man. Kemper praised his former commander's "ardent and overawing generosity of temperament, that beautiful unselfishness of heart, which preferred the cause of his country to his own." "He never forgot he was a Virginian," recalled Bishop Dudley. Indeed, Pickett's life provided a model for all Virginians. According to Captain Wise, "General Pickett was one who moved so noiselessly along that some of us had forgotten that we had a hero among us."[84] Eulogists praised "the simplicity, the modesty, and poverty that marked the later life of the patriot and hero." The grace with which he endured those privations signified "nobler treasures of wealth—a far richer and more enduring inheritance for his son—than the sum of the gold of California added to all the gems of Samarcand."[85] A Norfolk editor urged that a fitting monument to Pickett be built as soon as possible "so that future generations of Virginia may see what manner of man he was."[86]

In the late summer of 1875, Pickett's family made plans to move his remains from their temporary burial site to a final resting place among the Confederate dead at Hollywood Cemetery at Richmond. Controversy flared briefly, as Richmond's veteran community debated whether or not to allow black Virginia state militia units to take part in the funeral procession.[87] The Pickett family resolved it by requesting their participation.

"The removal of all that is earthly of the great and gallant Pickett took place" in Norfolk on October 22, 1875. A funeral procession that included clergymen, government officials, and Confederate and Mexican War veterans followed the cortege to the train depot. There, Lloyd J. Beall, former commandant of the Confederate Marine Corps, and an honor guard of eight members of the old 1st Virginia accepted the remains. Former generals Dabney H. Maury and Patrick T. Moore met the funeral train when it arrived in Richmond and accompanied the metal casket encased in wood to the capitol, where it lay in state at the southern end of the rotunda until the next afternoon.[88]

As chief marshal, General Maury had sent out a call to "all organizations, line and military" who might want to take part in Pickett's funeral procession.[89] He put together a simple, dignified contingent headed by a police honor guard and the 1st Virginia Infantry's band. Former general Bradley T. Johnson followed with a military escort from the 1st Virginia Infantry, mounted Knights Templar, and the Richmond Howitzers, all carrying furled Virginia flags tied with black crepe. The general's remains, borne on a platform over one of the Howitzers' guns, were followed by his family, his "war horse," and the clergy. The veterans of Pickett's division lined up next, with other Confederate veterans, Governor Kemper and other political leaders, the cadets of VMI, several smaller bands, and the general public falling in behind them. In peremptory fashion, the survivors of the 1st Virginia Infantry were advised that "all members of the old regiment are expected to be present."[90]

Newspapermen estimated that more than half the population of Richmond viewed Pickett's funeral procession and interment services on Sunday, October 24. The outpouring of public grief seemed somehow especially appropriate, for, as one editor wrote, "General Pickett was peculiarly Richmond's soldier." No matter where he had served on active duty and regardless of the perils he faced, "his heart ever turned to Richmond with pride and affection, and he treasured up pleasant memories of which our city was the scene." All of Richmond understood the special link. The 1st Virginia, Richmond's "pet regiment" belonged to his command, and "in his fate was merged the destiny of hundreds we dearly loved." The bond had remained strong. "His glory was our glory and his cause was our cause. News from Pickett was news from 'our boys.' The first dust-covered courier from the battlefield was asked, 'How have Pickett's men fared?'" Indeed, "Pickett and Richmond became inseparably connected, and men, women, and children spoke of them in one breath. He was proud to command Virginians."[91]

Pickett's remains, placed on a platform erected over "rifled gun no. 2" of the Richmond Howitzers and decorated with flags and flowers, proceeded slowly through the crowded city streets. At the cemetery, Rev. Charles Minnigerode officiated over the brief burial service. An honor guard fired three rounds in salute. Flowers bedecked the casket, and a correspondent took note: "Besides the Virginia State flag, the battle flags and the colors which covered the remains, there was one truly beautiful emblem which of itself was sufficient to remind one that a prominent officer of the Lost Cause was being buried": a Confederate flag of white and scarlet verbenas and blue dwarf ajuratum.

As the sun began to set, shadows made "by the forms of some of the soldiers who followed the dead chieftain over many hard-fought field" fell around the new grave on the summit of the Hollywood Cemetery's Gettysburg Hill. As one onlooker observed, "No other burial place could have been as appropriate."[92] While both North and South embraced the clump of trees as "the high water mark of the Rebellion," Pickett's defeated warriors had taken one further step on their own: they marched straight into the pantheon of the Old South's greatest heroes.

4

BINDING
THE WOUNDS
OF WAR

If in memory Pickett's men shone in time of war, in reality they nonetheless failed an important test in time of peace. As many of their fellow Virginians directed postwar efforts to recast Robert E. Lee as the Confederacy's greatest hero, Pickett's men did not join them. They had many reasons for charting this divergent course, but in so doing, they cut themselves off from some of the staunchest defenders of the Lost Cause and the self-appointed guardians of the "truth" of Southern history. This intrastate tension opened the way for Pickett's Charge to add yet another dimension to its place in popular memory as it helped lead the New South toward the cause of national reconciliation.

The wounds of civil war healed slowly. In 1874, the editors of the *Army and Navy Journal* hoped that "patriotic men, anxious to obliterate every trace of the war, and to begin a new era of good feeling between North and South" soon could meet together in friendship. Still, plans to reunite the Union IX Corps and James Longstreet's First Corps that year quickly fell apart when it was deemed too soon to "bury the hatchet together." [1]

Indeed, Southerners now seemed far more intent on using that hatchet on each other. In October 1870, Robert E. Lee died, opening the way for the Southern Historical Society, headed by virulently unreconstructed Jubal Early, to advance unimpeded in "vindicating the truth of Confederate History."[2] As its members saw it, part of that truth required the absolution of Robert E. Lee from any responsibility for the South's defeat.[3] The words of a eulogy charted their course: "His fame belongs to the world, and to history, and is beyond the reach of malignity."[4]

The defeat at Gettysburg required special explanation, of course, and Virginians led the hunt for a scapegoat to deflect responsibility from Lee. Jeb Stuart and Richard Ewell took fire early, but the greatest share of blame quickly shifted to James Longstreet, an easy target after William Swinton published the general's criticisms of Lee's command decisions at Gettysburg.

Early, along with former artillery chief William Nelson Pendleton and Lee's wartime staff, quickly closed ranks against Longstreet.[5] Contrived allegations of Longstreet's slowness on July 2 provided sufficient ammunition for the opening skirmishes in this war for control of Southern war history.[6] In 1877, however, Longstreet himself introduced July 3 as an additional point of contention. He defended his opposition to the charge to a national audience by explaining that his duty as Lee's second-in-command required him to express his professional opinion. "General," Longstreet had told Lee, "I have been a soldier all my life. I have been with soldiers engaged in fights by couples, by squads, companies, regiments, divisions and armies, and should know as well as any one what soldiers can do. It is my opinion that no 15,000 men ever arrayed for battle can take that hill." He had not hesitated to speak freely, feeling "that my record was such that General Lee would or could not misconstrue my motives."[7]

Many of Early's clique used Longstreet's words as evidence of insubordination, however, and heaped upon him not only blame for July 2 but for Pickett's destruction on July 3 as well. In the *Southern Historical Society Papers*—already touting itself as the preeminent authority on Confederate history—Early slammed Longstreet's lack of "the spirit of confidence so necessary to success."[8] Walter Taylor of Lee's staff insisted that the entire First Corps had been ordered into the assault and still wondered why only Pickett's men advanced while the rest of Longstreet's men watched "in breathless suspense, in ardent admiration and fearful anxiety . . . but moved not."[9] Lee's military secretary Armistead Long used the language of Pickett's own rejected report in which he "criticized the failure to furnish him with the supporting force which had been ordered" to blame Longstreet. He asserted that while Virginians never must forget the heroic charge of Pickett's division that already has "passed into history as 'one of the world's great deeds of arms,'" they also must remember that the Old War Horse had cost Virginia lives.[10]

Longstreet's Virginia critics may well have been relieved that Pickett

Lt. Gen. James Longstreet. Blamed for the failure of the July 3 charge by Jubal Early and his Virginia clique, he nonetheless retained the loyalty of Pickett's men. (Francis Trevelyan Miller, comp., Photographic History of the Civil War [New York: Review of Reviews, 1911], 10:179)

himself died before these attacks flowered fully in the late 1870s. Pickett's relief by Lee after Five Forks ruined his credibility as the general's champion. Moreover, rumors of his fondness for alcohol clashed with Lee's own abstemious character.[11] Just the same, Pickett always had remained a loyal Virginia Confederate. He served as an honorary pallbearer at Lee's funeral, and he helped to organize the Association of the Army of Northern Virginia. Indeed, he died in the middle of his term as president of the Southern Historical Society.[12] Virginia's Lost Cause advocates had reason to hope that Pickett's men would continue to follow the public path their general blazed.

But Pickett's men disappointed their fellow Virginians. For many reasons, they showed little willingness to celebrate the life of Lee if it also required them to turn on Longstreet. Most of Pickett's subordinates and staff members understood the strong bonds of personal and professional friendship that bound their general to Longstreet. The two fought side by side in Mexico. When Old Pete lost three children to scarlet fever during the war, Pickett had made the funeral arrangements to spare the bereaved parents that heavy burden.[13] Such ties deserve respect, and Pickett's intimates refused to tamper with them.

While personal loyalties may have determined the actions of Pickett's closest army friends, they do not explain why so few of the division's rank and file did not join the Old Dominion's attack on Longstreet. Their silence reveals a severely split veterans community in postwar Virginia.

By the early 1870s, former Confederates from Richmond and the Tidewater—home to Pickett and many of his men—resented the efforts of comrades in the western part of the state to wrest away their traditional control of state political matters, including, but not limited to, military affairs. The split opened in 1874, when Pickett's former brigade commander James L. Kemper won the governorship of Virginia on the Conservative ticket. Like most members of his party, he never apologized for his service to the Confederacy, but he also believed that it made more political and economic sense to deal with the present and look to the future than to dwell on the past. George Pickett's political sentiments lay with the Conservatives. Since Kemper was single, Pickett's wife recalled that "my Soldier and I often assisted him at his receptions" and other official functions.[14] Pickett worked for Northern economic interests as a Virginia agent for the Washington Insurance Company. He carried as a prized possession a pocket watch engraved with two crossed flags, the Stars and Bars and the Stars and Stripes. Most hard-line Lost Cause activists, including those western Virginians who led the anti-Longstreet crusade, remained loyal Democrats and looked upon conservative ex-Confederates like Kemper and Pickett as traitors to their heritage.

Certainly, not all of Pickett's men shared their commander's political views, but like it or not, they paid for his perceived heresy. Through the late 1870s and much of the 1880s, except in cases when the story of the July 3 charge might be manipulated to attack Longstreet, the editorial board of *Southern Historical Society Papers*—perhaps by coincidence, more likely by design—ignored Pickett's men. No substantive account of the charge by a survivor of the Virginia division appeared in the journal through that period.

As if to make clear their displeasure with Pickett's men, the editors actively solicited articles from Confederate veterans from other states whose views of July 3 took glory away from them. Board member Dabney H. Maury asked Col. B. D. Fry of Archer's brigade to answer historians who "created the impression that Pickett's division alone" reached the Union line. The colonel then cited the case of a Union soldier wounded by the spearhead of the 13th Alabama's colors to prove that his men indeed had closed with the enemy.[15] The editors allowed former general James Lane to decry the claim that Pettigrew only had supported Pickett's men and to declare his own brigade "as much the 'heroes of Gettysburg' as *any other* troops that took part in it." [16] Isaac R. Trimble used the pages of the *Papers* to condemn the many accounts of the July 3 charge that left the impression that "Pickett's men did all the hard fighting" and suffered the most severely.[17] The editors asked Henry Heth to respond, too, but his usefulness ended quickly when he declared the assault of July 3 a mistake and placed the blame on Lee.[18]

Using such tactics, Virginia's Lost Cause advocates cut off Pickett's men from the most authoritative outlet for Confederate history. They severed the tie completely. In 1881, when Abner Doubleday alleged in his *Chancellorsville and Gettysburg* that the mortally wounded General Armistead "saw with a clearer vision that he had been engaged in an unholy cause" and apologized for his treason, no loyal Southerner could let the slander stand.[19] To hurry Doubleday's assertion "into its merited oblivion," the editors of the *Papers* produced refutations from Hancock, his staff officer Henry H. Bingham, and even Theodore Gerrish of the 20th Maine, who only saw the wounded general later at the hospital.[20] If the editors asked even one of Armistead's own surviving senior officers or private soldiers for help to clear their general's name, they printed none of their responses.

If the slight bothered Pickett's men, they did not complain. They simply found other ways to preserve their image as the flower of Lee's army on their own terms, always refusing to embrace the anti-Longstreet vehemence of their fellow Virginians.

For example, they wrote unit histories. Charles T. Loehr's chronicle of the 1st Virginia—the "Old First" with roots back to the French and Indian War—praised Pickett's men and included not a single word of censure against James Longstreet. Defeat of Pickett's stalwarts occurred because reinforcements dared not enter "this death-trap," stranding the intrepid Virginia division, "or all that was left of it."[21] Richard Irby of the Nottoway Grays of the 18th Virginia also blamed their absent supports and asserted that "no commendation given by writers concerning this celebrated charge of Pickett's Division ever exceeded the truth."[22]

Personal memoirs also preserved the special character of Pickett's men. David E. Johnston, former sergeant major of the 7th Virginia, portrayed his comrades on the evening of July 2 as the epitome of Victorian heroes: "Happy, gentle, brave, jolly spirits, little do you anticipate the horrors of the next twenty-four hours!" Pickett's "specially selected" men were impatient to advance, for they believed that Lee would order them to charge only if certain that "victory was sure to perch upon their banners." Although they saw "guns, swords, haversacks, human flesh and bones, flying and dangling in the air," they willingly answered Pickett's call: "Up, men, and to your posts! Don't forget today that you are from old Virginia."[23] Royal Figg of Parker's battery in Alexander's battalion watched "that 'brave and gallant few,' . . . who stormed and *took* the heights at Gettysburg." The Old Dominion "need not be ashamed of her sons who walked so calmly through the fiery storm of that summer afternoon—calmly to wounds and death!"[24]

Unit histories and personal memoirs only found limited audiences, however. Pickett's men believed their prowess deserved greater applause.

Some may well have found such recognition by observing the growing popularity in the North of a new school of Virginia writers, who, beginning in the mid-1870s, infused into their writing the view that prosperity lay down the road of sectional understanding and national reunion. The Centennial celebration of 1876 resurrected Virginia's traditional place as the "mother of presidents." The commitment of her revolutionary statesmen to patriotic principles deserved special remembrance, since only a difference of opinion about the duties of a patriot had forced Virginia to secede in 1861. Adopted Virginian George Cary Eggleston hoped Northern veterans would come to see that "if you had been bred at the South, and had understood your duty as the Southerners did theirs, you would have fought quite as bravely for secession as you did against it."[25] In this way, Virginians began reforging common bonds without rejecting their Confederate heritage.

The new school of Southern writing caught on in many forms. Popular novelists such as Thomas Nelson Page became so successful in catching the fancy of the Northern reading public that toward the end of the 1880s a literary critic asserted that "the epoch of the war [is] the favorite field of American fiction to-day, but the Confederate soldier is the popular hero. Our literature has become not only Southern in type, but distinctly Southern in sympathy."[26] These "New South" Southern soldiers did not dwell on the past glories of the Lost Cause. In Page's *The Burial of the Guns*, a Confederate colonel at Appomattox bade his men farewell with this benediction: "The end may not be as we wanted it, prayed for it, fought for it; but we can trust God; the end in the end will be best that could be; even if the South is not free she will be better and stronger that she fought as she did."[27]

Pickett's Virginians, among others, took advantage of this new spirit. When the *Philadelphia Weekly Times* launched its "Annals of the Civil War" series in 1877 to bring together the literate commentary of combatants of all ranks in both armies, Pickett's men answered the call and positioned themselves for rediscovery by the entire nation. If the *Southern Historical Society Papers* had no room for their work, the "Annals" showed no such qualms. Capt. Henry T. Owen of the 18th Virginia adopted a tone that appealed to Northern audiences: the command of the attack was "given to General Pickett, a brave and fearless officer and a fit leader of this forlorn hope, thrown forward to retrieve disaster or turn by fierce conflict the waning fortunes of a dying cause." Then, the wartime images of the Richmond press flooded back again. In Pickett's division, "nearly every family of honorable mention in the history of the State as a Colony or Commonwealth, had its representative." Here, "men of learning, of wealth and refinement were scattered through every regiment" along with "the yeo-manry of the Old Dominion, the bone and sinew of the land."[28]

Pickett's men still placed the blame for their destruction just where the Richmond press had placed it in 1863—on Pettigrew and Trimble, not on James Longstreet. W. W. Wood recalled mounted officers "dashing franti-cally up and down" the lines of their supports, "apparently endeavoring to get them to move forward, but we could see that they would not move."[29] Owen had looked "far off toward the left flank, saw the supporting col-umns there were crumbling and melting rapidly away," and heard Pickett tell his brother, Maj. Charles Pickett, that if the supports failed, " 'my division will be cut to pieces.' " But the rout could not be stopped. Owen made a rare concession to "some brave Tennesseans and North Carolini-ans, who never wavered in the storm" and fought at the side of Pickett's men, but Thomas D. Houston refused to concede any such credit. Claim-ing that the supporting troops failed to do their duty, he quoted from a letter written by Lt. John James of the 11th Virginia, "We gained noth-ing but glory and lost our bravest men."[30] No other group of Confederate soldiers so successfully set themselves apart to so much popular acclaim.

The story of Pickett's men went out to still more Northern readers through the publications of various Union veterans groups. The old sol-diers of the Grand Army of the Republic and similar organizations will-ingly reprinted suitable accounts by old foes as they refought their battles in their newsletters and journals. Subscribers to the *Grand Army Scout and Soldiers' Mail*, for instance, found only a single substantive Southern ac-count of Gettysburg, but in it, Louisiana artilleryman William M. Owen perpetuated the image of a superbly mounted Pickett, who bore "the air of an old crusader" and, with "his long hair waving under his kepi, seemed the very incarnation of war."[31]

The willingness with which Pickett's men turned to Northern literary outlets contrasted sharply with the lingering suspicions of many former Confederates who believed the victors would never be fair to the van-quished South. Even into the 1880s, former general Lafayette McLaws warned, "The price of our reputations is eternal vigilance." He argued that "the North, knowing that it has wronged us, will never forgive us— and will not permit the truth be told, if they can help it."[32]

To quell such concerns, the editors of *Century Magazine*, a widely read national journal, launched its "Battles and Leaders of the Civil War" series in 1884. They hoped to reexamine some of the war's "cloudy ques-tions" now that "its heroic events are passing into our common history."[33] Gettysburg spawned many of the cloudiest questions, of course, but James Longstreet's main essay about July 3 resolved none of them, and he perpetuated the image of Pickett's men as the real heroes of the day. Longstreet, mostly responding to attacks made against him by "men who have claimed to have been the friends of General Lee," tried to repay the loyalty of Pickett's Virginians who had not joined the ranks of his critics. Pickett, with a "jaunty cap raked well over on his right ear and his long auburn locks, nicely dressed, hanging almost to his shoulders," Longstreet wrote, "seemed rather a holiday soldier than a general at the head of a column which was about to make one of the grandest, most desperate assaults recorded in the annals of war." Longstreet also dismissed the complaints of Pettigrew's and Trimble's men, who "seem to consider the less conspicuous part given them a reflection upon them as soldiers of true mettle and dash."[34] Even E. Porter Alexander, who discussed dispassionately many of the events of July 3 in his own essay, still could not resist noting that "no soldier could have looked on at Pickett's charge and not burned to be in it."[35]

Northern survivors who wrote about July 3 for the "Battles and Leaders" series further enhanced the reputation of Pickett's men. In many cases for the first time, interested readers could balance familiar Southern chronicles of the charge with graphic and detailed Northern accounts of its repulse. Edmund Rice of the 19th Massachusetts wrote vividly about the "never-to-be-forgotten scene" as Pickett's men "pushed on toward the crest, and merged into one crowding, rushing line, many ranks deep" that got "so near that the expression on their faces was distinctly seen." Col. Norman J. Hall's contemporary report about the fight at the Angle, full of specifics and generosity to other commands, fit well the editors' prescription for softening controversy. Lt. L. E. Bicknell's piece on the 1st Massachusetts Sharpshooters and the New Yorkers of Sherrill's brigade challenged the claim of the 8th Ohio that they alone deserved credit for the flank attack that wrecked Pettigrew's left.[36] These essays helped Northerners and Southerners find mutual respect and common ground for open dialogue. The editors admitted that everything they printed "is not all history," but, "in its errors, its bias, its temper, and its personalities, it is the material of history."[37] And memory.

Signs of progress toward national reconciliation took many forms, but veterans reunions offered the most obvious public displays of these feelings. Early in the 1880s, individual chapters of Northern and Southern veterans groups began to visit one another's hometowns, and Pickett's men had been among the first to sponsor such joint ventures. In October 1881, some of Pickett's veterans in the First Virginia Infantry Association played host to a delegation of New Jersey veterans visiting Yorktown; the following April, some of these same Virginians went to Trenton, New Jersey, as guests of a local Grand Army of the Republic (GAR) post. The final Northern toast of the event saluted the end of sectional animosity: "The American soldier—whether revolutionary, Mexican, federal, or confederate—he has ever displayed a bravery that has won the admiration of the world." One of Pickett's men answered, "Once again, with one common purpose, we march shoulder to shoulder toward one common destiny." [38]

Emotions still ran so deep, however, that neutral meeting sites seemed preferable to gathering on the old battlefields. Even though Union and Confederate veterans met at Fredericksburg, the Wilderness, and Chancellorsville in May 1884, the reunion did not include many soldiers who actually fought there. [39] In 1887, however, Pickett's men and Webb's Philadelphians decided to take this final step. The nation watched with rapt attention as the survivors of the two armies prepared to meet again at the stone wall at the Angle.

The road to reunion at Gettysburg would not be smooth. Not all agreed that the time for such a meeting had arrived. Some of the most vehement protests against returning captured Confederate battle flags to Southern states, first suggested in the early 1880s, came from the Vermonters who had wrecked Pickett's right flank at Gettysburg. "While we were loyal, they were traitors," one wrote, adding that the rebellion's leaders "ought to repent in sackcloth and ashes and thank God that a long-suffering and forgiving nation, permitted them to live." [40] Veterans of the 15th Massachusetts of Harrow's brigade made clear that they, too, opposed any such act: "We cannot confound the heroes and martyrs of a noble cause with those whom the twin furies of treason and slavery led forth to battle." No "sickly sentimental gush of reconciliation" could make them forget that the principles for which their comrades died "were right, and those against which they fought were deeply wrong." [41]

So long as these highly charged emotions held sway, a Southern return to the site of the Confederacy's high water mark seemed unlikely. As a Virginia veteran admitted in 1887, "Gettysburg is too sad a field to attract many Southerners." [42] Government historian John Bachelder tried to change their minds. He got South Carolina congressman and former Confederate colonel David Wyatt Aiken to enlist Southerners to support his efforts to obtain federal funding to mark the Confederate lines in a way that would "credit them with a valiant defense of conscientious convictions." [43] Gettysburg civic leaders opened the door wide to Southerners, too. They touted the physical beauty and the "health-restoring springs" of the area, as well as the "enthusiastic devotion and unfailing fidelity, the dauntless daring and ardent gallantry of the two hundred thousand Americans who here contended in deadly conflict for our nation's life."

They noted that "every tree marks the spot where a dying patriot gasped his last prayer for his country as he poured upon its altars his young life's blood"; but they remained purposefully vague about the sectional loyalties of that hero.[44]

The plan to bring Pickett's men back to Gettysburg flowed from all these general sentiments and one very specific stimulus. In 1886, survivors of the 69th Pennsylvania of the II Corps decided to erect a regimental monument at the Angle, where they had helped to repulse the great charge of July 3. Since most of the men came from "the humbler walks of life," however, they found themselves having to ask for financial assistance from the public. Its generous contributions paid for an impressive monument bearing inscriptions that "are a history themselves, placed there by survivors as they knew the story of Pickett's charge and repulse."[45] Buoyed by this strong evidence of public support, survivors of Brig. Gen. Alexander S. Webb's regiments—the 69th, 71st, 72nd, and 106th Pennsylvania—joined together in February 1887 to form the Philadelphia Brigade Association and began planning dedication ceremonies for new monuments to both the 69th and 71st Pennsylvania at Gettysburg.[46] At one of their first meetings, the Philadelphians learned that a delegation of Pickett's men intended to discuss with the Gettysburg Battlefield Memorial Association the placement on the battlefield of a marker honoring the Virginia division. Naturally interested in the Southerners' intentions, they wrote to Charles T. Loehr of the First Virginia Association to suggest that the Pennsylvanians and Pickett's men meet again at Gettysburg, this time "in a spirit of 'Fraternity, Charity and Loyalty.' "[47]

In Richmond, Pickett's men met in February 1887 as well. After years of informal association, they now incorporated the Pickett's Division Association to lend greater authority to their plans to salute their comrades' efforts at Gettysburg. William R. Terry, former colonel of the 24th Virginia, became its first president. Charles Pickett, the general's brother and former adjutant, was elected vice president. Early on, the association decided to accept the Philadelphians' invitation to join them at Gettysburg in July 1887, and Charles Pickett accepted appointment to the new organization's reunion committee.[48]

Plans for a division monument at Gettysburg, perhaps to be dedicated at this upcoming reunion, became both a labor of love and a source of considerable contention. Since Pickett's men intended this memorial to stand in lasting tribute to their sacrifice, even the smallest details raised serious questions. The wording of the inscription degenerated into heated debate. Some wanted to include Dearing's all-Virginia artillery battalion on the roster of component commands because it had supported Pickett's advance on July 3 and often acted in concert with the Virginia division, while others quibbled with the notion. Some suggested that Brig. Gen. Montgomery Corse's Virginia brigade be included on the monument since it did belong to the division. Others objected, however, since Corse's men had been detached in July 1863 and did not fight at Gettysburg.[49] After considerable debate over monument design, the organization finally approved a twelve-foot-high memorial made of Richmond granite.[50] On only one point no controversy existed: the marker had to be located on Cemetery Ridge, at their deepest penetration of the Union line.[51]

Predicting success for its venture, the committee sought an appropriate orator for the dedication. As the senior survivor of Pickett's Charge, General Kemper seemed the obvious choice, and the association's leaders chose him unanimously to unveil the memorial "in memory of the patriotism and devotion of those of our Division who fell in our famous charge." They knew of his fragile health, but they nonetheless impressed upon him their obligation to perpetuate "the gallant deeds of our glorious Virginia soldiers."[52] But Kemper begged off. "I should gladly and at any sacrifice exercise the noble privilege of greeting our surviving comrades at the proposed reunion," he wrote, admitting that in his declining health, "no one, so much as myself, can regret the fact that I cannot again see the field of Gettysburg." Still, Kemper assured the reunion committee that "on such an occasion even spontaneous utterances cannot err" in saluting Pickett's men, who advanced "with firm alignment, steadfast tramp and deliberate valor, to the death-grapple in which they expected to die and knew how to die."[53]

The general's refusal to speak became only the first in a series of problems the Pickett's Division Association now faced. A second stemmed from internal dissension. Deep emotional pain still made it impossible for some to return to Pennsylvania, even to dedicate a monument to fallen comrades, and they questioned the loyalty and motives of those who did intend to go. To resolve this problem, the First Virginia Regimental Association joined the list of Richmond's military hosts for a visiting delegation of Massachusetts veterans arriving on July 4. Those of Pickett's men who had become active in veterans affairs but did not want to go to Gettysburg now had an honorable excuse.[54]

A third problem nearly derailed the whole memorial project and the proposed reunion. The Gettysburg Battlefield Memorial Association rejected the Pickett's Division Association request to locate its monument on Cemetery Ridge. John Bachelder reported that he had received "bushels of letters" expressing incredulity that a Southern monument might be permitted within Union lines.[55] One-armed Lucius Fairchild, commander-in-chief of the GAR, blustered against the reunion. Governor Joseph B. Foraker threatened to use the Ohio National Guard "to prevent such 'sacrilege.'"[56]

Stunned at the unexpected turn of events, three prominent veterans of Pickett's division—Richard L. Maury, Judge William G. Clopton, and Edward Payson Reeve—went to Gettysburg in early May to plead their case.[57] After a long and heated meeting, the memorial association's leaders again turned them down. Formal monuments like the one the Pickett's Division Association envisioned had to be erected on original lines of deployment, not in advanced or temporary positions. They encouraged Pickett's men to give serious thought instead to building their monument on Seminary Ridge, where "it would occupy a commanding position, possibly attracting more attention than elsewhere and be a notable beginning of a new departure in the lines of memorials that are now encircling Gettysburg." The only concession the commissioners offered came in the form of begrudging permission to erect an inconspicuous marker where Armistead fell.[58] Stung by these decisions, the Pickett's Division Association resolved unanimously on May 7, 1887, not to go to Gettysburg at all.[59]

As soon as he heard of the Virginians' decision, John W. Frazier, secretary of the Philadelphia Brigade Association, wrote an open letter to Pickett's men to urge them to come anyway. He hoped they would put aside their disappointment and enjoy "the hospitality that we will extend to you" and "the fraternal feelings created by that re-union, the first of the kind held since the war." Frazier promised his group's help in placing a Pickett's division memorial on Cemetery Ridge. Nobody could take more pride in their accomplishments, Frazier assured them, than "they who withstood the shock of your charge—a charge not surpassed in its grandeur and unfaltering courage in the annals of war since time began."[60] Charles Loehr, the Pickett's Division Association secretary, thanked Frazier for his sentiments, but he expressed doubts that the Virginians would change their minds now. He could only hope that the day would come when Pickett's men and the Philadelphians could meet at Gettysburg to dedicate "a memorial to the gallant men of both sides, expressive of the true American motto, 'A large Country and a large Heart.'"[61]

Frazier refused to give up. He now pledged Pennsylvania's help to erect the marker where Armistead fell to "indicate for all time to come on the historic grounds of Gettysburg the position reached by Pickett's Division." Loehr published the appeal in the Richmond *Dispatch*.[62] Virginians responded so well to the open letter that just a few days later Loehr was able to send Frazier welcome news. It now seemed likely that Pickett's men would "succeed in getting at least a respectable delegation to join you in revisiting the spot where more history was made in three days than we can now make in thirty years."[63]

The planned reunion now drew considerable positive popular attention. Some Northern organizers wanted to end the ceremonies with the return of three Confederate flags captured by the Philadelphians at the Angle. Frazier himself wrote to the War Department to find out where the flags were stored and how the Union veterans could obtain them. An interested Northern observer noted that "whether or not it proves possible to comply with this request or not, the very fact that it is made is of the highest significance, as showing that there are plenty of Union soldiers who are ready to return rebel flags."[64]

Frazier's request showed just as clearly, however, that many other Northern veterans were not so enthusiastic at the prospect. As the Pennsylvanian tried to locate the banners, controversial "Corporal" James Tanner presented special resolutions to the Society of the Army of the Potomac to keep the flags under federal authority. Choosing his words carefully in order to sound like the advocate of reconciliation he certainly was not, Tanner argued that the captured flags were "holy relics of our common people," and thus, "Northern men and Southern men, Union men all to-day, all demand for those flags such care as will ensure their preservation."[65] Other disapproving Northerners did not disguise their sentiments. Former general Benjamin F. Butler asserted that a flag "is an 'archive,' an evidence of victory." Any effort to return the captured flags "is therefore a mutilation of public records, depriving our soldiers of their rightful place in history."[66]

Southerners tried to defuse the flag flap. Virginia governor Fitzhugh Lee made it clear that Pickett's men had not requested the return of the flags and that they knew the banners "are the property of the victors, and were content to let them remain in their charge." He insisted that the nation did not need to "be agitated again by pieces of bunting that mean nothing now." The South would work toward peace and prosperity "whether the flags rot in Washington or are restored to their former custodians." Former general John B. Gordon desired only "peace and goodwill, and prefer[ed] these to a return of even so cherished relics."[67] Even Jefferson Davis entered the fray, although with less conciliatory purposes, arguing that any War Department order to return the flags violated "all known military precedents." Since he doubted that the twenty-six regiments of regular troops in the Union army had captured the nearly 500 Confederate flags stored in Washington, he argued that the banners rightly belonged to the states whose troops had taken them. In any case, they "have no right to be in the National Capital." If the South could not reclaim them, Washington should not have them either.[68]

Davis's widely reprinted remarks inspired one Northern editor to comment in late June that any kind of conciliatory move had to give something to both sides, noting that "reconciliation, to be effective, has to be mutual."[69] What could the South offer in exchange for the return of its cherished banners? Frazier and his fellow Philadelphians could not get Pickett's flags back, and they watched carefully to see if this setback might yet cause the Virginians to back out.

Still uncertain but with only a week to go, Philadelphia veterans finally announced that they would sponsor an elaborate parade to the train station from which they would leave for Gettysburg. They still hoped that once they established "the principle of fraternal reunions between the Blue and the Gray" that such annual meetings would "do more to establish American fellowship and fraternity than anything else that has taken place since the war ended."[70] Their spirits soared even higher when, a few days before they departed for Gettysburg, the Union veterans learned that not only did the Virginians still intend to come, but also the Virginia general's widow LaSalle Corbell Pickett and her son would come with them.[71]

On July 2, 1887, about 500 Philadelphia Brigade veterans, friends, wives, children—fewer than the estimated 1,000 expected two weeks earlier—prepared to leave for Gettysburg.[72] Flags flew from every building near the train station. A cannon boomed out a salute. The Union veterans wore snow-white helmets, blue flannel shirts, and a distinctive memorial badge. "There were many old men in line, whose white beards and gray locks showed that they were close to the allotted age of man," exaggerated one observer.[73]

The train arrived in Gettysburg at about 6 P.M. Their Southern guests —about 200 in number—arrived at about 8:30. The weather was hot and uncomfortable "despite the hurrah business everywhere." The Southerners formed in ranks behind the Stars and Stripes, "the only flag in line," and a band played "Dixie." One Union veteran who toted around his three-year-old child bedecked in miniature canteens and blue and gray badges expressed pride in the Philadelphia Brigade, "but he was prouder of that baby than if he had captured the whole of Pickett's division alone and single handed." Rebel yells pierced the air, and the Union veterans waved their white helmets in response. At the town square, they faced each other in two lines and shook hands. As a Northerner wrote, "Pickett's Division, for the first time, was in undisputed possession of Gettysburg." The Virginians had "at last conquered the Philadelphia Brigade."[74]

Col. Charles H. Banes of the Philadelphia Brigade extended a soldier's greeting. Pickett's men "were brave soldiers in war; we welcome you because you are true citizens in peace." Edward Payson Reeve thanked the Pennsylvanians for their hearty welcome and suggested a new monument at Gettysburg. Some Northerners in the audience no doubt feared that Reeve was about to make one last pitch for a marker to Pickett's division within Union lines, but instead, he urged support for a newly proposed memorial to commemorate the high tide of the Confederacy.[75] Such a monument, he believed, "if properly carried out will do more to restore true friendship in the sections than any other one thing which could be done."[76]

The celebration quickly became an exercise in oratorical excess. With all the rhetorical flourishes at his command, editor A. K. McClure of Philadelphia extended to Pickett's men the formal greetings of the Commonwealth of Pennsylvania and ranked the events of July 3 at Gettysburg with Thermopylae, but added that the military prowess of the Spartans could not match that of "the volunteer soldiers of Hancock and Pickett who willingly dared and died for their convictions." Col. William R. Aylett responded for Virginia: "We come as survivors of a great battle, which illustrated the greatness and glory of the American people." He assured his hosts that "we have come forth from the baptism of blood and fire in which we were consumed, as the representatives of a New South, and we have long years ago ceased to bear in our hearts any residuum of the feelings born of the conflict." He was glad that "over the tomb of secession and African slavery we have created a new empire, and have built a temple to American liberty" over which the Stars and Stripes flew. Proud of his home, he hoped none would begrudge Virginia the right to add Lee, Jackson, Stuart, and Pickett to the state's roll of illustrious citizens that included Founding Fathers Washington, Henry, Mason, Jefferson, Madison, Marshall, and Monroe. Alluding to the recent controversy over captured banners, Aylett asserted that "Southern men don't care who keeps the flags—the past went down in war, and we recognize now the banner of our fathers."[77]

The speeches went on for hours, but the presence of Mrs. Pickett and young George on the speakers' platform frequently drew away attention from the orators. For many, Sallie made the meeting special. As one Northerner later claimed, "Mrs. Pickett bears the credit of having been the first woman who welded the Blue and Gray together." Another deemed her the fulfillment of the Old Testament prophecy that "'a woman shall crush the serpent's head.'" Now she could "crush the head of the serpent of hatred, sectionalism, and strife."[78]

The Northern press went wild. The *New York Times* hoped that the return of Pickett's men to Gettysburg in 1887 would be just a "small fore-runner" of the great silver anniversary reunion being planned for 1888. Delighted that the Virginians came despite their disappointments, some Northern journalists used the reunion to decry continuing efforts by "the Fairchilds and Tanners and other apostles of bitterness" to stir up the embers of sectional hatred.[79] The editor of the *Philadelphia Inquirer* argued that real veterans rarely gave in to "the prejudices and animosities of section and race," and politicians "who hope to turn a penny, honest or otherwise, by it, against the next national election day" needed to pay special heed to this soldiers reunion.[80]

Much of the Southern press also embraced the good feelings. Newspapers from Richmond to Charleston to Atlanta carried details of the entire proceeding.[81] The *Atlanta Constitution* deemed the occasion to be "the most remarkable one on record since Lincoln delivered his memorial oration at the dedication of the Gettysburg national cemetery in 1863." Such meetings of former foes on their old battlefields could only strengthen the "ties of a common country, a common lineage, a common tongue."[82]

The nearness of the reunion to the Fourth of July presented a special opportunity to look for deeper meaning in this unique celebration. The editor of the *Philadelphia Inquirer* recalled that in 1863 "the struggle was so momentous—on one side the perpetuity of the Republic, on the other the creation of a great Confederacy; the feeling was so intense, the excitement ran so high, the strain was so great while the contest continued as to temporarily obliterate from men's minds the past." Now the war was over, and it was appropriate, he believed, for Northerners and Southerners alike to prepare for celebrations of the national anniversary "more imposing than they have been for a full quarter of a century."[83]

Back in Gettysburg, the festivities continued. Early in the afternoon of July 3, the veterans of both armies marched to the Angle. To the tune of "Rally 'Round the Flag," the Union veterans took up their old positions. "The stone fence is still standing behind which the Philadelphia Brigade made its heroic stand," one onlooking journalist noted, and the new monuments to the 69th and 71st Pennsylvania stood only a few feet behind it.[84] The buzz that swept through the audience no doubt included critical comments about the 69th's obelisk, which some onlookers considered "neither appropriate for a battlefield memorial nor for a cemetery."[85]

The veterans of the 69th Pennsylvania dedicated their marker first. Regimental adjutant A. W. McDermott read a list of their Gettysburg dead. General Joshua T. Owen, once the Philadelphia Brigade commander, saluted Pickett's Virginians: "Neither Alexander nor Caesar, Charlemagne nor Frederick, Wellington nor Napoleon ever ordered so

LaSalle Corbell Pickett. The general's widow played a key role in transforming the Virginia division into a leader in the cause of national reunion. (VHS)

hazardous a charge as that which Gen. Robert E. Lee ordered Gen. Pickett to make with his partially-depleted division on the 3d of July, 1863." Then he praised the men of the 69th Pennsylvania who had withstood the charge "where Southern valor and Northern fortitude were put to their severest test." Owen felt strongly that the Virginians should be able to honor their soldiers as the Pennsylvanians now did and urged support for the efforts of Pickett's men to place their monument where they wanted it. His call for three cheers for Pickett's division met with a thunderous response.[86]

Poetry, song, and oratory filled out the program. John Bachelder formally accepted the 69th Pennsylvania's monument for the Gettysburg Battlefield Memorial Association and thanked all the Pennsylvanians for putting together this special reunion at "the scene of Pickett's Charge, because it was here that Lee made his last effort for success. How desperate that effort was, you 'boys' know best yourselves."[87] Adjutant McDermott then asked Mrs. Pickett to step forward to be presented with a three-foot-high spray of white flowers shaped into a trefoil, the color and shape of the badge of the Second Division of the II Corps. "Remembering that that brave band of foes who desperately fought us on this spot, was commanded by your late husband, the gallant General Pickett," McDermott tendered her this "token of our love, for the warm interest you have taken in our efforts to reunite in bonds of fraternity those sections of our country so unhappily estranged by the war." Sallie only bowed her head in thanks.[88]

Then the survivors of the 71st Pennsylvania took the stage. They were especially proud. Their regimental badges, combining blue and gray, had become the reunion's "happiest hit of all." Commenting on their shared bond, Gen. William W. Burns believed that while "Pickett's Charge will live in song, its sad requiem will echo 'the Philadelphia Brigade.'" These Pennsylvanians and Virginians deserved to recognize each other's bravery, because "history will record their deeds together."[89] Gen. William F. "Baldy" Smith wanted Pickett's men to build their monument within the Northern line, "where the foremost man in that division fell or turned back, finding his valor vain against the man that held the Union line here on that day." It would take nothing away from the victors' laurels, he asserted. Indeed, "would it not add new luster to those you won?"[90]

More ceremonies followed. New York artilleryman Andrew Cowan, near his battery's new monument just south of the copse of trees, returned to the Pickett's Division Association a sword he had captured on July 3, explaining that he took it from a young Southern officer who had fallen dead at his feet. Maj. J. F. Crocker of the 9th Virginia accepted the relic with a promise to try and restore the blade to the family of the slain officer.[91]

When the day's proceedings ended, Pickett's men and their Philadelphia hosts went into bivouac, many staying in small tents erected near the copse of trees. "This evening it is hard to tell which is the [Philadelphia] brigade and which the Pickett's division" camp, one observer noted.[92] Impromptu speeches filled the night air, as the men exchanged badges, hats, and other mementos, "even to the giving of a lock of Col. O'Reilly's white hair to Col. Aylett." At midnight, pandemonium broke out for ninety minutes as veterans of both armies launched early Fourth of July celebrations. A Virginia chaplain admitted, "I am the most conquered man you ever met—conquered here by love."[93]

At 7 A.M. on the nation's birthday, official festivities resumed. After Colonel Aylett asked each Virginian to contribute twenty-five cents to cover Mrs. Pickett's expenses, "the way the money rattled on the Secretary's desk was sufficient proof of the esteem" in which the division held her.[94] (H. S. Petty, her official host, later complained that he did not spend all the money collected and could have returned some of it to the association treasury, but "Mrs. Pickett liked to ride in Pullmans."[95]) Then, in a 100-carriage caravan, the Virginians went out to visit their battlefield. The first carriages carried Mrs. Pickett, her son, and historian John Bachelder. They stopped near the junction of the Emmitsburg Road and the Spangler Farm lane. Near the Spangler farmhouse, Pickett's men filed through a receiving line "on the very ground over which her husband's command had charged" to meet Sallie and her son.[96] Col. H. C. Cabell marveled at the coincidence: "I pointed out the spot where Genl. Pickett and his Officers were. It was almost on the spot on which Mrs. Genl Pickett stood when the surviving soldiers were introduced to her that day."[97] Bachelder then asked Pickett's men to take their July 3 positions and requested the senior officer from each of the fifteen Virginia regiments to step forward and verify the line his command occupied.[98]

Even after the tour continued on to the Union line, Sallie Pickett remained the center of attention. She gathered daisies and clover blossoms and handed them out to her husband's men as mementos. She gave autographs. Young George Pickett showed off his father's ornate watch with "the stars and stripes and the stars and bars crossed on the lid; on the inside are the names of the battles in which he participated in the Mexican War."[99]

Near the Angle, the white-helmeted Philadelphians met Pickett's men for official reunion photographs. As cameramen focused their lenses and the crowds temporarily hushed, Virginians and Pennsylvanians joined together to create a lasting image that symbolized the spirit of reunion and reconciliation. In 1887 as in 1863, men in blue and in gray met at the stone wall. And this time they shook hands.

It made for a wonderful image, inspiring Franklin W. Fish to write:

" 'Shake, Johnnie, shake!' 'Shake, Yankee, shake!'
    Gettysburg! At Gettysburg!
The ties we bind no foe shall break,
    Gettysburg! At Gettysburg!

From every mountain top and lake,
From Northern wood and Southern brake,
'Shake, Yankee, shake!' 'Shake, Johnnie, shake!'
    Gettysburg! At Gettysburg!' " [100]

Only one piece of unfinished business remained. Pickett's men still wanted a division monument. Buoyed by Union veterans' promises of support, the Virginians reached a tentative agreement with the memorial association to erect a monument on a site one Northerner described as being "about ten yards in front of our lines. This may be changed, but at this time the ground has been set apart for the men of Arm[i]stead's Brigade. . . . A plain post erected by General A. S. Webb, commander of the Philadelphia Brigade, now marks the place." [101] After all this, ironically, Virginia never did erect a permanent marker there.

Virginian and Pennsylvanian parted close friends. "NOW AND FOREVER! Reunited on the Battleground of Gettysburg" blared a headline in the *Philadelphia Inquirer*. Sallie Pickett thanked both the Virginians and her Northern hosts: "Regal entertainment has its expression in lavish expenditure of money—empty display of pomp and splendor—but our entertainment was a lavish expenditure of soul, a display of chivalry and heartfelt rivalry, wherein the men of Pennsylvania vied with our own cherished sons in doing honor to us." She felt sure that "the brave and loyal hearts of both North and South are firmly cemented under the old Stars and Stripes, the emblem of our fathers," and that the Stars and Bars now could be "laid away sacred only to memory." [102]

The bonds between the Philadelphians and the Virginians remained strong for years, a factor that helped to entrench the image of Pickett's Charge in national memory. The year after that first Gettysburg reunion, Pickett's Virginians invited Philadelphia Brigade veterans to come to Richmond to help them dedicate a monument to honor their commander. This meeting, like the one in 1887, tested both sections' commitment to national reconciliation. Northern foes of the Gettysburg ceremonies could not fathom why any Union veteran would even consider visiting the former Confederate capital. Likewise, a few Virginians protested the participation of Union veterans in these Southern rites and pointed to the problems surrounding the erection of a Pickett's division memorial at Gettysburg as solid evidence of Northern refusal to deal with "rebels" guilty of "treason." Indeed, many Virginians complained that this new memorial project smacked so badly of politics that some who did not participate in the charge seemed to enjoy more credit and prominence than did its survivors. [103]

Pickett's men ignored much of the controversy, however, inspired by a comrade's plea to "keep alive only the heroic courage and sublime devotion to duty which is the common heritage of the American people" so that "the Historian of the future will not fail to award the old Confederate his pale need of praise." [104] A hastily arranged committee, giving in to local demands, decided to hold the ceremony on October 5, 1888, the third day—"Veterans' Day"—of the state exposition in Richmond. [105]

The Pickett memorial committee found its commitment tested at every turn. Merely attempting to find a company to design and deliver an appropriate memorial in timely fashion nearly defeated the entire project. [106] Five days before its unveiling, several pieces of the monument had not yet been fitted into place. [107]

Even worse, the critics guessed correctly that the dedication of the Pickett monument would become a highly political event. Each detail of the day's events seemed fraught with small, yet potentially explosive, dangers. Reeve hoped that Aylett would repeat the oratorical performance he performed at Gettysburg, but some of Pickett's men in Aylett's hometown of Portsmouth announced that they opposed the colonel's selection on the grounds that they had "very little respect for him as a *soldier*" and encouraged Reeve to find an orator who had served "without fear and without reproach." [108] Kemper's health still remained fragile. [109] Reeve announced that Eppa Hunton would give the address, but loyal Democrat Hunton refused the invitation. [110] Democratic governor Fitzhugh Lee also begged off, explaining only that he might be out of town on the day of the ceremony. [111] Reeve finally got Pickett's former staff officer R. Taylor Scott to agree to speak. [112]

The military parade caused political problems, too. The Pickett-Buchanan camp of Richmond Confederate veterans readily agreed to participate, of course. [113] Delegations from Norfolk, Portsmouth, Hampton, Petersburg, Alexandria, and Fredericksburg Confederate veterans camps also decided to come. [114] The Philip Kearny GAR Post 10, made up of Union veterans living in Virginia, also wanted to march. [115] On the other hand, other prominent Virginia veterans groups—including the Richmond Howitzers, the Richmond Light Infantry Blues, and the Pegram Battalion Association—announced their intentions to send either a small detail or no official delegation at all. [116] Individual members of the aforementioned organizations could march if they desired, but only as part of some other association.

Despite all these problems, however, the ceremonies finally came together. A small contingent of Pickett's men met 150 Philadelphians at Fredericksburg and escorted them to Richmond. [117] Mayor J. Taylor Ellyson welcomed the Pennsylvanians officially and hoped they would enjoy being the "guests of that matchless infantry whom Pickett led so grandly down against the roaring heights of destiny." At the last minute, the funding drive came up $600 short, but at the conclusion of the mayor's greeting Pickett's veterans subscribed the needed sum the night before the dedication.[118]

On the morning of the ceremony, yet another crisis emerged. A few weeks earlier, Pickett's men had offered the post of honor in the parade to Hollywood Cemetery to the Philadelphia Brigade veterans.[119] But on the day of the parade, when the Philadelphians saw Southern veterans lining up under the Confederate flag, they refused to march. The Virginians did not understand why their guests became so upset; after all, the Southerners had marched under that same banner during recent visits to New York City, Boston, and Bunker Hill. A Philadelphian then explained that the ornate Stars and Stripes they carried this day had been lent to them on the condition "that it not be used in procession with a 'rebel' flag." Rescuing the moment, Mayor Ellyson convinced the Philadelphians to repack their borrowed flag, asked the Virginians to furl their Confederate flag, and got them all to march under the Stars and Stripes that belonged to the Robert E. Lee Camp of Confederate veterans.[120]

At the cemetery, after an invocation by the former chaplain of the 18th Virginia, former general Montgomery Corse unveiled Pickett's memorial. About twenty-five feet high and resting on a granite foundation, the monument featured a central cylinder surrounded by six pillars with bronze and copper tablets, all topped by a bronze urn wreathed in flowers. The monument stood close to Gettysburg Hill, where so many of Pickett's men had rested since the early 1870s. Engraved lists of the regiments in each of the four Virginia brigades in Pickett's division (Corse's men were included) and Dearing's artillery battalion filled the tablets on the granite pillars. A reporter estimated its cost at $1,800.[121]

The formalities did not last long. Afterward, Pickett's men and their Northern guests visited the Richmond Exposition and toured Libby Prison, Belle Isle, and other historic sites.[122] A fine banquet offered the most sumptuous foods of the region. Colonel Aylett, denied the chance to speak at the cemetery, again greeted the Pennsylvanians warmly: "May the aspiration ascend to Heaven from every bosom that God bless, hallow and prosper the work of reconciliation and love inaugurated by the Philadelphia Brigade and Pickett's Division."[123] The Pennsylvanians left their new friends with the prayer that "there come through this great war perennial peace."[124] The sword that Union artilleryman Andrew Cowan had returned to Pickett's men at the 1887 reunion was delivered to Thomas H.

The Pickett's division memorial over the general's grave in Hollywood Cemetery, Richmond (Author's collection)

Ford, who had identified it by the diminutive palmetto on the blade as that of his late brother, Lt. P. Fletcher Ford of the 57th Virginia.[125]

Through such public celebrations, Pickett's Charge became one of the first and thus one of the most lasting symbols of national reunion. The vivid image of former foes shaking hands across an old stone wall evoked powerful support for setting aside controversy and working together with a shared commitment for a common future. The cause of intersectional reconciliation took its inspiration from many sources, but the meeting of several hundred Virginians and Pennsylvanians at Gettysburg in July 1887 provided one of its most enduring symbols.

5

MONUMENTS
TO MEMORY

Not all Northerners shared the spirit of reconciliation that brought Pickett's men and the Philadelphians to Gettysburg in 1887. That reunion and the approach of the battle's silver anniversary in 1888 prompted thousands of Union veterans to reflect on the accomplishments of their youth, and some plainly did not like the way history remembered them. At the dedication of his regimental monument on the battlefield, one Pennsylvanian made two especially unsettling observations: First, "the battle of Gettysburg has served to magnify the glory of the rebels at the expense of the Union troops," and second, the only "great event of the battle in the popular mind is the magnificent charge of Pickett's Division."[1] This they could not tolerate.

As Northern veterans broke free of the postwar national amnesia that had stifled discussion of military affairs, interest in their wartime experiences revived. They looked with pride on their generation for conclusively resolving a national crisis.[2] As Daniel Sickles told veterans in July 1888, "The war of 1861–65 was our heroic age. It demonstrated the vitality of republican institutions. It illustrated the martial spirit and resources and genius of the American soldier and sailor." The war's "lavish sacrifices of blood and treasure, the unyielding tenacity of the combatants, the constancy and firmness of the people on both sides, men and women, old and young, rich and poor, signalized the great conflict as the heroic age of the Republic."[3]

No wonder, then, as they felt the press of advancing age, they began to commemorate their services to the nation and to honor fallen comrades. They erected monuments, held special rites, and published personal memoirs and unit histories that chronicled their days in uniform as honestly as memory would permit. For Army of the Potomac veterans in particular, and even for thousands of Union soldiers who did not fight there, evocative images of Gettysburg and Pickett's Charge provided useful emotional touchstones that helped them remind posterity that they had answered the nation's call to duty.

Union veterans now welcomed the authority of history. Many respected history's "truth," even when it caused discomfort. Many more, however, called up from memory the imperfectly remembered disconnected strands of battle experience and endowed them with the mantle of "truth" instead. Those most concerned with preserving the "truth" of the events of July 3, of course, were the many Northerners who had served on or near Cemetery Ridge that day. In the 1880s, they finally rediscovered a serious interest in the tactical details of the Union defense. Minor controversies once shunted aside in the afterglow of victory now blossomed anew in flurries of contentious rhetoric. Unwilling to languish unfairly in the wash of "the high water mark of the Rebellion," they entered into new literary wars with enthusiasm.

Just as compelling, many Northerners who took no part in the dramatic events of July 3 also cared deeply about the way posterity would recall this day's action. Veterans of the first and second days of battle at Gettysburg worried that the popular attention accorded Pickett's Charge would cast into obscurity their own efforts and sacrifices on that field. For others, the action on July 3 held far greater symbolic importance than mere military success; all Americans shared the real fruits of victory the Army of the Potomac won at Gettysburg. Still others believed that only a renewed commitment to the truth of history could mitigate the effects of recent misguided efforts to promote intersectional harmony; for them, reunions like that at the stone wall in 1887 trivialized the sacrifices of their youth and drowned in waves of contrived emotionalism the principles for which they fought and many of their comrades died.

Northern criticism of that recent "Virginia love feast" at Gettysburg revealed just how seldom Union veterans agreed on the wartime events that deserved commemoration, those who should be permitted to celebrate, and the conduct of those rites. The war still stirred strong emotions in many Northern towns where too many middle-aged men hobbled through life on crutches, with empty sleeves, or with consumptive coughs that somehow never went away. Thus, as the silver anniversary of the great battle approached, it came as no surprise that the editor of a veterans newspaper wrote, "No God-knows-who-was-right bosh must be tolerated at Gettysburg. The men who won the victory there were eternally right, and the men who were defeated were eternally wrong."[4]

Even a generation after Appomattox, a substantial portion of Northerners had not forgotten victory's cost. Most of the planners of the Gettysburg silver anniversary ceremonies had worn blue uniforms, and while enjoined to salute veterans of both armies, they appreciated strong sentiments against this notion.[5] One Northern veteran warned Southerners to "understand that the hallowed field of Gettysburg is no place to vaunt treason and glorify rebellion." Those appalled by the 1887 joint reunion wanted die-hard Confederates to "stay at home and gnaw the file of discontent in obscurity."[6]

Not all Union veterans wallowed in such deep vindictiveness, of course, but many did hope for a silver anniversary celebration that commemorated first and foremost the greatest victory of the Army of the Potomac. "There is something inexpressibly grand and touching in this visit, 25 years later, to the field of their fiery trial and immortal glory, of the men who fought at Gettysburg with a devotion and courage as sublime as that displayed at Marathon and Thermopylae," wrote one Northerner.[7] There would be time later for reforging intersectional ties.

One specific problem especially threatened the likelihood of a conciliatory celebration at Gettysburg in 1888. The proposed Pickett's division marker, endorsed even by many Union veterans the previous year, continued to draw the wrath of Northerners who opposed any such gesture. One man, so outraged that the memorial association's commissioners considered Virginia's request at all, complained that the South's rebellion was "the most causeless and unjustifiable war that ever disturbed the peace and wasted the lives and treasure of a contented and happy people." So certain that Virginians simply must "restrain themselves from extolling treason" with monuments on Northern soil, this veteran's views show that memories of Pickett's Charge served opponents of reconciliation just it did its proponents.[8]

In the end, those who preferred that the silver anniversary remain a Northern celebration got their way. Union veterans attended in great numbers. "The roads—and all roads lead to Gettysburg—are crowded with men on foot, men in wagons, men in carriages," wrote an impressed correspondent, adding that "the Grand Army of the Republic has turned

The field of Pickett's Charge in the 1880s, viewed from the position of the Philadelphia Brigade at the time when Union veterans began to erect monuments here. The 69th Pennsylvania held the wall in the foreground, along the line marked sparsely by small trees. Pickett's Virginians advanced directly toward the photographer's position, their lines breaking around the Codori farm in the center. (Charles B. Tower Album, USAMHI)

its face toward the great battlefield of the war and, poor or rich, those of its members who live within reach of Gettysburg are on their way."[9] Congress had turned down a request for funds to defray transportation costs, a move that had "a depressing effect on old Confederates, who felt insulted."[10] Only about three hundred Southern veterans attended.

Only about twenty of Pickett's men, and not an official delegation from the Pickett's Division Association, went to the 1888 reunion. Thomas A. Hutchins of the 14th Virginia thought they should go, believing that "as a Political move, it is a good one for the destruction of section hatred & issues."[11] Few agreed, however. Even Sallie Pickett, who received a personal invitation to come as "a link in the chain of unity between the sections broken by civil war," sent her regrets. Still hoping for "the perfect union of the survivors of the blue and gray upon the field consecrated by the blending of the blood of the bravest men ever upon God's footstool," she cited health concerns to explain her absence.[12] The few Virginians who went decided to dress entirely in gray, but except for the state coat of arms on their jacket button and their "Army of Northern Virginia" badges, they wore no other military regalia.[13]

So, while Southerners mostly stayed home, dignitaries from the North flooded into Gettysburg in great numbers. Dan Sickles, who touted the III Corps fight of July 2 and not Pickett's Charge of July 3, was the most visible Union veteran present. An entourage of former Union generals and senior officials from various veterans organizations followed him nearly everywhere. A correspondent noticed all the gold braid and mused: "Had a shell patterned after the shells that did such awful execution on the battlefield of Gettysburg 25 years ago burst on any part of that field today, the havoc among Generals, Colonels, and other wearers of high military titles would have been simply sickening."[14] With prominent Northern political leaders, military detachments of U.S. Regulars and National Guardsmen, and special reunions of the I and XII Corps, the 1888 reunion truly became an Army of the Potomac celebration.

Only one prominent Southerner with strong ties to the history of July 3 came to Gettysburg in 1888. James Longstreet represented the interests of his Virginians very well, yet he did not forget the sensibilities of Northern veterans. The charge of July 3, Longstreet proclaimed, "has no parallel nor is likely to have [one] in the annals of war." He recalled "the elastic steps" of Pickett's men "whose half-concealed smiles expressed pleasure in their opportunity" to "fill the measure of a soldier's pride, and well did they meet their promise." He saluted the Northern defenders, too, noting that Pickett's men fell "at the feet of the foe who, standing like their own brave hills, received with welcome the shock of this well-adjusted battle."[15]

Former Union general Dan Butterfield escorted Longstreet to Cemetery Ridge, where he could look out at the battlefield of July 3 from the Northern troops' perspective. Reporters pressed close to catch the Southern general's every word, but as he gazed out to the west toward the treeline of Seminary Ridge, he grew noticeably quiet. At the copse of trees, a Philadelphian told him about the recent efforts of Pennsylvanians and Virginians to win approval for a permanent Southern marker near that site. Longstreet knew that Pickett's men wanted to place a memorial there, and the temporary marker already in place interested him. When he finally made his first comments about the charge, he called it a mistake. He then pointed out a few topographical changes in the landscape but admitted that "the field looked to him much as it had looked on the day of the battle. The mental photograph taken on that day was as clear as on the day of the battle." Reporters sensed growing tension in the crowd: "Thinking of Pickett's fatal charge begot silence, and the party moved toward Cemetery Hill."[16]

Even if the anniversary ceremonies had not centered around the events of July 3, the celebration could not end without some kind of commemoration at the stone wall. After all, wrote a Philadelphia correspondent, that was the point at which "the flower of the rebel army, consisting of Pickett's division of Virginia troops and men who had been engaged in many desperate struggles during the war," made their most desperate attack. When the Pennsylvanians held their ground, that action became "the turning point of the rebellion."[17] Perhaps in reaction against the previous year's reunion, the 1888 festivities at the Angle lasted only a short time. Photographers snapped a few frames, and the crowds quickly broke up. Since no special events were planned for July 4, attendees headed elsewhere to continue their holiday weekend.[18]

In the end, the 1888 ceremonies did not live up to the events that inspired them. Nor did they draw much popular interest. The only truly controversial issue seemed to be a poem written for the occasion, Will Henry Thompson's "High Tide at Gettysburg." Virginians were not happy that he called positive attention to troops other than Pickett's men: "Ah, how the withering tempest blew / Against the front of Pettigrew!" He also permitted Tennessee to share center stage with those who "fell where Kemper led" and those who "died where Garnett bled." No ex-Confederate wanted to believe that the charge ended with "the death cry of a nation lost."[19] The poet's praise of Confederate military prowess also won condemnation from Northerners. For years, however, the strongest protest came from Lost Cause advocates who wondered how any so-called "Southern poet" could write such things as: "They smote and fell who set the bars / Against the progress of the stars."[20]

The 1888 meeting had provided an opening for Northerners hostile to national reconciliation to vent their feelings, however. Many simply could not understand how brothers-in-arms could expect them to forget the sacrifice of so many of their comrades' lives. Northern critics of the 1887 joint reunion now turned their vehemence against the members of the Philadelphia Brigade who chose to go to Richmond for the dedication of the Pickett's division memorial just a few months after Gettysburg's silver anniversary. One critic damned the Philadelphians' participation in the ceremony as "another exhibition of unrepentant and blatant rebelism such as seems inevitable whenever that organization and the organized survivors of Pickett's Division meet." Citing the words of a Southern speaker who had "insolently proposed to quarter the rebel flag on the Star Spangled Banner," he expressed disgust that no Philadelphian protested the suggestion "in the name of his comrades who had died vindicating the righteousness of the cause and the stainlessness of the flag." They should have refused emphatically to take part in any rite in which "the abhorrent emblem" of the Confederacy was displayed. More to the point, Philadelphians should not have considered participating in any unveiling of a monument to George E. Pickett, "a man whose only distinction was gained fighting the Government which had educated him; which supported him 20 years, and which he had solemnly sworn to defend." No true Union man should ever salute "a man conspicuous only for his efforts to make treason successful." [21]

Such sentiments survived well beyond the silver anniversary of the battle. Some GAR posts, such as the Henry I. Zinn post of Mechanicsburg, Pennsylvania, responded to a plea for money to build a statue of Robert E. Lee on Seminary Ridge by asserting that it "could not, would not, and will not give its consent and agree to place a monument at the expense of the State of Pennsylvania, at Gettysburg nor elsewhere in the State of Pennsylvania to his memory, being a rebel and a traitor whose shoulders were crimsoned and stained with the blood of thousands who gave their loyal lives in support of the flag." [22] When Lee's statue on Monument Avenue in Richmond was unveiled, hard-line Union veterans made fun of the ceremony's "hysteria of maudlin sentiment," and one expressed relief that Virginia women had not been asked "to contribute their locks for tackle to haul and raise the statue," or else "there would have been more short-haired women in Virginia to-day than could be seen in a hundred Women's Rights Conventions." [23]

Many Northerners refused to tolerate further what they perceived to be continual blatant expressions of Lost Causism. Even more than they disliked monuments to Confederate heroes, they despised the feeling that they were losing the literary war for the history books. "A few more Confederate histories, and it will be made to appear that all that ever confronted the Army of the Potomac was Gen. Lee, occasionally assisted by an Orderly, and a casual gentleman armed with a shotgun," wrote one Northern editor.[24] For Union veterans of Gettysburg, the manner in which the history of the battle passed down to future generations began to take on greater importance than ever before. With the image of the copse of trees as the "high water mark of the Rebellion" firmly entrenched in popular memory, service at Gettysburg on July 3—however direct or tangential—became a badge of honor for any soldier. It spoke well of their military prowess. Abraham Lincoln's benediction validated their sacrifice. For these and many other reasons, in speeches, at reunions and dedications of monuments, and in their memoirs and regimental histories, many agreed that repulsing Pickett's Charge, merely witnessing

Pickett's Charge, being on the same battlefield as Pickett's Charge, and—as the years passed—even having the common bond of a blue uniform with those who turned back Pickett's Charge helped to measure their worth as soldiers. No Lost Cause bombast should ever be allowed to take that away.

In order to connect to that pivotal moment in the nation's fortunes, Union veterans called up hazy recollections and inspiring popular images and recast them all as "history." Old themes burst forth anew, now more stirring than ever before. And all recorders of history concurred: at Gettysburg on July 3, a day of national crisis, the defenders of the Union faced an awesome foe. "The veterans of Virginia, the flower of the rebel army, under its idolized commander," prepared to write "another bloody chapter in the history of the rebellion" that day, wrote the historian of the 16th Maine.[25] A man in the 14th Connecticut recalled that at every step the enemy showed "determination and resolute defiance, the line moving forward like a victorious giant, confident of power and victory."[26] The sight had awed a spectator from the 73rd Ohio: "The scene is like a pageant rather than a battle."[27] "Like incarnate demons the rebels charge[d]," recalled Pvt. Theodore Gerrish of the 20th Maine, "six gigantic brigades—the flower of the Confederacy—the old imperial guard of Lee's army."[28] A Minnesota sergeant recalled the "magnificent spectacle [of] steel crested billows" as "an intensely interesting sight; especially to us who must face it, breast it, break it—or be broken by it."[29] Indeed, the stakes had been so great, a Vermont survivor wrote, that Pickett, "the one of all the veteran officers of the great Army of Northern Virginia personally selected by General Lee," led "the flower of his army in whom was centered all his hopes." They were to Lee "like Napoleon's body guard at Waterloo."[30]

Intensely interested in the smallest details of their defense, Northern veterans gave in to hyperbole and literary or rhetorical excess. Descriptions of the great bombardment now might impress the most skeptical. "Only a *Milton* could find and put language together that would give even a faint idea of the 'confusion worse confounded' of such a scene," wrote a veteran of the 126th New York.[31] The history of the 118th Pennsylvania (a regiment that had been posted far from the worst of the cannonade) recalled that Southern gunners "would send the solid shot along with the fury of a maddened bowler."[32] The spectacle inspired eloquence, not merely terror. All the way over near Spangler's meadow, the men of the 13th New Jersey huddled behind their breastworks and "philosophically awaited the *denouement*" while Confederates continued "to deluge us with all the old iron they could spare."[33] Few Northerners downplayed the effectiveness of the Southern cannonade now. Perhaps it spoke well of the

15th New Jersey's chaplain that he still admitted that "much of this cannonade was but a noisy demonstration, and less decisive than the musketry firing."[34]

Union veterans also got caught up in a numbers game. Their line on Cemetery Ridge appeared more and more often to be the "thin blue ribbon" Carleton C. Coffin had described at war's end. Still, even this appellation suggested greater strength than the veterans wished to convey. Now they made the point that units of the II Corps already had suffered great losses in earlier battles and even on July 2. Early on July 3, for instance, "the little battalion called by courtesy the First Minnesota, was moved up to its place in Harrow's brigade line. In appearance it resembled one of the many skeleton Confederate regiments after the battle of Antietam."[35]

Similarly, the greater the numbers of the advancing foe, the better it suited Northerners' purposes. At first, Longstreet's words set the standard. The chaplain of the 125th New York, for one, wrote: "See! from the woods covering Seminary Ridge that magnificent line of men—a mile long, three lines deep, and each line a double line—upwards of fifteen thousand strong . . . as on dress parade."[36] But Union accounts usually increased the odds. As early as 1864, one of Stannard's Vermonters had insisted that they were attacked by "an overwhelming force of seventeen thousand rebels," but their "charge was gallantly repulsed by this brigade alone."[37] In the 1870s and 1880s, a spate of Northern regimental histories insisted that the South came with an attacking column of 18,000 men. But Lt. William Lochren of the 1st Minnesota recalled, "We estimated the force as twenty thousand."[38] A survivor of the 19th Maine in Harrow's brigade recalled "a force estimated from 18,000 to 25,000 men."[39]

Some estimates defied reality. Many Northerners wrongly believed that Lee greatly outnumbered Meade at Gettysburg, and this misperception shaped their interpretation of the cost of the South's great charge. A veteran of the 106th Pennsylvania believed that the Confederate army lost 16,000 men in the assault, a number that likely exceeded that of the entire attacking column.[40] An otherwise quite reliable guidebook, written by a Gettysburg native and army veteran, claimed that Garnett's brigade alone suffered over 3,000 casualties, for what would have been a loss of about 150 percent.[41]

When Northern veterans could not quantify what they saw, they found other ways to explain the spectacular scene the Southern attack presented. A spectator from the 55th Ohio on Cemetery Hill recalled " 'acres of soldiers in solid mass.' "[42] Imprecisely, but with great imagery, a man in the 12th New Hampshire described the attack of Pickett's men as "the most

Veterans of the 13th, 14th, and 16th Vermont remembered their flank attack this way.
(Massachusetts Commandery, MOLLUS, USAMHI)

threatening battle-cloud of the Rebellion, rolling up from the Southern horizon like a billow of fire."[43]

Curiously, while great odds mattered tremendously, few other details about the Confederate force seemed quite so important. Northerners often wrote as if the Virginians charged alone and quickly and uncritically accepted the popular name "Pickett's Charge" for the July 3 attack. Even worse, when Northerners mentioned any other Southern command other than Pickett's men, they showed an unnerving tendency to misrepresent or misidentify them. One Vermonter insisted that his brigade had taken on Carnot Posey's Mississippians, not Perry's Floridians.[44] The 16th Maine's historian asserted that McGowan's South Carolinians and Thomas's Georgians were part of the attacking column.[45] J. W. Nesbit of the 149th Pennsylvania named Trimble as commander of the brigades of Wright, Mahone, and Posey while omitting all reference to Scales and Lane.[46] Another Northern writer no doubt made every Virginian cringe when he wrote of "Pickett's North Carolinians."[47]

Even the Northern troops who actually had faced Pettigrew's and Trimble's men on July 3 frequently failed to acknowledge this fact. Many veterans of Hays's division bought into the seductive imagery of Pickett's

Charge completely. When Col. Clinton MacDougall spoke at the dedication of the 111th New York's monument in 1891, he referred so frequently to Pickett's Charge that editors inserted into the published version of the talk a footnote that explained that the regiment actually had fought Pettigrew's division, not Pickett's.[48] Very few Northerners took time to point out, as did the veterans of the 90th Pennsylvania, that the "strong column consisted *not only* of Pickett's Division, as we hear it so often erroneously stated, which included the Virginia contingent—the flower of his army, but Pettigrew's Division and two Brigades of Pender's Division of Hill's Corps."[49] Only a few would assert forthrightly that "the term Pickett's charge, as applied to the entire movement, is a misnomer."[50]

The impact of images first crafted by the wartime Richmond press also showed through clearly in Northern regimental histories. The historian of the 3rd Wisconsin declared that while the "North Carolinians turned and fled in terror, Pickett's men alone remained," and those brave Virginians "tempered in the fire of many battles quailed not."[51] Union veterans seemed to accept as truth every accolade the Richmond press ever heaped on Pickett's men, and romanticized notions of their old foemen found their way into numerous memoirs. A piece in a Vermont unit history portrayed Pickett's division "as made up of the best blood of Virginia, and . . . nearly all the adventurers of the army who made war a profession and a means of livelihood." The author added that Pickett's men included old soldiers who had fought under Taylor and Scott in Mexico, filibusterers in Central America, veterans of service under Garibaldi in Italy, and "members of the celebrated British Legion which served against Don Carlos in Spain. All these were accustomed to war and loved its excitement as the gambler loves his game." All this flowed from the pen of former Union general Abner Doubleday.[52]

If Pickett's men represented the flower of the Southern army, then surely a special sense of accomplishment accrued to Northern troops for defeating such soldiers. For those who could accept the spirit of national reunion, praise of former enemies became absolutely essential. "We can honor the brave, though misguided, men who took part therein. They were Americans. None other than Americans could make such a charge," claimed the Honorable Ira M. Hedges at the dedication of the 95th New York's monument.[53] It was all the easier to salute their foe, because, as Colonel MacDougall explained, "It was not the men who fought and died here that brought on the war. We cannot blame the men who bore the brunt of the battle on the Confederate side. . . . We honor their splendid courage; we honor the 'Wild charge they made' here."[54] Pvt. Mark Nickerson's 10th Massachusetts played no active role in the repulse; still

Nickerson "always maintained that Picket[t]'s Charge at Gettysburg was a braver charge than the Charge of the Light Brigade." If he ever met one of those men, Nickerson insisted, "I would take off my hat to him as one of the bravest men who ever lived." [55] At the dedication of the monument to the 1st New York Battery at the copse of trees, the Honorable Sereno Payne praised "the unequaled charge of Pickett's men," some of whom sat in the audience. He could not repress "the proud exclamation, 'These too, are Americans!'" [56]

Praising worthy enemies inspired great rhetorical and literary excess. An audience of Marylanders learned in 1888 that Gettysburg "was the scene of the grandest charge recorded in history—that of Macdonald and his twenty thousand at Wagram not excepted, for they were not marching against Americans. What Marathon was to Greece, Blenheim to Germany, Hastings to England, more was Gettysburg to America." [57] The 44th New York recalled that from their position on Little Round Top, they watched as Pickett's 15,000 men copied "a favorite plan of Napoleon." For their unit history, they appealed to the ancients for descriptive inspiration: "Tacitus wrote that the first object of an attacking army, is by noisy and spectacular demonstration to carry fear to the minds of the opposing force. Pickett's charge was well calculated to accomplish that purpose." But, "unlike Caesar, they came, they saw, they were conquered." [58]

Not all Union veterans could treat their former foes with such gracious praise, however. The Pennsylvanian who complained of chronicles of Gettysburg that glorified the Southern soldiers at the expense of Northerners believed it was time to destroy the "halo of glory around a charge which does not appear around the men who firmly stand to resist it." [59] Some Northerners laughed at any notion of exceptional Southern bravery, even insisting they had repulsed the great attack with amazing ease. A Delaware veteran rejected all "talk about the gamecock qualities of the Southern troops" as "pure, unadulterated rot," adding, "I have often heard with feelings that made me tired, the account of Pickett's charge at Gettysburg, and their splendid courage. I went over the ground on the morning of July 5, 1863, and I know whereof I speak when I say that three-fourths of those men were shot while running to the rear." [60] Capt. Robert G. Carter of the 22nd Massachusetts, certain that no man could stand up to the massed artillery and infantry fire unleashed from Cemetery Ridge— even in the face of all evidence to the contrary—decided that "all the drivel about the Union center being pierced is too absurd . . . to entertain for a moment." Any future historians who accorded Pickett's men even partial success he classified in advance as "*buncombe writers who were not there*" who nonetheless continued "to hand down and perpetuate historical lies." [61]

Still, even as they grumbled about the inaccuracy or the pro-Southern bias of some historical literature on the repulse of great charge, veterans of the I and II Corps troops who played a role in it ranked it high among their most important memories. It became a highlight not just of their military careers but of their entire lives. So much had been at stake that it deserved special commemoration. For Keystone State soldiers the issue had been especially clear: "It is death or victory, and the soil is Pennsylvania."[62] The men of the 69th Pennsylvania had understood their special obligation; every man felt "that he had more courage to meet the enemy at Gettysburg, than upon any field of battle on which we had as yet been engaged."[63]

In answering the call of duty, they handed down an important lesson in civic responsibility to future generations. "The Union forces realized that the life of the Nation was in peril, and on that battle hinged the future destiny of the Republic," the Honorable John M. Davy reminded the veterans of the 108th New York, and "every beat of the heart, every thought of loved ones at home, encouraged them to hold their ground and to fight with renewed vigor."[64] They had held the moral high ground, too. When the "mightiest surge of the slaveholders' rebellion was shattered," the 14th Connecticut was proud to have been "part of the living bulwark that broke it."[65] With its work at Gettysburg, the 111th New York helped to decide such grave issues as "the right of an undisputed majority to rule, as against the right of a factious minority to rebel."[66]

Unquestionably, the fighting had been severe. A Maine officer remembered that the Southern infantry advanced "hot with passion born of war, stained and blinded with blood, the living fail[ing] to see the terrible harvest of death in their rear, and, utterly reckless of personal results, they press on and on."[67] A Pennsylvanian who had laid in close support of the defenders of the ridge recalled that "carnage is here and now personified." The Confederates advanced in a "compact mass of human beings, which, all covered with blood, seems to be driven by an irresistible force superior to the individual will of those composing it."[68] One of the few survivors of the battered 1st Minnesota asserted that "if men ever become devils, that was one of the times. We were crazy with the excitement of the fight. We just rushed in like wild beasts."[69] An officer in the 8th Ohio graphically described how, when Union artillery and infantry fire opened up on the Southern ranks, "arms, heads, blankets, guns and knapsacks were thrown and tossed into the clear air," and even though a "moan went up from the field, distinctly to be heard amid the storm of battle," the Southerners had pressed on.[70] The men of the 126th New York wondered if on July 3 they became all too "familiar with the 'devilish enginery' of modern warfare" that destroyed "the flesh and bones of the very flower of our country's young manhood."[71]

Now, as the preservation of special memories grew in importance, even the most evocative and emotionally satisfying prose could not appease many Northern participants if it did not work toward establishing the "truth of history." Formerly irrelevant discrepancies now demanded resolution, and controversies revived with a vengeance. A Philadelphia editor observed with interest: "New facts and assertions concerning the battle here are cropping out continually, but even the generals differ as to their positions, and as to what they or the adjoining command did at certain times or on certain days."[72]

Union soldiers jockeyed for position in the history books, and not even senior officers seemed immune. During the cannonade, Hancock had ordered his II Corps artillery to return the Confederate fire, but army artillery chief Henry Hunt told gunners to save ammunition. The battery commanders had followed Hancock's directions. Hunt used the "Battles and Leaders" series to reopen the issue of command jurisdiction, asserting that if his orders had been obeyed, the Southern infantry never would have reached the stone wall.[73] Hancock had died in 1886, but Francis A. Walker of his staff took up a defense of his late commander's right to control all II Corps batteries.[74]

Not surprisingly, jealousies now divided soldiers and units that once fought together on Cemetery Ridge. More than ever before, Union veterans demanded acknowledgment of their special contributions to victory.

Some boasted confidently. Capt. John E. Burton of the 11th New York Independent Battery believed that "it was the moral effect" of three batteries coming up late in the action that broke the Southerners' charge.[75] Lt. Tully McCrae of Woodruff's battery agreed that "our artillery came in, saved the day, and won the battle" and complained, "I have always been of the opinion that the Artillery has never received the credit which was its due for this battle."[76]

Infantrymen, of course, saw it differently. Individual units advanced for themselves—not for the whole Union line—special claims for credit. The "Battles and Leaders" series had given Hall's men a chance to explain what they did on July 3, and veterans of the 19th Massachusetts in particular bragged that they had been the real "keystone of the Union" that day.[77] The Pennsylvanians of the Philadelphia Brigade, of course, chafed at any suggestion that they had given less than their best effort at the clump of trees. "There have been accounts carelessly published in some of the histories of the war" guilty of "grossly misrepresenting the heroic efforts of the brigade," wrote the unit historian.[78]

The Philadelphians especially resented the critical commentaries on their conduct contained in Lt. Frank Haskell's long letter about the battle. Circulated unofficially in pamphlet form even before its publication as a book in the early twentieth century, the manuscript spawned a firestorm of protest from angry Pennsylvanians.[79] "Haskell might, with equal truth and egotism, have written: 'To Dick and his rider belong the honor of meeting and repulsing Pickett's Division,'" one complained. Time did not soften perceived insults. When both the Massachusetts Commandery of the Military Order of the Loyal Legion and the Wisconsin History Commission gave their strong endorsement to the book, the Philadelphians openly challenged Haskell's honesty about many incidents. They took special note of his claim to be "the one solitary horseman between the Second Division of Hancock's Corps and Pickett's Division." With biting sarcasm, the Pennsylvanians asked just how the Virginians, "any one of [whom] could kill a jay bird at a distance of 150 yards . . . were able to make such a slaughter in *our ranks at long range*" but "could not even disable First Lieutenant Frank Aretas Haskell, or his horse, and they not forty yards distant."[80]

Survivors of Alexander Hays's division of the II Corps also grew increasingly sensitive about the way their day's work appeared in the historical record. Like Pettigrew's Confederates, they too often disappeared in accounts that devoted greatest attention to the Confederate penetration on Gibbon's divisional front. They no doubt cringed to read such items as a New Jersey veteran's comment that "three Pennsylvania regiments received the full force of the blow."[81] Hays's veterans tried to make clear that the fight on their front had been just as tough as that down at the clump of trees. Indeed, but for an accident of geography—the angled stone wall—the attack would have hit them squarely. A senior officer of the 126th New York believed that the true object of the north-shifting formation of Pickett's men was "to march through my command and seize Cemetery Hill, which, no doubt, *was* their intention."[82] Colonel MacDougall of the 111th New York agreed that "the greatest point of attack seemed to be Ziegler's Grove, just on our right and rear."[83]

The Southerners' purposeful shifting to their left, the number of casualties Smyth's and Sherrill's men inflicted on the attackers, and the number of prisoners they took all provided Hays's men with further evidence of the Confederate intention to pierce their front. Still, they had permitted no penetration of their line. The regimental historian of the 1st Delaware claimed that "the rebel ranks melted away like wax" in front of his unit, and "none of them reached a point in our front nearer than fifty yards."[84] The Southern troops "came on in companies and squads quite up to our

Veterans of the 126th New York in Hays's division preserved this unusual perspective of the July 3 charge that focuses on the fight near Ziegler's Grove and the Bryan barn. (Wilson, Disaster, Struggle, Triumph)

lines (as many fell within twenty paces of us)," but the 12th New Jersey did not break.[85] Major Richardson of the 126th New York asserted that "we poured our volleys from rifled muskets so hotly that, although most desperately rallied by their officers, they came no nearer than twenty rods."[86]

The soldiers of Hays's main line grew angry that others—and not just Gibbon's division—stole their fairly won glory. Men of the 125th New York used the cover of a fence line to position themselves at right angles to the Southern troops before pouring "a murderous fire into the rebel flank, comprising Pettigrew's men." The New Yorkers resented the 8th Ohio for taking sole credit for the flanking fire that played so prominently in many Southern accounts, and they insisted that the "distinct record" of the 125th's action "should go into the general history" of the battle.[87]

Hays's men accorded their general much of the credit for steeling his command. The general's charismatic personality and his subsequent death in battle at the Wilderness in May 1864 made this easy to do. They took pride in recounting a conversation—possibly fabricated since the principals disliked one another—in which Webb yelled, "Hays, they got through my line," only to have Hays reply fiercely, "I'll be damned if they got through mine."[88] Almost as popular with Hays's men was the story of the captured Confederate officer who asked the general, "Where are your men?" When Hays waved his hand toward his thin line, the Southerner said, "If I had known that this is all you have, I would not have surrendered." Hays had replied—"in speech more emphatic than pious"—"Go back and try it over."[89]

Hays's men were not the only participants in the events of July 3 who felt that history had ignored their efforts. Veterans of the I Corps—exclusive of Stannard's Vermonters—had provided close support; some of its units actually fought on the front lines. Col. Theodore Gates always insisted that his 80th New York and 151st Pennsylvania "met the onset of Pickett's attack—that they broke his line and killed and wounded a large number of his troops and that hundreds surrendered to them."[90] He and other I Corps survivors demanded justice. Sgt. Patrick DeLacy complained that while he often heard that the 143rd Pennsylvania did nothing to repel this famous charge, "every survivor here knows that Dana's brigade opened fire upon Wilcox and upon the advancing column under Pickett, as it hove in sight across the plain." Convinced that their fire had forced Pickett's men to bunch up and shift to the left, where II Corps infantry and massed artillery destroyed the assault, DeLacy found it fitting that the I Corps "should strike the decisive blow."[91]

Hays's survivors and the I Corps participants often feigned modesty about the importance of their contribution to victory—in part because the bragging of Gibbon's men irritated them—but they made their point nonetheless. Colonel MacDougall noted that "many claims have been made as to who bore the brunt of Pickett's Charge," but he assured his men that they did not need to stoop to shameless self-promotion. "The most you have ever claimed was that you had assisted in repelling the greatest charge ever made upon a battlefield. In the language of the immortal Lincoln, you felt that 'there was glory enough at Gettysburg to go all around.'"[92] Similarly, W. C. Dunton did not claim for the Vermont brigade all the credit for the victory, since "nearly all the loyal states had their soldiers there, and they all did their duty faithfully and fought equally well. But," he added, "by the fortunes of war, under the Providence of God, these three Regiments of the Second Vermont Brigade occupied the pivotal point at the most critical time of that great battle," and their actions there became "a turning point of history and of human destiny."[93] Making such claims carried some danger. After a Vermonter made a similar statement, another Union veteran poked fun at the whole state, which seemed "ready and willing, regardless of party, to rise and affirm that to the best of their knowledge and belief Gen. Stannard saved Gettysburg."[94]

When they looked beyond the competing claims for various units, nearly all of the participants agreed that this had been the common soldier's victory. This kind of leveling became an important part of understanding the special nature of war fought by armies of volunteers. As a veteran of the 71st Pennsylvania noted, "Generals and admirals win high renown for the military achievements of their men, but personal deeds of heroism by simple privates or subalterns are rarely recorded."[95] The historian for the 1st Delaware marveled at the "degree of bravery or efficiency of the part of soldiers" in his brigade. "Not a straggler nor a skulker could be seen; every man was in the ranks, and . . . although ordered to crouch close behind the low stone wall, most of the men stood upright, as unsheltered as the enemy, and fired with regularity and deadly precision."[96]

As time passed, actual participation in the repulse of the charge became less and less of a prerequisite for calling upon its memory as validation of military prowess. Veterans of a number of Union regiments who never fired a shot yet had lain in close reserve behind Cemetery Ridge began to endow with great importance the small roles they played. Their very willingness to respond to duty's call spoke well of their commitment to the Union. The regimental chaplain asked veterans of the 1st Pennsylvania Cavalry, who had been posted on July 3 right behind the II Corps line, to reflect upon what "might have been" had they been ordered to advance: "To charge under such circumstances, a whole division of infantry flushed as it would have been with success," would have been "awful (and doubtless your last charge)." The call had not come, but that "was not your fault, you were here" to answer it.[97] The men of the 12th New Hampshire also knew that "they might be called upon to help stay the flood-tide of the Rebellion," and even though they did not go into the fight, "each one felt, as never before, an individual responsibility commensurate with the magnitude of the struggle and the consequences of the issue."[98]

The great charge and its repulse held such popular appeal that even distant eyewitnesses preserved the memory, sometimes making it seem that they had taken a far more active role. The men of the 57th New York, which suffered heavily the day before in the Wheatfield, joked with each other as they watched bits of the attack through the smoke, spending much of their time yelling " 'Come on Johnie, we long to embrace you,' 'They must be hungry for lead,' 'As they drop on our bayonets we will help them to the rear,' " and anything else "that could be thought of to heighten the occasion."[99] Reverence for the past usually commanded considerably more solemnity, however. Gen. James Wood reminded survivors of the 136th New York, which fought on Cemetery Hill, how Pickett's men fell "as autumnal leaves fall from a forest tree, and cover the ground. In our mind's eye we see it now, as we saw it then. *Memory* vividly recalls it."[100]

Not all Union survivors of the battle felt comfortable with the increasing tendency for the events on Cemetery Ridge on July 3 to eclipse the other two days of fighting, in history or in memory. Veterans of the clashes of July 1 and July 2, as committed to seeking the "truth" as survivors of July 3, balked at any suggestion that the fight at the copse of trees deserved special designation as "the high water mark of the Rebellion." Fearing that their own efforts and sacrifices would be forgotten if they did nothing, they challenged the seductive pull of selective memory that threatened to consign them to obscurity.

At monument dedications all over the battlefields of July 1 and July 2, orators struck a common chord. During Michigan Day at Gettysburg in June 1889, L. S. Trowbridge regretted the "curious fact that in popular estimation the whole thought of the Battle of Gettysburg seems to center about Pickett's Charge on the third day." He wished to call attention to "other services on other portions of the field which, in my judgement, have not received the attention which they have justly deserved." [101]

Certainly the veterans of the III Corps agreed with this sentiment. Dan Sickles and his men had held several reunions at Gettysburg—even before the Philadelphians and Pickett's men met there—and they came each time "to renew the memories of the part taken by our corps in the great conflict of Thursday, July 2, 1863—the decisive day at Gettysburg." [102] The theme appeared repeatedly in III Corps memoirs, regimental histories, and monument dedications. When the 40th New York unveiled its memorial near Devil's Den, the orator regretted that "the student of the current magazine literature, the observer of the numerous cycloramic exhibitions of the battle of Gettysburg," may never understand that "Pickett's Charge was a thirty minute incident in a three days' contest, and not all of the battle." [103] Sickles himself took up the familiar cant at the dedication of the New York State monument in 1893: "There is a day and an hour in the life of every nation when its fate hangs on the issue of a battle; such a day and hour—thirty years ago—was the crisis of the battle of Gettysburg on the afternoon of the 2d day of July, 1863." [104]

Survivors of other corps who did not fight on Cemetery Ridge took up Sickles's refrain. A veteran of the 22nd Massachusetts, a V Corps unit that had reinforced the III Corps line on July 2, took special aim at the popular writings of journalist Coffin, who made the repulse of Pickett's Charge famous as "the high water mark of the Rebellion." He challenged the fundamental validity of this "sentiment of a non-combatant," arguing that the slopes of the Round Tops, where "the most desperate of the three days' fighting took place, where rebellion might have succeeded but for the opportune arrival of the Fifth Corps . . . *was* the '*high water mark of the Rebellion.*'" [105]

Other Gettysburg veterans felt that in their efforts to redirect attention to July 2 Sickles and his partisans only traded one inaccuracy for another. Survivors of the fight of July 1 felt the slight especially keenly. At the dedication of the monument of the 147th New York near the Railroad Cut, Capt. J. V. Pierce mused that "but for the heroism and staying qualities of Reynolds and his men the first day, General Sickles would never had the opportunity to make the handsome boast that the Third Corps fought the battle of Gettysburg." With notable perceptiveness, Pierce added: "There were fifty battles of Gettysburg fought on these hills and plains,—each sanguinary and terrific in character." [106]

The XII Corps had fought one of those battles on the slopes of Culp's Hill earlier on July 3, and its veterans feared that the clash on Cemetery Ridge threatened to cast them into the shadows, too. A survivor of the 27th Indiana's unsuccessful advance across the Spangler meadow complained that Pickett's Charge had "about it certain theatrical, as well as tragical features, well calculated to awaken popular interest and applause." But this had not been "the battle of Gettysburg, at least not all of it. It was not even as conspicuous in actual blood-letting as is sometimes thought." [107]

Union veterans of the Western campaigns could not understand the hoopla at all. "It is claimed by nearly all writers on the battle of Gettysburg that it was the decisive battle of the war," one Ohio soldier later wrote, adding that "we out West never thought we had gained a victory unless the enemy left before they rested after the battle." [108] He found plenty of support even among veterans of the Eastern campaigns. When a prominent historian of the war pronounced the fighting and the losses on July 3 as "phenomenally severe" and "murderous," a Northerner argued that Gettysburg was "no bloodier or more desperately contested" than many others battles during the war. Hancock's men who withstood the July 3 charge so splendidly "went forward to equally desperate fighting on future battlefields." Indeed, Gettysburg was "merely a sample of what came before and followed after." [109]

In the end, however, most Union veterans looked beyond the rival claims of various units to find deeper significance in the events of July 3. Some chose to look at its short-term military implications. "The great interest of the battle of Gettysburg centres about the charge of Pickett's division," wrote a New Jersey veteran. "Up to that hour it had been a drawn battle. But in the destruction of this command, Lee had suffered a defeat which thwarted all his lofty expectation." [110]

Some saw more indirect military benefits accrue from their battlefield success. As Col. Daniel B. Allen of the 154th New York explained it, "The grandest, proudest, most enthusiastic feeling which can ever visit the heart of man is the moment at the end of a hard fought field when the enemy finally gives way and surrenders the field of battle. The Union soldier who witnessed the final repulse and flight of Longstreet's Corps upon this field . . . can never again experience the feeling of joy and pride which then thrilled his soul." [111]

Still others steered the opposite course. They feared that all the attention accorded to Pickett's Charge would set an unfairly high standard against which other battlefield exploits would be measured, and inevitably, they would be found wanting. A survivor of the frontal attacks against the stone wall at Fredericksburg complained especially bitterly that while "Pickett's Charge has been eulogized and painted as the most phenomenal exhibition of courage and soldiership during the whole war," his own experience "towers high above the much vaunted" events of July 3. At least at Gettysburg, he argued, Pickett's men had "strong hopes of success," while even the "dullest man in the Army of the Potomac" knew their assault at Fredericksburg would fail.[112] Partisans of the VI Corps, perhaps because the command played so small a part at Gettysburg, also took special exception to comparing all frontal assaults with Pickett's Charge, arguing that "the simple facts are, a few of the Sixth Corps charged up Marye's Heights [in May 1863] over the same ground, in the same way as Burnside did, in as gallant a manner as Pickett's men did, and they got there, too; though one never hears of it." [113]

In an interesting twist on the same theme, some of the nine-month Pennsylvania volunteers of Brig. Gen. Andrew A. Humphreys's division, who viewed the charge on Marye's Heights as the single most riveting moment of their brief military careers, found ways to make their effort and Pickett's Charge share the limelight. One wrote that "the European world sounds and re-sounds, echoes and re-echoes with plaudits for the Rebel grand charge on the third day at Gettysburg," but this was "unjust to the many similar exhibitions of Union determination. The assaults of French and of Hancock, but *particularly of Humphreys*, were much more desperately brilliant." The work of the 131st Pennsylvania that day "was not exceeded on any of the historic battlefields—not by the charge at Balaklava, immortalized by Tennyson, nor by that of Pickett's men at Gettysburg." When the survivors of Humphreys's division dedicated its monument in the national cemetery at Fredericksburg in 1908, the keynote speaker did not make points with his audience when he reminded them that "next to Pickett's Charge," the Pennsylvanians' charge at Marye's Heights "was the most bloody and disastrous of our Civil War." [114]

In time, the results of July 3 took on even more symbolic meanings that went far beyond mere victory for Union armies. Many survivors forged links between battlefield success, the salvation of the Union, and traditional notions of spiritual salvation.[115] Relying heavily on Christian themes of redemption, one orator suggested that a brief rain shower and a rainbow after the repulse reiterated God's covenant "not only to the natural world, that the waters of the deluge should never return to destroy the earth, but of his gracious promise, that Truth and Right should triumph among men." The events of July 3 assured all good Union men "that our country should prevail in its struggle for Nationality and Liberty." [116]

The war generation used the events of July 3 to hand down to posterity a legacy of civic obligation. A veteran of the 125th New York wrote that "the price paid in blood was none too great for the fruitage to the Nation and the world. Some things are evermore costly; and they are the more prized because their price is paid in blood and death." [117] To call Gettysburg merely a "Mecca," a phrase the "guide-books and more talkative veterans have got hold of," suggested a "sad poverty in terms of reverence." [118]

Thus, men of the 5th New Hampshire of the III Corps, so badly battered in the Wheatfield, still could admit that "when the broken ranks of Pickett's Virginians rolled back from the low stone-wall of Cemetery Ridge, the hitherto doubtful balance of the war began to incline in favor of the Union and the Constitution." Like many Northerners, they had come to believe as an article faith that which was only a hopeful portent on July 3, 1863: "The certainty of Appomattox lay in the defeat at Gettysburg." [119] The historian of the 15th New Jersey agreed that the "charge of Pickett may be used as a date—for, from that hour when he moved forth to sure destruction, the Confederacy was doomed to go down." [120] At the dedication of the 145th New York's monument, Col. Edward Price noted that "the battle was the turning point, and is its own panegyric. Up to that time there was doubt mixed with hope on both sides," but "after the repulse of Pickett's gallant and desperate charge, the skilled leader of the foe retreated with his baffled and bleeding braves, [and] fear and doubt were with the enemy and hope and confidence with us." [121] A veteran of the 90th Pennsylvania summed up succinctly the true importance of July 3: "The God of Battles decided for Liberty and Nationality." [122]

Some especially reflective Northerners perceived in the failure of Pickett's Charge a definitive line of demarcation separating two distinct periods in national development. Capt. Asa W. Bartlett of the 12th New Hampshire felt so strongly about that moment that he described the spot where Armistead fell as "the real Itasca from which overflows and shall continue to flow for centuries to come, a stream that shall purify her cities and replenish her fields; and make even her mountain tops and her desert plains furnish sustenance for millions now unborn, and her valleys and prairies to blossom as the rose." If the soldiers who died here could have

seen what "their life's blood was to purchase and secure for the count-
less generations of coming time, they would have died, as some of them
did, with a smile of satisfaction upon their countenances."[123] Col. John
Danks of the 63rd Pennsylvania offered this benediction: "When we think
of Humanity as being crushed with sin, and look for a remedy, we begin
at the Garden, and find the conclusion at Calvary. When we think and
speak of the government of England as threatened with dismemberment
and ruin, and look for the remedy, we find it at Waterloo. So, when we
think and speak of oppression, class and caste in America, and look for
the remedy, we begin at Harper's Ferry, with old John Brown, and find
the answer in Pickett's Charge at Gettysburg."[124]

When Union soldiers were honest with themselves, they suspected that
the cause of preserving an accurate historical record had become a lost
cause. To many, however, it did not matter that much. Indeed, as one
Pennsylvania soldier suggested, Gettysburg needed one more memorial,
"a monument surmounted by a statue entitled 'Memory.'"[125]

The pull of memory prevented the complete commitment of Pickett's
Charge to the realm of history. No matter how careful and intent on preserving the "truth" these veterans professed to be, thousands of personal
perspectives, perceptions, and prejudices invariably colored and shaped
their memories of July 3. Sgt. Frederick Fuger, whose personal memoir of
service with Cushing's battery was powerful stuff, found it impossible in
later years "to reconcile the many disputed questions which have arisen.
Indeed, it is almost doubtful to the minds of many of the participants in
the battle whether they were even present—so different from their recollections of the events do recent recollections appear."[126] Still, a former
Union captain warned his comrades about their special obligation to keep
separate history and memory: "Though it was so real, so impressive, so
fraught with excitements and filled with scenes so surprisingly beyond any
we had ever witnessed . . . it nevertheless seems after this lapse of years to
be invested with a haze which casts upon the picture as we reproduce it in
our memory, a semblance of unreality, which almost makes us doubt our
waking senses, and we ask ourselves, 'Can these things have really happened?'"[127] In memory, the answer was a resounding "Yes." History could
not answer with the same confidence, and Union veterans did not mind.

6

SOUTHERN
DISSENTERS
SPEAK OUT

Shortly after the Gettysburg silver anniversary ceremonies, an unsigned, unobtrusive filler article appeared in the *National Tribune*. Its author noted, "After an inexplicable silence of nearly 25 years, the North Carolinians are beginning to assert themselves in regard to the charge on the third day at Gettysburg. Every student of the history of the war knows that it was not Pickett of Virginia but Pettigrew of North Carolina who was entitled to the principle credit for that charge. Pickett started out in command of the charging column, but stopt when within half a mile of our line, while Pettigrew went on with his North Carolinians, and reached the farthest point attained by any rebel troops."[1]

The *Tribune*'s editor did not get all the facts right either, but his most egregious error lay in assuming that Pettigrew's and Trimble's survivors and partisans had suffered in silence.

Thousands of ex-Confederates in North Carolina, Alabama, Mississippi, Tennessee, and Florida despised Virginia's version of Pickett's Charge. But only in the 1880s, and with uneven success, did they launch literary counterassaults worthy of the men they sought to honor. In the end, they did emend bits of the historical record. In the equally important war for popular memory, however, they won very little.

First impressions are hard to forget, and even in 1863, many Southerners recognized that the Virginia bias of the Richmond press would color memories of the war. Just after Chancellorsville, for instance, a North Carolinian complained that lightly engaged Virginia regiments "will have a column or two devoted to their exploits" but of battle-shattered regiments from the Old North State "there is great probability that not one line will ever be published."[2] When postwar writers began to base their books on these slanted reports, a Tar Heel editor remarked that the volumes "would make very pretty reading," if they carried "the caption '*story* of the *war*—founded on fact,' but when 'tis called *history*, 'tis positively nauseating!"[3]

Any effort to change popular notions about Pickett's Charge had to begin by discrediting Virginia's well-entrenched version of the story. Unfortunately, champions of Pettigrew's and Trimble's men failed to find an effective way to disturb the aura of glory that glowed around Pickett's men alone. During the war, no newspaper in Florida, Tennessee, North Carolina, Alabama, or Mississippi possessed sufficient influence to invalidate the Virginia dailies' damaging assertions. From the end of the war through the 1880s, then, editors of local newspapers and regional periodicals throughout the former Confederacy made clear their unrestrained resentment of the way Virginia journalists treated them. As an author for Wilmington's short-lived *South-Atlantic* wrote, "No fool [is] so complete a fool as the Virginia fool, and Richmond [is] the Virginia fool *par super-excellence*."[4]

Southerners outside Virginia did more than simply cry foul, however. In more constructive fashion, they worked hard to preserve their versions of important historical events such as that of July 3 at Gettysburg. North Carolinians in particular showed great zeal in their early efforts to challenge perceived errors in the historical record. Former North Carolina governor Zebulon Vance made his state's case to the one body that he hoped might care the most, the Southern Historical Society. "North Carolina is entitled to stand where her troops stood in battle—behind no State," he argued. Available records proved that "North Carolina furnished more soldiers in proportion to white population, and more supplies and material in proportion to her means" than any other Confederate state. Those biographers of "the great and illustrious leaders which Virginia gave to the Confederacy" who "have been too anxious to eulogize their heroes to give due attention to the forces which wrought their plans into such glorious results" frustrated him terribly.[5]

The deafening silence that met his plea only worried Vance further. If the Southern Historical Society was committed to preserving a true history of the Confederacy, it did not seem to have done much to rein in the excesses of its fellow Virginians. Tar Heel editor T. B. Kingsbury wrote in 1875, "The Virginia historians, Pollard, McCabe, *et id omne genus*, set the example of doing injustice to North Carolina soldiers, and we have but little hope that their example will cease to be followed."[6] Former captain Joseph J. Davis of the 47th North Carolina read John Esten Cooke's popular biography of Lee, which included a colorful depiction of Pickett's men in the July 3 charge, and averred that "Cooke is a better novelist than historian" and in his gross misrepresentations of fact "slanders men whose devotion and whose bravery on the field of battle were equal (and that is all that is claimed for them) to any engaged in the war."[7]

Our Living and Our Dead, a Raleigh-based journal of the mid-1870s devoted to "North Carolina—her past, her present and her future," became the official organ of the state's branch of the Southern Historical Society. Its editor expressed outrage that most books about the war "almost entirely ignored the presence and deeds of the soldiers of North Carolina," and he announced plans to compile and preserve a complete and accurate collection of historical source material for future scholars to mine. He urged his fellow citizens not to "turn a cold shoulder upon this effort to do justice to the sons of North Carolina." If they did not follow his lead now, the effort might well die and "prove another lasting monument to that want of State pride which has ever characterized our people" and distinguished them from Virginia.[8]

Even as North Carolina led the earliest attempts to break the Old Dominion's stranglehold on the history and memory of July 3, most of its first counterattacks proved to be as provincial and self-interested as the Virginia accounts they condemned. Some tried to salvage only the reputations of Tar Heel troops, even blaming the bad conduct of other elements of Pettigrew's division—especially the quick withdrawal of Brockenbrough's Virginians—for besmirching the North Carolinians' reputation. According to editor Kingsbury, even the usually reliable William Swinton had failed to realize that Pettigrew's North Carolina brigade "advanced as far as did Pickett's men and *lost twice as many men* as any brigade under Pickett's command."[9] If Pollard and others had bothered to make distinctions between Pettigrew's division (an organization under his temporary leadership that included troops from several states) and his permanent Tar Heel brigade command, Swinton might not have made "the infamous reflections he makes upon North Carolinians."[10]

Despite this penchant for self-promotion, North Carolina quickly rallied supporters to its cause. Former general Isaac Trimble congratulated editor Kingsbury for alerting the public to the errors about the July 3 charge that Northern and Southern authors alike "still blindly adhered to."

Brig. Gen. James Johnston Pettigrew, North Carolina's champion on July 3 at Gettysburg (Francis Trevelyan Miller, comp., Photographic History of the Civil War *[New York: Review of Reviews, 1911],* 10:153)

While he feared that impressions left by "mistakes, misstatements, or even intentional perversions of truth" in wartime press accounts might prove difficult to erase, he hoped that journals such as *Our Living and Our Dead* would remind North Carolinians of their troops' courage, endurance, acceptance of military discipline, and, as displayed at Gettysburg, "their daring valor."[11] Former general James H. Lane, a Virginian who had led a North Carolina brigade into the charge on July 3, asked a Richmond editor, "for the sake of *truth*, [to] allow a Virginian, through your columns, to state a few facts" that might correct misperceptions about the fight that appeared in Dabney McCabe's biography of Lee. After explaining how his men bravely filled gaps in Pettigrew's battered line, Lane expressed regret that "the historians from my native State are so very partial to Pickett's Division."[12] As if to make amends for his home state's wrongs, Lane shared special memories of service with North Carolina troops. On the morning of July 3, when Lee visited his bivouac, he told Lane that "North Carolina has cause to be proud of such troops." One of Lane's men subsequently taken prisoner at Gettysburg told him that "the Yankee ambulance corps reported that dead North Carolinians were found farther in the Union lines than any others."[13] Virginian Randolph Shotwell, one of Pickett's men who moved to North Carolina after the war, told his new neighbors that when he thought "the North Carolinians had made a lodgement on the crest, I picked up a musket and started to move toward the left."[14]

These compliments changed few minds, however. As Virginians took over control of the Southern Historical Society and solidified its role as the sole authority on Confederate history, the initial images of the wartime Richmond press established themselves even more enduringly. In the late 1870s, Walter Taylor of Lee's staff outraged Pettigrew's and Trimble's veterans by slandering them in his memoirs and in the "Annals of the War" series. A Tar Heel reviewer censured Taylor for suppressing important information and for perpetuating inaccuracies that resulted in "a very great injustice to the commands of Pettigrew and Trimble."[15]

Although Taylor had not aimed the worst of his vitriol at Pettigrew's or Trimble's men—Longsteet was the real target—the editor of the Raleigh *Observer* declared that the time had come to settle the issue and requested local survivors to submit their own accounts of the action of July 3. The veterans responded enthusiastically, and the editor could not resist remarking that "if the cloud of witnesses we have presented do not vindicate the honor of North Carolina soldiers on that fatal day, human testimony is utterly worthless."[16]

The soldiers wanted to establish several points. First, they expressed great dismay that even at this late date they still had to resort to unusual measures in their efforts to right the historical record. Captain Davis understood that all writers carry a bias toward the troops of their own states but avowed that while "we can afford to be neglected by them, we cannot afford to be misrepresented by them." Taking aim at the wartime Richmond press, Adj. D. M. McIntyre of Scales's brigade agreed that it was time to end the placing of the "blood-bought laurels" of his fallen comrades "on undeserving brows by those who were not participants of the great conflict, but were simply observers of the occasion."

Second, Pettigrew's and Trimble's men tried to destroy entirely the notion that they had been assigned a mere supporting role on July 3. They had served as integral elements of the assault force. An officer in the 47th North Carolina explained how his regiment originally deployed behind Pickett's men but then moved to the left "and advanced simultaneously with and on the same line" as the Virginians. The move "caused no 'confusion' in Pettigrew's brigade" but apparently " 'confounded' the historians" and many Virginia writers, including Colonel Taylor. Capt. J. G. Harris of the 7th North Carolina never "did know who was to have done the supporting part of that day's work, but one thing I do know, there was devilish little of it sent round our way." Lt. Thomas Malloy of the same unit simply wanted Virginians to tell the truth: "Col. Taylor knows of other and more probable causes for our want of success at Gettysburg than the failure of the N.C. troops to support Pickett."

North Carolinians claimed that they, too—not only Pickett's Virginians—had reached the brink of success when forced to fall back. A wounded survivor recalled seeing a Yankee color-bearer break for the rear "trailing his flag and followed by his regiment," leaving nothing to prevent the North Carolinians "from going right into the enemy's works." Col. W. G. Morris of the 37th North Carolina argued that six of his officers "were wounded in the enemy's works and captured," an impossibility if they broke as early as the Virginians charged. Lt. Thomas Norwood may have been one of those captured officers; he was "dragged over the breastworks" by a blue-coated sergeant. Capt. B. F. Little of the 52nd North Carolina "found some of my men killed and wounded immediately at the works" when he was captured there.

These North Carolinians also asserted that when they fell back they did so under specific orders and on their own terms. There had been no panicky rout. "I never knew Lane's men to give way without orders, and I don't believe they did at Gettysburg," wrote Capt. J. W. Vick of the 7th North Carolina. Lt. P. C. Carlton could not identify who gave the order to pull back, but he insisted that "the command was actually given." Perhaps taking his cue from the postbattle assertion of the 26th North Carolina's Lieutenant Colonel Jones that orders "came from the right to fall back" (and Pickett was to Jones's right), another recalled that after crossing to a road "some ten steps in the rear of the Rock fence," they were ordered back by "some officer in Pickett's command. Know not the rank."

North Carolinians tried hard to shift the onus for the defeat to the Virginians. Even before his own unit reached the Emmitsburg Road, Lieutenant Malloy caught a glimpse of Pickett's men already "very much broken" and not appearing as "an organized body of men, such as would be likely to succeed in a charge." The first Yankees Lt. D. F. Kinney of the 7th North Carolina saw "were in our rear and right coming up the turnpike," already vacated by Pickett's men. Judge B. F. Carpenter, a veteran of the 34th North Carolina, entirely outraged by "serious mistakes made by the writers from Gen. Pickett's division of Virginians," asserted that while his own men nearly captured the enemy works, "Pickett's Division ran, what did not surrender." If they had held their ground, "the day would have been ours. I believe their running caused the loss of the battle of Gettysburg."

A few Carolinians vented their anger against a different set of Virginians: Brockenbrough's brigade on Pettigrew's left flank. Capt. A. S. Haynes recounted how an injured man from that command had told him that he was his company's only casualty. "Here is a marked difference between the two companies, his and mine. The statistics of the casualties will certainly show who gave way and who fought. If our command had run off so many of them would not have been killed."

General Scales, a decidedly interested partisan now sitting in the U.S. House of Representatives, turned to John Bachelder, "the best informed man in all the details that make up the Battle of Gettysburg," for official resolution of the issue. He had reason to hope that Bachelder would take the side of his men. When Scales had visited the field previously, the historian had told him that most accounts of the July 3 fight did not treat North Carolina troops fairly, and the general himself remembered "distinctly to have heard the NCa boys laugh at the idea of Pickett going further than others in this assault." [17] Bachelder issued no specific corrective at this time, however.

The frustration of North Carolinians festered unabated into the 1880s. Few people outside the state read those wonderfully detailed, if self-promoting, memoirs in the Raleigh *Observer*. Most Tar Heel veterans preached only to the converted.

For nearly 25 years, North Carolina fought against the tide of history almost alone. Most of North Carolina's troops fought in the Army of Northern Virginia and had a vested interest in a correct history of that organization. By comparison, the three regiments each from Tennessee and Mississippi, or the seven hundred Floridians, or even Wilcox's Alabama brigade, represented relatively small contingents from states whose soldiers fought mostly in the Western theater. In July 1863, Mississippians, Tennesseans, and Alabamians had looked with greatest interest upon the action at Vicksburg, not the campaign in Pennsylvania. It took time for Army of Northern Virginia veterans in those states to rally to North Carolina's cause and join the fray. They finally did so at a time when opportunities to right the historical record of July 3 had begun to increase. After Congress in 1880 appropriated $50,000 to complete a comprehensive study of each unit's correct lines and movements, John Bachelder made a special plea for assistance from all Southern commands, not just those traditionally accorded the most prominence. An even more useful opening came in 1882, when the editor of the "Annals of the Civil War" series published two unusual pieces about July 3.

In "Pickett's Men at Gettysburg," North Carolinian William R. Bond took aim at a Northern author who in an earlier article had repeated "with probably the best intentions" the slanderous comparisons between Virginia troops and North Carolina units "which originated in Richmond nineteen years ago." The tarnished image of Pettigrew's and Trimble's men, "though refuted time and time again, still seems to flourish," he complained. So he counterattacked with praise for the stalwart efforts of Tar Heel troops on July 3 and accused Pickett's men of running away panic-stricken. Despite all "the outcry they raised about their slaughter," Bond wrote, "Pickett's Division of dead men drew more rations than any division in the army" only two weeks later.[18]

Shortly thereafter, the editor of the "Annals" presented a piece entitled "Longstreet's Assault," penned by J. H. Moore of Archer's Tennessee brigade. Moore avowed that he had not intended to write at all, but he expressed astonishment that even at this late date material errors still existed in most histories of the July 3 assault. "Was this Pickett's charge?" he asked bluntly. "If it was made by Pickett's division it is proper to call it Pickett's charge," he argued, but in this case, the "chief participants and those who have suffered most heavily are never mentioned." Moore knew that soldiers often tried to embellish their accomplishments, but he insisted that in truth the "Tennessee Brigade was the only one in Heth's division that carried their standards into the fortifications on the hill." Using the authority of Bachelder's maps to clinch his point, Moore claimed that "the memorable charge can with more propriety be denominated Heth's or Pettigrew's, rather than Pickett's."[19]

Despite Moore's powerful advocacy of the Tennessee brigade, his essay also illustrated a major reason why Pettigrew's and Trimble's men failed to change Virginia's popular version of events. Just as the North Carolinians tended to write only of specific commands from the Old North State, Moore only wrote on Archer's Tennesseans. Indeed, he did not even mention the two Alabama units in Archer's brigade. While Pickett's men spoke with a single voice, and one that increasingly incorporated national values, the veterans and partisans representing the different states and commands in Pettigrew's and Trimble's commands never forged a united front.

The Tennesseans remained in the forefront of the fight for historical revisionism when a mysterious writer who used the name William H. Swallow developed Moore's ideas even more. Revealing to the reading public only that he was an engineer "attached to Early's division" during the battle and that he had attended school nearby before the war, he wrote several detailed essays on Gettysburg for the Louisville-based *Southern Bivouac*. He did not launch impassioned tirades against those who disparaged the men of Pettigrew's and Trimble's commands, but he challenged a few specific points. Most notably, since most of the attacking troops on July 3 belonged to the Third Corps, "the movement ought more properly be called the 'Assault of A. P. Hill's corps.'" With some reluctance, Swallow might accept the name "Longstreet's assault," since Lee had placed him in tactical command of the advance, but it "would be a misnomer to call this assault, as many writers have done, 'The charge of Pickett's division.'"[20]

In dramatic detail, Swallow constructed a picture that seemed to dismantle point by point the Richmond press's version of the day's events. After describing the advance of the three Virginia brigades individually in vivid detail, he then turned his attention "to a dense column whose front seemed to cover twice the front of Pickett's division." These men under Trimble and Pettigrew did not falter. Northern artillery forced a brief halt for realignment, but then "some mighty unseen power, over which they had no control and whose influence they could not resist, impelled them forward." Swallow wanted to tell "the truth." He sought help from Bachelder, the only student of the battle who had "struck the right trail of investigation."[21] He even asked General Kemper for his memories of the moment when Tennessee and Virginia entered the Union works, but the answer disappointed him. "From first to last," Kemper wrote, "I saw nothing of Archer, or of Pettigrew, or of Davis, or of Heth's Division . . . or of any Confederate commands excepting only the three brigades of Pickett's Division," which found itself thrust into a "*cul-de-sac* of death."[22] Kemper no doubt told the truth as he saw it, too; he fell wounded before the moment that Swallow described. Undaunted nonetheless, Swallow gave credit for first penetration of the Union line to Garnett, soon followed by the Tennesseans, with some of Armistead's Virginians and the Tar Heel brigades of Scales and Lane close behind. At the wall, men of Virginia, Tennessee, Alabama, and North Carolina "fell as leaves fall."[23]

More distinctive, Swallow provided a wonderfully detailed account of parts of the fight of Pettigrew's division just north of the Angle. He recounted a conversation after the battle with the wounded Union brigade commander Smyth, who told him how the Southern troops "fought with a fiery determination that he had never seen equaled." If Pettigrew's men had failed to breach the Northern line, "the answer is, that there were scarcely any left to stand." As further evidence of the intensity of their fight, Swallow described a plank of fencing along the Emmitsburg Road on their front perforated with 836 bullet holes.[24]

These dissenting accounts drew interest but made little headway in the correction of the historical record. Thus, as the silver anniversary of the charge grew closer, Tennesseans tried harder to break Virginia's version of the events of July 3. Tennessee's J. B. Smith criticized New York artilleryman Andrew Cowan for a speech in which he had said that "beyond the wall" was "nothing but gray-clad Virginians." Smith demanded fairness. "Some writers have gone so far as to say Pickett made the immortal charge with five thousand Virginians," while omitting entirely the services of Pettigrew's and Trimble's men. The 14th Tennessee lost heavily on July 1 but still "planted its colors on the stone wall and left them there." The conduct of the 13th Alabama and Scales's and Lane's Tar Heels also merited all praise. The courage of the 2nd Mississippi in Davis's brigade on July 3 "has become a matter of history." Smith's comments found their way into the book edition of the "Battles and Leaders" series but only in small print as a filler.[25]

Taken collectively, the Tennesseans' essays accomplished something that all of North Carolina's bluster to date had failed to do. They brought the case for Pettigrew's and Trimble's men to a national audience. Still, they had not yet convinced the American people of the truth of their assertions. Moreover, Tennessee did not fire the single most telling shot of that early literary war. That honor went to a North Carolinian after all.

The continued slanders aimed at Tar Heel troops for their conduct on July 3 so incensed William R. Bond that in 1888 he published at his own expense an inflammatory pamphlet entitled *Pickett or Pettigrew? An Historical Essay*. A quotation from Ralph Waldo Emerson on the title page hinted at what would follow: "Tell the truth and the world will come to see it at last." The former Confederate staff officer dedicated the work to "the memory of the brave men of HILL'S CORPS, who were killed while fighting under the orders of General Longstreet" and "whose fame has been clouded by the persistent misrepresentation of certain of their comrades."[26]

Bond introduced few new charges, but he stated his case far more strongly than the Tennesseans had. "Longstreet's assault on the third day at Gettysburg, or what is generally, but very incorrectly known as 'Pickett's Charge,' has been more written about in newspapers and magazines than any event in American history," he wrote. "Some of these accounts are simply silly. Some are false in statement. Some are false in inference. All in some respects are untrue." He did not care to debate the wisdom of the charge. He merely planned "to compare and contrast the courage, endurance and soldierly qualities" of the units in the assault, especially the troops of Pickett and Pettigrew.[27]

Bond believed it imperative to correct the historical record not only to honor the men who fought and died on July 3 but also to preserve the truth for future generations. He was outraged by a recent article in *St. Nicholas*, the most popular children's magazine of the era, that claimed that: "those on the left [Pettigrew] faltered and fled. The right [Pickett] behaved gloriously. Each body acted according to its nature, for they were made of different stuff. The one of common earth, the other of finest clay. Pettigrew's men were North Carolinians. Pickett's were superb Virginians." Such "ignorance, narrowness, and prejudice," Bond asserted, had to be stopped.[28]

It pained Bond that false images of the events of July 3 inspired so many speeches and essays. But if history were not corrected, those "falsehoods will soon become intrenched in poetry and art" as well. At the Centennial Exposition at Philadelphia, he saw a large painting of the fight at the Angle, probably James Walker's canvas. "Of course," Bond wrote, "I knew that the subject of the painting was founded upon a myth." But he had to keep up the fight. Truth, he wrote, is " 'a Krupp gun, before which falsehood's armor, however thick, can not stand.' One shot may accomplish nothing, or two or three." But if he kept firing his literary blasts, he finally might win a battle for truth.[29]

The name "Pickett's Charge" particularly outraged Bond. He could find only a single historical example that demonstrated equal injustice. At Thermopylae, 300 Spartans and 700 Thespians died in defense of all the Greek states. History heaped praise on Leonidas and his Spartans, but, Bond wondered, "How many have ever so much as heard of the equally brave Thespians?"[30] He did know, however, how the events of July 3 had become so distorted. "When the subject is peculiarly Southern," Northern authors turn almost exclusively to Pollard, McCabe, Cooke, and other prominent Virginians. These men, however, "merely reflected the opinions of the Richmond newspapers," and the Virginia capital was "the most provincial town in the world." Troops from states other than Virginia seldom won admiring prose. "A skirmish in which a Virginian regiment or brigade was engaged was magnified into a fight, an action in which a few were killed was a severe battle," Bond complained, and if a Virginia unit took heavy losses, then "troops from some other state were to blame for it." Virginians had mastered the cultivation of reporters who gave them the "excessive indulgence of a silly parent."[31]

Pickett's division, Bond asserted, excelled at "the habit of 'playing possum.' " They had caused little damage to the enemy at Gettysburg. While viewing Walker's painting, he heard an old soldier say, "Tut! I'll agree to eat all the Yankees Pickett killed," and noted that the man "was neither remarkably large nor hungry-looking." He even admitted that the veteran may have engaged in some hyperbole, since "I have since heard that among the dead men in blue, near where Armistead fell, there were six, who had actually been killed by musket balls."[32]

"To how many does the name Gettysburg suggest the names of Tennessee, Mississippi or North Carolina?" Bond wondered. Somehow, he had to counter the arrogance of Pickett's Virginians, who believed that "their division stood to Lee's army in the same relation, that the sun does to the Solar system." He turned to Pettigrew's casualty lists for evidence of their valor. Citing a recent study of Civil War casualties that listed twenty-seven Confederate regiments in order of greatest loss in a single fight, he noted that the 26th North Carolina, with 588 men lost at Gettysburg, headed the roster. Six of the list's twenty-seven regiments came from North Carolina. For their losses at Gettysburg, the 2nd and 42nd Mississippi regiments also made the roll. Bond pointed out to readers of Pollard, Cooke, and McCabe that "not one regiment from Virginia is mentioned in this list." [33]

Bond also condemned Virginians for blaming Pettigrew's and Trimble's men on Pickett's left or the Alabamians and Floridians on Pickett's right for the defeat. But in some cases, Bond missed the mark. He portrayed the Virginians' purposeful oblique march toward the copse of trees as a terrible error that led to the annihilation of Wilcox's and Lang's men "when they attacked where Pickett should have been." He wondered if this explained why "shortly after this battle General Wilcox was promoted and General Pickett and his men were sent out of the army." Did Virginians dare curse Pettigrew's or Trimble's men, "the choice troops of A. P. Hill's old division, ever famous for its fighting qualities?" If so, it was like "Achilles cursed by Tersites! A lion barked at by a cur!" [34]

Still, in his enthusiasm to promote North Carolina and Pettigrew's command, Bond made too many provable errors to win the credibility for his cause he so deeply craved. He wrongly insisted that Union losses on Pickett's front were so light that "not one regiment in Gibbon's or Doubleday's commands, which after the shelling, lost one-fourth of one per cent." [35] Stannard's Vermont brigade, he argued, had "not one man killed, not one wounded" in its flank attack on Pickett's division. He also fixed the average number of dead in each of Pickett's regiments at fifteen, a total sufficiently low to refute any claim that Virginia suffered "a carnage so appalling as to amount to butchery." [36] (A modern study of the rosters of the fifteen Virginia regiments in the charge shows the number of killed and mortally wounded to range from 24 to 55. [37]) Bond's pamphlet, an interesting and occasionally outrageous polemic, appeared again in 1900 and in expanded form the next year, full of new "evidence" and strident claims.

By the end of the 1880s, North Carolina seemed poised to launch a counterattack on the Virginia version of Pickett's Charge. Supporters rallied to the call. The depths of their commitment can be seen in the way T. J. Cureton, a veteran of the famed 26th North Carolina, closed letters to his friends: "In hope history will yet do Justice to the charge of our Brigade (Pettigrew's) on 'Cemetery Ridge' on 3rd July 1863." [38]

As the turn of the century approached, those new recruits found a variety of opportunities to participate actively in the cause. Individual endeavors such as Bond's pamphlets gave way to more organized institutional efforts. The new *Confederate Veteran* magazine, first published in 1893 in Nashville, and several new or reactivated state historical societies joined in the battle.

As a semiofficial publication of the new United Confederate Veterans, *Confederate Veteran* drew sufficient subscribers to make it a successful financial venture. Editor S. A. Cunningham wanted to use his publication to "gather authentic data for an impartial history" of the Southern war effort. Portraying the Southern Historical Society, his chief rivals in this task, as elitists, he set himself up as the unchallenged spokesman of the common soldier and plain folks.

Early on, a Virginia veteran suggested that Cunningham give equal coverage to operations in both the Eastern and Western theaters. Since his friends served in the Army of Northern Virginia, "they naturally feel slighted when they find most of your reading matter referring to the men and movements of the Tennessee army."[39] Nonetheless, although articles from familiar Virginia writers appeared occasionally, *Confederate Veteran* primarily reflected the editor's interests in the Western armies and soldiers. This bias opened a door for critics of Virginia's version of the events of July 3.

At first, the new journal did not enter the controversy. A lengthy biographical sketch of A. P. Hill did not even mention the events of July 3. A Mississippi veteran of Barksdale's brigade wrote an article in which he reminisced about watching Lee and Longstreet near the Peach Orchard early on July 3. He recounted only what he saw from his perspective as passive observer and in so doing told a familiar tale: "It was one of the grandest sights ever mortal eyes looked upon. It makes me shudder now, as I see the shells plow through the ranks of that gallant band."[40]

Tennessee veterans of the charge, however, quickly turned to *Confederate Veteran* to attempt to rewrite the history of July 3. Thirty-seven years after the fact, J. B. Turney, one-time captain of the 1st Tennessee, still "watched and waited in vain" for a truthful version of the great assault. He especially regretted writers' "manifest disposition to ignore the gallant work of the First Tennessee in the last charge upon the Federal lines."

Turney claimed that the 1st Tennessee advanced with the main column of attack, on line with Pickett's Virginians. "For three miles from right to left we charged in unbroken line," he wrote, "bent on victory or death." As senior officers fell, he took command of the regiment and double-quicked his men over the last 150 yards to the Union line, holding fire until "we were within about fifteen steps of the stone wall." His men's first volley shattered resistance in his front. He then ordered a bayonet charge. Quickly, his Tennesseans found themselves in "desperate hand-to-hand conflict for the possession of the fragile wall of masonry." A Federal officer threatened to skewer Turney with his sword, but "I parried it just in time."

Turney did not attack or reject the Virginia version of Pickett's Charge so much as he found a way to place the 1st Tennessee—not even all the Tennesseans—in the middle of its most famous moments. Indeed, he claimed that as he neared the stone wall, he "found everything successful to my right," where Pickett's men fought, while much of his own brigade had failed. Only a strong enfilading fire by Turney's men cleared the way for some men of the 7th Tennessee, 13th Alabama, and 5th Alabama Battalion to join them. When time came to go over the wall, the 1st Tennessee and a few of Garnett's Virginians crossed first.

Turney told a great story. As the Tennesseans fought on at the Angle, Armistead "noted the importance of the position held by the First Tennessee" and obliqued to the left to help them. The general crossed the wall, sword flashing, with Turney "by his side, and with us went the colors of the First Tennessee." When Armistead went down with a mortal wound, Turney caught him as he fell. After seeing to the general's care, Turney then called a conference of his surviving company commanders. A courier from no less than Robert E. Lee himself interrupted the meeting, carrying orders to the senior commander (Turney assumed this role) to hold his position. Finally, artillery fire from right and left forced them out of their dearly won position. "Some of the Virginians on our right had already yielded," Turney recalled, and he regretted that when "a white flag was reluctantly hoisted by a Virginia regiment to my right," some of his own 1st Tennessee became prisoners, too.[41] Combat veterans rightly found much of this hard to believe. Indeed, some of Turney's fellow Tennesseans found fault with it. A brother officer in Archer's brigade who Turney admired criticized him for insulting the leaders of the 7th Tennessee.[42] An officer in that regiment punned, "The most unkind shot of all is therefore from the archer in our own camp."[43]

Turney's flights of fancy illustrate only one kind of exaggeration and self-promotion that passed for history in *Confederate Veteran*. Easily correctable inaccuracies plagued many of the journal's accounts of the July 3 charge. The editor proclaimed a piece written by Dick Reid, a Nashville police sergeant, proved "that he 'was there.'" His fanciful account included thirty-pounder Parrott cannons (there were none at Gettysburg) and Gen. Robert Toombs's Georgia brigade (Toombs resigned six months earlier and his brigade—now Benning's—fought at Devil's Den). He portrayed Armistead as "an old man, seventy years old, with his white hair hanging over his shoulders" as "the first man, mounted on his horse, to reach Cemetery Heights, and just as he hallooed at Archer's Tennessee brigade to stand by Virginia he was shot dead in his saddle." The forty-six-year-old, balding, and dismounted Armistead who actually participated in the attack does not appear in Reid's version of events. His story ended with praise for Archer's brigade, which fought so hard their "terrible loss shows how the sons of old Tennessee immortalized themselves at Gettysburg." Truth apparently rests with the ten Confederate generals Reid claimed lay dead or wounded in front of the enemy's works after the charge.[44]

For years, Tennesseans continued to turn to *Confederate Veteran* as the most accessible outlet for their version of what happened on July 3. Fergus S. Harris of the 7th Tennessee wrote of a recent visit to Gettysburg when a guide pointed out where Archer's Tennesseans scaled the stone wall. Delighted that his comrades "had at least received proper recognition," Harris cried as he spoke of a comrade killed by a shell near there. A farmer plowing the field just then uncovered a iron fragment, and Harris was "satisfied, from the very nature of the circumstances, that this piece of shell killed this brave Tennesseean."[45] June Kimble of the 14th Tennessee feared that "so much has been controverted" about the charge that he merely reinforced the notion that Archer's brigade set the axis of advance for the assault, and all the troops in the charge—including Pickett's men—dressed on them. With pride and sorrow he recalled the withering volleys and double-charged canister that "shattered and mutilated as fine a body of Southern heroes as ever trod a battlefield."[46]

Pettigrew's and Trimble's veterans from other states used *Confederate Veteran* as well. In 1896, Mississippian Andrew J. Baker argued that the time had come to honor their dead "who, also, made the same charge and under a more galling and deadly fire, by at least having their memories perpetuated along with those of General Pickett's command." Citing Bachelder's maps as evidence, Baker argued that some of Davis's Mississippians went farther up the slope of Cemetery Ridge than the men under Armistead, "whose death it is said marked the high watermark of the Confederacy." He hoped that Henry Heth, the senior survivor of Pettigrew's division, would take up their cause more actively, especially since no one could know "how soon we who went to Pennsylvania are to join those who are still there on that field."[47]

Mississippians aimed their diatribes at several targets. W. D. Reid of the 11th Mississippi rejected accusations from North Carolinians that Trimble's left flank had been exposed to enemy fire by the premature withdrawal of Davis and Brockenbrough. "I do know that I went to that rock fence and was shot down there," he asserted. Only three of the twenty-seven men in his company on the morning of July 3 came back unscathed, strongly suggesting that Davis's men at least did not break early.[48] Surgeon B. F. Ward of the same unit took aim at James Longstreet, who, in his speeches on Gettysburg, "praises Pickett's and Trimble's troops, but carefully ignores Heth's. Why is this?"[49]

The Mississippians primarily targeted the Virginia version of that day's events, of course. Even if they were slow to enter the literary war, they felt proud of their accomplishments at Gettysburg. In 1905, the P. F. Liddell chapter of the United Confederate Veterans dedicated a monument to the soldiers of Carroll County, Mississippi. The orator read a long poem about Gettysburg, full of references to Pickett's Virginians and their great charge. When his audience grew surly, he smiled, then explained why he chose that ode: "It illustrates my theme. It pays splendid tribute to the sublime courage of Pickett's Virginians in their charge upon Cemetery Ridge, and Pickett's Virginians were made up largely of Mississippians, a fact which the historians and poets seem often to overlook."[50]

Mississippi veterans also turned to the newly established Mississippi Historical Society for support. When J. C. Rietti compiled the *Military Annals of Mississippi* under its auspices, he noted that while the "world has sounded the fame of Pickett's charge," it "has not known that it was Mississippi's troops who went furthest up those fatal heights and broke the enemy's line of defence at the only point it was carried in the charge." Citing support from official reports and the testimony of Mississippi veterans, he argued that "the dead of Davis['s] Brigade were found at a greater distance up the heighths [*sic*] than any other brigade participating in the charge."[51]

The Mississippi Historical Society's journal took up their cause, too. Baxter McFarland argued that the July 3 losses of the 11th Mississippi exceeded those of any one of Pickett's fifteen regiments, a comparison that deserved special attention since the 11th had taken no part in the fight at the Railroad Cut on July 1 and took all its casualties in the charge. Company rosters revealed that the regiment suffered 103 men killed and mortally wounded in the July 3 assault and when the wounded and missing were added in, the unit lost 310 out of the 350 men in ranks that morning.[52] He did not doubt that Davis's men advanced to the stone wall. Indeed, Capt. William T. Magruder of the brigade staff was killed "whilst cheering the men over the wall." This evidence, McFarland hoped, would silence Virginia writers whose literary outpourings "have little or no basis of historical truth,—no small part of it being fiction, pure and simple."[53] McFarland reinforced the assertions of William A. Love, whose study of

Davis's men a decade earlier also concluded that the Bryan barn "is the 'high water mark' of the Confederacy and is forty-seven yards beyond the place reached by Pickett's men."[54]

Mississippians took every opportunity to acknowledge the valor of its heroes at Gettysburg. Surgeon Joseph Holt of the 2nd Mississippi contributed a stirring bit of battle lore with his tale of the wounding and death of the 11th's "singularly self-confident and manly" Sgt. Jere Gage and his efforts to write a farewell letter to his family. Ward also turned to another kind of quantitative evidence to make sure that the Virginia version of Pickett's Charge would not become "the crowning act of glory in the tragic drama of Gettysburg": by his own count, Pickett's division hospital contained 279 wounded too badly to remove to the South; by contrast, Heth's hospital held 693.[55] And like Pickett's men in the 1880s, still other Mississippians tried hard to mark the spot of the alleged breakthrough by the 11th Mississippi at Ziegler's Grove. On the eve of World War II, the Gettysburg park superintendent still had to explain to Maud Brown that "a Mississippi monument on Cemetery Ridge would confuse and not clarify the action" and "would also set a bad precedent."[56]

Alabama and Florida veterans contributed little to the turn-of-the-century literary war. Floridian W. D. Burtchaell seemed resigned to viewing July 3 as "Virginia's gala day and her sons showed the best that was in them on that famous and terrible field." He could only regret that although Wilcox's and Lang's men "displayed an equal valor[,] they are rarely mentioned by writers who have described 'Pickett's Charge.'"[57] Capt. C. Seton Fleming's memoir of service in the 2nd Florida appeared in book form in 1884, and the *Southern Historical Society Papers* published the Floridian's Gettysburg chapter soon thereafter. But since Fleming did not blame Longstreet for the destruction of the small fragment of Florida brigade left after July 2, did not criticize the performance of Pickett's men, and did little to support the cause of Pettigrew and Trimble, he contributed little to the resolution of controversy. Unfortunately, these few items and some wartime letters of Col. David Lang, also published in the *Papers*, comprise the bulk of the defense of the Floridians's accomplishments.[58]

Similarly, Alabamians did not enter the literary battle in force. Nothing had come of wartime legislation to create a historical bureau to record the deeds of Alabama troops. Col. Hilary Herbert wrote a history of the 8th Alabama of Wilcox's brigade shortly after the war, but he left it in manuscript form for years, fearing that publishing it might "seem like self-laudation." He wrote little about July 3, in any case: "What we could have been expected to effect has always remained a mystery. . . . Every private saw at once the madness of the attempt. But never was their courageous

Judge Walter Clark, editor of the North Carolina regimental history series (North Carolina Dept. of Archives and History, Raleigh, N.C.)

devotion to duty more nobly illustrated by their calm and quiet obedience to orders on this day." [59] Colonel Fry's dissenting voice that described "Pettigrew's Charge" for the readers of the *Southern Historical Society Papers* in 1878 seemed mostly a curiosity. Wilcox, who wrote much about Confederate history, wrote little on his brigade at Gettysburg. The silence puzzled Colonel Herbert, who always wondered why nobody kept them from advancing after Pickett's repulse. "Gen. Wilcox never explained it—if he knew, and I suppose he did not." [60] A few memoirs of individual Alabama soldiers added only bits of color to the July 3 story. George Clark of the 11th Alabama, for one, remembered an artillery bombardment so intense that gunners could be seen "bleeding at both ears from the effect of concussion." He had heard rumors of orders stopping their advance but concluded that "the whole affair is involved in mystery even until today." [61] John Abbott of the 8th Alabama left a confused account in which his brigade went into the charge at the same time as the Virginians "to draw some of the fire from Pickett's troops." [62]

Even with the help of these allies, North Carolina still continued to fly Pettigrew's and Trimble's banner highest. In 1894, the North Carolina State Confederate Veterans Association approved the appointment of Judge Walter Clark, former lieutenant colonel of the 70th North Carolina, as editor of what became a five-volume history of every Tar Heel command in Southern service. When he completed the ambitious project in 1901, Clark proudly asserted that it was no longer true that while "North

Carolina has grandly known how to make history," its citizens had "till now always left it to others to write it." These pages, he continued, preserved authentic and reliable information for "some yet unborn Thucydides or Macaulay of the future" who would "transmit to all time the story of this most memorable struggle."[63]

Several common threads wove through these regimental narratives. First, North Carolinians deserved greater credit than they ever received for their services at Gettysburg and elsewhere; second, the partisan editorial policies of the Richmond press denied them those laurels; and third, Pettigrew's and Trimble's commands on July 3 at Gettysburg performed outstandingly in the egregiously misnamed "Pickett's Charge."

Veterans wrote of their wartime exploits with unrestrained pride. Maj. J. A. Weston of the 33rd North Carolina vented his anger against the author in *St. Nicholas* "whose name I am glad I do not know" who had favored the Virginians over the Tar Heels: "This man ought to be sent to the insane asylum. I cannot reply to such childish twaddle." A survivor of the 47th North Carolina claimed that "the respective numbers of dead men in the correctly recorded spots where they fell" supplied all necessary evidence of their valor at Gettysburg, and Pettigrew's men filled the most advanced spots, not Pickett's men, who had "claimed for themselves pre-eminence in this bloody affair."[64]

North Carolinians still resented the Richmond press coverage that left North Carolina troops out of Gettysburg's pantheon of heroes. William McLaurin of the 18th North Carolina took some solace in the sage advice his comrades had lived by during the war: "Wait till you hear from General Lee was the rule with the North Carolina troops, leaving to others to make reputations by printers ink."[65]

Survivors of units that had participated in the charge took the opportunity to make a compelling case for North Carolina valor. McLaurin reminded readers that the selection of Heth's division and Pender's two brigades for the July 3 charge had been a "high compliment" extended by Lee because Pickett's division "had not had a good whiff of powder" since Gaines' Mill in June 1862. No one could question the commitment of Tar Heel soldiers that July day. Octavius Wiggins of the 37th North Carolina took special inspiration from Lt. Iowa M. Royster, who, mortally wounded, still led his company into the charge. "Children of the South," he implored, "can you hear of these noble feats of your countrymen without having your hearts swell with pride?"[66]

Important controversies demanded resolution. How far up the slope of Cemetery Ridge did the North Carolinians advance? Some claims were modest. The 7th North Carolina, one historian asserted, "went as far as any other command, and was among the last to leave the field." The 11th North Carolina claimed to have penetrated the Union line, but a counter-attack had soon forced them to leave behind a large number of prisoners; still, they kept their flag, the only one saved in Pettigrew's brigade. The color-bearer of the 47th North Carolina fell "not ten steps from the rock wall," and its men stopped that close to the Union line. After crossing at least three fences, the men of the 38th North Carolina were stopped only "a few feet in front of the enemy's infantry," where Union troops flanked them.[67]

Other units claimed much more. The 18th North Carolina and each other regiment in its brigade "broke the enemy at some point in its front." North Carolina dead and wounded could be found in Ziegler's Grove and "at the stone fence, the height of a man's chin, *eighty yards further in their front* than the stone fence about 2½ feet high, in front of Pickett's line." The fates of Capt. E. Fletcher Satterfield and two other officers of the 55th North Carolina provided an especially macabre bit of evidence to support the Old North State's claim to farthest advance up the slope. The three men fell near the Bryan barn in a position that was "*more advanced than that attained by any other of the assaulting columns.*" Two comrades later visited the field to verify the spot, and Bachelder marked it. As Charles M. Cooke argued, the historian's measurements proved that "those killed *farthest to the front* belonged to the Fifty-fifth North Carolina" at a spot seventy-three yards beyond the point where Pickett's men pierced the Union line. Asserting that no Virginian who broke into the Angle advanced more than forty yards beyond that wall, Cooke claimed that the 55th marched thirty-one yards farther east than any of Pickett's men.[68]

Why the charge failed was another crucial point of contention. The Tar Heels of Pettigrew's division tended to blame the Virginians in their own command. One North Carolinian wrote that the conduct of the charge was "not what it ought to have been" because Brockenbrough's Virginia brigade "did not come up to its usual standard." Octavius Wiggins asserted that the 37th North Carolina had to oblique to the left to take the Virginians' place. Even General Lane took aim at the Virginians in Pettigrew's division, noting that the 28th North Carolina — his original command — moved into the front line after "Davis' brigade was repulsed and Brockenbrough's did not get beyond the position occupied by General Thomas."[69] If they could change few minds about Pickett's men, they vented their frustrations on more vulnerable Virginians.

Two of the four essays in the fifth volume of the series that directly addressed the Gettysburg controversy offered perhaps the most objec-

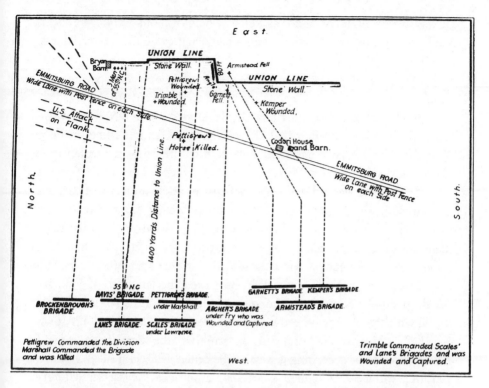

A typical map offered in defense of North Carolina's claim to have advanced farther on July 3 than any other command. Note the location where the three North Carolinians—Capt. J. Fletcher Satterfield and two comrades—fell in front of their commands. (Five Points in the Record of North Carolina)

tive statements of North Carolina's case. Maj. William McK. Robbins, a native North Carolinian who served with the 4th Alabama in 1863 and a Gettysburg Battlefield Commissioner since 1894, used the authority of his position to affirm that "two or three hundred Virginians, a number of Archer's Tennesseans and Alabamians, and a few of Pettigrew's North Carolinians" followed Armistead into the Angle. The rest of Pettigrew's and Trimble's men farther to the north could not storm the more substantial stone wall on their front. Thus, while Robbins did not validate the most strident North Carolina versions of the events of July 3, he gave them considerable credit nonetheless: "Pickett's Virginians did as nobly as they and their friends have ever claimed, and the North Carolinians, Tennesseeans, Alabamians, and Mississippians, under Pettigrew and Trimble, did fully as well." [70] Samuel A. Ashe, a committed North Carolina partisan more subtle in his rhetoric than most, drew heavily on Bachelder, Swallow, official reports, and the Raleigh press to reach similar conclusions.

"It was indeed a field of honor as well as a field of blood," and "the sister States of Virginia and North Carolina had equal cause to weave chaplets of laurel and of cypress."[71]

North Carolina's regimental series illustrated only one part of the state's counterattack on Virginia's version of the events of July 3. Private efforts yielded a few individual Tar Heel memoirs about Gettysburg. James S. Harris, a survivor of Lane's brigade in Trimble's line, made it clear that North Carolinians could attack each other just as virulently as they criticized Virginians. He recalled the arrogance of one of Pettigrew's staff officers who warned them against disturbing the integrity of the first line unless it wavered but added "with an apparent feeling of pride 'the men in front never waver.'" In short order, Harris wrote, his own regiment advanced unchecked to the Angle when the men in front indeed broke and ran.[72] James I. Metts, a North Carolina staff officer who did not participate in the July 3 assault, borrowed the language of William Bond's pamphlet to criticize Richmond writers who had "so persistently flirted with the truth" about the "Spartan Virginians" and the "Thespian North Carolinians." He felt it time to state that "the valor of the one will not be dimmed by according justice to the other."[73] D. H. Hill Jr.'s North Carolina volume of Clement A. Evans's ambitious *Confederate Military History* criticized "people ignorant enough to believe" that either Pettigrew's division only supported Pickett or the assault failed because North Carolina did not support Virginia; their long casualty lists provided the best evidence "that on this field the North Carolinians measured squarely up to every soldierly obligation."[74]

In addition to these individual literary efforts, a state-sponsored campaign to right the historical record flourished well into the twentieth century. For a new series of "North Carolina Booklets," which were first issued in 1901, Samuel Ashe prepared "The Charge at Gettysburg," an easily distributable reprint of his essay in the regimental history series, in which he praised the North Carolinians who "accomplished as much as any other troops, suffered greater losses[,] penetrated the farthest and remained the longest."[75] North Carolina adopted an unofficial new motto that graced the cover of historical society publications: "First at Bethel, Farthest to the Front at Gettysburg and Chickamauga, Last at Appomattox." North Carolina writers argued as well that the Old North State provided more troops for the Confederacy than any other and that its citizens held proportionately fewer positions of power or prestige that exempted them from fighting. To salute "another glorious anniversary to North Carolina veterans"—the successful charge of Cooke's, Lane's, and MacRae's troops at Reams Station in 1864—the historical society commissioned a pamphlet entitled *Five Points in the Record of North Carolina in the Great War of 1861–5* in which Bond and others justified anew each claim made in the new state motto. They adopted a new tactic: Strident rhetoric gave way to systematic evaluation of the public writings and speeches of all Virginians and others such as James Longstreet and Porter Alexander, whose wartime service with Virginia troops tainted their credibility.[76]

Only one question remained: Would any of this make any difference? More adept at interstate infighting now, Bond took North Carolina's case to anybody who would print it. In 1901, he convinced the editors of the *National Tribune* to offer their Northern audience a six-week serialized version of "Pickett or Pettigrew."[77] Unfortunately, it drew little response, and few North Carolinians tried again at this time to push Virginia's Pickett's Charge out of the national limelight.

In July 1903, Col. John R. Lane of the 26th North Carolina addressed the North Carolina Society of Baltimore. He borrowed the theme of national reunion that had worked so well for Pickett's men since 1887. To his Tar Heel friends he said, "Your valor is coming to be regarded as the common heritage of the American nation. It no longer belongs to the South; it is the high water mark of what Americans have done and can do." To his fellow survivors of the 26th in the audience he offered "the highest tribute—a comrade's tears."[78] Despite their best efforts to right the wrongs in the historical record, North Carolinians had every reason to wonder if their sacrifices of July 3 at Gettysburg would ever be accorded any more than such symbolic gestures.

7

VIRGINIA
VICTORIOUS

The ardency of the discordant voices emanating from many parts of the old Confederacy quickly drew the wrath of the Old Dominion. Virginians simply refused to tolerate any tampering with their version of the events of July 3, images accepted as truth since 1863. Thus, with great energy, they silenced their challengers, by both discrediting their motives and arguments and overwhelming all doubts with a new flood of heroic images of Pickett's men buffed to an even higher sheen. The Virginians had no new points to make. They simply indulged themselves by taking time to draw larger-than-life portraits more sharply, to exaggerate old exaggerations. Now, indeed, image was everything.

Just as they had for years, in wonderfully evocative and emotional ways, Virginians continued to remind the entire South just how perfectly Pickett's men represented the spirit of all truly faithful Confederate soldiers. At the same time, they sustained their appeal to all Americans to embrace Virginia's heroes as their own.

Virginia veterans impressed upon their comrades that history must not forget their sacrifices for noble principles. Col. Richard L. Maury, after working so hard for a Virginia monument inside the Angle at Gettysburg, reminded the George Pickett Camp of Confederate Veterans in August 1893 that they must uphold their obligation to perpetuate for their children and all America the memory of "the valour, loyalty, and merit of those heroic Virginian soldiers of Pickett's Division." It was not enough to keep alive the name of Pickett, Longstreet, or even "the mighty Lee himself." The private soldier of Pickett's division deserved an equally honored place since he had won "the most conspicuous place in song and verse and picture and story of all the millions who stood to arms in those momentous days."[1]

This message went forth in a host of new journals published in the 1890s for veterans and their families and designed to promote the spirit of conciliation. Factual accuracy hardly mattered in these romanticized accounts of old glories; thus, readers could forgive the false assertions of Sgt. James H. Walker of the 9th Virginia that Hood's Texans attacked Cemetery Ridge on July 1 and McLaws repeated it the next day. Far more important was that, after a July 3 cannonade that shook the earth "such as probably the younger Pliny mentioned in his description of the eruption of Vesuvius," Pickett's men undertook "to win for Virginia and the Confederate states a name which would be handed down to posterity in honor, and which would be spoken of with pride, by not only Virginia, but by all America." Indeed, Lee chose Pickett's men "because they were Virginians," but now the whole country "should look upon this charge as showing the valor of the American soldier."[2] Similarly, the maudlin tale of "The Hero of Pickett's Division" told of two soldiers, believed to be father and son, who advanced with Pickett over the works. The elder of the pair—a color-bearer—fell, and the "fair, sweet-faced young soldier" waved the banner defiantly until he dropped dead beside him. Litter-bearers discovered that the pair was not father and son, but husband and wife. An old man and a little boy searching for the place where the two died found that flag, "embroidered by the fair hands of Virginian women—embroidered with their hair," covering two skulls. The author intoned: "Greece has her Marathon, Sparta her Thermopylae, Europe her Waterloo, America her Bunker Hill, but the Confederacy has her charge of Pickett's division."[3] With such florid rhetoric at their command, Virginians easily quieted the storm of criticisms swelling up from the South before it seriously damaged the image of Pickett's men as national heroes.

No one was more shocked than Pickett's men, then, when some of their fellow Virginians turned on them once more. Beginning in the mid-1890s and lasting well into the next century, controversy swirled around an unexpected nexus: George E. Pickett himself.

One particularly telling shot started this intrastate war, a blow all the more shocking because it came from inside the ranks of Pickett's division. In July 1863, when Maj. Kirkwood Otey had submitted the 11th Vir-

Kirkwood Otey, as a member of the VMI Class of 1849. Forty-five years later he accused his former division commander George Pickett of improper conduct on July 3, 1863. (Virginia Military Institute, Lexington, Va.)

ginia's casualty list to the Richmond press, he had praised Pickett's conduct on July 3 as "fully worthy of the occasion." In 1887, he had traveled to Gettysburg with others of Pickett's men for that first great reunion of the Blue and Gray. In November 1894, Otey changed his story dramatically: "Whoever will take the trouble to make inquiries will find that there is an underground rumor, narrative, or whatever you may call it, that General George E. Pickett did not take part in the immortal performance of his division" on July 3. Reflecting back, he could not recall ever hearing "a positive statement as to where General Pickett was in that charge, never heard him located or placed." Otey then argued that no one could place Pickett on the field because the general, in fact, was not there. After getting his wounded hand dressed, Otey had stopped at the "whiskey wagon" to get something for his pain and saw "two officers of General Pickett's staff (their names can be furnished if desired)" there, "each with a tin cup, awaiting their turn for a ration of whiskey." While Otey did not see his division commander in person, the presence of the staff officers "naturally suggested that General Pickett might be in the neighborhood."[4]

Otey's own post-Gettysburg court-martial for drunkenness on duty might well have cast doubts on the veracity of his accusations, and he never did explain why he waited until the 1890s to spring his surprise attack on the memory of his former commander.[5] Nonetheless, a Virginian had opened for close scrutiny an important element of the Pickett's Charge story. Had Pickett really led his men into action, as so many early accounts asserted and so many Virginians believed? "Armistead was killed, Garnett was killed and Kemper as good as killed," Otey asserted, thereby turning the fact that Pickett and his staff came out of the fight unhurt from apparent good fortune into evidence of cowardice.

Not surprisingly, others among Pickett's men quickly rallied to their commander's defense. Only four days after Otey lodged his charges, Charles Pickett, the general's brother and former adjutant, rejected as unfounded any suggestion that any member of the commander's official party had not done his entire duty on July 3. The general and his staff had positioned themselves exactly where they could act most efficiently, "as closely in the rear of the line of battle as was possible to do," where Pickett could "observe the advance and movement of his own Division, as well as, those of the troops on his left (Pettigrew & others)." One-third of the way across the valley, Pickett had sent three staff officers—one at a time—for reinforcements. Sending three men to deliver a routine message revealed physical danger so great that the general "deemed it hardly within the bounds of reason that more than one of them could reach Wilcox." When the general finally sent Charles for still more reinforcements, the fire near the Emmitsburg Road had grown so hot that Charles was certain that "it was our final parting in this world."[6]

Charles Pickett's effort to silence his brother's detractors failed. For at least the next twenty years, Otey's accusations reappeared in various forms and opened up Pickett's character to pointed criticism. Even prominent Virginians stepped forward to cast doubts on the general's heroic image. Eppa Hunton, colonel of the 8th Virginia in 1863, harbored ill feelings toward Pickett since at least that spring, when the general—in Hunton's mind—did not push sufficiently hard to win his promotion to command the brigade Garnett led on July 3. He never joined Pickett's men at Gettysburg reunions and turned down the invitation to speak at the dedication of the Pickett monument in the Hollywood Cemetery in 1888. Hunton remained deeply devoted to the Lost Cause and the Democratic Party after the war, putting him at odds with many of the leaders of the Pickett's Division Association. One of the few people to whom he agreed to comment about the charge was Jubal Early's associate John W. Daniel, "a dear friend who at a tender age spilled his blood for the cause we love so well—one who still loves the dear cause and has never failed to defend it—who has never said *he was glad it failed*."[7] Perhaps all these factors help explain why Hunton invariably asserted that Pickett faced no danger on July 3. Indeed, Hunton claimed, the general had a penchant for dodging fire; at Suffolk, he had slid off his saddle so his horse could shield him from Union musketry.[8]

At least Otey and Hunton had participated in the July 3 attack. Not all of Pickett's new critics could claim that much. Implying censure, Third

Corps artilleryman William T. Poague related that on July 3 he saw the general only once, "on the line of my guns on horseback" at about the time the Virginia division reached the Angle, placing him well west of the Emmitsburg Road and behind Pettigrew's command at the attack's most crucial moment.[9] Former cavalryman Thomas Rosser wondered why Pickett did nothing to counter Stannard's Vermonters: "If Gen'l Pickett were there, why did he not make a change of front, with at least a portion of his command to meet this flank attack?" With no hard evidence but plenty of venom—perhaps the result of his own efforts to salvage his reputation at Pickett's expense after Five Forks opened both of them to criticism—Rosser felt sure that Pickett "had been detained in the rear, from some unknown cause, and was not on the field, near enough to command the attacking column, when the enemy was reached."[10] Perhaps that "unknown cause" might be inferred from Virginian John S. Wise's insight that Pickett "was a high and free liver, and often declared that, to fight like a gentleman, a man must eat and drink like a gentleman."[11]

Former Confederate partisan ranger John Singleton Mosby did not make forthright allegations about Pickett's fondness for alcohol, but he did recount several times over in unflattering terms Pickett's only face-to-face meeting with Lee after the war. In 1870 Mosby had accompanied Pickett to a brief, cold meeting with their former commander. When Pickett cried that Lee "had my division massacred at Gettysburg," an unsympathetic Mosby replied, "Well, it made you immortal." Mosby also claimed that when Lee spotted Pickett still marching with his men a few days after Five Forks, he had asked loudly in a tone of voice he rarely used, "Is that man still with this army?"[12] Mosby's comments encouraged other critics from Pickett's own division. Edmund Berkeley, former major of Hunton's 8th Virginia, praised Mosby's honesty and asserted that "Pickett took good care not to have himself or any of his staff hurt in the charge . . . as he was not in it." Berkeley had marched "in the exact centre of Picketts Div., & could sweep the entire field." When Hunton had asked Berkeley after the war if he thought Pickett was in the charge, "I replyed I did not and he said neither do I." He also related to Mosby that a courier had told Hunton that all during the charge he carried "canteens of water to Gen Pickett & his staff who were behind some boulders in the wood."[13]

Word already had circulated in Virginia that Mosby intended to expand an earlier work on Confederate cavalry at Gettysburg to encompass the whole battle. Eppa Hunton's son asked him how he intended to treat the July 3 charge and its major actors, fearing that Mosby would take Pickett's side and somehow shift blame for the failure of the attack to subordinates such as his father. Trying to forestall any such possibility, the younger

Hunton even suggested that there had been a close relationship between his father and Pickett. Mosby calmed the worried son: "You need not have any fear of my mentioning your father in print—nor have I any intention of writing anything about Pickett and Gettysburg." He even called the young man's bluff: "I have made no charge against Pickett but I have heard your father speak in an uncomplimentary manner of him," adding, "I think you are very much mistaken in saying that your father was fond of Pickett."[14]

Not surprisingly, North Carolinians picked up on this new twist right away. James Metts's study of the charge stated bluntly that "Pickett remained behind." He cited as his source Charles Venable of Lee's staff, who, perhaps seeing a chance to strike out at Virginians who had not helped the Lee cause, had written, "I will say all honor can be given to Pickett's brigade [sic], although the general was not with it." Venable even asserted that only "Pettigrew was well to the front, leading his men."[15] Col. Charles Marshall of Lee's staff, who had damned Pickett with the faint praise that he did nothing improper on July 3, prompted one of Pettigrew's officers to observe that if Pickett was in the right place, then "Pettigrew and Trimble, who were with their commands, were in the wrong place."[16]

Pickett's friends, of course, did not take these attacks lightly. Soon after Charles Pickett jumped to his brother's defense, the general's orderly Thomas Friend pledged his support, claiming that "it is our duty to defend the name of Gen. Pickett against such calumny." How "anyone, who wore the 'gray,' [could] be guilty of such traitorous lies" confounded Friend, who proclaimed himself "willing and ready at all times to defend [Pickett], whatever the cost may be." No "base slanderers" would "take one laurel from the crown of Gen. George E. Pickett, as long as his Soldiers and his Soldiers Children live."[17]

More of Pickett's men soon joined him. Former sergeant W. W. Wells of the 14th Virginia recalled how "I naturally looked for Genl. Pickett under such trying conditions as we were then placed at Gettysburg." During the advance "he changed his position from the Front to the rear of the Line and when I saw him last he was within a short distance of the Stone Fence."[18] Martin Hazlewood, historian of the George E. Pickett Camp of the United Confederate Veterans, finally introduced the Virginia division to readers of the *Southern Historical Society Papers* by defending his general against the charges of Otey and "superficial writers in search of a scapegoat for the untoward results of this fatal battle."[19]

Renewed interest in Pickett's unpublished report fueled still more speculation. What was in it? Hazlewood recognized its value and asked Charles Pickett, "Can you get it? It would be very helpful" in clearing the general's good name.[20] Just a few years earlier, James Longstreet learned that Sallie Pickett claimed to have the original document, but he believed the general had obeyed Lee's orders to destroy it.[21] Charles Pickett suggested that even if his brother had not torn it up, the report likely burned with other family documents when Richmond fell or got captured with the rest of Pickett's division records.[22]

Charles Pickett did not need that document, however, to rally the rest of the general's wartime staff to the defense of his brother's reputation. He and former captains Robert A. Bright and W. Stuart Symington already had injected their version of their general's actions on July 3 into Northern author J. H. Stine's history of the Army of the Potomac, in which "Pickett's staff is quite prominent." Stine included the full text of several letters written by Pickett's friends.[23] Bright, Symington, and another former staff officer, Edward R. Baird, also agreed to Charles Pickett's request that they cooperate with Longstreet, who appreciated the fragility of individual memory and wanted "to get a more intelligent view, and by comparison weed out errors or reconcile discrepancies" about July 3 for his memoirs.[24] Agreeing with Longstreet that "the Pickett charge was the crowning point of Gettysburg & Gettysburg of the war—So regarded at least," Pickett's military family had already reached consensus on a number of contentious issues.[25]

Even before Otey's accusations, they had considered the general's whereabouts on July 3. Symington claimed he saw Pickett riding "in rear of Garnett and Kemper's Brigade," the proper place for a division commander. A few days later, he added detail: Pickett was "with Garnett & Kemper as a front line & Armistead as a second line," then he "was between the two lines."[26] He did not recall how far the general advanced, but Bright remembered that he had brought him a message "on the side of the Hill" well toward the front, at "the last descent before the ascent to the stone wall."[27]

They also agreed that Pickett did all he could to control the entire advance. Baird asserted that "some troops on our left gave way" and Pickett sent him and Symington to rally them.[28] He did not identify them, but Symington did: "When I carried one of their flags trying to get them to rally the few who did stand said they were N. Carolinians." He took the banner back to Longstreet's headquarters, where, so he claimed, the 11th North Carolina picked it up later.[29] When Pickett discovered Union troops trying to turn his left, he ordered artilleryman James Dearing "to open with every gun on the flanking column."[30] In each case, Pickett's staff portrayed the general as an active field commander.

Longstreet used this information sparingly when he wrote about July 3

Capt. W. Stuart Symington, a member of Pickett's staff on July 3 and one of his strongest postwar defenders (VHS)

in *From Manassas to Appomattox*. His narrative of the artillery bombardment and the charge covered fewer than six pages, and he gave greater attention to criticizing "the knights of peaceful later days" who "have been busy in search of points on which to lay charges or make innuendoes of want of conduct" against him.[31] More important in the long run, however, in their efforts to help Stine and Longstreet, the reconstitution of Pickett's staff proved very useful when Otey took aim at their general in 1894. These veterans and the allies they attracted launched a stout defense of Pickett against the slings and arrows of his fellow Virginians; moreover, they discredited all critics who challenged their version of Pickett's Charge.

The most important recruit in this war to preserve Pickett's good name never wore a gray uniform. Sallie Pickett, already active in reunions, a favorite of the Virginia division, and a force to be reckoned with, added to the cause her pen and her sheer presence. She always loved her husband's veterans, but she did more for her husband's defense by taking his case to new audiences. Through essays, novels, memoirs, and such Victorian standards as compiled love letters designed to touch hearts, she wrote for all American women, North and South. Her tales of heroic actions in exciting times also reached younger Americans for whom the war had become little more than a colorful story.

Sallie did not take up her pen until the 1890s, but well before the turn of the century she had tailored a perfect image of the man she called "My Soldier." He possessed "the sweetest and the tenderest of natures, and no man was more beloved of men, women and children of every degree and station" than George E. Pickett. Appointed to West Point by national hero Abraham Lincoln—so she wrote—Pickett showed "the keenest sense of justice, the most sensitive consciousness of right, and the moral courage to do it." Ulysses S. Grant had tendered to Pickett the federal marshalship for Virginia after the war in recognition of his strength of character, and Pickett adhered to his principles in refusing the offer. Alluding to recent critics, Sallie admitted "a wee, sma' few of those of his own comrades of the Lost Cause" envied the "glory of his short, unfinished life," but she knew that most of his men loved him and that "to-day a whole nation of true soldiers everywhere give veneration to his memory."[32]

Sallie wanted to dedicate her first book, *Pickett and His Men*, to her Soldier alone, but she felt certain that her husband would have said, "I did not do it—my men did it all."[33] James Longstreet wrote a gracious introduction that erased all doubts about Pickett's generalship. At Five Forks, Longstreet wrote, he had not failed; others had failed him, leaving "that brilliant and heroic leader and his Spartan band to the same hard straits they so nobly met at Gettysburg." For Pickett, *"duty was his polar star."*[34]

In colorful vignettes, Sallie revealed Pickett's strength of character. During the Mexican War, he had displayed great bravery while carrying the first American flag over the parapets at Chapultepec. He had stared down the British and secured the American claim to San Juan Island on the eve of the Civil War. If anyone doubted George Pickett's glory, Abraham Lincoln—an unquestionably great man—had validated it. When he stood on Cemetery Ridge on the day of his great address, a bystander said, "Think of the men who held these heights!" "Yes," Lincoln replied, "but think of the men who stormed these heights!"[35] Pickett's men.

For those in Democratic strongholds of the South who might resent her husband's link to the Great Emancipator, Sallie provided lengthy excerpts of Union general and Democratic presidential candidate George McClellan's eulogy. With true McClellanesque hyperbole, Pickett emerged as "the purest type of the perfect soldier." He may even have become "the best infantry soldier developed on either side during the Civil War." In a comparison that must have stunned the Lee cult, McClellan avowed that Pickett would "live in history as nearer to Light Horse Harry, of the Revolution, than any other of the many heroes produced by old Virginia."[36]

Sallie handled her husband's critics by complimenting them or ignoring them. Although Hunton had not yet made public his feelings about Pickett, she knew from his refusal to speak at the Pickett's division monument dedication to treat him generously. Thus, she did not find "his long experience in poring over musty files in a law-office any obstacle to a gallant military career" and hinted that Hunton's health, not Pickett's lack of confidence in him, prevented his early promotion to brigade command.[37] She wrote nothing critical of Otey personally, but she attempted to destroy the credibility of his hints about Pickett's drinking on July 3 in a particularly gushy vignette, replete with language that probably no soldier going into battle ever uttered. According to Sallie, Wilcox rode up to Pickett and offered him his flask, saying, "Pickett, take a drink with me. In an hour you'll be in hell or glory." Pickett declined, recalling his promise to Sallie that he "would keep fresh upon my lips until we should meet again the breath of the violets she gave me when we parted." Thus, he hoped to reach "either glory or glory."[38]

Sallie tried to treat even Pettigrew's and Trimble's men and their partisans generously. Pettigrew himself, she wrote, had attempted "to reach the post of death and honor, but he was far away, and valor could not quite annihilate space." Worse, three of his four brigades did not know their new division commander and did not respond to his leadership with unquestioning obedience. Indeed, she ended her brief commentary on these units by repeating her belief that each soldier on the field on July 3 did "what the most profound sense of duty and patriotism, controlled by the emergencies which surrounded him, suggested that he should do."[39]

Reviewers treated Sallie's effort graciously. It possessed a "particular charm."[40] John Chase celebrated her "rare gift in a woman,—she is a good historian,—clear in the presentation of her facts, and at the same time unflaggingly picturesque and entertaining."[41] Some showed less enthusiasm, however. Another literary critic decided that its chapters on home life in wartime Virginia would prove far more valuable to historians than its "military narrative, carefully as it has been prepared."[42]

Sallie did not write only about Gettysburg or even George Pickett, but all her literary efforts worked toward a common purpose. Her short stories portrayed life in old Virginia, the environment that shaped her Soldier.[43] Her flowery style drew in readers of new popular magazines, to whom she could admit with feigned modesty: "It has been easy for me to write of Lincoln and Davis, of Grant and Lee and Jackson and the rest, because I knew them and admired them." But, mostly, she loved to relive "those pregnant moments—those sharpest bas-reliefs" that illustrated best "the character, quality, and contour" of George Pickett. She claimed she knew her Soldier "from babyhood," and the first words she learned to write, with his kind assistance, "were 'Sally' and 'Soldier.'" Only a strong, compassionate man could lead his men up the slopes of Cemetery Ridge, seek no personal laurels, and confront his commander with this reality: "Not all the glory in the world, General Lee, could atone for the widows and orphans this day has made."[44]

Sallie's active partisanship helped to breathe new life into the image of Pickett and his men. New cockiness emerged in Virginians' narratives of the events of July 3. They showed no fear of the criticism heaped on them by North Carolina and her allies. Nor did they respond to the barbs of fellow Virginians. They simply dismissed all challenges. Richmond's wartime version of the charge had proved sufficiently durable to suggest its entire truthfulness.

A new wave of genuine pride in the accomplishments of Pickett's men emerged in the twenty years before the golden anniversary, and Virginians found plenty of opportunities to uphold their heroes' virtues. Reunions offered arenas to tout their achievements. "Has Lee 'grown so great that he embarrassed God?'" asked one orator who considered the grandeur of Pickett's advance and decided that while God had willed their repulse, the Virginians' bravery had "sanctified their defeat."[45] Veterans from other Southern states who came to reunions in Richmond were stunned by the bias in Old Dominion hero worship. In 1907, a South Carolinian complained that the orator at one reunion had singled out for special praise "the names of but three Confederate officers, and they Virginians—Jackson, Stuart, and Pickett, the trio attached to the Army of Northern Virginia."[46] George Pickett had broken new ground, now mentioned in the same sentence as the other two.

Other Virginians spread the glory of Pickett and his men on the public lecture circuit, talking to veterans groups, women's groups such as the new United Daughters of the Confederacy, or any civic organization—North or South—committed to preserving the nation's history. As Captain Baird told the Essex Chapter of the United Daughters of the Confederacy, Pickett's men performed "a *simple miracle* of valor."[47] Capt. John Lamb noted in the dedicatory address for a monument to the Confederate soldiers of Charles City County, Virginia, that a full history of its local Southern Guards reflected "the glorious deeds of Arm[i]stead's Brigade, Pickett's Division." Mixing dreams of "what might have been" with the political realities of the day, Lamb asserted that Pickett's success would have meant that "two governments instead of one would be exercising control of the magnificent domain over which the Stars and Stripes float proudly today." Still, he did not want to teach the children of Pickett's men "that their fathers were wrong in the struggle for Southern independence."[48]

The postwar political disagreements that had split Lost Cause Democrats such as Jubal Early from Virginia Conservatives such as James Kemper largely had disappeared, facilitating the emergence of this new spirit. Death and the passage of time resolved or softened old squabbles, and a new alliance now bound old foes against a common enemy: the Republican Party. Finally, even a stalwart Lost Cause advocate such as Fitz Lee could explain why the July 3 charge could carry no name but "Pickett's Charge": "The operation of a detached force generally takes the name of the commanding officer. Pickett was the senior officer in rank," and "the appellation refers to the whole body of nine brigades, and should not be limited to the three Virginia brigades which belonged to Pickett's division." If either of the other permanent commanders led their divisions that day and outranked Pickett, "the assault would have been known as Heth's or Pender's charge, as the case might be."[49]

Along with the political denouement the *Southern Historical Society Papers*, after more than twenty years of relative silence about the July 3 charge, now welcomed contributions from veterans of Pickett's division. Many of the Lost Cause advocates who steered the journal's early course had died or at least moderated their tone, opening the way for Pickett, his men, their battles, and anything connected with them to appear regularly. Moreover, reminiscent of its original role in constructing the story of Pickett's Charge, the Richmond press again printed many articles about the assault that ultimately graced the pages of the *Papers* and reached many readers outside Virginia.

No matter how they expressed it, Pickett's men invariably portrayed their endeavor on July 3 as a uniquely high measure of courage, commitment to principle, and military prowess. "The story of Pickett's charge will ever be remembered and generations yet to come will point to it as one of the grandest acts of heroism in American history," wrote Charles T. Loehr of the 1st Virginia.[50] Col. Rawley Martin of the 53rd Virginia believed that "if those men had been told: 'This day your lives will pay the penalty of your attack upon the Federal lines,' they would have made the charge just as it was made."[51] According to the 9th Virginia's James Crocker, Pickett's "intelligent soldiers" knew the success of their cause rested on them, and "all were willing to die, if only their country could thereby triumph."[52]

In addition, Pickett's men addressed the great losses they absorbed, a task that was essential to successfully countering North Carolina's accusation that relatively few Virginians died on July 3. Descriptions took on an air of melodrama. According to one account, as they stood near the Southern artillery line before the charge, they knew "it was to be another Malvern Hill, another costly day to Virginia and to Virginians."[53] The horrific became commonplace. Col. Joseph C. Mayo of the 3rd Virginia described the results of a single Union shell hitting a nearby apple tree: "First Lieutenant A. P. Gomer, legs shattered below the knee; of the

Arthur brothers, second and third lieutenants, one killed and the other badly hit; Orderly Sergeant Murray mortally wounded, and of the privates, one killed and three wounded." He saw his color-bearer fall with "a hideous hole sheer through his stalwart body, and his right hand closed in a death grip around the staff of that beautiful new flag."[54] Lt. William Wood recalled that when he got close to the stone wall, "I looked to the right and left and felt we were disgraced," so few men were still in line; then he realized how many lay dead and wounded behind him.[55] The 8 survivors of the 100 men on the 18th Virginia's skirmish line still convinced Pvt. John W. Clay of his regiment's hard fight.[56] On July 4, Charles Loehr of the 1st Virginia counted only thirty men in his regiment.[57]

All of Virginia had paid the high cost of its soldiers' heroism. Crocker described "the mournful lamentations of Virginia itself, the mother of us all, over the loss of so many of her bravest and best sons." Who could believe Tar Heel slanders as Crocker reeled off the names of the division's dead leaders? "The loss of company officers are in equal proportion," Crocker wrote. "It is a sad, mournful summing up."[58] Long-delayed eulogies to these slain leaders now appeared regularly in the *Southern Historical Society Papers*. The 57th Virginia's 24-year-old colonel, John Bowie Magruder, fell at Cushing's guns shouting, "They are ours."[59] Col. James Gregory Hodges of the 14th Virginia helped to fulfill with his own death a promise delivered just before the Gettysburg campaign: "You may expect to hear a grand account of the regiment." The colonel's family had tried to recover his remains, but they could not be identified: "He sleeps in the trenches with those who made that charge of Pickett's division immortal."[60]

Junior officers and even enlisted men won similar tributes. James Crocker reeled off a list of twelve sons of Portsmouth, Virginia, who died on July 3, all heroes who "gave new lustre to the prowess of arms, and laid a new chaplet of glory on the brow of Virginia, brighter and more immortal than all others worn by her."[61] Mayo saluted an unknown Virginian who died beyond the spot where Armistead fell, proclaiming him "the foremost hero of them all, a humble private, without a name."[62]

And perhaps to strengthen new ties to those who tolerated no criticism of Lee, Pickett's men no longer accepted Marse Robert's own injunction: "It is all my fault!" James Clay explained that he and a number of new recruits from Maryland who had joined the 18th Virginia just before the battle volunteered as skirmishers on July 3 "in the presence of General Robert E. Lee, who seemed to personally look after this hazardous duty in our three brigades."[63] Colonel Mayo recalled Kemper's earnest injunction on July 3: "The commanding general had assigned our division the post of honor that day. He was a Virginian; so were they." When Mayo's men fell back and saw Lee, "followed by his faithful aides, the two Charleses — Venable and Marshall," he seemed "a very anointed king of command, posing for the chisel of a Phidias, and looking on him we knew that the army was safe."[64]

Pickett's men now sustained the image that Lee's composure had been "perfectly sublime." Captain Bright recalled Lee's wonderful tribute to Pickett: "The men and officers of your command have written the name of Virginia as high to-day as it has ever been written before."[65] Loehr had seen that Lee "felt the repulse and slaughter of the division, whose remains he viewed" when he heard him say, even though the blame was not his to bear, " 'General Pickett, your men have done all that men could do; the fault is entirely my own.' "[66]

It took a rare Virginian indeed to break ranks against Lee now. William Mahone, long a pariah in the eyes of many of his fellow Virginians, sounded more like Longstreet than a son of the Old Dominion when he asserted that it "was plain to my mind — that no troops ever formed a line of battle that could cross the plain of fire to which the attacking force would be subjected, and live to enter the enemy's works on 'Cemetery Hill' in any organized force." He could not understand why "General Lee would insist on such an assault after he had seen the ground."[67]

Lee had seen the ground, of course, and he did order the charge. Nonetheless, if he was not responsible for the day's results, the guilty parties had to be named. When Pickett's survivors considered the question, James Longstreet still did not become their target of reproach. Crocker believed that "the disastrous result of the campaign, in my opinion, was not due to the generalship of Lee, but wholly to the disregard of his directions by some of his generals," especially cavalry chief Jeb Stuart.[68] Rawley Martin concurred that "somebody blundered at Gettysburg but not Lee." The fault rested with unnamed "others, who failed to execute his orders."[69] Among Pickett's survivors, only Crocker suggested Longstreet's guilt in print; even then he limited his criticisms to July 2, the day before the great charge.[70]

If Pickett's men accorded responsibility for the failure of the attack to no senior general, their resentment toward other troops in the charge thrived anew. John H. Lewis watched his comrades in Armistead's brigade as they "fell in heaps, still fighting, bleeding, dying," waiting "for the assistance that should have been there." But when their supports "vanished from the field," the sad fragment of Pickett's division fought the whole Union center alone.[71] Charles Loehr raised the issue as a prelude to personal loss. A close friend, Pvt. "Monk" Wingfield, looked back and asked,

"Where are our reinforcements?" When Loehr said he did not see any, Wingfield replied, "We are going to be whipped, see if we don't." They were his last words.[72] Captain Bright praised the willingness of the 52nd North Carolina's Col. James K. Marshall to press on after a piece of shell mortally wounded him. If all the men on Pickett's left had gone on like Marshall, "history would have been written another way."[73]

Pickett's men also renewed their assault on the Alabamians and Floridians who were to have protected their right flank. Loehr asserted that Wilcox's brigade "fell back faster than it came, adding only to the losses and accomplishing naught."[74] As the third of the three staff officers sent to bring up Wilcox, Captain Bright saw the result of the Alabamians' and Floridians' slowness: Stannard's Vermonters hitting the Virginians' flank.[75]

Nothing connected with Pickett and his men seemed too insignificant for public notice. Even heroes' relics commanded great reverence. When a New Yorker contacted Virginia editor John W. Daniel to give back some of Colonel Hodges's personal possessions, the journalist oversaw the return of the officer's sword belt, which "is the same that Col. Hodges wore when his picture was taken, which now hangs in Mrs. Hodges' room."[76] Former Confederate general George H. Steuart had found Garnett's sword in a Baltimore pawnshop, and after Steuart's death, the blade was returned to Garnett's niece. Since his body was never identified, the general's last moments drew considerable curiosity; one of his men still found it "inexplicable that his remains were not identified."[77]

Emotion overflowed at the unveiling of a portrait of Lewis Armistead at a United Confederate Veterans camp in Richmond. The brave officer, "linked by ties of blood with many of our best, the son of a soldier," had needed only "a fit opportunity to prove himself the hero he was." On July 3 at Gettysburg, his hat on the tip of his sword, "borne aloft with matchless courage," became "a standard as glorious, as worthy to be sung, as the plume that floated at Ivry above the helmet of Navarre."[78] All hints of Armistead's alleged disloyalty vanished. Sgt. D. B. Easley recalled that, believing the general to be dead, he "fired several shots over his body" and heard no treasonous word.[79] If Virginia ever again had to answer a call to arms, Armistead's example could still "nerve their hearts with unflinching determination to do or die in her defence."[80]

Now, George E. Pickett merited only praise. Rawley Martin acknowledged the earlier controversy surrounding the general's whereabouts and sided with his staff: "I am sure he was where his duty called him throughout the engagement. He was too fine a soldier, and had fought too many battles not to be where he was most needed on that supreme occasion of his military life."[81] The accolade came when it was needed most. In late 1903, the "Where was Pickett?" debate reopened when North Carolinian Samuel A. Ashe asked in an article in a Richmond newspaper why Virginians continued to slander Pettigrew's and Trimble's men even though they all knew that the day's reverse could be blamed in large part to Pickett's being "well to the rear."[82]

Ashe ignited a firestorm of protest with that one article. Courier Thomas Friend again took up his commander's defense, repeating that Pickett rode only "a few feet in the rear of the advancing column." He came within a short distance of the Union line, always keeping "his eye on the left [toward Pettigrew], never looking for a moment to the right of the column, showing that he feared for the left." Friend even recalled Pickett's complaint that "General Lee had put on his left 'a division that was whipped the day before.'" The courier assured readers that he had seen North Carolina troops fight bravely in other battles; still, "in the interest of truth and history, and in defense of the immortal name of Pickett," he felt compelled to defend his general against Tar Heel slander.[83] Captain Bright of Pickett's staff quickly challenged Ashe's assertions, too. Since 1892, he had continued to compile information from fellow staff members about July 3. Some minor details changed, but not Bright's stand on Pickett's whereabouts: "General Pickett and his staff were about twenty yards in rear of the column."[84]

Like never before, the fate of mounted men in Pickett's Charge carried great implications. It stood to reason that a man on horseback made a better target than one on foot, and what had happened to others who rode into the attack might suggest how far forward Pickett or his staff went. Everyone knew what happened to Garnett and Kemper; both had been mounted. The ill Col. Lewis B. Williams of the 1st Virginia, also mounted, fell mortally wounded. At least two of Kemper's staff officers killed in the battle had been on horseback. Controversy raged, but Bright dismissed its relevance, countering that all officers who rode into the charge — except for the division commander and his staff — had disobeyed Pickett's explicit orders to advance on foot.[85] Before the debate ran out of steam, even a professional cavalry journal reprinted a short article entitled "Equine Heroes of Pickett's Charge."[86]

At last, and in many ways, Pickett's men had secured their special niche in history. A spate of military memoirs by senior Confederate officers — whether they served in Pickett's division or not, whether they came from Virginia or not — held up the Virginia division for special praise. Georgian John B. Gordon, still a virulent critic of James Longstreet, nonetheless saluted his Virginians with the admission that "the point where Pickett's

Virginians, under Kemper, Garnett, and Armistead, in their immortal charge, swept over the rock wall, has been appropriately designated by the Government as 'the high-water mark of the Rebellion.'"[87] E. Porter Alexander apportioned blame for the failure of the charge among Lee, Longstreet, ordnance and quartermaster problems, reconnaissance shortcomings, poor staff work, and, especially, badly deployed artillery. Still, even in his analytical prose, he praised the Virginians and their leader, "who was riding with his staff in rear of his division."[88] Longstreet's chief of staff Moxley Sorrel described Pickett as "a singular figure indeed"; and his assault deserved to rank among "the greatest feats of arms in all the annals of war." He knew that the story of July 3 still inspired deep feelings of pride: "Well do we know that amid all things to happen, the memory of Pickett's charge will forever live in song and story of that fair land for which the Southern soldier poured out his blood like water."[89] Longstreet died in 1904, but his widow Helen Dortsch Longstreet carried on the fight to clear his name of any stain of responsibility for the South's defeat at Gettysburg, reiterating always his praise for the Virginians he sent across the valley.[90]

So tightly had Virginians closed ranks around Pickett's men that any criticism aimed at them or their leader was quashed before it could do any harm. In 1908, in explaining why he did not publish his detailed study of the battle at Five Forks, Virginia cavalryman Thomas T. Munford described how difficult it had become to write about Pickett and other Confederate leaders who had absented themselves from their commands to attend Gen. Thomas Rosser's infamous shad bake and feasted on fresh fish when the Northern attack broke. "Gen. Pickett was the rashest officer commanding the whole, Gen. Fitz Lee ranking cavalry officer and Rosser the *entertaining officer* at the *shad lunch*," Munford explained. The irresponsible commanders left their subordinates "like *tin soldiers*, to hold their position without orders for any emergency," and the Confederate lines around Petersburg crumbled when Five Forks fell into Union hands. Three of Munford's associates read and commended his study of the fight that put Lee's army on the road to Appomattox, but they feared publishing it would do more to promote controversy and draw criticism from friends of Pickett and Fitz Lee than it would add to historical knowledge. Not wanting to make himself a target of the partisans of deceased "officers who could *not answer* for themselves," Munford regretfully adhered to the suggestion of his friends, who "advise me not to *print*."[91]

Undoubtedly, Munford understood the power that friends of Pickett and his men commanded. They had rallied to silence both the internal

Virginia threat and the external challenge of North Carolina and its allies. They had learned how to use a full range of weapons, from shows of outrage to subtle nuance. They had always been skilled storytellers. They had become superb debaters and defeated all critics with remarkable ease.

Appearing gracious in victory, some Virginians generously accorded occasional tidbits of acknowledgment or praise to those who had lost the literary war. Captain Bright admitted that some of Garnett's men told him that perhaps sixty men from Alabama and North Carolina, "without formation of any military kind," had fought at the wall with them.[92] Similarly, Robert W. Douthat of the 11th Virginia explained that he called the attack "Pickett's Charge" simply because "the world has chosen to give it" that name. He would not boast that the Virginians served more heroically than the Tennesseans, Alabamians, North Carolinians, or Mississippians that day, since there was "certainly glory enough in the Charge for all."[93] At this point, these were harmless concessions.

The sentiments they expressed may have been genuine, but such comments too often came off as mockery when buried among more general criticisms of the conduct of troops other than the Virginians. Bright, for one, briefly praised a few individual North Carolinians but only after recounting in fine detail his meeting with "English Gordon," a former British officer who told Pickett, "My men are not going up today." When Pickett ordered Gordon to hold his men to their duty, he had replied, "You know, Pickett, I will go as far with you as any other man, if only for old acquaintance sake" (they allegedly had opposed each other during the San Juan affair in 1859–60), but he just could not guarantee the conduct of his men. Bright neglected to add that Lt. Col. George T. Gordon of the 34th North Carolina suffered a severe leg wound while he was leading his veterans nearly to the wall.[94]

More typically now, of course, Virginians used a Pickett's Charge–style frontal assault to destroy the credibility of all potential critics. George L. Christian spearheaded the most direct counterattack on North Carolina's version of the events of July 3 when his report for the history committee of the Grand Camp of Confederate Veterans of Virginia took on—item by item—nearly every major contention the Tar Heels ever made. Christian urged all Virginians to stick to their well-established war record so it could not be "misunderstood or misrepresented by either friend or foe." The inflammatory North Carolina Historical and Literary Society's pamphlets especially "*demand* consideration and attention," since these works promoted the image of the Old North State "at the expense of Virginia."

Christian tore apart key North Carolina assertions. When the Old

North State claimed to provide 126,000 soldiers for the Confederate army —as compared with Virginia's 76,000—Christian cited Bureau of Conscription figures: 153,876 Virginians in the ranks and 88,475 North Carolinians. He also demanded that North Carolina subtract from its rolls the 13,000 South Carolinians who crossed state borders for a higher bounty. To the charge that Virginians held too many civil appointments, Christian cited the Conscript Bureau's list of men relieved of military service by virtue of their civilian positions; only 25,063 Virginians won exemptions compared to 38,166 North Carolina residents who did. North Carolinians who wanted to believe that the stout work of its 1st Infantry at Big Bethel helped to hold a wavering Old Dominion in the Confederacy had to remember that "*Virginia was a 'battle-ground' from the beginning to the close of the war*," and "*Virginia was the only state dismembered by the war*." Christian doubted that any part of North Carolina's "First at Bethel, Farthest to the Front at Gettysburg and Chickamauga, Last at Appomattox" motto could survive objective scrutiny. Recent claims that " 'Chancellorsville' was a 'North Carolina fight' " bothered him, too.

Christian reserved much of his strongest argument to dispute North Carolina's claim for deepest penetration of the Union line on July 3 at Gettysburg. "We were there," he wrote, and "we did not think then, and do not think now, that Pettigrew's and Pender's went so far." He used official reports to strengthen his own case and cited inconsistencies in reports from Pettigrew's and Trimble's commands to reach his predictable conclusion: "*Every one of the official reports*, both Federal and Confederate (with the exception of Colonel Shepherd, of Archer's Brigade, not composed of Carolinians), which refer to the troops who entered the enemy's works, *point unmistakably to those of Pickett's Virginians. . . . None of the official reports from the officers commanding the North Carolina troops make any such claim for their troops*—a claim that would certainly have been made if the facts had warranted it." He dismissed outright the 55th North Carolina's claims for farthest advance up Cemetery Ridge based on the location of Captain Satterfield's corpse. "Every soldier knows that the *'front' of an army is wherever its line of battle is (whether that line is zigzag or straight), and the opposing troops which penetrate that line are farther to the front, than those which do not*." [95]

Christian could be just as guilty as the North Carolinians he attacked when it came to bending the historical record to his own needs, however. Still, as time passed, the aging Virginians could not limit their concerns to the preservation of their own cherished memories. It became equally essential to hand down these glories unsullied to future generations. The persistence of cherished images in a wide variety of historical works, biographies, and literary anthologies written early in the twentieth century had to please them. They found the story of Virginia's finest moment in a secure place in the nation's memory.

Virginians took pleasure in how well Northerners with no veterans' constituency to satisfy embraced Pickett's men and their charge. A New Yorker asked Rawley Martin to recount the attack because "the charge of Pickett's Division outrivals the storied heroism of the Old Guard of Napoleon," adding that he believed "the old First Confederate Army Corps could have whipped the best two corps in Napoleon's army, taken in the zenith of his fame." [96] *Confederate Veteran* reprinted "Pickett's Division at Gettysburg" by Massachusetts author Charles A. Patch, who wrote that the Virginians "were blown away from the cannon's mouth, but the line did not waver" while "Pettigrew's weak division was broken, fleeing, and almost annihilated." If Pickett's men had been properly supported, the Northerner concluded, they would "possibly have established the Southern Confederacy." [97]

Better still, standard American history texts, even those written by Northerners, seemed to have accepted Virginia's version of the event, even while they still did not master its factual foundations. John Clark Ridpath wrote of the "18,000 men, in three divisions, under Armistead, Garnett, and Pettigrew," all led by Pickett in "the most memorable charge ever witnessed in America." [98] Benson Lossing's encyclopedia described a Southern battle line three miles in length, with Pickett and his 15,000 Virginians in the vanguard. [99] Even prominent New England historian James Ford Rhodes described Union soldiers watching the advance of "Pickett and his fifteen thousand with suspense, with admiration," until Hancock "showed the same reckless courage as Pickett" and repelled them. [100]

The Virginia Historical Committee displayed far greater interest in children's textbooks than they showed in popular or general histories. Members gave Philip A. Bruce's *School History of the United States* only weak approval, for instance, because he did not "state the South's position in reference to the late war as strongly as it can or should be stated to our children," a serious mistake for a Virginia author to make. [101] No doubt a work such as *Half-Hours in Southern History* suited many Virginians better. It considered questions such as "Why did Longstreet not reinforce Pickett in his famous charge?" As "all the World Wondered," a reviewer rhymed in explanation that the charge failed because "some one had blundered." Proving that anti-Longstreet sentiment died slowly in some parts of Virginia, the committee asserted that on July 3 "the South would have won the battle of Gettysburg and with that her independence, if General Lee's wishes had been obeyed as [Stonewall] Jackson would have obeyed them." [102]

The same committee also reviewed books that touched on Southern culture as well as its history. They criticized a volume entitled *Stepping Stones to Literature* for its failure to include sufficient examples of Southern writing and rhetoric. Alluding to Pickett's Charge, they argued that "the South has produced orators whose impetuous eloquence has made men rush with a glad cheer into the very jaws of death." [103] They had a point. Ever since the late 1880s, when the American literary world had rediscovered the South, Virginians had taken full advantage of the interest. When Thomas Nelson Page began "Run to Seed" with "Jim's father died at Gettysburg; up against the Stone Fence," no one wondered what fence he meant. They also understood why "this fact was much to Jim, though no one knew it; it tempered his mind; ruled his life." [104]

According to historian Sheldon Van Auken, the Southern historical novel of the early twentieth century "was the fruit of the Virginia culture rather than of the South as a whole." [105] By this time, moreover, Page and his romantic literary style had given way to other writers—those who found in the Civil War the inspiration to experiment with newer, more realistic literary forms. Mary Johnston set her novels in the dirty camps and on the bloody battlefields of the Army of Northern Virginia. She may well have drawn inspiration from the wartime Richmond press coverage of Pickett's Charge to produce this kind of prose: "Out from the ranks of the gray fortress's defenders rushed a grey, world-famous charge. It was a division charging—three brigades *en echelon*,—five thousand men, led by a man with long auburn locks." They marched on toward "a curious, unearthly light, the light of a turn in human affairs, the light of catastrophe, the light of an ending and a beginning." In other offerings, she described the charge as "fit to draw the fierce eyes and warm the gloomy souls of all the warrior deities. Woden may have watched" as Pickett's men swept up the slope of Cemetery Ridge. But she wrote of gore, not of glory. When the charge was repulsed, the "fields were all carpeted, a beautiful carpet, a costly carpet, more costly than Axminster or velvet. The figures were horses and men all matted and woven together with skeins of scarlet thread." [106]

Northerners could not muster up a similar literary style, although their images shared important similarities with those constructed by their Virginia counterparts. They, too, wrote as if only Pickett's men had made that great charge. Poet T. C. Harbaugh saluted the "Five thousand by Generals heroically led / And after the battle three thousand lay dead." With wonderful irony, he portrayed a child "at play 'mid the blossoms that blew, /

With never a sigh for the brave Pettigrew."[107] Novelist Elsie Singmaster wrote of Pickett's men charging on, lured by the silence of the Union artillery, until the guns suddenly reopened. In traditional Northern style, she savored the results: "The joy in the Union army was indescribable. Shouting their triumph, they forgot the long marches, the privations, the miseries; they even forgot their comrades lying all about them in terrible positions of agony. The battle of Gettysburg was won."[108]

As the golden anniversary celebration neared, Virginia had secured a special place in history and memory for Pickett and his men. James Crocker understood why they had needed to do this:

> Before our dead are counted, there arose from that bloody immortalized field, Fame, the Mystic Goddess, and from her trumpet in clarion notes there rang out upon the ear of the world the story of Pickett's charge at Gettysburg. All over this country, equally North and South, millions listened and returned applause. Over oceans Fame wings her way. Along the crowded population and cities of Europe she rings out the story. The people of every brave race intently listen and are thrilled. Over the famous battlefields of modern and ancient times she sweeps. Over the ruins and dust of Rome the story is heralded. Thermopylae hears and applauds.

As he strained for every bit of eloquence he could muster, Crocker finally concluded: "The intrinsic merit of the charge of Pickett's men at Gettysburg, is too great, too immortal of sections, of states, or of local pride."[109] All of Virginia—and *most* of the nation—heartily concurred.

8

HAND-GRIPS
AT THE
SACRED WALL

"If there is one spot on the battlefield that should be sacred it is this stretch from where Hancock fell, wounded, to the Brian House, along which Pickett's Division of Virginians beat in vain in the grandest charge of the century, and which has gone into history as designating the 'high-water mark of the rebellion,'" a Northern editor proclaimed.[1] In July 1913, fifty years after they faced each other as enemies, thousands of aging warriors from both armies reassembled at Gettysburg as if to validate that claim. When old men in blue reached across the low stone wall to shake the hands of old men in gray, few present could resist the power of the emotionally charged scene.

But what did that scene represent? For fifty years, efforts to preserve and mark that bloody battleground had been aided and hindered alike by the forces of both history and memory. Those charged with the stewardship of the field discovered over and over again that postbattle reports and the physical conformation of the terrain did not mesh always with "certainties" in old soldiers' minds. Thus, while they had done all they could to protect historical truth, they had not resolved every controversy, including some that swirled around the events of July 3. The golden anniversary ceremonies would measure how much that did, or did not, matter.

The preservation effort at Gettysburg included two main elements.

The first, land acquisition, included securing control of the battle's key terrain features and then building roads, paths, and bridges to make it accessible to visitors while protecting it from excessive wear. The second, the accurate marking of the battle lines, required strict supervision over the location and design of the memorials, which included ensuring that the inscriptions on all markers explained objectively the events that took place on that bit of Pennsylvania landscape. Neither task proved easy.

The drive to preserve the conflict's military geography began shortly after the smoke of battle cleared. In August 1863, David McConnaughy of Gettysburg decided that "there could be no more fitting and expressive memorial of the heroic valor and signal triumph of our Army . . . than the Battle-field itself, with its natural and artificial defenses preserved and perpetuated in the exact form & condition they presented during the Battle."[2] The cemetery that Abraham Lincoln consecrated in November 1863 made a small first step toward saving part of the Union position, and in 1864, Pennsylvania chartered the Gettysburg Battlefield Memorial Association and appropriated $6,000 for the purchase of land on Cemetery Hill, Culp's Hill, and Little Round Top.[3]

This initial preservation effort flagged in the late 1860s and early 1870s. As early as 1867, a visitor to Gettysburg noted that the passage of even one more year would "obliterate all traces of where so many Rebel leaders and followers lay buried" on the slopes of Cemetery Ridge, especially because "the ground is cultivated without regard to the remains of the misguided men who lie beneath it."[4] Finally, in the late 1870s, Pennsylvania's Department of the Grand Army of the Republic helped the memorial association revitalize its preservation efforts, chiefly by supporting the purchase of additional acreage.

Buying the land was an essential first step. Maintaining it as it looked in 1863 proved far more difficult. Just after the battle, a New York reporter described the ground of the July 3 charge: "It must not be supposed that the space between the ridges is an even plain, shaven with the scythe and levelled by the roller." Indeed, the land between the ridges "rises and falls gently and with little regularity, but in no place is it steep of ascent. Were it not for its ununiformity and for its occasional sprinkling of trees over its surface, it could be compared to a patch of rolling prairie in miniature."[5] It would be difficult to preserve the 1863 contour lines in an area that continued to be farmed actively. Some old soldiers understood the inevitability that the ground on which they fought would not remain undisturbed. As a Union veteran looked out over the scene of the fighting of July 3, he told some Southern visitors, "Oh, it's all changed." He pointed to a spot where Confederate troops had taken shelter in a depression "and

Union veterans return to the high water mark on November 19, 1885, to help mark their lines. Historian John Bachelder is second from the left, II Corps historian F. A. Walker is third from the left, and General Hancock is sixth from the left. (Massachusetts Commandery, MOLLUS, USAMHI)

my company just poured shot into you and slaughtered you like flies. But the hole isn't there now. It has been filled in in the course of years. Everything is different now."[6]

But not every veteran who returned to Gettysburg chose to accept that reality, and they often superimposed faded memories on terrain features that did not exist in 1863. The passage of time, changes in natural terrain, even the addition of roadways to the battlefield, all helped to confuse the historical record. In 1885, when he saw a plan for an avenue along Cemetery Ridge on the southern fringes of the field of Pickett's Charge, Winfield S. Hancock expressed the fear that the road might be mistaken for the line of battle, adding, "I think the actual lines were somewhat in advance of the road, between the Vermont position and the Stonehouse."[7]

All these changes greatly complicated the second task facing the battlefield's stewards: marking the battle lines. That effort, too, began soon after the fighting ended. Even before the dead were buried, John B. Bachelder—often called "the government historian"—began to interview wounded soldiers, especially Southerners, to gather specifics about the battle. By 1873, he had talked to thousands of enlisted men and "the officers of every regiment and battery of the Army of the Potomac." In addition, he walked over the battlefield with more than 1,000 officers who fought at Gettysburg, "forty-six of them generals in command."[8]

Bachelder tried hard to reconcile the physical evidence of the battlefield with hundreds of soldiers' memories about July 3. In a battlefield guidebook he published in 1873, he seems to have reached some preliminary conclusions: Aimed at "a peculiar, umbrella-shaped copse of trees" on the II Corps front, the assaulting force's front line "consisted of Pickett's division, on its right; Pettigrew's division, on the left. Trimble's division advanced in the second line." Some confusion still remained in his mind, too; he placed Anderson's division in a third line, and while he rightly deployed Lang and Wilcox on Pickett's right, he also put Thomas and McGowan on Pettigrew's left. The Confederates pierced the Union line at the copse of trees, but Northern forces quickly closed that gap and counterattacked on both flanks to turn back the Southerners. Those trees, he wrote, marked "unquestionably the *high water mark of this battle, and of the war!*"[9]

The flaws in Bachelder's early assessment of the July 3 action revealed the existence of great numbers of disputed points about the charge and its repulse, most of which emerged from his interviews. He wondered, for instance, how much credit to give Stannard's Vermonters for their attack against Pickett's right flank. Could their claim of collapsing the Virginians' line stand objective scrutiny? Vermonters certainly thought so. Even before the end of 1863, G. G. Benedict, the Second Vermont Brigade's champion on all questions related to Gettysburg, already had warned Bachelder against taking seriously a "rebel statement that our 'flanking party' was dispersed and scattered in confusion."[10] Bachelder had to weigh the Vermonters' claims against the reliability of Col. Theodore Gates, who asserted that the 80th New York and the 151st Pennsylvania did the real fighting "in front of the left of the 2nd Corps."[11] How should he deal with the concerns of Col. George N. Macy of the 20th Massachusetts, who felt that too many battle accounts had extended the "left of Stannard's troops . . . too far to the front" noting that "they did not run so far towards the Emmitsburg Road—or so much at right angles"?[12] And these variants concerned only one small bit of action on July 3.

Bachelder found his efforts to relate personal recollections to the physical evidence on the ground of the July 3 fighting hampered by several problems he could not solve. Most trying in the first decade after the war was that Confederate survivors showed little interest in helping him.

In November 1865, James L. Kemper, Pickett's surviving brigade commander, refused to cooperate with Bachelder's quest for information. "It is obvious, from his own showing that ninety-nine hundredths of his material is drawn from Northern sources," Kemper complained to a friend, fearing as well that "any such prominence of my command in a Northern version of the Battle of Gettysburg would bear too much resemblance to the exhibition of the captive behind the triumphal ear of the Roman Imperator—to suit either my taste or my principles." The general concluded: "The day for the history of that battle is not yet. It will come." Bachelder no doubt cheered when James Longstreet agreed to be interviewed at about the same time Kemper refused. He knew that time was an enemy, when as early as 1865, Kemper raised concerns that "the facts assumed or implied in the questions which Col. B. proposed to me, in reference to the movements of my division and brigade are almost wholly imaginary and mythical." [13]

Bachelder feared that if he could not get Southerners to cooperate, his efforts to mark their battle lines would fail and render the historical record biased and incomplete. Most of his efforts in the 1860s and 1870s to bring Confederate veterans to Gettysburg to walk the ground of July 3 proved unsuccessful. When he invited senior officers from both armies to tour the field with him in August 1869, Walter Harrison of Pickett's staff came, but he later noted that "there was no general officer of the late Confederate army there, and consequently no effort made to establish the position of those troops by any landmarks." [14] For years, Bachelder simply could not soften Southern veterans' reluctance to come back to Gettysburg. An officer in the Jeff Davis Legion informed him curtly that the soldiers he most needed to talk to could not play the role of "professional veteran" since most of them were killed in action. [15] More to the point, as a South Carolinian noted, "We old Confederates are too poor to make such a trip." [16] For reasons they could not explain, plenty of Pickett's men—including Captain Bright and Colonel Hunton—never could make themselves return to Gettysburg.

Bachelder's second big problem stemmed from the highly selective memories of those veterans who did agree to cooperate with him. As if to warn Bachelder about this likelihood, George G. Meade himself admitted to a bit of uncertainty about his actions on July 3. His own mental haziness showed "that in the excitement of battle no individual's memory unsupported by corroborative evidence is to be relied on, however honest and truthful the individual may be." [17] True to Meade's prediction, many veterans told Bachelder stories that revealed the taint of the wartime press, overactive imaginations, or wishful thinking.

George G. Meade Jr., the Union commander's son and a member of his staff, explained the quandary in which many returning veterans found themselves. When he visited Gettysburg in 1882, "everything came back to me as if it had only just occurred," but he also "could not locate the exact points, and the impression left on my mind, was how much smaller and more contracted the fields and ground were than my recollection of them." [18] So many old soldiers assured Bachelder they recalled events as clearly as if they had occurred the previous day, no wonder he grew increasingly skeptical. By the early 1890s, when two North Carolina officers offered to show Bachelder their lines, he warned them that "entirely new data is always looked upon with distrust." He knew by now that when veterans came to the battlefield, they already "have talked the subject over, adding little by little, until unintentionally, their story is not historically correct." [19]

Bachelder's third challenge came from veterans and veterans groups who disagreed with his conclusions about their role in the battle. As Superintendent of Tablets and Legends until 1887, he possessed the authority to control the placement of monuments and the wording of the memorials' inscriptions. [20] Some Pennsylvania veterans believed Bachelder allowed himself to be misled by "men who undertook to describe the position miles from the scene" and as a result misplaced many of their state monuments. [21] Still others disputed his analysis of the historical record and pushed for specific emendations that would enhance their actions. Pvt. John Buckley of the 69th Pennsylvania wanted Bachelder to emphasize "how so few men behind the wall made themselves so effective" on July 3 by loading discarded rifles the previous evening with rounds of English-made "buck and ball" ammunition; when they fired these specially loaded rifles at a range of fifty yards, "the slaughter was terrible." [22] Thomas Galwey sent an article he wrote about the 8th Ohio's attack against Pettigrew's left flank to Bachelder with the strong suggestion that he look again at an action "so singular . . . that it seems to me worthy of special notice." [23]

Until the War Department took administrative authority over Gettysburg in the 1890s, Bachelder tried hard to live up to the memorial association's commitment to historical accuracy. One special project became his personal legacy. Just before the silver anniversary, association leaders asked him to plan a monument to commemorate the "high water mark of the Confederacy." His design, an open book of bronze—"the record of history"—supported by piles of cannonballs, became the first truly national memorial at Gettysburg. Here, officially recorded, Pettigrew's and Trimble's men and all the troops of the Union I Corps that took part in the action of July 3 shared the stage with Pickett's Virginians and Hancock's II Corps. Significantly, Bachelder chose as its most prominent legend, "High Water Mark of the Rebellion. This copse of trees was the landmark towards which Longstreet's assault was directed, July 3, 1863." He would not call the attack "Pickett's Charge." [24]

Bachelder died in 1894, and both irony and justice attach to the War Department's acceptance of administrative responsibility for the newly designated "national military park" at about the same time. Everything Bachelder tried to do to mark troop positions took on greater importance now that military and congressional leaders had begun to tout the utility of Civil War battlefields as "classrooms" for instructing army and National Guard officers. Many Civil War veterans strongly supported the completion of the historian's work. Cavalryman J. Irvin Gregg suggested that the marking of the Southern lines finally would make the lessons of Gettysburg "not only cogent but conclusive."[25] Dan Sickles argued that once both armies' positions were marked, Gettysburg "should be a military post, garrisoned by Artillery. With all its movements preserved it would be an object lesson of patriotism through untold centuries."[26] Former Confederate cavalryman Joe Wheeler offered an extra incentive; with the Southern lines formally marked, "the States to which these troops belonged would gladly go to the expense of erecting suitable monuments."[27]

War Department officials appreciated the importance of promoting the nation's military heritage with appropriate memorials, but it understood the greater need to get the facts straight. At Gettysburg, the responsibility for preparing the text for the hundreds of government markers erected around the turn of the century fell to a board of three commissioners. To ensure objectivity, at least one had to be a Confederate veteran. William McKendree Robbins, former major of the 4th Alabama, accepted the primary responsibility for the tablets commemorating the Southern units in the July 3 charge.

Robbins's commitment to objectivity, strong as it was, could have been colored by his personal feelings. Although he served with Alabama troops, Robbins was born in North Carolina. When Gen. Stephen D. Lee wanted a copy of Bond's *Pickett or Pettigrew*, Robbins put him in direct contact with its author.[28] When Walter Clark asked him to write about the charge for the North Carolina regimental series, Robbins had complied.[29] He also recommended disapproval of a request for a marker to Garnett's brigade near the alleged spot where the general died outside the Angle, citing precedents that limited the placement of monuments to main battle lines.[30] As George L. Christian prepared to write his scathing critique of North Carolina claims at Gettysburg, he sought Robbins's opinions but did not use his comment that "the left of Pickett & the right of Pettigrew and Trimble pushed forward & went equally far, as the testimony of impartial Union witnesses proves & the front lines of Confed. dead indicated to all observers."[31] When Robbins read staff officer Robert A. Bright's 1904 article on Pickett's Charge, he called it "interesting, but like everything written on this subject by Virginians [it] is lacking in fairness to soldiers of the other States." He shared his feelings with Bright: "Yankees in that battle have told me that the commands from other States left their dead as far to the front & close to the Union lines as the Virginians."[32]

Regardless of his personal feelings, Robbins relied upon Bachelder's voluminous data and talked to veterans himself to prepare the inscriptions for the official battlefield markers. In explaining his conclusion that Pickett's and Pettigrew's men advanced equally far, he wrote former artilleryman Porter Alexander that "Union officers who viewed the grounds that same evening have told me often that Pettigrew's dead west of the wall and Pickett's dead east of the wall formed one straight north and south line, this showing where both stopped."[33] It should come as no surprise, then, that no battlefield marker for either Pickett's three brigades or Pettigrew's and Trimble's commands makes extravagant claims or offers hostile criticisms. Nor does the phrase "Pickett's Charge" appear. Robbins made the "Pickett-Pettigrew-Trimble Assault" the official designation for the charge. Robbins's influence could be detected further in a comprehensive history of the battlefield published during his tenure, a work that specifically praised Pettigrew's and Trimble's men.[34]

Perhaps there is some sad justice in that Robbins did not live to see so much of this turn-of-the-century interpretation effort overwhelmed by the emotional appeal of Virginia's version of events. In the years leading up to the golden anniversary ceremonies, it became increasingly clear that historical inaccuracy, unfairness and all, had not prevented Americans from embracing the Old Dominion's images of Pickett's Charge.

By now, when history and popular memory clashed, history rarely won. In September 1906, about 800 members and friends of the Pickett's Division Association and the Philadelphia Brigade Association met at Gettysburg one last time. "No such reunion could be held by British and Boer veterans, by the soldiers of Russian and Japan or by those of France and Germany," a Northern veteran bragged. "Only here in the United States could former foes meet as friends."[35] Pennsylvanian Joseph McCarroll returned to Pickett's men the captured sword of Lewis Armistead, which had been stored with care since July 1863. Capt. Thomas D. Jeffress of the 56th Virginia accepted the blade, and Pickett's men resolved to display it in the Confederate Museum at Richmond, next to a small American flag and with a legend bearing the general's last command: "It is the Philadelphia brigade; give them the cold steel, boys."[36] Watching with approval were Sallie Pickett and her son, now Maj. George E. Pickett, U.S. Army.[37]

As the ranks of the "old soldiers" thinned rapidly, the most active period of building memorials passed with them. Reflective observers did not miss its cumulative effect: "Gettysburg is the one great battlefield in this country—or in the world for that matter—which has been scrupulously preserved and turned into an easily studied and tastefully marked and embellished military park." The federal government and individual states had spent millions of dollars to consecrate "a place steeped in inspiring associations and a true shrine of American patriotism."[38]

This last comment summed up Americans' truest perception about the importance of Gettysburg. Despite the commissioners' intentions to right the historical record, "Pickett's Charge"—and whatever sentiments that name evoked—struck a deeper chord with most people than the realities of July 3 ever could. Preparations for the golden anniversary unleashed both practical and interpretive problems for the newly formed Battle of Gettysburg Commission, and in the end, even after all the effort to preserve an accurate history of the battle, the ceremonies played chiefly to memory.

Before any celebration could begin, however, the committee had to find ways to finance it. Pennsylvania National Guard Lt. Col. Lewis E. Beitler, the commission's field secretary, carried most of the administrative load. He wooed the governors and state legislatures of the Northern and Southern states whose soldiers fought at Gettysburg. To promote the idea that this anniversary truly belonged to the entire nation, he helped to guide legislation for federal funding through Congress and watched President William H. Taft sign a bill to match the $150,000 Pennsylvania had already committed. When money ran short, he successfully convinced Pennsylvania legislators to increase the state's contribution.[39]

Not wanting to waste a cent of the funds he raised, Beitler broke from the usual practice of allowing veterans groups to run their own gatherings. To care for the estimated 40,000 expected to attend, he cobbled together a team from the Regular U.S. Army, the Pennsylvania National Guard, and the Boy Scouts to operate the encampment. The army's quartermaster department supplied cots, blankets, mess equipment, food, medical supplies, and sanitation facilities. Using an estimate of ten deaths per day among the old soldiers, they even brought fifty coffins.[40] Brig. Gen. Hunter Liggett accepted formal command of the encampment.

Matériel arrangements could be complicated, but, in many ways, unforeseen problems of another sort that surfaced during the planning caused more worry. When some Southerners expressed a desire to wear their old uniforms and bring their battle flags, some Union veterans voiced their opposition. Gov. John Tener of Pennsylvania, official host of the ceremonies, defused the controversy by issuing a public statement that "whether the uniform be blue or gray, the wearer will be heartily welcome." GAR posts united behind Tener. Former Union artilleryman

Andrew Cowan, whose guns had blasted Pickett's men with double canister, wanted to see both flags fly again: "The starry banner and the Southern cross—unfurl them again at Gettysburg. The celebration would be colorless without them."[41]

Southerners, too, did their part to assure Northerners that they intended to celebrate the completion of national reunion. Even though Colonel Beitler won their special praise for silencing rumors "that the Confederate flag and the gray uniforms would be objectionable at Gettysburg," United Confederate Veterans (UCV) leader C. Irvine Walker made sure everyone knew that they were coming to Pennsylvania "not to battle, but to seal a lasting peace." He asserted that Southerners "will show that we are willing to bury forever the bitterness of the past."[42]

Among the most visible Southerners promoting the celebration as an end to sectional rivalry was Sallie Pickett. She told national audiences that she perceived her frequent visits to Gettysburg as neither an insult to the North nor an embarrassment to the South. "Three phases of loyalty sway the Southern heart to-day," she argued, "loyalty to memory, loyalty to present duty, loyalty to hope." She saw no rivalry among these sentiments, for "he who is untrue to the past is recreant to the present and faithless to the future."[43]

Sallie drew attention to the golden anniversary celebration in many ways. She republished *Pickett and His Men* in time to promote both popular interest and profits. "Stirring history Pickett and his men made, and Mrs. Pickett has recorded it remarkably well," wrote a reviewer, who expressed delight that she wrote more on "the doings of Pickett's men than on their leader's."[44] Sallie also wrote a novel entitled *The Bugles of Gettysburg*, employing every Victorian literary device and excess imaginable, to tell the tale of a brother officer of her Soldier, who served with him in the Old Army and returned to Virginia with him in 1861. "Like most romances of the war time there is a big Virginia mansion, and a slim, dark-haired girl in white," wrote the rare reviewer who did not pan the work as unrelievedly sappy. Sallie described Pickett's Charge "from within, as it were," the Virginians following "their slender, long-haired general into the valley of smoke and bursting shells."[45] If literary critics hated the book, Pickett's men loved it, and at $1.10 a copy, advertisers touted it as "a book every veteran will want."[46]

Sallie even promoted the spirit of reunion in *Cosmopolitan Magazine*. "The Wartime Story of General Pickett by Mrs. General George E. Pickett" appeared as a serial almost monthly for the year before the golden anniversary ceremonies at Gettysburg. Her stories were familiar to those who had read her earlier literary efforts, but that hardly mattered. In a slightly more restrained tone than she usually used, Sallie produced yet another effusive monument to her husband. "Great events often hang on small incidents," she wrote of Heth's search for shoes that allegedly brought the armies to Gettysburg. After reviewing the fights of the first and second days, she botched the July 3 deployments: "Pickett's three brigades were to attack in front where there was a bristling hedge of artillery and infantry; Pettigrew and Trimble to charge in second and third lines of battle; Wilcox to join Pettigrew. Anderson was behind the two supporting divisions to take Trimble's place."[47]

Even if she got her facts wrong, Sallie knew exactly how to keep the spotlight on her husband. With great deliberation, she described how "Pickett, with Lee and Longstreet," made a long reconnaissance of the Confederate line. After the artillery stopped, he penned a final missive to her and mounted his spirited charger. "His long, dark-auburn hair floated backward in the wind as he rode down the slope of death." No doubt state pride made her write in error that "at the head of each regiment floated the dark-blue flag of Virginia"; Pickett's men actually marched under their square Confederate battle flags. But few cared. Her final comments saluted something far more important: the courage, coolness, discipline, and endurance that "has made the story of Pickett's charge the glory of American arms."[48]

Sallie further sentimentalized the golden anniversary when she compiled *The Heart of a Soldier; as Revealed in the Intimate Letters of General George E. Pickett, C.S.A.*, a series of forty-four letters from Pickett to Sallie between September 1861 through the postwar years, to "stir the heart of every American."[49] These notes, wrote one reviewer, had earned "their place as a vital part of the courage and heroism that lives in the history of our great war."[50] Somehow Pickett found time to write Sallie a six-page letter just before his great charge. His well-documented confidence on the field clashes sharply with his words: "A wail of regret went up from my very soul that the other two brigades of my old division had been left behind. Oh, God!—if only I had them!—a surety for the honor of Virginia." When the artillery stopped, Pickett prayed, "Oh, God in mercy help me as He never helped before!"[51] His letter of July 4 mourned the men who "eagerly offered up their lives on the altar of duty." At least one edition of the work included Sallie's editorial footnote informing readers that much had been excised from this letter, since her Soldier had written "material similar to General Pickett's [first] report to General Lee," which had been returned "to guard against dissensions."[52] Two days later, Pickett bemoaned the "sacrifice of life on that blood-soaked field on the fatal third" that "was too awful for the heralding of victory, even for our victorious foe, who, I think, believe as we do, that it decided the fate of our cause."[53] Eloquent words, indeed. The only problem, of course, is that in all probability, Pickett did not write them. Historians have debated their authenticity for years, and the weight of evidence bears decidedly toward Sallie as their true author because their content is based heavily on Harrison's *Pickett's Men*.[54]

The popularity of Sallie's work revealed a sentimental refrain that anniversary planners—consciously or not—embraced as well. Simply stated, this would not be a celebration of the "truth of history." The ceremonies needed only to provide tangible evidence of shared honor, the end of sectional ill will, and the commitment of both North and South to a common future. What kind of gesture could best get this message across? Robert W. Douthat, a captain in the 11th Virginia on that July 3 so long ago, wished that the veterans of both armies could face each other in two long lines, twenty feet apart. Then, as the two lines marched forward to meet each other, each soldier should grasp the hand of a former foe in a hearty handshake "and if possible utter the words: 'I forgive.'"[55] Gettysburg provided the perfect backdrop for a timely healing of old wounds.

As the time for the celebration neared, however, more somber notes sounded, too. The Progressive Era reform impulse inspired, among other things, a rebirth in peace activism. Peace advocates asserted that wars served no good purpose, devoured a nation's most valuable economic and human resources, and rarely solved the problems that started them. Believing that "no indictment of war is complete without an exhibit of a battle scene," J. Frank Hanly described the July 3 battle at Gettysburg: Cannons "vomit an avalanche of fire and iron" while destiny beckons the "gray, bellipotent hosts to death and glory." As the Southerners advance, "fearful missiles tear them to fragments. All seem to have become food for powder." Although "fragments of bodies, arms, legs, caps, and guns are thrown as from a caldron," they proceed on until the "colossal, monstrous crime is finished."[56] Expressing similar sentiments, a South Carolina editor urged his readers to think about Gettysburg's cost: "Let us realize, if we can, the horror of those three days. Let us picture, if we can, the carnage at the Bloody Angle. Let us feel, if we can, the grief that settled down upon thousands of hearts in the North and in the South when the lists of the dead were published." He reminded readers, "At Gettysburg men butchered one another. At Gettysburg thousands died in utmost agony. At Gettysburg good and gentle women were widowed and the happiness of homes was destroyed. Let us try to see the thing as it was—to see it in all its crimson horror and all its ghastly cruelty."[57]

Yet many more Americans believed that the war's unspeakable horrors held important lessons. An editor from Maine described the monuments that dotted the field of the July 3 charge as "really hideous and grotesque," but then he asked his readers to remember that their ugliness was "their first merit." Many of those statues had been carved by the village stone-cutter who "was sincerely and honestly commemorating in his best fashion the glory of common men like himself who left the plow and counter to go out and be great." Those who could not understand that should "go home and be made sound again."[58]

As July approached, a few hard-liners still refused to come around. At least once, the editor of *Confederate Veteran* refused to call the Gettysburg celebration a reunion because he felt the term had been taken over by Northerners and Southerners who "generally have no record back of them to elicit admiration, and the best soldier-veterans are repulsed by it on each side."[59] Black leaders also criticized the gathering. In their eyes, the trumpeting of the end of sectional ill will rejected the Union's war aim of emancipation. Organizers invited black veterans to participate fully in the celebrations, and a few went, but in Jim Crow America, they were housed on their own separate street in the tent camp. White veterans noticed them only in the evening, when they would "tune up a banjo, and they sing the old plantation melodies."[60]

After the nation had debated the great reunion's merits and its meaning, it began early in July with the arrival at Gettysburg of at least 35,000 Union veterans. Estimates of the total number of attendees ran as high as 56,000, but only a few more than 7,000 former Confederates attended; Virginia sent the largest group—estimated at 3,270—with North Carolina's 1,265 a distant second.[61]

The 1913 anniversary celebration took place during a stretch of the hottest weather south-central Pennsylvania had seen in years. Crowds mobbed specially installed water fountains and the vendors of ice cream and cold drinks. The heat did not spoil the good spirits of the attendees, however; a young spectator admired the "wonderful double army of old men" who enjoyed a reunion that "might have been theatrical if it had not been so spontaneous."[62]

With an eye to passing down to future generations the legacy of an honorable past, journalists took care to note the old soldiers' every word and action. The presence of distinguished visitors forged proud links to those long-ago days. Confederate generals Evander M. Law and Felix H. Robertson (son of the Gettysburg commander of the Texas Brigade) attended, along with Union general Lewis A. Grant. At a dignitaries' tent at the Lutheran Theological Seminary, a visitor met "two grandsons of George Pickett, undemonstrative lads of high school age," along with sons and grandsons of Generals Longstreet, Meade, and A. P. Hill. He could find no better symbol of national reunion than the moment in which a band played the national anthem, and all those "upon the dusky lawn— the Picketts, the Longstreets, the daughter of General Hill, the Meades, the long row of men in gray and gold—became silent, rose to their feet, and uncovered."[63]

On "Newspaper Row," two tents had been set aside for the only woman permitted to have quarters in the encampment: Helen Dortsch Longstreet, the widow of Lee's "Old War Horse." A guest of Pennsylvania, she wrote commentaries on the celebration that appeared in over fifty newspapers across the nation. She sounded a discordant note, complaining at this late date—and despite her late husband's frequent comments to the contrary—that the battle's "famed charge was Longstreet's." Reportedly, Dan Sickles had told her that "it is improper to call it Pickett's charge. It was made under the immediate command of Gen. Longstreet, who protested against it." Longstreet had told Sickles that " 'I obeyed Gen. Lee's positive command, a command issued against my protest, for I knew that the charge would cost a useless sacrifice of thousands of lives.' " Now his widow "felt his dumb agony as he looked upon the marching columns and knew that it was their death march." No one seemed interested in taking up her case for historical accuracy, however; her pleas generally were ignored.[64]

Almost any connection of the past to the present and future inspired the many photographers and journalists who swarmed the encampment. Hundreds of Boy Scouts who served as orderlies and runners listened for hours to the old soldiers' stories. "It is in the vital link thus forged between the passing and the coming generations that the great value of the Boy Scout contact with the veterans of the two armies really lies," wrote one observer. The reunion made it possible for the boys to enjoy the "heart-to-heart confidences of men who had faith in a cause, and showed their willingness to die for the faith," which "cannot but count for more than any printed page."[65] One Union veteran who shared his tales hoped they would "take away the last excuse for the young people to cherish any sectional hatred."[66]

The spirit of completed reunion flowed through dignitaries' speeches. Vice President Marshall noted, "There is now no difference between North and South except cold bread and hot biscuits."[67] Speaker of the House Champ Clark, who was eleven years old when Fort Sumter was fired on, told the audience how Gettysburg inspired his own generation: "Cold must be the heart of that American who is not proud to claim as countrymen the flower of the southern youth who charged up the slippery slopes of Gettysburg with peerless Pickett, or those unconquerable men in blue, who through three long and dreadful days held these beetling heights in face of fierce assaults. It was not Southern valor, or Northern valor. It was, thank God, American valor."[68] A visiting clergyman, noting on July 3, 1913, that "it is to the minute just fifty years ago by the stroke of the clock since Pickett's charge came to an end," feared that too many Americans failed to understand the reunion's full significance: "Never before in the world's history have two armies that stood against each other like two castles with cannon shotted to the muzzle, met in friendship, good will, and with a common enthusiasm for the same flag" only fifty years later.[69]

Only a few events disappointed the crowd. President Woodrow Wilson's address won few plaudits from some former Confederates who had looked forward to hearing the first postwar Southern president.[70] Still, the address did impress an Ohio editor who recorded that the president's "clear, patriotic voice" could clearly be heard at "that sacred spot . . . the Bloody Angle, where the flower of Virginia veterans under Pickett went to their doom, carrying the hopes of the Confederate cause with them."[71]

The veterans carried forward the theme of national reunion spontaneously. When one old Virginian got lost in the Union section of the tent camp, he met some of the veterans of the 1st Minnesota, which had helped to push back Pickett's men on July 3. He told them that he had served in the 28th Virginia. "That would be Olmstead's [Armistead's] forces, wouldn't it?" a Minnesotan asked. When the Virginian nodded, the Northerner asked with a gleam in his eye, "Comrade, what became of your flag that day up yonder?" "You Yanks got it, that's all I know," he replied. "Right! We got it then and we've got it right now," the Minnesotan said. "It's in St. Paul, you old son-of-a-gun, did you know that?" The Virginian stayed with them that night, and before he left the next morning, he admitted, "As long as some of you Yanks had to get that flag I'm mighty glad it was you-all. You-all are pretty good people."[72]

The scene replayed itself in reverse as well. "Old Man Clark" from the Philadelphia Brigade found his way into the Virginians' camp. To some of Pickett's survivors, he crowed, "We saw you coming, and we licked you, didn't we?" They admitted, "Yes, you-all licked us, but we crowded ye some." "All right, we did it," Clark replied, "and, Lord God, how I like to tell you about it!" The observer who witnessed the exchange noted with pride, "What greater proof that the war is over is required than the ability to accept such badinage good-naturedly!"[73]

A small contingent of men from the 111th New York of Hays's division took special pains to acknowledge that soldiers from commands other than Pickett's—without identifying Pettigrew's or Trimble's forces by name—"also gave their bravest and their best." They had not forgotten "that upon their regimental and company rolls are also often written the words, 'Killed at Gettysburg.'" A few Southerners especially appreciated that this tribute came from a Northern regiment "which lost seventy-one percent of its number" in that same fight.[74]

Standing out among the Confederate attendees, Pickett's men always attracted big crowds. Robert McCulloch, a veteran of Garnett's brigade and now president of the St. Louis Railway Company, told over and over how he and a "little knot wearing Pickett badges" met a group of Union veterans near the spot where "fifty years ago almost to the minute we had been almost as close together, but each seeking the other's life."[75] Those badges—each made of six inches of white silk about 2½ inches wide, topped with a gilt strip and a star, and emblazoned with the words "PICKETT'S MEN, 1863-1913"—became instant collectibles. The seal of Virginia with the state motto "*Sic Semper Tyrannis*" and "July 3rd, GETTYSBURG" finished off the design. The Latin motto raised eyebrows, since John Wilkes Booth had shouted those words at Ford's Theater after he shot Abraham Lincoln, but, as Virginians quickly explained, the motto had appeared on the state seal "long ere Booth was ever born."[76]

Edward G. Freeley, one of Pickett's men, drew a crowd nearly each time he claimed to be the man who actually "marked the highest place to which the spray of that charge of Southern chivalry reached." He pointed to one special spot and said, "There it is, right there, sir. No one got any further than that, and there three of them beat me down with the butt ends of their muskets." New Yorker Ross E. Graydon spoke up from the throng around Freeley: "Comrade, I wouldn't be a bit surprised if I was one of those fellows who banged you over the head, for I remember slamming one Johnnie who had got out ahead of his crowd and come romping right up here to the very guns of the battery we were supporting." Peering closely at Freeley, Graydon said, "Maybe you're that fellow—now, I wonder." Then the two clasped hands and gazed out over the field together.[77]

It somehow seemed appropriate that Virginian A. C. Smith and Pennsylvanian Albert N. Hamilton chose to visit the wall at the same time. In July 1863, Smith and some comrades of the 56th Virginia had just climbed over it when he was hit. He remembered that a Union soldier gave him some water and took him to the hospital. With a catch in his voice, Smith sighed, "He's gone to his reward by this time, I reckon." Hamilton, a veteran of the 72nd Pennsylvania, arrived at the wall with a different group of visitors just as Smith ended his story. He related how "it was right here that a Johnny fell into my arms. I lifted him up and gave him a swig of water, and then got him on my shoulders and carried him off, but . . ." At that point, Smith—who had been listening—looked closely at Hamilton's face. "Praise the Lord! Praise the Lord, it's YOU, brother!" he shouted. Then, the "two old foes fell into each other's arms, embracing."[78]

Naturally, all kinds of quaint items caught the interest of the reporters. I. E. Tibben of the 71st Pennsylvania wore his wartime uniform, including canteen, knapsack, blanket roll, and "a big cap that must have been sweltering hot" that day. Virginian William H. Turpin of the 53rd Virginia made an even more striking sight with his heavy blanket roll and "the same old suit, the coat tied together with strings and his feet bound up in burlap bagging, instead of shoes," just as he had been dressed on July 3, 1863. C. P. Deering of the 28th Virginia, taken prisoner at the wall, praised his captors: "The Yankees were sho'ly very nice to us." He had spent most of the next two years at Fort Delaware, but even there, they "had the finest hospital you ever saw, and they gave us different stuff every meal."[79]

A few of Pettigrew's men apparently slipped in with Pickett's veterans, but they won no special attention for their old command. Only a few individuals drew the reporters' notice. After an old Tar Heel veteran named John Caisan explained to a rapt audience near the Angle what he had done fifty years earlier, a man in blue interrupted to ask him to repeat his name. When Caisan complied, the Union veteran clasped the Southerner's hand. "What a singular coincidence, for my name is John Caisan, and I, too, come from Burlington, but it's Burlington, N.J., instead of North Carolina."[80] One of Lane's men probably won few friends at home after a reporter printed a recollection of his fears going into the charge: "Boys, we aren't going to take it. It's too far across."[81]

Soldiers who fought on other parts of the field clamored to see the site of the July 3 fight. "Interest centers about this, because the spot was accessible and well defined. It was the finish of the three days of bloody and fierce struggle, which in turn was the beginning of the end of the Confederate cause," wrote one reporter. "There is no American soldier—real soldier I mean—whether he wore the gray or whether he wore the blue, whose heart does not throb with pride at the valor and courage of his brother who made this deadly march and fierce fight."[82]

The reenactment of the great charge itself helped to sum up for many of the attendees all the many emotions of the day. About 3 P.M. on July 3, 1913—as close to the minute, fifty years later, as they could surmise—crowds gathered to watch about "500 all told, survivors of Pickett's Charge and the resisting forces" line up to face each other once more.[83] Pickett's men marched in double column, without arms, from the Emmitsburg Road to the stone wall. The 24th Virginia's Maj. William W. Bentley, who was wounded three times on that long-ago July 3, served as

*Virginia and Pennsylvania fly their flags at the stone wall at the golden anniversary ceremonies, July 1913. (*Fiftieth Anniversary of the Battle of Gettysburg*)*

their commander this day. Capt. T. C. Holland of the 28th Virginia served as adjutant. As they advanced, spectators swarmed around Pickett's men. Thomas O'Brian marched at the head of the column, carrying the only Confederate flag seen during the reunion. That flag, recalled one observer, "was a history in itself—aye, and a tragedy, too. . . . Nineteen standard bearers had dropped in bloody succession beneath those Stars and Bars on that awful day half a century before."[84]

As they climbed the slope, they approached the stone wall where fifty years ago had waited "the hated Yanks," and "behind that stone wall waited the Yanks to-day!" Maj. Robert Stokes and his adjutant, longtime Philadelphia Brigade Association leader John Frazier, led the Union contingent.[85]

One reporter described that final ascent as so steep that some young men found it a hard climb, "but the old men didn't seem to regard it as a difficult thing at all." Mark Boone of the 57th Virginia, aged 78, reached "that ancient, disputed wall" first. J. L. Rockwell of the 106th Pennsylvania, aged 72, helped him over.[86] Southerners clasped hands with smiling Northerners across the barricade. "Hand-grips! Hand-grips that spelled: *'One Nation; One Flag,'*" wrote one man.[87] After the Virginians climbed over the wall, a few walked over to the stone marking the place where Armistead fell. "They were the men who broke into the Union lines with him and saw him die," explained an onlooker, and as they gathered around the little monument, Northern men stood in silence with them.[88]

*Pickett's Virginians and Webb's Pennsylvanians shake hands at the stone wall,
July 1913. (Fiftieth Anniversary of the Battle of Gettysburg)*

Festivities resumed when the Southern veterans broke out in cheers
and the Northern soldiers quickly joined in. Pennsylvania congressman
J. Hampton Moore greeted them: "You meet again here at the 'Bloody
Angle,' the very zenith of the mighty current of the war, not as furious,
fighting champions of State or Section, but as messengers of peace." He
presented an American flag to Pickett's men: "With shot for shot and
bayonet for bayonet you met each other then. Now you know, on either
side, the foeman you met were worthy of your steel." At the wall, Capt.
Robert Douthat raised up the Confederate flag again, "crossed it with
the triangular flag of the Philadelphia brigade, and between the two em-
blems he planted the brand new *Stars and Stripes!*" The significance of
the action was not lost on the crowd, and a shout of approval "fairly split
the air."[89] Each of Pickett's men received a bronze medallion bearing the
words "Philadelphia Brigade" and "Pickett's Division," courtesy of the
John Wanamaker Company of Philadelphia.[90]

The stifling hot weather inflicted the only casualties this July 3. Several
of the old soldiers collapsed from the heat and the emotions of the day.
Most, however, just walked slowly back to the tent city, discussing a new
plan "which has run like wildfire all over camp to-day" for a new monument "to commemorate both the first and the second charge of Pickett's
Division."[91]

Journalists, many of whom were too young to remember much about
the war, found both the recreation of the charge and the following cere-

monies impressive. "'Dramatic' seems an overworked and unsatisfying word when applied to the incidents that marked the week of the Gettysburg reunion," wrote one correspondent, who nonetheless assured readers that there "was no 'staginess' about any of the proceedings."[92] A *New York Times* correspondent went to see if Meade's headquarters looked anything like the way Samuel Wilkeson had described it so colorfully in the aftermath of the artillery bombardment on July 3; he noted that "the hollyhocks and roses that Wilkeson describes are blooming again to-day."[93]

Enterprising photographers got their share of contrived shots.[94] By and large, however, the veterans themselves decided what was appropriate and what was not. When a small group of Southerners started across the field of Pickett's Charge by themselves, a man with a camera hailed them. The Southerners deduced what the photographer wanted, and "with one common impulse they raised their canes, turned tail and fled like a lot of scared rabbits, the dreaded 'Rebel Yell' reverberating down the hillside." The resulting photos had "plenty of action in them—'all rear views!'"[95]

Veterans of both armies wanted critics of the ceremonies to understand that they sincerely meant to celebrate the end of sectional bitterness. Two old soldiers bought a hatchet at a local hardware store and then literally buried it out near Devil's Den "to show the world that between North and South no bitterness survives."[96] As explained by C. Irvine Walker of the UCV, the reunion was not meant as "a glorification of the heroic charge of Pickett's and Pettigrew's men, or the magnificent gallantry with which the Blue line of Cemetery Ridge repulsed that charge," but simply as a salute to the valor of the American soldier.[97] As a correspondent for the *San Francisco Examiner* claimed with some historical inaccuracy but plenty of emotion, "We know that it is well that the cause which lost did lose; that it is well that Pickett's gallant, glorious, heroic men wasted all their valor against the guns of Doubleday; that it is well that it was the men in Blue and not the men in Gray who slept that night on a field of victory," all in "a necessary, useful, splendid sacrifice whereby the whole race of men has been uplifted."[98] The American people required no further evidence of the success of national reunion. A Mississippian recalled a comrade who called the July 3 assault "the charge which saved the Union," and this "epigrammatic characterization of this valorous charge" seemed "to define in some degree the sentiments that swelled in many hearts."[99]

He could have added historians and partisans of the Southern commands from states other than Virginia to the list of those who could learn from the mood of the ceremonies. "Fame has been kind to General Pickett," one visitor wrote. "Never mind the questions which the military historians argue." It did not matter that the supports did not arrive. It did not matter that Lee, or Longstreet, or somebody else, erred in sending Pickett's men forward from Seminary Ridge. Just the same, "all the States of the Union claim those men to-day, and the veterans of the North, no less than those of the South, pay them their tribute of admiration. The Old Guard at Waterloo, the Light Brigade at Balaklava, and Pickett's men at Gettysburg—these three. Are there any others?"[100]

Still largely missing from all the panoply were Pettigrew's and Trimble's men or Wilcox's and Lang's troops. Tennesseans, Alabamians, Mississippians, and Floridians could not even share in the satisfaction some North Carolinians must have felt to read the *Cincinnati Enquirer*'s editorial: "Martial story contains no more thrilling narrative than that effort of the Virginians and North Carolinians under Pickett and Pettigrew" on July 3.[101] Herbert Francis Sherwood of *Outlook* almost got it right. He had wandered through the Confederate encampment at the reunion and climbed to the crest of Seminary Ridge about where Lane's North Carolina brigade of Trimble's command had rested early on July 3. Sherwood described how Lane's Tar Heels deployed for the attack fifty years earlier, but he still called the assault by Virginia's name for it: "Pickett's Charge."[102]

Diehard cynics still could find things to complain about. Even Virginians, who should have been entirely delighted by the proceedings, could find fault. Virginia governor William H. Mann rejected a suggestion that he host another great reunion planned for 1915. Such a meeting would coincide with the fall of Richmond and the Confederacy's surrender, and Mann opposed marking that event with any such celebration. "The Gettysburg reunion was an entirely different affair," he argued. "The spirit of Gettysburg was of friendship and of kindly relations," not a celebration of victory or defeat, and "any reunion which celebrated the fall and burning of Richmond would be woefully inappropriate."[103]

The golden anniversary also brought out those who continued to argue that too much emphasis had been put on George Pickett, his Virginians, even Gettysburg itself. After giving the great reunion full coverage, the editor of *Confederate Veteran* felt compelled to comment that he still believed that "thousands of others deserved like applause with Pickett's men at Gettysburg." It meant nothing that "the final test of human strength and courage was assigned to that Virginia division," since "Pickett's Division was composed of typical Confederate soldiers, and it was that command that proved the test."[104] Mississippian G. B. Gerald of Barksdale's brigade recalled the ferocity of the day: "One of my officers said to me [during the bombardment] that he had never believed the story about the world coming to an end, but that he'd be damned if he didn't believe it now and that it was going to take place within less than fifteen minutes." He had admired the steadiness of the troops in the advance "sometimes called the charge of Pickett's division and at other times the high tide at Gettysburg," but he thought the writer who had asserted that "the century trembled in the balance" went way too far.[105]

Of course, cringing most as they observed the proceedings were thousands of North Carolinians. A few months after the reunion, New York artilleryman Cowan recalled that a delegation of Tar Heels had attended the celebration to strengthen their claim to being "farthest at the front at Gettysburg." A quick reading of Hays's official report convinced him that "the Claim of NC is unwarranted." He argued that "none of Hill's corps advanced as far as Webb's front in the angle, so Va., not NC was foremost there." The tunnel vision of combat precluded his seeing anything north of the copse of trees even fifty years later.[106] Still, some could be swayed. A Rhode Islander wrote to a North Carolina friend shortly after the reunion that some artillerymen from his state "told me that two men of a North Carolina regiment lay dead at the wall evidently killed by the canister fired at the command of Sergeant Olney." He now believed that "the stone marking the high water mark as the farthest north that the confeds. reached on the field of Gettysburg is in the wrong." [107]

Perhaps some of these comments reached Richmond, where, in October 1913, the George E. Pickett Camp of Confederate Veterans formed a committee to consider formally "the facts bearing upon the presence and participation" of their general and his troops on July 3 at Gettysburg. The results could be predicted even before the committee issued its report: Pickett had served in "actual and active command of his division," they alone broke the Union line, and he deserved the mantle of "the hero and idol of the Gettysburg charge." [108]

In the end, however, all the critics' gripes and complaints were ignored. Organizers of the great reunion did not set out to right the wrongs of history. Mostly, they succeeded in their main purpose: The celebration "forged the last link in the reunion of the North and the South, and wiped out the last remnant of bitterness and hostile feeling." Over the field of Pickett's Charge, "it would not be a great stretch of imagination to picture the heavens opened, and looking down on this scene the spirits of Abraham Lincoln, and . . . the great commanders and leaders on the Union side in this titanic struggle, and the spirits of Lee and Longstreet . . . joined in a perfect and eternal reunion in that world where war is unknown." The meeting had honored the nation, the fallen, and all those many veterans "soon to be mustered out of the army of the living and mustered into the army of the unforgotten." [109]

As the veterans wended their way back home and the army packed up its tents—and many of its coffins, too, since only eight of the old men died—each American could find his own personal meaning in this reunion. John C. McInnis of North Carolina complained that "we boys always cald it Pickets newspaper charge[.] the Richmond Papers Blowed it [up] and it has got into history but it is wrong. . . . Pettigrews lost more men than his whole Division[.]" [110] But even McInnis would have to concede on one point: In the war for popular memory, in 1913 as surely as in 1863, Pickett and his men decisively won.

EPILOGUE

THE OLD
BRIGHT WAY OF
THE TALES

Today's visitor to Gettysburg cannot escape it. The clump of trees, the target of Pickett's Charge, complete with the bronze book commemorating the "high water mark of the Rebellion" concludes almost every tour. The vista between the valleys still compels our attention and awe.

Perhaps the public forum of the T-shirt best illustrates the power of the memory of Pickett's Charge today. Garments bearing the popular name of the July 3 assault show three Southern infantrymen advancing to the attack. (Identical shirts with a "Stonewall Brigade" label probably rest nearby, a second tribute to Virginia valor.) A preshrunk cotton commemorative to Richard B. Garnett entitled "Red Eye Returns" features his riderless horse. Fans of Lewis Armistead can wear the image of his hat on the tip of his sword to answer his call, "Who Will Follow Me?" Can a silk-screened salute to James Kemper be far behind?

Winfield Scott Hancock shirts have found a niche in the market, but fans of Gibbon or Hays go away frustrated. Smyth, Sherrill, Webb, Hall, and Harrow have been ignored. The possibility of Pettigrew- or Trimble-ware—or Joseph Davis, James K. Marshall, or James Lane prints—have not captured the imagination of local marketeers either. David Letterman fans can purchase a shirt bearing a top-ten list of reasons why Pickett's

Charge failed, however. The T-shirt concern has captured entirely the essence of popular memory about July 3.

The shirts tell us, too, that George E. Pickett's memory is secure. As poet Stephen Vincent Benet wrote of the general on July 3, Pickett had "Dreamt of a martial sword, as swords are martial in dreams, / And the courtesy to use it, in the old bright way of the tales. / These days are gone with the blast. He has his sword in his hand. / And he will use it today, and remember that using long."[1] Pickett certainly did not forget July 3, and the American people have not forgotten him either. What we remember about him, however, mostly comes from the "old bright way of the tales."

In the years after the golden anniversary, Pickett's Charge immersed itself even more deeply into the American memory. In traditional ways and in imaginative new ones, which drew on the attack's symbolic value as well as its historical importance, the July 3 charge's legacy of valor, sacrifice, and commitment has been well preserved for future generations.

In 1917, long after most Northern states had dedicated their monuments at Gettysburg, Virginia erected one, too. Its very site near the spot where Lee met Pickett's survivors and accepted blame for their mauling illustrates the primacy of the July 3 charge in Virginia's memory. There, the great commander still sits astride Traveler, gazing toward the clump of trees. The Old Dominion's aristocrats and farmers are frozen in bronze at the monument's base, or else, as one veteran wrote, "General Lee [would] be quite lonely at Gettysburg without his army and his flag."[2]

On July 3, 1929, North Carolina dedicated its own state memorial, appropriately enough, on Pettigrew's line. Mount Rushmore sculptor Gutzon Borglum set the eyes of its bronze color-bearer and stalwart soldiers toward the clump of trees, too. At the dedication, Gov. O. Max Gardner asserted with confidence that the Southerners at the Confederacy's high water mark "were North Carolina boys, members of the immortal 26th North Carolina regiment."[3] Another speaker felt honored to salute them, too, since "the very word 'Gettysburg' has come to symbolize courage and carnage."[4] A second, smaller marker placed nearby restated North Carolina's claim that one of every four Southern soldiers who fell at Gettysburg came from the Tar Heel State. As the ceremonies ended, an airplane piloted by a North Carolinian flew overhead and dipped its wings in tribute.[5]

North Carolina's usual allies did not follow her lead this time. In 1933, Alabama dedicated its memorial but placed it way off on the Confederate right flank, where Law's brigade jumped off for Little Round Top. Florida erected no monument at all until the centennial year, and Mississippi waited until 1973 to dedicate its jarring statuary on Barksdale's July 2 line.

Tennessee's memorial—originally intended for a site on the July 1 field—foundered with funding problems until the monument was completed in 1982.[6] The newest monument to evoke memories of July 3 recalls Virginia's version of events; the Masonic monument commemorating the moment when Capt. Henry H. Bingham succored mortally wounded Lewis Armistead stands in the National Military Cemetery annex.

As the period of memorial building wound down, the flow of soldiers' memoirs reduced to a trickle as well. In 1920 and 1921, the editor of *Confederate Veteran* revisited the controversy over Armistead's last words as if it were something new, but he added nothing to the historical record.[7] By now, both the passage of time and temper of the times worked against the old warriors. Growing pacifist sentiment after the Great War killed off much popular interest in most things military. Lack of subscribers and veteran authors forced the venerable *Southern Historical Society Papers* to end its long publishing run in 1927. Five years later, *Confederate Veteran* ceased publication. The Northern veterans' *National Tribune* folded in 1940.

Diehards in North Carolina still tried to fight the power of popular memory. Into the 1920s, state chapters of the Daughters of the American Revolution published pamphlets full of patriotic essays, including Judge Walter Clark's reminder that "there was no reason why the [July 3] assault should have ever been styled 'Pickett's Charge,' except that the Richmond papers were anxious to boost him for promotion to Lieutenant-General."[8]

But fewer and fewer remained to beat that old drum. Dr. Henry E. Shepherd suggested that if the South had adopted a staff system like that used in the German army in World War I, it "might have averted our disaster" on July 3, when "the dance of death at Gettysburg was forever ended." But if it was too late to change history, then art, poetry, and "the gift of historic reproduction" still could make certain that "Pickett's Charge" was "absorbed into the inner consciousness of the American nation." The popular memory of the charge—however one perceived its reality—possessed value as a unifying factor in a rapidly changing world: "Whatever our standard of political morality, we may at least concur in the judgment of Mr. Lincoln, who, upon surveying the field in November, 1863, exclaimed in a burst of mingled wonder and admiration: 'I am proud to be the countryman of the men who assailed those heights.' "[9]

As critics of Virginia's version of the events of July 3 realized that they could not remove Pickett's men from their foremost place in popular memory, they scrambled to secure places for soldiers from North Carolina, Alabama, Mississippi, and Tennessee alongside them. As Alabamian John Purifoy wrote, he refused to "engage in the dastardly effort of attempting to pluck a single leaf from the laurel crown of achievement" that adorned the heads of Pickett's men. All he could do is hope that Americans would remember that all descriptions of the Virginians' "splendid valor" at Gettysburg applied just as well to "the fighting of the two divisions, Heth's and Pender's of Hill's corps."[10]

Memory transcended history even more readily as the old soldiers faded away. In July 1938, 1,800 Civil War veterans came to Gettysburg one last time. *Newsweek* illustrated its story about the event with Philippoteaux's painting, which depicted "Pickett's charge: one of history's outstanding military episodes." A photo of the North Carolina monument bore the ironic caption, "Scene of Pickett's Charge."[11] Baltimore journalist Robert Littell looked out over the field of the great charge and marveled at the "great and deathless thing in men which bids them fear not to be slain." But now, in the midst of economic depression and an increasingly unsafe world, he wondered what it all had meant.[12] In answer, historian Bernard DeVoto saw "more technical splendor in Chancellorsville, more irony in Shiloh, more obstinate incandescence in Chickamauga, more hypnotic horror in the Wilderness," but in July 3 he saw something special: "the certainty that the Confederacy would lose the war." Before that day, he wrote, "there had been no mold for the future in America, but now there was one—and for the Western world as well."[13] Maybe this notion explained why the war generation took such care to preserve the memory of this great moment. Maybe this explained why their descendants still honored it. In any case, an unbearable sadness was attached to one observation: "There will be no seventy-sixth reunion. This one is the last."[14]

If the old soldiers really worried about being forgotten, they worried unnecessarily. However, they may very well have been surprised to learn just how many different ways July 3 would leave its mark on the nation's historical consciousness.

Their battles inspired and instructed future generations of American soldiers. Just as predicted, Gettysburg did become an open-air military classroom. Pennsylvania National Guardsmen regularly encamped there, and beginning in 1902, firstclassmen from West Point toured the field as part of their coursework in the art of war. By 1915, the Department of Military Engineering at the U.S. Military Academy had developed a textbook on the battle for classroom use.[15] Before World War I, officers attending more senior military schools at Fort Leavenworth and the U.S. Army War College took staff rides to Gettysburg to study the lessons that Lee and Meade, Longstreet and Hancock, Pickett and Pettigrew could teach them.[16] About July 3 they learned that "caution and daring are valuable attributes of command, but they must be used with discretion."[17] They wondered if modern smoke shells might have improved the South's chances for success, estimating that over 90 percent of the Confederate assault force could have come within 100 yards of the Union line under proper concealment.[18] In the post–World War II years, of course, General Eisenhower took to the field of Pickett's Charge a small parade of prominent military men, including Field Marshal Bernard Montgomery, who shook his head in disbelief at the sight.[19]

The U.S. Marines learned from Gettysburg, too. In 1922, they twice re-enacted Pickett's Charge to try to answer, "What would have happened at Gettysburg if the armies of Meade and Lee had met with modern weapons and equipment?"[20] The first time, they advanced in the same shoulder-to-shoulder formation Pickett's men had used fifty-nine years earlier. The second time, they advanced with air scouts, tanks, rifle grenades, and other modern weaponry. They concluded that both attacks would have failed. Senior Marine commanders also suggested, however, that Lee likely would not have launched his attack under modern conditions, since "he would have known from his airplane observers that the entire Army of the Potomac was mustered against him."[21]

Helen Dortsch Longstreet witnessed the Marine maneuvers. "The battle was staged to-day with marvelous accuracy in every detail, exactly as I have heard General Longstreet describe it hundreds of times," she wrote. She almost felt she "stood in the living presence of the South's audacious hope." Avowing again her husband's opposition to the assault, she still expressed awe at the courage of the Virginians, who, even though "mowed down like grass, smilingly closed the columns to show the world how Southern men could fight and die for principles for which they were willing to pay the supreme price." An elderly one-armed veteran standing nearby complained about losing his limb in that charge: "It was powerful hard to lose my arm and be whipt, too; and what was the use of it?" A bystander pointed to the Stars and Stripes and said, "The stars on its blue field are all the brighter, its red stripe all the deeper, its white stripe all the purer, because you left an arm in front of Cemetery Hill in Pickett's charge. That was the use of it. That was the good of it."[22]

Helen Longstreet's observations about the Marines at Gettysburg appeared in a seemingly unlikely source: *Literary Digest*. Still, she apparently knew she would find interested readers there. Even in the twentieth century, poets, novelists, essayists, and other chroniclers who did not aspire to write history continued to employ the drama of Pickett's Charge to good effect.

In 1931, the *Chautauquan* sponsored an essay contest that required entrants to decide: "What is the most dramatic incident in American history, and why?" E. D. Warfield, the second-prize winner, waxed philosophical on "The Repulse of Pickett's Charge." Warfield had looked for a moment that represented "the climax and catastrophe" of a great historical confrontation. Considering slavery to be "the essential climax of the age-long conflict with the forces antagonistic to freedom" and Gettysburg the turning point of the war to abolish it, Pickett's Charge had to be the nation's most dramatic moment: "The success of the Confederacy, which had trembled in the balance up to the charge of Pickett on the field of Gettysburg, was never again possible." [23]

Not even Sallie Pickett's execrable *Bugles of Gettysburg* dulled the reading public's interest in fictionalized or nonhistorical accounts of her Soldier's great charge. Stephen Vincent Benet's *John Brown's Body* used the events of July 3 to tell a story that Jubal Early and his cronies would have liked. "Dutch Longstreet, the independent, / Demurs, as he has demurred since the fight began. / He had disapproved of this battle from the first / And that disapproval has added and is to add / Another weight in the balance against the gray." On Cemetery Ridge awaiting the Confederate advance were Hancock's men from eleven states, "the metals of all the North, cooled into an axe of war." George Pickett appeared first as a friend of Abraham Lincoln, "the strange shawled man / Who would talk in a Springfield street with a boy who dreamt of a sword." In Benet's charge, only the Old Dominion commanded center stage: "You could mark the path that they took by the dead that they left behind, / Spilled from that deadly march as a cart spills meal on a road, / And yet they came on unceasing, the fifteen thousand no more, / And the blue Virginia flag did not fall, did not fall, did not fall." And when it did fall and Pickett pulled back, "The sword was still in his hand," but "a thing was cracked in his heart." [24]

Popular Southern novelist William Faulkner reminded all Americans about the demarcative quality of the events of July 3. In *Intruder in the Dust*, Pickett's Charge became a metaphor to describe such a moment in human experience:

> For every Southern boy fourteen years old, not once but whenever he wants it, there is the instant when it's still not yet two o'clock on that July afternoon in 1863, the brigades are in position behind the rail fence, the guns are laid and ready in the woods, and the furled flags are already loosened to break out and Pickett himself with his long oiled ringlets and his hat in one hand probably and his sword in the other looking up the hill waiting for Longstreet to give the word and it's all in the balance, it hasn't happened yet, it hasn't even begun yet, it not only hasn't begun yet but there is still time for it not to begin against that position and those circumstances which made more men than Garnett and

Kemper and Armistead and Wilcox grave yet it's going to begin, we all know that.[25]

Pickett and his men continue to appear in twentieth-century Civil War fiction in both dramatic and trivial ways.[26] In Ben Ames Williams's *House Divided*, Lee had told Longstreet "those Virginians of Pickett's will do anything men can do," and when Pettigrew's men broke, Longstreet wondered if, indeed, "those Virginians [were] going to stay there till the last of them died."[27] Readers of Michael Shaara's Pulitzer prize–winning *The Killer Angels*, a tautly drawn psychodrama featuring the clash of wills between Lee and Longstreet, find as well a vibrant image of George Pickett, drawn larger than life in a way that would have pleased Sallie. Character sketches of his three brigadiers are studies in contrast: the haunted, doomed Garnett; the courtly "Lo" Armistead, whose best friend is Union general Hancock; and the ambitious politician James Kemper. Shaara's charge is Pickett's Charge. Pettigrew and Trimble hardly appear. For that matter, the Yankees remain shadowy figures on July 3 as well.[28]

Pickett also appears as a member of Jeb Stuart's fictional court-martial board in Robert Skimin's *Gray Victory*.[29] And he is a very interested hostile onlooker in Douglas Savage's *The Court Martial of Robert E. Lee*, in which, from a back row, he whispers to an aide-de-camp a line repeated many times over: "That old man had my division massacred."[30] In Ted Jones's *Hard Road to Gettysburg*, twin brothers separated at birth—one raised in the South and educated at VMI, and one raised in the North who attended West Point—meet again inside the Angle on Cemetery Ridge, where the brother in gray dies saving the life of the brother in blue.[31] Harold Coyle bucks tradition a bit with his use of the "divided brothers" theme: His Virginian comes from Brockenbrough's brigade and meets his brother in the 12th New Jersey on Hays's front.[32] Even humorist Richard Armour found the events of July 3 worthy of this rather dubious notice: "The most decisive of these battles [of the Civil War] was Gettysburg, where the Confederates, who by this time were low on ammunition, swept up the hill with sharpened stakes in what was called Pickets Charge."[33]

Just as the soldiers and the literary community have continued to find something of interest in Pickett's Charge, so too, of course, have historians. In both the Pulitzer prize–winning *R. E. Lee: A Biography* and *Lee's Lieutenants*, Douglas Southall Freeman brought Pickett's Charge—in full-blown Virginia colors—to a twentieth-century audience as convincingly as the Lee cult and Pickett clique had done fifty years and more before. Freeman's Lee was not quite so infallible as Jubal Early's Lee, but he came close. Freeman's Longstreet remained sufficiently petulant, recalcitrant, and insubordinate to a degree that Early would have approved; in language Old Jube might have used, the historian insisted that Old Pete on July 3 "was so depressed by his conviction of the unwisdom of an attack that he was not conscious of any failure in preparation." [34]

When Freeman wrote of the three brigades of Virginians, he evoked the old wartime images: "Pickett's troops were charging gloriously. They even might reach the blue line without losing their formation. They were within canister range; they defied it; they kept straight on." In a major concession to the historical record, he added this single sentence about other commands in the charge to his comments about the Virginians: "So did the right Brigades of Heth's Division." [35] But that was all. Freeman preserved largely intact the Virginia version of Pickett's Charge and buttressed it with extensive use of the official records, firsthand accounts from the *Southern Historical Society Papers*, and new materials from some unpublished manuscript resources. No student of the Eastern theater ignored Freeman's efforts, still among the most useful analyses of Lee's army.

Freeman blazed a path that became well worn in the years leading up to the Civil War Centennial. Fairfax Downey, Clifford Dowdey, and a host of others worshiped at the altar of Lee and the Virginians. Dowdey's *Death of a Nation: The Story of Lee and His Men at Gettysburg*, for instance, includes little new information and even less new interpretation in its eloquent and easy-to-read narrative. Dowdey's Lee made no mistakes, but Old Pete's surliness when denied his own way reduced him "to a state of incompetence for command." The Virginia version of Pickett's Charge reigned nearly as pervasively in the historical world as it did in the realm of literature.[36]

In the 1950s, however, a dissenting voice made itself heard. Glenn Tucker, a North Carolina writer, took Longstreet's side on many key controversies about Gettysburg in his *High Tide at Gettysburg*, thus raising serious questions about Lee's generalship, especially on July 3. About Pickett's Charge Tucker raised more pointed concerns. He insisted that "the impression often conveyed that only Armistead's soldiers stormed the wall and penetrated the Northern works does not spring from the events of the battle. The 'high water mark' is more symbolic than actual." With an eloquence usually reserved for Virginians alone, Tucker mourned the losses of the 14th Tennessee, which had entered the battle on July 1 with 365 men, took only 60 into the charge, and came out with 3.[37] Tucker became Pettigrew's and Trimble's Douglas Southall Freeman. In this and subsequent works, he did his job so well that many students of the Civil War began to reconsider their earlier perceptions about Gettysburg and Pickett's Charge.[38]

Perhaps most stunning of all, Tucker demanded that James Longstreet be reconsidered, too. And in history as in life, where Longstreet went, Pickett was sure to follow. The approach of the Civil War Centennial inspired George R. Stewart's *Pickett's Charge: A Microhistory of the Final Confederate Attack at Gettysburg, July 3, 1863*. Given the highly partisan nature of so much writing about the great charge and the title of the book itself, Stewart provided a balanced treatment of the day's events that included *all* of its actors, both Northern and Southern. His work, however, illustrated all too well the ensnaring webs of state pride, great joy and destroyed hopes, dreams of personal glory, and the deep hurt of justice denied that dogged objective analysis of the attack since July 1863. Mostly, Stewart had an eye for catchy vignettes. Unfortunately, it seems he treated all those disconnected threads as equally valid historical sources; readers never learned that it mattered a great deal who told the original story, when he told it, and why. Alan M. Hollingsworth and James M. Cox may well have understood this when they compiled *The Third Day at Gettysburg: Pickett's Charge*, a collection of wartime reports, excerpts from the postwar writings of partisan participants of all sorts, and Freeman's modern views, all designed to teach the skill of critical thinking; the University of North Carolina was among the first to adopt it.[39]

Critical study of the crucial events of July 1863 has benefited greatly from Edwin B. Coddington's *The Gettysburg Campaign: A Study in Command*. Building on the solid foundation of John B. Bachelder's voluminous manuscript sources, he acknowledged the contentious issues concerning July 3 and tried to resolve them as objectively as his eyewitness accounts would let him. He added much to our knowledge of the battle, except in one area: for the July 3 charge, he still gave overweening credence to standard sources. During the explosion of studies published during the centennial years, James Sefton reminded students of military history that frequently cited items such as battle dispatches often suffered from "unintentional exaggeration, inaccuracies of timing, lack of clarity in geographical description, and incompleteness," while official reports nearly always "lack critical evaluation of the actions of others and frequently attempt to claim a bit too much credit for the commands of the respective writers."[40] All students of Gettysburg still need to pay attention to a most telling comment one veteran wrote to Bachelder: "What a herculean task to separate the truth from the falsehood in the multitude of reports that have rained down on you since 1863."[41]

The ongoing tension between memory and history—and the manner in which it shapes the way we remember the events of July 3—still suggests itself at every turn. The theme of the centennial anniversary celebration in 1963, "A Nation United," recalled that of the reunion of Pickett's men and the Philadelphians in 1887. And just as in 1887, some dissented from that notion. A few months before the celebration, agrarian author Allen Tate told a Minnesota audience, "I cannot imagine any enlightened Southerner—such as one usually imagines oneself to be—rejoicing in the defeat of the South. Can defeat ever be a good thing for the defeated?" If he had lived in the South in 1861, he continued, he likely would have found himself at the stone wall "with three men whose presence at Gettysburg has from boyhood given the battle a direct impact on my imagination, such as no other action of that war could give." The three were Lew Armistead, Col. Robert C. Allen of the 28th Virginia, and his own maternal grandfather, who survived the charge. Arguing that only one Federal war aim was achieved—perpetual Union—he looked at the uncertain future of the civil rights movement of the early 1960s and feared that, despite Lincoln's benediction, even the Union dead had died at least partly in vain.[42]

Predictably, the program for July 3, 1963, called for a "Reunion at the High Water Mark." Perhaps a bit wary of the recent signs of change in Gettysburg historiography, chairman E. J. Stackpole prepared program notes designed to offend no one. "An important date in United States history will be memorialized in a dramatization of the decisive climax of the three-day battle," he wrote. Lee "had determined to risk 15,000 of the Confederacy's best soldiers," Stackpole added, but he omitted entirely all commanders' names. And he did not call the attack "Pickett's Charge." He wrote that after the great bombardment, "the stage was set for the famous Confederate charge!" Lee's attack was repulsed, Lee's invasion was halted, and "the High Water Mark of the Confederacy had been reached."[43]

Stackpole shied away from naming the charge after George Pickett, but other centennial celebrators did not. James Van Alen, for example, penned the ceremonial ode and titled it "Pickett's Charge." All the old images were there: The "spearpoint of a vital thrust, George Pickett's tough division" was the "pick of Old Virginia trained in every skill of war" and "the very essence of a first-class combat corps." Pettigrew and Trimble received no mention; indeed, the only allusion to any other troops appeared in a horrendously inaccurate reference to 10,000 men "from Carolinas in the East, from Georgia, Louisiana, on to Texas in the West."[44]

But all this was prelude. At 3 P.M. on July 3, 1963, nearly 30,000 spectators watched 500 men in gray uniforms march toward the stone wall, where 500 men in blue uniforms awaited them. There, they joined "in brotherhood and amity to pledge their devotion to the symbol of their common unity—the Stars and Stripes." Many spectators agreed that the ceremony lacked dignity. Just as in 1863, casualties quickly mounted, including a "14-year old Union 'general' who was trampled by a horse" and an expensive sound system that was supposed to carry recorded cannon fire and music. Reenactors "photographed better than they performed," too; during the advance "several rebels broke ranks to snap pictures."[45]

Reenactments of Pickett's Charge have continued to be integral parts of Gettysburg anniversary commemorations. For serious reenactors, the ongoing historical controversies have informed their participation. In 1988 at the 125th anniversary ceremonies, twentieth-century Tar Heels representing the 26th North Carolina of Pettigrew's brigade grew livid when organizers denied them permission to charge as a unit over the stone wall. When told that they could cross over as individuals under the flags of Virginia regiments, one disgruntled Carolinian stated, "We agreed to a man to 'die' in front of the wall rather than to assist the Virginians in perpetuating such a lie."[46] Spectators had a tough choice, too. They had to pick between two lapel pins: a gray one inscribed with "I Charged with Pickett," or a blue one emblazoned with "I Sent Pickett Packing."

The Tar Heel reenactors had a valid gripe. Or did they? In 1986, Gettysburg National Military Park officials had finally approved the placement of a monument to the 26th North Carolina on the slopes of Cemetery Ridge, at a point north of the Angle where its men closely approached the stone wall. The memorial places North Carolinians perhaps forty yards farther up the slope than the monument at the alleged site of Armistead's fall.[47] Today the accuracy of the historical evidence that validated the marker's placement has been challenged. The 26th could not have been as far south as the marker suggests it was, one student of the fight argues; if any North Carolinians attacked the wall at that point, he suggests, they most likely belonged to Scales's command under Colonel Lowrance.[48] If Maud Brown were still alive, she would no doubt use this challenge as inspiration to increase her efforts to mark the 11th Mississippi's advance into Ziegler's Grove.

Others have tried to draw the line between history and memory in other ways. Using arguments reminiscent of Dan Sickles's rhetorical flourishes, several modern historians have tried to argue that the successful defense of Little Round Top marks the true turning point of the war, echoing the claims of V Corps partisans in the 1880s.[49] Army War College staff ride leaders have made a case for the battle turning on a misdirected advance by Benning's Georgians that brought them out at Devil's Den instead of at Little Round Top, where their role as Law's supports should have taken them and where their timely arrival might have broken the line of the 20th Maine.[50] Allen Tate argued that the part played by the 1st Minnesota "turned the tide of battle," a fact obscured by the more spectacular

Pickett's Charge.[51] Perhaps such debate serves a good purpose; the objectivity of the historical method occasionally must reassert its intellectual muscle over the power of memory.

But it probably will not. Entrepreneurs know they can only sell what appeals to the mass market. The T-shirt concession is not the only way to measure the endurance of Pickett's Charge in the national imagination. Most of July 3rd's action can be followed in the paintings of the major Civil War artists working in the field today. In *Remember Old Virginia!* Dale Gallon depicts the deployment of Kemper's brigade in the hollows near the Spangler farm and in another painting, he groups Pickett with Armistead and Kemper as Old Dominion troops undergo a final rifle inspection. The advance of Garnett and his men hold the central focus of Keith Rocco's *Pickett's Charge: Hell for Glory*. Lewis Armistead crossing the stone wall remains as popular an image now as when Rothermel and Philippoteaux rendered the scene on canvas a century or more earlier. Mort Kunstler's *The Bloody Angle* depicts the fight between Virginia and Pennsylvania near the copse of trees. And the meeting between Lee and Pickett's returning survivors is portrayed in his *It's All My Fault*. Gallon offers two important Northern viewpoints, one from Cushing's Battery at the stone wall and the other featuring Hancock and the 69th Pennsylvania at the copse of trees. In *The High Water Mark*, featuring the 26th North Carolina's assault on the stone wall north of the Angle, Kunstler gives a rare glimpse of some of Pettigrew's men; and Don Troiani's *Emmitsburg Road* offers a grim view of Pettigrew's advance, too.

Most of the major painters today employ historians to check the details they put to canvas, but not all artistic renderings put historical accuracy first. Sculptor Francis J. Barnum cast Pickett's Charge in pewter, but his advertising copy describes unaccountably "one of General Lewis Armistead's Alabamans" as mounting the stone wall; indeed, pictured also is one of Cushing's cannoneers swinging his rammer in an effort to "beat off the bayonet-bearing Alabaman."[52] The Hamilton Collection offered the "Robert E. Lee Presentation Tankard," a dubious salute to the abstemious Lee; perhaps there is some bitter irony that one of the two incredibly inaccurate scenes depicted on the vessel is "General Picket [*sic*] leading his fateful charge against Union forces during the historic battle."[53]

And so it goes. The memory of Pickett's Charge is up for sale. Preservationists used it to good effect in their fund drives to bury the utility lines that mar the military landscape along the Emmitsburg Road. Battlefield guidebooks feature the high water mark prominently, if not always accurately; one notoriously bad effort so confused the battle that the authors have Pickett's men crashing through a gap in a strong Union trench line and being repulsed by the newly arrived 1st Minnesota, which lost 82 percent of its 3,200 men—about ten times its actual strength—in the effort.[54] In souvenir shops all over Gettysburg, coffee mugs, key chains, and license plates bear the image of Confederate soldiers under the banner of "Pickett's Charge." Busloads of hungry tourists eat at General Pickett's Buffet, most blissfully unaware that the building sits squarely in Pettigrew's part of the line. For only $35, the ecologically aware can own a "Pickett's Charge tree," a seedling from an actual battlefield tree germinated in a private nursery.[55] Virginia's charge is alive, well, and for some, apparently quite lucrative.

In yet another interesting blending of history and memory, Ted Turner's extravaganza "Gettysburg" has perpetuated the Virginia version of Pickett's Charge for a wide audience of moviegoers. Reflecting the impact of the new scholarship, Tom Berenger's Longstreet—hat, beard, and all—appears as the embodiment of rationality and responsible command. Martin Sheen's Lee is Michael Shaara's Lee—physically ailing, at times irresolute, utterly devout, and perhaps a bit too confident and unyielding after reaching a decision. But the third day belongs to Virginia. There is no doubt, Turner filmed *Pickett's* Charge. Richard Jordan's Armistead takes James Lancaster's Fremantle up and down his brigade's ranks and tells of his Virginians' lineage in words of praise that Captain Owen might well have used a century before. The images shine brightly: Armistead's own military family stretching back to the Revolution; Aylett, the Virginia colonel, descended from Patrick Henry; the young Virginia color-bearer whose grandfather was president of the United States. We hear Stephen Lang's Pickett yell, "Up Virginians." We hear Armistead remind his men that they are from Old Virginia. And Pennsylvania and Virginia meet in close combat at the Angle.

Fans of Pettigrew's and Trimble's men find little to cheer them here. "Pettigrew" appears only briefly, primarily to accept compliments about his grades at the University of North Carolina and to promise Longstreet a copy of his book. An appropriately excitable "Trimble" has his best moments on July 1 when he damns Ewell's lack of aggressiveness and demands transfer to another command. To add insult to injury, in the initial cut of the film, "Longstreet" drew lines in the dirt to show the generals how to deploy their troops for the charge—and he did it wrong, placing Trimble in the first line with Pettigrew in the second.

During the Civil War Centennial, historian Oscar Handlin commented that Americans' "persistent fascination with that great conflict reveals that it has become a symbol, to which significant meanings adhere." Nonetheless, he admitted, "it is still difficult to make out the character of that symbol."[56] In many of Gettysburg's souvenir shops, tourists can plunk down two dollars and validate Handlin's observation with what remains the most versatile bit of kitsch to be inspired by the memory of Pickett's Charge. The "Pickett's Charge" ballpoint pen contains a tube of liquid in the upper half of its barrel. When one tilts the pen, three sturdy Confederates—one apparently Lew Armistead with his hat on his sword (and, it would seem, another on his head)—"charge" down the pen toward a stone wall protecting several blue coated soldiers. Depending on how much one tilts the pen, sometimes the Southerners get hung up a little way down the barrel, satisfying Yankee owners; other times they stop about halfway over, offering a dubious salute to Brockenbrough's Virginians. Sometimes they make it almost to the wall, illustrating the fight on Hays's front. Occasionally, the Confederates replay the fight at the Angle and crash through the Union line completely. The Lost Cause lives!

Just what do twentieth-century Americans think about Pickett's Charge? Everyone, from the most earnest student of the battle to the casual tourist, can pick and choose their version of "history" from the tangled web of truths, both intentional and unintentional half-truths, exaggerations, and out-and-out lies the war generation left. So long as glossy generalizations, unresolved controversies, and unanswered questions remain—and they will—the historically minded among us will study, research, and rethink yet again the events that transpired between those two ridges. For most Americans, however, details about unit commanders and tactical maneuvers never held much attraction. Something else inspires awe. Just what that "something else" is remains essentially an individual matter. The popular memory of Pickett's Charge had many architects—Northern, Southern, Virginian, North Carolinian, and more—and they certainly did not share a common vision. Twentieth-century Americans need not demand it fit any specific intellectual or emotional niche, either. Pickett's Charge thrives on in our memories at least in part because it possesses sufficient versatility to resonate even in today's fast-paced world. George Will likened Georgia's efforts to keep the Confederate battle flag on its state banner to "Pickett's Charge" in its "melancholy glory that attends predestined futility."[57] When Disney's plans for an American history theme park near Manassas fell through and Gettysburg briefly emerged as a possible replacement, a political cartoonist depicted several ranks of mouse-eared infantry aiming at a clump of trees; the caption read "Pickett's Charge, 1994."[58]

Frustration will likely remain the lot of the purists. As a disgruntled veteran noted in 1913, "Pickett's charge has been so grossly exaggerated and misrepresented as to give some color to the oft-repeated axiom that 'history is only an agreed-upon lie.' "[59] Perhaps Lieutenant Haskell guessed correctly from the start about the lasting impact of an unsuccessful Southern infantry attack on July 3: "Tradition, story, history—all will not efface the true, grand epic of Gettysburg."[60]

NOTES

ABBREVIATIONS

The following abbreviations are used in the notes and illustration credits.

B&L   Buel, Clarence C., and Robert U. Johnson, eds. *Battles and Leaders of the Civil War*. 4 vols. New York: Century Printing Co., 1888.

BP   John B. Bachelder Papers, New Hampshire Historical Society, Concord, N.H.

DU   Perkins Library, Duke University, Durham, N.C.

GNMP   Gettysburg National Military Park

MOLLUS   Military Order of the Loyal Legion of the United States

NC Regs   Clark, Walter A., comp. *Histories of the Several Regiments and Battalions from North Carolina in the Great War, 1861–1865*. 5 vols. Raleigh, N.C.: E. M. Uzzell, 1901.

NY at Gbg   New York Monuments Commission for the Battlefields of Gettysburg and Chattanooga. *Final Report on the Battlefield of Gettysburg*. [Cover title, *New York at Gettysburg*.] 3 vols. Albany, N.Y.: J. B. Lyon Co., 1902.

OR   U.S. War Department. *The War of the Rebellion: A Compilation of the Official Records of the Union and Confederate Armies in the War of the Rebellion*. 127 vols. Washington, D.C.: Government Printing Office, 1880–1901. (All citations to *OR* are to series 1.)

Pa at Gbg   Nicholson, John Page, comp. *Pennsylvania at Gettysburg. Ceremonies at the Dedication of the Monuments Erected by the Commonwealth of Pennsylvania to Mark the Positions of the Pennsylvania Commands Engaged in the Battle*. 2 vols. Harrisburg: E. K. Meyers, 1893.

SHC   Southern Historical Collection, Wilson Library, University of North Carolina, Chapel Hill, N.C.

SHSP   *Southern Historical Society Papers*

USAMHI   U.S. Army Military History Institute, Carlisle Barracks, Pa.

VHS   Virginia Historical Society, Richmond, Va.

PROLOGUE

1. Frank Aretas Haskell, *The Battle of Gettysburg* (Madison, Wisc.: Wisconsin History Commission, 1908), 181–82.
2. Address of Maj. William B. Wight, June 12, 1889, in O. B. Curtis, *History of the Twenty-Fourth Michigan of the Iron Brigade, Known as the Detroit and Wayne County Regiment* (Detroit, Mich.: Winn & Hammond, 1891; Gaithersburg, Md.: Olde Soldier Books, 1988), 424.
3. David Thelen, "Memory and American History," *Journal of American History* 75 (March 1989): 1123.
4. Ibid., 1120.
5. James H. McRandle, *The Antique Drums of War* (College Station, Tex.: Texas A&M Press, 1994), 53–54.

6. For an explanation of the utility of history to support popular memory, see Michael Kammen, *Mystic Chords of Memory: The Transformation of Tradition in American Culture* (New York: Vintage Press, 1993), 3–14.

7. McRandle, *Antique Drums of War*, 52–53.

8. William H. Jones to wife, July 13, 1863, William H. Jones Papers, DU.

9. George R. Stewart, *Pickett's Charge: A Microhistory of the Final Confederate Attack at Gettysburg, July 3, 1863* (Boston: Houghton Mifflin Co., 1959; Greenwich, Conn.: Fawcett Publication, 1963), xv.

10. For studies of these events, see Stewart's *Pickett's Charge*, which rarely discriminates between the processes of history and memory, and the more scholarly and careful Edwin B. Coddington's *The Gettysburg Campaign: A Study in Command* (New York: Charles Scribner's Sons, 1968; Dayton, Ohio: Morningside, 1979), ch. 19.

11. A good account of the council of war may be found in John Gibbon, *Personal Recollections of the Civil War* (New York: G. P. Putnam's Sons, 1928; Dayton, Ohio: Morningside, 1988), 140–45.

12. *OR* 27, (2):320.

13. Ibid., p. 359.

14. Ibid., p. 623.

15. See Stewart, *Pickett's Charge*, 159, and Kathy Georg Harrison and John W. Busey, *Nothing But Glory: Pickett's Division at Gettysburg* (Hightstown, N.J.: Longstreet House, 1987), 9–13, for modern assessments of the question.

16. See Harrison and Busey, *Nothing But Glory*, 9–13. Walter Harrison, a member of Pickett's staff, argued that fewer than 4,500 muskets went into the charge; when he added in the officers, he reached a total of approximately 4,700. Walter Harrison, *Pickett's Men, A Fragment of War History* (New York: D. Van Nostrand, 1870), 90.

17. *OR* 27 (2):320 (Lee), 359 (Longstreet), 608 (A. P. Hill).

18. For details, see Hancock's report, *OR* 27 (1):372–75.

19. See Gibbon's report, *OR* 27 (1):416–18.

20. See Hays's report, *OR* 27 (1):453–55.

21. See report of II Corps artillery chief Capt. John G. Hazard, *OR* 27 (1):477–80, especially his map on 479.

22. *OR* 27 (1):258.

23. See Stewart, *Pickett's Charge*, 120–21, and William P. Haines, *History of the Men of Co. F, With Description of the Marches and Battles of the 12th New Jersey Vols* (Camden, N.J.: C. S. McGrath Printer, 1897), 40–41.

CHAPTER ONE

1. D. B. Easley to Howard Townsend, August 15, 1913, D. B. Easley Papers, USAMHI.

2. Address of O. W. Norton, September 11, 1889, in *Pa at Gbg*, 1:432–33.

3. Quoted in Richard Holmes, *Acts of War: The Behavior of Men in Battle* (New York: Free Press, 1985), 149.

4. Ibid., 79.

5. Quoted in Michael Kammen, *Mystic Chords of Memory: The Transformation of Tradition in American Culture* (New York: Vintage Press, 1993), 31.

6. Entry for July 3, 1863, Samuel A. Firebaugh Diary, USAMHI.

7. Quoted in [Maine Commissioners], *Maine at Gettysburg, Report of the Maine Commissioners Prepared by the Executive Committee* (Portland, Maine: Lakeside Press, 1899), 136.

8. O. W. Norton address, 1:432.

9. J. M. Stone to Joseph R. Davis, [undated], in BP.

10. Charles H. Banes, *History of the Philadelphia Brigade* (Philadelphia: J. B. Lippincott & Co., 1876), 193.

11. Joseph Graham, "Gettysburg: Remembering Pickett's Charge, 'An Awful Affair,'" Max R. Williams, ed., *Civil War Times Illustrated* 23 (April 1984): 48.

12. J. L. Bechtel to Miss Connie, July 6, 1863, copy at GNMP. The comment is all the more stunning since the 59th New York suffered seventy dead and mortally wounded in the West Woods at Antietam. The regiment's dead and mortally wounded at Gettysburg numbered only twelve.

13. Robert Garth Scott, ed., *Fallen Leaves: The Civil War Letters of Major Henry Lawrence Abbott* (Kent, Ohio: Kent State University Press, 1991), 86.

14. Alexander McNeil to David E. Porter, August 16, 1863, Civil War Times Illustrated Collection, USAMHI.

15. *OR* 27 (2):645.

16. Holmes, *Acts of War*, 175.

17. Frank Aretas Haskell, *The Battle of Gettysburg* (Madison, Wisc.: Wisconsin History Commission, 1908), 181–82.

18. Address of Edwin B. Wight, June 12, 1889, in O. B. Curtis, *History of the Twenty-fourth Michigan of the Iron Brigade, Known as the Detroit and Wayne Country Regiment* (Detroit, Mich.: Winn & Hammond, 1891; Gaithersburg, Md.: Olde Soldier Books, 1988), 424.

19. William J. Hatchett to Parents, July 7, 1863, Civil War Times Illustrated Collection, USAMHI.

20. Michael W. Taylor, ed., *The Cry is War, War, War: The Civil War Correspondence of Lts. Burwell Thomas Cotton and George Job Huntley, 34th Regiment North Carolina Troops* (Dayton, Ohio: Morningside, 1994), 147.

21. Ralph Orson Sturtevant, *Pictorial History, Thirteenth Vermont Volunteers, War of 1861–1865* (n.p., [after 1908]), 307.

22. Anne C. Rose, *Victorian America and the Civil War* (New York: Cambridge Press, 1992), 237–44, speaks to the mind-set of at least one social type in American society during the war years for whom restraint seemed to be an imperative character trait. See also Joseph Allan Frank and George A. Reaves, *"Seeing the Elephant": Raw Recruits at the Battle of Shiloh* (New York: Greenwood Press, 1989), esp. 91–93, 119–27, which analyzes the postbattle writings of approximately 450 combat veterans.

23. Paul Fussell, *The Great War and Modern Memory* (New York: Oxford University Press, 1975), 169–70.

24. Gerald Linderman, *Embattled Courage: The Experience of Combat in the American Civil War* (New York: Free Press, 1987), 1. For an enlightening discussion of

soldier disillusionment with civilians who stayed home, see ch. 11, appropriately titled "Unraveling Ties."

25. Milo P. Quaife, ed., *From the Cannon's Mouth* (Detroit, Mich.: Wayne State University Press, 1959), 196.

26. Quoted in Gregory A. Coco, *A Strange and Blighted Land, Gettysburg: The Aftermath of a Battle* (Gettysburg, Pa.: Thomas Publications, 1995), 51.

27. For explication of the unexceptional nature of many military duties, even in a combat situation, see James H. McRandle, *The Antique Drums of War* (College Station, Tex: Texas A&M Press, 1993), 36–37.

28. Graham, " 'An Awful Affair,' " 48.

29. Letter of Captain C. A. Phillips, July 6, 1863, quoted in *History of the Fifth Massachusetts Battery* (Boston: Luther E. Cowles, 1902), 652.

30. Fussell, *The Great War and Modern Memory*, 327.

31. Henry P. Clare to Brother William, July 5, 1863, copy in GNMP.

32. "John W. Plummer's Account," in Frank Moore, ed., *The Rebellion Record: A Diary of American Events* (New York: Putnam, 1862–1865), 10:180.

33. Quoted in G. T. Fleming, comp., *Life and Letters of Alexander Hays, Brevet Colonel United States Army, Brigadier General and Brevet Major General United States Volunteers* (Pittsburgh: Gilbert Adam Hays, 1919), 442.

34. J. L. Bechtel to Miss Connie, July 6, 1863, copy at GNMP.

35. William B. Hoitt to "Friend Mary," July 13, 1863, Lewis Leigh Collection, USAMHI.

36. *OR* 27 (1):437.

37. Ibid., (2):650.

38. Terrence Winschel, "The Gettysburg Diary of Lieutenant William Peel," *Gettysburg Magazine*, no. 9 (July 1993): 105.

39. *OR* 27 (2):385.

40. Granville Belcher to wife, July 16, 1863, Granville W. Belcher Papers, DU.

41. *OR* 27 (1):451; (2):435.

42. *OR* 27 (1):239, 373; J. R. Bechtel to Friend Connie, July 6, 1863, GNMP.

43. Winschel, "The Gettysburg Diary of Lieutenant William Peel," 105; W. B. Taylor to ?, July 29, 1863, William B. Floyd Collection, copy in Robert L. Brake Collection, USAMHI.

44. Graham, " 'An Awful Affair,' " 48.

45. General Davis actually measured his forward progress by the fence lines his men hit. See *OR* 27 (2):651.

46. Holmes, *Acts of War*, 141.

47. *OR* 27 (1):373, 454.

48. Letter of Chauncey L. Harris, undated but immediately post-Gettysburg, printed in George H. Washburn, *A Complete Military History and Record of the 108th Regiment New York Volunteers from 1862 to 1894* (Rochester, N.Y.: E. R. Andrews, 1894), 52.

49. Entry for July 3, 1863, William J. Burns diary, Save the Flags Collection, USAMHI.

50. *OR* 27 (1):373, 461, 467.

51. G. G. Benedict to John B. Bachelder, December 24, 1863, in John B. Bachelder Papers, Massachusetts Historical Society, Boston, Mass.

52. *OR* 27 (2):469.

53. Entry for July 3, 1863, William J. Burns diary, Save the Flags Collection, USAMHI.

54. Entry for July 3, 1863, Charles W. Belknap Diary, copy in box 10, Robert L. Brake Collection, USAMHI.

55. Mead to wife, July 6, 1863, copy in box 7, Robert L. Brake Collection, USAMHI.

56. Alexander McNeil to David G. Porter, August 16, 1863, Civil War Times Illustrated Collection, USAMHI.

57. *OR* 27 (1):439.

58. McRandle, *Antique Drums of War*, 138.

59. *OR* 27 (2):386.

60. William H. Jones to wife, July 13, 1863, William H. Jones Papers, DU.

61. *OR* 27 (1):239, 373.

62. Ibid., pp. 349, 353.

63. *OR* 27 (2):386; Haskell, *Battle of Gettysburg*, 117.

64. Capt. W. W. Bentley to Capt. W. Fry, July 9, 1863, George E. Pickett Papers, DU.

65. *OR* 27 (2):319.

66. The map is reprinted in *OR* 27 (1):438.

67. "Fighting Them Over," *National Tribune*, August 20, 1885.

68. Captain George D. Bowen diary, entry for July 3, 1863, quoted in Richard Rollins, comp., *Pickett's Charge: Eyewitness Accounts* (Redondo Beach, Calif.: Rank and File Publishers, 1994), 269.

69. *OR* 27 (1):470.

70. Ibid., p. 465.

71. Ibid., p. 473.

72. George Bowen diary, entry for July 3, 1863, in Rollins, *Pickett's Charge*, 269.

73. Quoted in ibid., 269; also quoted in Fleming, comp., *Life and Letters of Alexander Hays*, 443.

74. *OR* 27 (1):454.

75. Ibid., p. 462.

76. Surprisingly enough, the most straightforward statement about such a movement comes from Union general Hancock. See *OR* 27 (1):373–74.

77. See Frank and Reaves, *"Seeing the Elephant,"* 88–89, for insights on the visual and psychological impact of a geographically restricted battlefield.

78. *OR* 27 (1):431.

79. Quoted in Rollins, *Pickett's Charge*, 294.

80. Haskell, *Battle of Gettysburg*, 121–22.

81. *OR* 27 (1):428.

82. Ibid., p. 431.

83. Quoted in Rollins, *Pickett's Charge*, 294.

84. Haskell, *Battle of Gettysburg*, 119.

85. *OR* 27 (1):431.

86. Haskell, *Battle of Gettysburg*, 120.

87. Entry for July 3, 1863, William J. Burns diary, Save the Flags Collection, USAMHI.

88. *OR* 27 (1):443.

89. Ibid., p. 446.

90. Ibid., p. 439.

91. Ibid., p. 444.

92. Ibid., p. 425.

93. Letter of Sgt. John Plummer, in Moore, ed., *Rebellion Record*, 10:180.

94. See the day-by-day breakdown of casualties in John W. Busey, *These Honored Dead: The Union Casualties at Gettysburg* (Hightstown, N.J.: Longstreet House, 1988), 39–42 (19th Maine), 57–59 (15th Massachusetts), 130–32 (82nd New York).

95. *OR* 27 (1):422.

96. Ibid., p. 423.

97. Haskell, *Battle of Gettysburg*, 127–30.

98. Letter of Sgt. John Plummer, in Moore, ed., *Rebellion Record*, 10:180.

99. *OR* 27 (2):374.

100. Haskell, *Battle of Gettysburg*, 127; Capt. A. N. Jones after-action report, July 5, 1863, in George Edward Pickett Papers, DU.

101. Alexander Webb to wife, July 5, 1864, copy in box 4, Robert L. Brake collection, USAMHI.

102. Report of Col. Joseph Mayo, July 25, 1863, in George Edward Pickett Papers, DU.

103. *OR* 27 (2):386.

104. Quoted in Rollins, *Pickett's Charge*, 205–6.

105. *OR* 27 (1):350, 353.

106. Gilbert Wright, ed., "Some Letters to his Parents by a Floridian in the Confederate Army," *Florida Historical Quarterly* 36 (April 1958): 365.

107. Haskell, *Battle of Gettysburg*, 130.

108. Holmes, *Acts of War*, 154–55.

109. Charles S. Wainwright, *A Diary of Battle: The Personal Journals of Colonel Charles S. Wainwright*, ed. Allan Nevins (New York: Harcourt, Brace & World, 1962; Gettysburg, Pa.: Stan Clark Military Books, 1993), 249.

110. Entry for July 4, 1863, in William J. Burns Diary, Save the Flags Collection, USAMHI.

111. See McRandle, *Antique Drums of War*, 41, for the formalities of this stage of "battle ritual."

112. Quoted in Coco, *A Strange and Blighted Land*, 88.

113. Pvt. Loren Goodrich to unknown, July 17, 1863, quoted in Charles P. Hamblen, *Connecticut Yankees at Gettysburg* (Kent, Ohio: Kent State University Press, 1993), 113.

114. Quoted in Coco, *A Strange and Blighted Land*, 58.

115. Garrett Deacon to "Frend Middleton," July 31, 1863, in possession of Mrs. Miriam G. Wurst, Marlton, N.J.

116. Banes, *History of the Philadelphia Brigade*, 192.

117. Abbott to father, July 6, 1863, in Scott, ed., *Fallen Leaves*, 184.

118. Charles E. Nash to unknown, July 29, 1863, in John Day Smith, *The History of the Nineteenth Regiment of Maine Volunteer Infantry, 1862–1865* (Minneapolis: Great Western Printing Co., 1909), 100.

119. McRandle, *Antique Drums of War*, 42.

120. *OR* 27 (1):469.

121. Ibid., p. 452.

122. William B. Hoitt to "Friend Mary," July 13, 1863, Lewis Leigh Collection, USAMHI.

123. Nash to unknown, July 29, 1863, in John Day Smith, *History of the Nineteenth Regiment of Maine Volunteer Infantry*, 100.

124. *OR* 27 (1):1042.

125. Ibid., p. 468.

126. Ibid., p. 440.

127. Albert S. Emmell to aunt, July 17, 1863, in Albert S. Emmell *"Now Is the Time for Buck and Ball": The Life and Civil War Experiences of Albert Stokes Emmell* (n.p., 1991), n.p.

128. *OR* 27 (1):441.

129. Ibid., p. 420.

130. Ibid., pp. 418, 421, 440, 446.

131. Alexander S. Webb to wife, July 27, 1863, copy in box 4, Robert L. Brake Collection, USAMHI.

132. H. H. Bingham to sister, July 18, 1863, copy at GNMP.

133. William B. Hoitt to "Friend Mary," July 13, 1863, Lewis Leigh Collection, USAMHI.

134. [Samuel Fiske], *Mr. Dunn Browne's Experiences in the Army* (Boston: Nichols & Noyes, 1865), 205.

135. Wainwright, *A Diary of Battle*, 250.

136. [Fiske], *Mr. Dunn Browne's Experiences in the Army*, 187. Despite the publication date, Fiske wrote these comments not long after Gettysburg; he was killed in action in the battle of the Wilderness in May 1864.

137. Boston *Journal*, July 6, 1863.

138. A. S. VandeGraff to wife, July 8, 1863, copy at GNMP.

139. For an overview of the quite disparate range of Southern responses to the defeat at Gettysburg, see Gary W. Gallagher, "Lee's Army Has Not Lost Any of Its Prestige," in *Third Day at Gettysburg and Beyond* (Chapel Hill, N.C.: University of North Carolina Press, 1994), 1–30.

140. David E. Maxwell to mother, July 12, 1863, in Wright, ed., "Some Letters to his Parents by a Floridian in the Confederate Army," 367.

141. Granville Belcher to Caroline, July 16, 1863, Granville W. Belcher Papers, DU.

142. W. H. Proffitt to Miss R. L. Proffitt, July 9, 1863, Proffitt Family Papers, SHC.

143. Edgeworth Bird to Sallie, July 7, 1863, in John Rozier, ed., *The Granite Farm Letters: The Civil War Correspondence of Edgeworth and Sallie Bird* (Athens: University of Georgia Press, 1988), 115.

144. John S. Lewis to mother, July 21, 1863, in Harry Lewis Papers, DU.

145. Susan Leigh Blackford, comp., *Letters from Lee's Army* (New York: A. S. Barnes, 1947), 190.

146. James W. Silver, ed., *A Life for the Confederacy* (Jackson, Tenn.: McCowat-Mercer, 1959), 153.

147. Stephens C. Smith to Father and Mother, July 12, 1863, typescript in Stephens Calhoun Smith Papers, DU.

148. H. T. Holladay to ?, July 7, 1863, in Holladay Family Papers, University of Virginia Library, Charlottesville, Va.

149. Jedediah Hotchkiss, *Make Me a Map of the Valley: The Civil War Journal of Stonewall Jackson's Topographer*, ed. Archie P. McDonald (Dallas, Tex.: Southern Methodist University Press, 1973), 157.

150. Entry for July 3, 1863, James J. Kirkpatrick Diary, copy in box 7, Robert L. Brake Collection, USAMHI.

151. William Calder to mother, July 8, 1863, copy in box 8, Robert L. Brake Collection, USAMHI.

152. William Henry Cocke to William Cocke, July 11, 1863, Cocke Family Papers, VHS.

153. James J. Phillips to Ben. F. H. Smith, July 18, 1863, copy at GNMP.

154. James Dearing to mother, July 20, 1863, Dearing Family Papers, University of Virginia Library, Charlottesville, Va.

155. E. Porter Alexander to father, July 17, 1863, in Alexander-Hilhouse Papers, SHC.

156. This percentage is based on the largest number of men Pickett may have carried into action (6,100); the actual proportion may have been considerably higher if this number overestimates Pickett's actual strength that day. See also R. K. Krick, *The Gettysburg Death Roster: The Confederate Dead at Gettysburg*, 3rd ed. (Dayton, OH: Morningside, 1993), 7.

157. Blackford, comp., *Letters from Lee's Army*, 188.

158. Entry for July 3, 1863, Charles Edward Lippett Diary, SHC.

159. William H. Jones to wife, July 13, 1863, William H. Jones Papers, DU.

160. Entry for July 3, 1863, George K. Griggs Diary, Museum of the Confederacy, Richmond, Va.

161. William J. Hatchett to Parents, July 7, 1863, Hatchett Family Papers, Civil War Times Illustrated Collection, USAMHI.

162. R. F. White to Ross cousins, August 2, 1863, Ross Family Correspondence, Virginia State Library, Richmond, Va.

163. William Henry Cocke to ?, July 11, 1863, Cocke Family Papers, VHS.

164. Henry T. Owen to wife, July 24, 1863, Henry T. Owen Correspondence, Virginia State Library, Richmond, Va.

165. William Fitzgerald to Mrs. Jones, July 11, 1863, George W. Jones Papers, DU.

166. E. M. M. to sister, [ca. late July–early August 1863], and James M. Magruder to Eva, August 8, 1863, John Bowie Magruder Papers, DU.

167. B. F. Little to wife, July 9, 1863, Little to wife, July 20, 1863, both in Benjamin Franklin Little Papers, SHC.

168. W. B. Taylor to ?, July 29, 1863, in William B. Floyd Collection, copy at GNMP.

169. W. F. Fulton to Sister, July 27, 1863, copy at GNMP.

170. Captain Fleming W. Thompson to ?, undated letter, copy in 11th Alabama file, box 7, Robert L. Brake Collection, USAMHI.

171. Raymond J. Reid to Hal, September 4, 1863, copy at GNMP.

172. Isaac S. Barrineau to sister, July 10, 1863, and Barrineau to sister, August 6, 1863, in Isaac S. Barrineau Papers, Civil War Miscellaneous Collection, USAMHI.

173. The need for a certain degree of security to promote the healing process among soldiers is well explained in Jonathan Shay, *Achilles in Vietnam: Combat Trauma and the Undoing of Character* (New York: Athanaeum, 1994), 59–61.

174. Joseph C. Haskell to mother, July 26, 1863, in Rachel Susan Cheves Papers, DU.

175. Lt. William A. Miller to sister, August 28, 1863, vol. 168, Fredericksburg National Military Park Library.
176. Douglas Southall Freeman, *Lee's Lieutenants: A Study in Command*, 3 vols. (New York, Charles Scribner's Sons, 1944), 3:162.
177. Henry T. Owen to his wife, December 21, 1863, Henry T. Owen Papers, Virginia State Library, Richmond, Va.

CHAPTER TWO

1. [Samuel Fiske], *Mr. Dunn Browne's Experiences in the Army* (Boston: Nichols & Noyes, 1865), 205.
2. B. F. Little to wife, July 9, 1863, in Benjamin F. Little Papers, SHC.
3. For more on the concept of the media's role in contextualization, see Philip Jenkins, *Intimate Enemies: Moral Panics in Contemporary Great Britain* (New York: Aldine De Gruyter, 1992), 216.
4. For insights on the press coverage of the Gettysburg campaign, see J. Cutler Andrews, *The South Reports the Civil War* (Princeton, N.J.: Princeton University Press, 1970), 302–36, and Emmet Crozier, *Yankee Reporters, 1861–65* (New York: Oxford University Press, 1956), 345–61.
5. *New York Herald*, July 6, 1863.
6. See J. Cutler Andrews, "The Press Reports the Battle of Gettysburg," *Pennsylvania History* 31 (1964): 177–78.
7. Whitelaw Reid, "The Battle of Gettysburgh," in Frank Moore, ed., *The Rebellion Record: A Diary of American Events* (New York: D. Van Nostrand, 1864), 7:90.
8. Ibid.
9. *New York Times*, July 6, 1863.
10. *Harrisburg Daily Telegraph*, July 6, 1863.
11. *Philadelphia Inquirer*, July 6, 1863.
12. *Harrisburg Daily Telegraph*, July 6, 1863.
13. *New York Times*, July 6, 1863.
14. *New York World*, July 6, 1863.
15. *New York Times*, July 6, 1863.
16. Reid, "Battle of Gettysburgh."
17. *New York Times*, July 6, 1863.
18. *New York Herald*, July 10, 1863.
19. Reid, "Battle of Gettysburgh."
20. *New York Herald*, July 10, 1863; *Philadelphia Public Ledger*, July 7, 1863.
21. *New York Times*, July 6, 1863.
22. *Baltimore American*, July 6, 1863.
23. *New York Herald*, July 9, 1863. While neither Pickett nor Pettigrew won mention in this article, the next sentence noted that the great charge of July 3 took place near the same hill "where occurred the charge of the famous brigade of Louisiana Tigers."
24. Reid, "Battle of Gettysburgh."
25. *Philadelphia Public Ledger*, July 7, 1863.
26. *New York Herald*, July 6, 1863.

27. Henry Clare to Brother William, July 5, 1863, copy at GNMP.

28. *Philadelphia Public Ledger*, July 7, 1863.

29. *New York Herald*, July 10, 1863.

30. *New York Times*, July 6, 1863.

31. *Baltimore American*, July 6, 1863.

32. *New York Herald*, July 6, 1863.

33. Ibid.

34. Ibid., July 9, 1863.

35. Reid, "Battle of Gettysburgh."

36. *New York Herald*, July 6, 1863.

37. *Baltimore American*, July 6, 1863.

38. Ibid.

39. *New York Times*, July 6, 1863.

40. Ibid.

41. *Philadelphia Public Ledger*, July 7, 1863.

42. *Philadelphia Inquirer*, July 8, 1863.

43. *New York Herald*, July 6, 1863.

44. Ibid.

45. *New York Times*, July 6, 1863.

46. *Harrisburg Daily Telegraph*, July 6, 1863.

47. *Philadelphia Public Ledger*, July 7, 1863.

48. *New York Times*, July 6, 1863; *Philadelphia Public Ledger*, July 7, 1863.

49. *New York Times*, July 6, 1863.

50. *Philadelphia Inquirer*, July 8, 1863.

51. *New York Herald*, July 6, 1863.

52. *New York Times*, July 6, 1863.

53. Reid, "Battle of Gettysburgh."

54. *New York Herald*, July 6, 1863.

55. Reid, "Battle of Gettysburgh."

56. *Philadelphia Inquirer*, July 10, 1863.

57. H. M. Wagstaff, ed., *The James A. Graham Papers, 1861–1884*. James Sprunt Historical Studies, vol. 20, no. 2 (Chapel Hill: University of North Carolina Press, 1928), 150.

58. *Richmond Daily Dispatch*, July 7, 1863.

59. Ibid., July 8, 1863.

60. Sumter, S.C., *Tri-Weekly Watchman*, July 13, 1863.

61. *Charleston Daily Courier*, July 15, 1863.

62. *Richmond Daily Dispatch*, July 7, 1863.

63. Ibid., July 8, 1863. See Andrews, *The South Reports the Civil War*, 315, on the pervasiveness of outrageous exaggeration after Gettysburg.

64. *New York Times*, July 11, 1863.

65. *Richmond Daily Dispatch*, July 10, 1863.

66. Ibid., July 13, 1863.

67. Ibid., July 10, 1863.

68. *Baltimore American*, July 6, 1863; reprinted in *Richmond Daily Dispatch*, July 10, 1863.

69. *Richmond Whig*, July 12, 1863.

70. *Richmond Daily Dispatch*, July 13, 1863.

71. Samuel Hoey Walkup Diary, first entry for July 10, 1863, Samuel Hoey Walkup Papers, DU.

72. W. B. Stinson [Pickensville, Ala.] to Josiah Staunton Moore, July 17, 1863, in Josiah Staunton Moore Papers, VHS.

73. *Richmond Daily Dispatch*, July 13, 1863.

74. Ibid.

75. Richmond *Sentinel*, July 27, 1863.

76. *Richmond Daily Dispatch*, July 13, 1863; Richmond *Sentinel*, July 16, 1863.

77. *Richmond Daily Dispatch*, July 13, 1863.

78. Richmond *Sentinel*, July 16, 1863.

79. *Richmond Enquirer*, July 21, 1863.

80. Richmond *Sentinel*, July 20, 1863.

81. Albertson is tentatively identified in Andrews, *The South Reports the Civil War*, 543.

82. "The Battle of Gettysburg," *Richmond Enquirer*, July 23, 1863.

83. Ibid.

84. "Battle of Gettysburg—Pickett's Division," *Richmond Enquirer*, July 23, 1863.

85. General Ambrose Wright to wife, July 7, 1863, printed in Augusta, Ga., *Daily Constitutionalist*, July 23, 1863, and reprinted in *Richmond Daily Dispatch*, July 28, 1863.

86. *Savannah Republican*, July 20, 1863; *Mobile Daily Advertiser and Register*, July 21, 1863. This widely clipped piece also appeared in the *Charleston Mercury*, July 23, 1863; Atlanta, Ga., *Southern Confederacy*, July 29, 1863; Columbia, S.C., *Daily Southern Guardian*, July 31, 1863; and New Orleans *Picayune*, August 1, 1863.

87. Richmond *Southern Illustrated News*, vol. 2, no. 4, August 1, 1863.

88. *Richmond Enquirer*, August 7, 1863.

89. Ibid., August 14, 1863.

90. Lang's views on Gettysburg press coverage have been reprinted in Francis P. Fleming, "Gettysburg. The Courageous Part Taken in the Desperate Conflict, July 2–3, 1863," *SHSP* 27 (1899): 192–205. See also Bertram Groene, ed., "The Civil War Letters of Colonel David Lang," *Florida Historical Quarterly* 54 (1976): 340–66.

91. "A Private," August 6, 1863, prepared for Richmond *Sentinel*, undated clipping at GNMP.

92. The *Raleigh Register* carried Albertson's article on July 25, 1863. The Raleigh *Standard* carried it the same day, and the *Fayetteville Observer* printed it on July 28, 1863.

93. *Raleigh Register*, July 26, 1863. Reprinted in the *Richmond Enquirer*, July 28, 1863. For more on North Carolina's protest against Virginia's press coverage of the Gettysburg campaign, see Glenn Tucker, *Zebulon Vance: Champion of Personal Freedom* (Indianapolis, Ind.: Bobbs-Merrill, 1965), 266–72.

94. See, for instance, Brig. Gen. Bradley T. Johnson's praise of North Carolina troops in the Seven Days battles in the *Richmond Enquirer*, August 26, 1862.

95. *Richmond Enquirer*, August 13, 1863.

96. William Norwood to "My Dear Wm," July 15, 1863, Tillinghast Family Papers, DU.

97. *Richmond Examiner*, August 1, 1863.

CHAPTER THREE

1. *New York Herald*, July 6, 1863.
2. Michael Kammen, *Mystic Chords of Memory: The Transformation of Tradition in American Culture* (New York: Vintage Press, 1993), 3.
3. Quoted in ibid., 30–31.
4. See Arthur James Lyon Fremantle, "The Battle of Gettysburg and the Campaign in Pennsylvania," *Blackwood's Magazine* 94 (September 1863): 380–83.
5. See Arthur James Lyon Fremantle, *Three Months in the Southern States: April– June 1863* (Edinburgh and London: William Blackwood & Sons, 1863; New York: Bradburn, 1864; Mobile, Ala.: S. H. Goetzel, 1864).

   Two other foreign observers who accompanied Longstreet to Gettysburg left memoirs that essentially reinforce the accounts of events offered by the Richmond press. These include Austrian officer FitzGerald Ross's *Cities and Camps of the Confederacy*, originally published in London, and Prussian Justus Scheibert's *Sieben Monate in den Rebellen-Staaten Wahrend des Nordamerkanischen Kreiges 1863*, published in Stettin in 1868, neither of which were translated into English until the mid-twentieth century.
6. Edward A. Pollard, *The Second Year of the War* (New York: Charles B. Richardson, 1864), 282–83. An earlier edition of this work was printed in Richmond in late 1863.
7. Edward A. Pollard, *The Third Year of the War* (New York: Charles B. Richardson, 1865), 32–36. After the war, Pollard repeated his diatribes all over again in *The Lost Cause: The Standard Southern History of the War of the Confederates* (New York: E. B. Treat, 1867), 408–10.
8. W. J. Baker to Louis G. Young, December 14, 1863, printed in Louis G. Young, "Pettigrew's Brigade at Gettysburg," *Our Living and Our Dead* 1 (February 1875): 552–53.
9. *Richmond Enquirer*, March 18, 1864.
10. M[ichael] Jacobs, *Notes on the Rebel Invasion of Maryland and Pennsylvania and the Battle of Gettysburg, July 1st, 2d and 3d, 1863* . . . (Philadelphia: J. B. Lippincott & Co., 1864), 42–43.
11. Patriot Daughters of Lancaster, *Hospital Scenes after the Battle of Gettysburg, July, 1863* (Philadelphia: Henry B. Ashmead, 1864), 18.
12. John Y. Foster, "Four Days at Gettysburg," *Harper's New Monthly Magazine* 28 (1864): 385.
13. John C. Williams, *Life in Camp: A History of the Nine Months' Service of the Fourteenth Vermont Regiment* (Claremont, N.H.: Claremont Manufacturing Co., 1864), 143.
14. [Edwin F. Palmer], *The Second Brigade; or, Camp Life, by A Volunteer* (Montpelier, Vt.: E. P. Walton, 1864), 179.
15. Michael Jacobs, "Later Rambles over the Field of Gettysburg," *United States Service Magazine* 1 (January 1864): 66–67.
16. Foster, "Four Days at Gettysburg," 388.
17. Theodore Ditterline, *Sketch of the Battles of Gettysburg, July 1st, 2d, and 3d, 1863* . . . (New York: C. A. Alvord, 1864), 20–21.

18. George J. Gross, *The Battle-field of Gettysburg* (Philadelphia: Collins, Printer, 1866), 18.

19. Foster, "Four Days at Gettysburg," 382.

20. Michael Jacobs, "Later Rambles over the Field of Gettysburg," *United States Service Magazine* 1 (February 1864): 165.

21. Gross, *The Battle-field of Gettysburg*, 18–19.

22. William Parker Snow, *Southern Generals, Who They Are, and What They Have Done* (New York: Charles B. Richardson, 1865), 104–5.

23. Thomas P. Kettell, *History of the Great Rebellion* (Hartford, Conn.: L. Stebbins, 1865), 463–64.

24. Horace Greeley, *The American Conflict*, 2 vols. (Hartford, Conn.: O. D. Case & Co., 1866), 2:382–87.

25. Charles Carlton Coffin, *Four Years of Fighting* (Boston: Ticknor & Fields, 1866), 295–97.

26. William Swinton, *Campaigns of the Army of the Potomac* (New York: Dick & Fitzgerald, 1866), 356–61.

27. William Swinton, *The Twelve Decisive Battles of the War: A History of the Eastern and Western Campaigns, in Relation to the Actions that Decided Their Issue* (New York: Dick & Fitzgerald, 1867), 344–45, 351–53.

28. Ibid., 355.

29. Kammen, *Mystic Chords of Memory*, 9.

30. Edmund C. Stedman, "Gettysburg," *Army and Navy Journal* 9 (May 11, 1872): 623.

31. John C. Kensil, "The Battlefield of Gettysburg, After Twenty Years," *Grand Army Scout and Soldiers' Mail*, September 8, 1883.

32. Warren H. Cudworth, *History of the First Regiment (Massachusetts Infantry)* . . . (Boston: Walker, Fuller & Co., 1866), 398–99.

33. Edwin B. Houghton, *The Campaigns of the Seventeenth Maine* (Portland, Maine: Short & Loring, 1866), 95.

34. D. G. Crotty, *Four Years Campaigning in the Army of the Potomac* (Grand Rapids, Mich.: Dygert Bros. & Co., 1874), 92–94.

35. Miss E. Latimer, *Idyls of Gettysburg* (Philadelphia: George Maclean, 1872), 37–38.

36. "Steel Engraving of the Battle of Gettysburg (Repulse of Longstreet's Assault)," in John B. Bachelder, *Gettysburg Publications* (Boston: John B. Bachelder, n.d.), 2–3.

37. Jenkins to Bachelder, January 7, 1864, BP. Reprinted in Mary Geneve Green Brainard, comp., *Campaigns of the One Hundred and Forty-Sixth Regiment New York State Volunteers* (New York: G. P. Putnam's Sons, 1915), 124.

38. John B. Bachelder, *Descriptive Key to the Painting of the Repulse of Longstreet's Assault at the Battle of Gettysburg* (New York: John B. Bachelder, 1870), 9n.

39. Ibid., 26, 32.

40. "Painting and Engraving of the Battle of Gettysburg," in Bachelder, *Gettysburg Publications*, 2, 8.

41. "Steel Engraving of the Battle of Gettysburg," 6.

42. See Edwin B. Coddington, "Rothermel's Paintings of the Battle of Gettysburg," *Pennsylvania History* 27 (1960): 1–27.

43. The entire ceremony was covered extensively in the *Philadelphia Inquirer*, December 21, 1870.

44. H. E. Brown, "Cushing's United States Battery at Gettysburg," *Grand Army Scout and Soldiers' Mail*, December 19, 1885.

45. *Philadelphia Inquirer*, December 21, 1870.

46. A. K. M. Storrie, "Gettysburg," *Grand Army Scout and Soldiers' News*, March 6, 1886.

47. John Ritchie for the *Boston Daily News*, October 24, 1883, quoted in program for the public display of the cyclorama painting at Boston. Copy in library at USAMHI.

48. "School Histories of the United States," *Southern Review* 3 (1868): 155.

49. See Thomas L. Connelly, *The Marble Man: Robert E. Lee and His Image in American Society* (New York: A. A. Knopf, 1977), 57–61.

50. James Dabney McCabe Jr., *Life and Campaigns of General Robert E. Lee* (Atlanta: National Publishing Co., 1866), 401.

51. Edward A. Pollard, *Early Life, Campaigns, and Public Service of Robert E. Lee* (New York: E. B. Treat, 1870), 113, 519.

52. McCabe, *Life and Campaigns of Robert E. Lee*, 401.

53. Pollard, *Lee and His Lieutenants* (New York: E. B. Treat, 1867), 512–13, 517–18.

54. John Esten Cooke devoted an entire chapter to Lee after the charge in *A Life of Gen. Robert E. Lee* (New York: D. Appleton & Co., 1871), 325ff.

55. John Esten Cooke, *The Wearing of the Gray, Being Personal Portraits, Scenes and Adventures of the War* (New York: E. B. Treat, 1867), 258.

56. See the characterizations in John Esten Cooke, *Surry of Eagle's Nest* (New York: G. W. Dillingham, 1866), 482, and especially Cooke, *Mohun* (New York: G. W. Dillingham, 1867), 87–91.

57. "Bacon and Greens," in George W. Bagby, *The Old Virginia Gentleman and Other Sketches* (New York: Charles Scribner's Sons, 1910), 45–68.

58. John Esten Cooke, *Hammer and Rapier* (New York: Carleton, 1870), 225.

59. Gorton Carruth and Eugene Ehrlich, *American Quotations* (New York: Wings, 1988), 274.

60. Henry Alexander White, "The Battle of Gettysburg. Some Literary Facts Connected Therewith," *SHSP* 27 (1899): 52.

61. Albert Bledsoe, "The Battle of Gettysburg," *Southern Review* 5 (April 1869): 440.

62. D. H. Hill, "Washington," *The Land We Love* 1 (1866): 92–93.

63. [D. H. Hill], "The Haversack," *The Land We Love* 3 (June 1867): 157.

64. Walter Harrison, *Pickett's Men, A Fragment of War History* (New York: D. Van Nostrand, 1870), 3.

65. Ibid., 3–4.

66. Ibid., 90–107.

67. John E. Edwards, *The Confederate Soldier, Being a Memorial Sketch of George N. and Bushrod W. Harrison* (New York: Blelock & Co., 1868), 136.

68. John Lipscomb Johnson, *The University Memorial: Biographical Sketches of Alumni of the University of Virginia Who Fell in the Confederate War* (Baltimore: Turnbull Bros., 1871), 435, 443–46, 450, 455.

69. Harrison, *Pickett's Men*, 101.

70. Mary H. Mitchell, *Hollywood Cemetery: The History of a Southern Shrine* (Richmond: Virginia State Library, 1985), 87–91.

71. LaSalle Corbell Pickett, *The Heart of a Soldier as Revealed in the Intimate Letters of General George E. Pickett, C.S.A.* (New York: Seth Moyle, 1913), 203–7.

72. "A Story of Gettysburg," *Southern Magazine* 12 (1873): 654–61.

73. Mrs. Garland Jones, "Ladies Memorial Association of Raleigh, North Carolina," ca. 1883, copy at GNMP.

74. Richard Irby, *Historical Sketch of the Nottaway Grays, Afterwards Company G, Eighteenth Virginia Regiment, Army of Northern Virginia* (Richmond: J. W. Furgusson & Son, 1878), 29.

75. Norfolk *Landmark*, August 1, 1875; reprinted in *Richmond Daily Dispatch*, August 2, 1875.

76. *Richmond Daily Dispatch*, August 2, 1875.

77. *Atlanta Constitution*, August 3, 1875.

78. *Richmond Daily Dispatch*, August 2, 1875.

79. Norfolk *Landmark*, July 31, 1875.

80. *Philadelphia Inquirer*, July 31, 1875.

81. *Richmond Daily Dispatch*, August 3, 1875.

82. Norfolk *Virginian*, July 31, 1875.

83. *Richmond Daily Dispatch*, August 3, 1875.

84. Ibid.

85. Ibid.

86. Norfolk *Landmark*, July 31, 1875.

87. See Virginius Dabney, *Richmond: The Story of a City* (New York: Doubleday & Co., 1976), 232–33. A similar squabble erupted over the participation of black state militiamen in the dedication of a monument to Stonewall Jackson, which was scheduled to take place within days of the Pickett funeral.

88. *Richmond Daily Dispatch*, October 23, 25, and 26, 1875.

89. Ibid., October 16, 1875.

90. Ibid., October 23, 1875.

91. Ibid., October 26, 1875.

92. Ibid.

CHAPTER FOUR

1. *Army and Navy Journal* 11 (May 16, 1874), 632.

2. "Our First Paper," *SHSP* 1 (1876): 39.

3. For the role of the Southern Historical Society in the shaping of Confederate history, and especially its tailoring of the image of Robert E. Lee, see Thomas L. Connelly, *The Marble Man: The Image of Robert E. Lee in American Society* (New York: A. A. Knopf, 1977), ch. 3.

4. J. William Jones, comp., *Army of Northern Virginia Memorial Volume* (Richmond: J. W. Randolph & English, 1880), 9.

5. See Connelly, *The Marble Man*, ch. 3. For Longstreet's perspective on the first attacks launched against him, see William Garrett Piston, *Lee's Tarnished Lieu-

tenant: James Longstreet and His Place in Southern History (Athens: University of Georgia Press, 1987), 118-31.

6. See, for example, Jubal A. Early, "Leading Confederates on the Battle of Gettysburg," *SHSP* 4 (1877): 241-81, and William Nelson Pendleton, "Personal Recollections of Robert E. Lee," *Southern Magazine* 15 (1874): 603-36.

7. James Longstreet, "The Campaign of Gettysburg," *Philadelphia Weekly Times*, November 3, 1877; reprinted as "Lee in Pennsylvania" in *Annals of the War, Written by Leading Participants North and South* (Philadelphia: Times Publishing Co., 1879), 414-46.

8. Jubal A. Early, "Letter from Gen. J. A. Early," *SHSP* 4 (1877): 64.

9. See, for example, Walter H. Taylor, "The Campaign in Pennsylvania," *Philadelphia Weekly Times*, August 25, 1877 (reprinted in *Annals of War*, 305-18), and variant versions in *Four Years with General Lee* (New York: D. Appleton, 1878), 103-8, and "Memorandum by Colonel Walter H. Taylor of General Lee's Staff," *SHSP* 4 (1877): 84-85.

10. Armistead Long, "Letter from General A. L. Long, Military Secretary to Gen. Robert E. Lee," *SHSP* 4 (1877): 118-23.

11. Rumors of Pickett's fondness for alcohol have dogged his reputation for years with no definitive resolution. The suggestion that a drinking problem kept him out of the Lee clique's inner circle appears in Dixon Wecter, *The Hero in America: A Chronicle of Hero Worship* (New York: Charles Scribner's Sons, 1941), 301.

12. See Pickett's appointments to various veterans committees in J. William Jones, *Army of Northern Virginia Memorial Volume*, 12, 42, 88.

13. See Jeffry D. Wert, *General James Longstreet: The Confederacy's Most Controversial Soldier—A Biography* (New York: Simon & Schuster, 1993), 48-49, 97.

14. See LaSalle Corbell Pickett, "My Soldier," *McClure's Magazine* 30 (1907): 569.

15. General B. D. Fry, "Pettigrew's Charge at Gettysburg," *SHSP* 7 (1879): 91-93.

16. James H. Lane, "Letter from General James H. Lane," *SHSP* 5 (1878): 38-40.

17. Isaac R. Trimble, "History of Lane's North Carolina Brigade—The Gettysburg Campaign—Letter from General Trimble," *SHSP* 9 (1881): 35.

18. Henry Heth, "Letter from Major-General Henry Heth," *SHSP* 4 (1877): 151-60. Heth's reticence may also stem from the fact that he and George Pickett were cousins and he, too, had known Longstreet for years. See James L. Morrison, ed., *The Memoirs of Henry Heth* (Westport, Conn.: Greenwood Press, 1974), 237.

19. Abner Doubleday, *Chancellorsville and Gettysburg* (New York: Charles Scribner's Sons, 1882), 195.

20. See several installments of "Notes and Queries" in *SHSP* 10 (1882): 284, 335, 423-29, and *SHSP* 11 (1883): 284-86.

21. Charles T. Loehr, *War History of the Old First Virginia Infantry Regiment, Army of Northern Virginia* (Richmond: William Ellis Jones, 1884), 36-38.

22. Richard Irby, *Historical Sketch of the Nottaway Grays, Afterwards Company G, Eighteenth Virginia Regiment, Army of Northern Virginia, Prepared at the Request of the Surviving Members of the Company at Their First Reunion at Bellefont Church, July 21, 1877* (Richmond: J. W. Furgusson & Son, 1878), 29.

23. For an enlisted man's view of the charge (although he was wounded in the cannonade and did not advance with the rest of the 7th Virginia), see David E. Johnston, *Four Years a Soldier* (Princeton, W.Va.: n.p., 1887), 244-64.

24. R. W. Figg, *"Where Men Only Dare to Go!" or the Story of a Boy Company by an Ex-boy* (Richmond: Whittet & Shepperson, 1885), 140.

25. George Cary Eggleston, *A Rebel's Recollections* (New York: Riverside Press, 1875), 4.

26. Albion W. Tourgee, "The South as a Field for Fiction," *Forum* 6 (1888–89): 405.

27. Thomas Nelson Page, *The Burial of the Guns* (New York: Charles Scribner's Sons, 1894), 74–75.

28. Henry T. Owen, "Pickett at Gettysburg," *Philadelphia Weekly Times*, March 26, 1881.

29. W. W. Wood, "Pickett's Charge at Gettysburg," *Philadelphia Weekly Times*, August 11, 1877.

30. Henry T. Owen, "Pickett at Gettysburg"; Thomas D. Houston, "Storming Cemetery Hill," *Philadelphia Weekly Times*, October 21, 1882. Houston's article includes a letter from Lt. James, 11th Virginia, dated July 9, 1863.

31. William M. Owen, "Pickett's Charge," *Grand Army Scout and Soldiers' Mail*, December 17, 1885.

32. Lafayette McLaws to J. B. Kershaw, July 17, 1888, Joseph B. Kershaw Papers, South Caroliniana Library, Columbia, S.C.

33. "Battles and Leaders of the Civil War," *Century Magazine* 28 (October 1884): 943.

34. James Longstreet, "Lee's Right Wing at Gettysburg," in *B&L*, 3:339–54.

35. E. Porter Alexander, "The Great Charge and the Artillery Fighting at Gettysburg," in *B&L*, 3:357–68.

36. Edmund Rice, "Repelling Lee's Last Blow at Gettysburg: I," in *B&L*, 3:387–90; Norman J. Hall, "Repelling Lee's Last Blow at Gettysburg: II," ibid., 390–91; L. E. Bicknell, "Repulsing Lee's Last Blow at Gettysburg," ibid., 391–92.

37. "The Century War Series," *Century Magazine* 29 (1885): 788.

38. "The Blue and the Gray," *National Tribune*, April 22, 1882.

39. "Battles and Leaders of the Civil War."

40. G. G. Benedict, *A Short History of the 14th Vermont Regiment* (Bennington, Vt.: C. M. Pierce, 1887), 32.

41. David M. Earle, *History of the Excursion of the Fifteenth Massachusetts Regiment and Its Friends, to the Battlefields of Gettysburg, Pa, Antietam, Md, Ball's Bluff, Va, and Washington D.C., May 31–June 12, 1886* (Worcester, Mass.: Charles Hamilton Press, 1886), 26.

42. R. L. Maury report on efforts to build Pickett's Division Monument at Gettysburg, ca. 1887, copy in Edward Payson Reeve Papers, SHC.

43. David Wyatt Aikin, "The Gettysburg Reunion. What is Necessary and Proper for the South to Do," Charleston *News and Courier*, June 21, 1882.

44. "The Grand Army Encampment Upon the Battle Field of Gettysburg," *Grand Army Scout and Soldiers' Mail*, August 18, 1883.

45. Anthony W. McDermott and John E. Reilly, *A Brief History of the Sixty-ninth Regiment Pennsylvania Veteran Volunteers from Its Formation Until Final Muster Out of United States Service. Also, an Account of the Reunion of the Survivors of the Philadelphia Brigade and Pickett's Division of Confederate Soldiers, and the Dedication of the Monument of the Sixty-ninth Regiment Pennsylvania Infantry at Gettysburg, July 2d and 3d, 1887, by John E. Reilly.* (Philadelphia: D. J. Gallagher, 1889), 52.

46. John Tregaskis, *Souvenir of the Re-Union of the Blue and the Gray on the Battlefield*

of Gettysburg, July 1, 2, 3 and 4, 1888 [sic, *1887*] (New York: American Graphic, 1888), [2–3].

47. Ibid., [3].

48. Ibid., [3, 5].

49. P. L. Terry, J. I. Lee, and N. H. Hazelwood to Gen. William R. Terry, May 7, 1887, in Edward Payson Reeve Papers, SHC.

50. This description is included in "The Picket[t] Memorial at Gettysburg," *National Tribune*, May 12, 1887.

51. R. L. Maury report on efforts to build Pickett's Division Monument at Gettysburg, ca. 1887, in Edward Payson Reeve Papers, SHC.

52. Richard L. Maury to James L. Kemper, April 5, 1887, James Lawson Kemper Papers, University of Virginia Library, Charlottesville, Va.

53. James L. Kemper to Richard L. Maury, April 7, 1887, Richard L. Maury Papers, DU.

54. An account of the Union veterans' visit can be found in *Philadelphia Inquirer*, July 5, 1887.

55. Tregaskis, *Souvenir of the Re-Union of the Blue and the Gray*, [5].

56. John W. Frazier, *Reunion of the Blue and Gray. Philadelphia Brigade and Pickett's Division, July 2, 3, 4, 1887, and September 15, 16, 17, 1906* (Philadelphia: Ware Brothers., 1906), 41.

57. *Philadelphia Inquirer*, May 6, 1887.

58. R. L. Maury report on efforts to build Pickett's Division Monument at Gettysburg, ca. 1887, in Edward Payson Reeve Papers, SHC; *Philadelphia Inquirer*, May 7, 1887. See also "Picket[t] Memorial at Gettysburg."

59. Tregaskis, *Souvenir of the Re-Union of the Blue and the Gray*, [5].

60. Ibid., [6].

61. Ibid., [6–7].

62. Ibid., [7].

63. Ibid., [7–8].

64. Untitled editorial, *The Nation*, June 23, 1887.

65. Copy of resolutions printed in Charleston *News and Courier*, June 26, 1887.

66. *The Nation*, June 23, 1887.

67. Lee's and Gordon's comments are contained in "The Battle-Flag Flurry," *The Nation*, June 23, 1887, 524.

68. Jefferson Davis to Col. Phocian Howard, June 20, 1887, printed in Charleston *News and Courier*, June 24, 1887, and elsewhere.

69. "The Battle-Flag Flurry," 524.

70. *Philadelphia Inquirer*, June 25, 1887.

71. Ibid., June 30, 1887.

72. Ibid., June 17, 1887.

73. *New York Times*, July 3, 1887.

74. See McDermott and Reilly, *A Brief History of the Sixty-ninth Pennsylvania*, 53–55; *Philadelphia Inquirer*, July 4, 1887.

75. The high water mark memorial, designed by John Bachelder himself, would be dedicated in 1891.

76. *New York Times*, July 3, 1887.

77. "North and South at Gettysburg," *Army and Navy Journal* 24 (July 9, 1887), 1001.

78. McDermott and Reilly, *A Brief History of the Sixty-ninth Pennsylvania*, 76.

79. *New York Times*, July 3, 1887.

80. *Philadelphia Inquirer*, July 5, 1887.

81. See, for instance, the several columns devoted to the reunion in the Charleston *News and Courier*, July 3, 1887.

82. *Atlanta Constitution*, July 2, 1887.

83. *Philadelphia Inquirer*, July 4, 1887.

84. Ibid.

85. Ibid.

86. *New York Times*, July 4, 1887.

87. *Philadelphia Inquirer*, July 4, 1887. The Philadelphians also presented Bachelder with a gold watch at this time.

88. Tregaskis, *Souvenir of the Re-Union of the Blue and the Gray*, [11–12].

89. *Philadelphia Inquirer*, July 4, 1887; *New York Times*, July 4, 1887.

90. *New York Times*, July 4, 1887.

91. Tregaskis, *Souvenir of the Re-Union of the Blue and the Gray*, [12].

92. *Philadelphia Inquirer*, July 4, 1887.

93. McDermott and Reilly, *A Brief History of the Sixty-ninth Pennsylvania*, 76; Tregaskis, *Souvenir of the Re-Union of the Blue and the Gray*, [13].

94. *Philadelphia Inquirer*, July 5, 1887.

95. H. S. Petty to Edward Payson Reeve, July 8, 1887, in Edward Payson Reeve Papers, SHC.

96. *Philadelphia Inquirer*, July 5, 1887; *New York Times*, July 5, 1887.

97. "A Visit to the Battlefield of Gettysburg," by Col. H. C. Cabell, copy in Cabell Family Papers, VHS.

98. *Philadelphia Inquirer*, July 5, 1887.

99. Ibid.

100. "Hand-Clasps at the Wall," in Tregaskis, *Souvenir of the Re-Union of the Blue and the Gray*, [16].

101. *Philadelphia Inquirer*, July 4, 1887; Tregaskis, *Souvenir of the Re-Union of the Blue and the Gray*, [18–20].

102. "Mrs. Pickett's Thanks," *Army and Navy Journal* 24 (July 16, 1887), 1011.

103. B. L. Farinholt to Editor of *Richmond Whig*, July 20, 1888, copy in Edward Payson Reeve Papers, SHC.

104. W. H. Young to E. P. Reeve, July 24, 1888, in Edward Payson Reeve Papers, SHC.

105. *Richmond Dispatch*, August 28, 1888.

106. See Cherry Street Granite and Marble Works to Reeve, June 1 and 4, 1888, and Agreement to Construct Monument in Hollywood Cemetery, June 26, 1888, by Hutcheson and Donald, Quarrymen and Cutters of Virginia Blue Granite; undated order for statuary from Monumental Bronze Company of Bridgeport, Conn., all in Edward Payson Reeve Papers, SHC.

107. *Richmond Daily Dispatch*, September 30, 1888.

108. C. T. Phillips to E. P. Reeve, July 7, 1888, in Edward Payson Reeve Papers, SHC.

109. James L. Kemper to E. P. Reeve, July 16, 1888, in Edward Payson Reeve Papers, SHC.

110. *Richmond Daily Dispatch*, August 30, 1888.

111. Eppa Hunton to E. P. Reeve, August 31, 1888, and Fitzhugh Lee to E. P. Reeve,

September 11, 1888, in Edward Payson Reeve Papers, SHC. Lee did happen to be in town the following day when Democratic clubs enjoyed a special day at the Virginia Exposition, however.

112. R. Taylor Scott to E. P. Reeve, June 6, 1888, in Edward Payson Reeve Papers, SHC.

113. [Pickett-Buchanan camp] to E. P. Reeve, September 26, 1888, in Edward Payson Reeve Papers, SHC.

114. *Richmond Daily Dispatch*, October 4, 1888.

115. Philip Kearny GAR Post 10 to E. P. Reeve, September 25, 1888, in Edward Payson Reeve Papers, SHC; *Richmond Dispatch*, October 4, 1888.

116. Richmond Howitzers [Veterans Association] to E. P. Reeve, September 25, 1888, [Pegram Battalion Association] to E. P. Reeve, September 26, 1888, and [Richmond Light Infantry Blues Association] to E. P. Reeve, September 27, 1888, all in Edward Payson Reeve Papers, SHC.

117. *Philadelphia Inquirer*, October 1, 5, 1888.

118. *Richmond Daily Dispatch*, October 5, 1888.

119. *Philadelphia Inquirer*, October 6, 1888.

120. Ibid.

121. *Richmond Daily Dispatch*, September 30, 1888.

122. *Washington Post*, October 6, 1888; *Philadelphia Inquirer*, October 1, 1888.

123. Quoted in *Philadelphia Inquirer*, October 6, 1888.

124. Capt. John E. Reilly, quoted in *Philadelphia Inquirer*, October 6, 1888.

125. *Richmond Daily Dispatch*, October 5, 1888.

CHAPTER FIVE

1. Address of Maj. J. W. Slagle, September 11, 1889, in *Pa at Gbg*, 2:742–43.

2. This mind-set is nicely dissected in Anne C. Rose, *Victorian America and the Civil War* (New York: Cambridge University Press, 1992), 245–55.

3. "25 Years Later," *National Tribune*, July 12, 1888.

4. Unsigned editorial comment, *National Tribune*, June 14, 1888.

5. *Army and Navy Journal* 25 (December 10, 1887): 387, and ibid., (December 17, 1887): 397.

6. "The Gettysburg Celebration," *National Tribune*, June 14, 1888.

7. Ibid., May 31, 1888.

8. Ibid.

9. *New York Times*, July 1, 1888.

10. "Gettysburg Reunion," *Army and Navy Journal* 25 (June 30, 1888): 980.

11. Thomas A. Hutchins to Edward Payson Reeve, May 28, 1888, in Edward Payson Reeve Papers, SHC.

12. *Philadelphia Inquirer*, July 3, 1888; *New York Times*, July 3, 1888; "25 Years Later."

13. *New York Times*, July 3, 1888.

14. Ibid., July 2, 1888.

15. Ibid.; "25 Years Later."

16. *New York Times*, July 4, 1888.

17. *Philadelphia Inquirer*, July 4, 1888.

18. Ibid., July 5, 1888.
19. Will Henry Thompson, "High Tide at Gettysburg," *Century Magazine* 86 (1913): 410–12.
20. See Kate Mason Rowland, "High Tide at Gettysburg," *Confederate Veteran* 11 (1903): 365–55.
21. "More Rebel Impudence," *National Tribune*, October 11, 1888.
22. Undated resolution of Henry I. Zinn Post, GAR, Mechanicsburg, Pa., copy in Harrisburg Civil War Round Table Collection, USAMHI.
23. "Unveiling of Lee's Monument," *National Tribune*, June 5, 1890.
24. "Valuable Historical Matter," *National Tribune*, June 12, 1890.
25. A. R. Small, *The Sixteenth Maine Regiment in the War of the Rebellion* (Portland, Maine: B. Thurston & Co., 1886), 124–25.
26. Charles D. Page, *History of the Fourteenth Regiment, Connecticut Volunteer Infantry* (Meriden, Conn.: Horton Printing Co., 1906), 151.
27. Samuel H. Hurst, *Journal-History of the Seventy-Third Ohio Volunteer Infantry* (Chillicothe, Ohio: n.p., 1866), 74.
28. Theodore Gerrish, *Army Life: A Private's Reminiscences of the Civil War* (Portland, Maine: Hoyt, Fogg & Dunham, 1882), 117.
29. Sgt. James A. Wright Memoir, undated, copy in 1st Minnesota file, box 10, Robert L. Brake Collection, USAMHI.
30. Ralph Orson Sturtevant, *Pictorial History, Thirteenth Vermont Volunteers, War of 1861–1865* (n.p., [ca. 1910]), 301.
31. Mrs. Arabella M. Wilson, *Disaster, Struggle, Triumph: The Adventures of 1,000 "Boys in Blue," from August, 1862, to June, 1865* (Albany, N.Y.: Argus Company, Printers, 1870), 181.
32. Survivors Association, *History of the Corn Exchange Regiment, 118th Pennsylvania Volunteers from their First Engagement at Antietam to Appomattox* (Philadelphia: J. L. Smith, 1888), 258–59.
33. Samuel Toombs, *Reminiscences of the War, Comprising a Detailed Account of the Experiences of the Thirteenth Regiment New Jersey Volunteers in Camp, on the March, and in Battle* (Orange, N.J.: Journal Office, 1878), 81.
34. Alanson A. Haines, *History of the Fifteenth Regiment New Jersey Volunteers* (New York: Jenkins & Thomas, 1883), 88.
35. Return I. Holcombe, *History of the First Regiment Minnesota Volunteer Infantry 1861–64* (Stillwater, Minn.: Easton & Masterman, 1916), 364.
36. Ezra D. Simons, *A Regimental History. The One Hundred and Twenty-Fifth New York State Volunteers* (New York: Judson Printing Co., 1888), 135–36.
37. J. C. Williams, *Life in Camp: A History of the Nine Months' Service of the Fourteenth Vermont Regiment* (Claremont, N.H.: Claremont Manufacturing Co., 1864), 145.
38. Lt. William Lochren, "The First Minnesota at Gettysburg," read before the Minnesota MOLLUS on January 14, 1890, in *The Gettysburg Papers*, comp. Ken Bandy and Florence Freeland, vol. 2 (Dayton, Ohio: Morningside, 1978), 612.
39. *Reunions of the Nineteenth Maine Regiment Association* (Augusta, Maine: Sprague, Owen & Nash, 1878), 13.
40. Joseph R. C. Ward, *History of the One Hundred and Sixth Regiment Pennsylvania Volunteers, 2d Brigade, 2d Division, 2d Corps, 1861–1865* (Philadelphia: F. McManus Jr. & Co., 1906), 201.

41. J. Howard Wert, *A Complete Hand-Book of the Monuments and Indications and Guide to the Positions on the Gettysburg Battle-field* (Harrisburg: R. M. Sturgeon, 1886), 51.

42. Hartwell Osborn et al., *Trials and Triumphs: The Record of the Fifty-fifth Ohio Volunteer Infantry* (Chicago: A. C. McClurg & Co., 1904), 104.

43. Asa W. Bartlett, *History of the Twelfth Regiment, New Hampshire Volunteers in the War of the Rebellion* (Concord, N.H.: Ira C. Evans, 1897), 132.

44. G. G. Benedict, *A Short History of the 14th Vermont Regiment* (Bennington, Vt.: C. A. Pierce, 1887), 12.

45. Small, *The Sixteenth Maine Regiment*, 125.

46. J. W. Nesbit, "Gettysburg," *National Tribune*, November 16, 1916.

47. "Saving the Nation," *National Tribune*, May 21, 1885.

48. Oration of Col. Clinton MacDougall, June 26, 1891, in *NY at Gbg*, 2:802.

49. A. J. Sellars, comp., *Souvenir, Survivors' Association, Gettysburg, 1888-9* (Philadelphia: John W. Clark's Sons, [ca. 1889]), 91.

50. Wert, *A Complete Hand-book of the Monuments*, 34, 36-38.

51. Edwin E. Bryant, *History of the Third Regiment of Wisconsin Veteran Volunteer Infantry, 1861-1865* (Madison, Wisc.: Veterans Association of the Regiment, 1891), 201.

52. Abner Doubleday, "Stannard's Men at Gettysburg," in Benedict, *A Short History of the 14th Vermont Regiment*, 38.

53. Address of Hon. Ira M. Hedges, July 1, 1893, in *NY at Gbg*, 2:735.

54. Ibid., 2:804.

55. Mark Nickerson, *Recollections of the Civil War by a High Private in the Front Ranks* (n.p., 1991), 70-71.

56. Address of Serano M. Payne, July 1, 1887, in *NY at Gbg*, 3:1273.

57. Oration of Col. James C. Mulligan, October 25, 1888, in [Maryland Gettysburg Monument Commission], *Report of the State of Maryland Gettysburg Monument Commission to His Excellency E. E. Jackson, Governor of Maryland, June 17th 1891* (Baltimore: William K. Boyle & Sons, 1891), 72.

58. Eugene Arus Nash, *A History of the Forty-fourth Regiment New York Volunteer Infantry in the Civil War, 1861-1865* (Dayton, Ohio: Morningside, 1988), 149.

59. Oration of Maj. J. W. Slagle, September 11, 1889, in *Pa at Gbg*, 2:742-43.

60. James C. McCoughtry, "Not Particularly Game," *National Tribune*, August 4, 1892.

61. Robert G. Carter, *Four Brothers in Blue* (Washington, D.C.: Press of Gibson Brothers, 1913), 317.

62. Oration of Brig. Gen. Henry H. Bingham, September 11, 1889, in *Pa at Gbg*, 1:51.

63. Andrew W. McDermott to John B. Bachelder, June 2, 1886, in BP.

64. Address of Hon. John M. Davy, September 4, 1888, in *NY at Gbg*, 2:783.

65. Oration of Chaplain Stevens, July 3, 1883, quoted in Charles D. Page, *History of the Fourteenth Regiment, Connecticut Volunteer Infantry* (Meriden, Conn.: Horton Printing Co., 1906), 336.

66. Address of Benjamin B. Snow, June 26, 1891, in *NY at Gbg*, 2:797.

67. Small, *The Sixteenth Maine Regiment*, 125.

68. Horatio N. Warren, *Two Reunions of the 142nd Regiment, Pa. Vols. . . .* (Buffalo, N.Y.: Courier Co., 1890), 114.

69. Lt. William Harmon, "Co. C at Gettysburg," Minneapolis *Journal*, June 30, 1897, copy in 1st Minnesota file, box 10, Robert L. Brake Collection, USAMHI.

70. Franklin Sawyer, *A Military History of the 8th Regiment Ohio Volunteer Infantry; Its Battles, Marches and Army Movements* (Cleveland: Fairbanks & Co., 1881), 131.

71. Wilson, *Disaster, Struggle, Triumph,* 183.

72. *Philadelphia Inquirer,* July 4, 1887.

73. Henry J. Hunt, "The Third Day at Gettysburg," in *B&L,* 3:369–84; and his rejoinder to Francis A. Walker's comments in ibid., 3:386.

74. See Francis A. Walker, "General Hancock and the Artillery at Gettysburg," in *B&L,* 3:385. Demonstrating just how quickly this controversy erupted, Walker made no mention of it in his *History of the Second Army Corps in the Army of the Potomac* (New York: Charles Scribner's Sons, 1887), published just before Hunt's outburst.

75. Address of Capt. John E. Burton, July 3, 1893, in *NY at Gbg,* 3:1308.

76. Tully McCrae Reminiscence, March 30, 1904, copy in box 12, Robert L. Brake Collection, USAMHI.

77. "The Nineteenth [Massachusetts]," *The Bivouac* 3 (November 1885): 413.

78. Charles H. Banes, *History of the Philadelphia Brigade* (Philadelphia: J. B. Lippincott & Co., 1876), 180.

79. Although Haskell's *Battle of Gettysburg* did not find wide circulation until 1908, a limited-issue pamphlet version was printed about fifteen years after the war and reprinted in 1898 as part of the history of Haskell's Dartmouth College's Class of 1854. See *Battle of Gettysburg* (Madison, Wisc.: Wisconsin History Commission, 1908), xxi–xxii.

80. "Reply of the Philadelphia Brigade Association to the Foolish and Absurd Narrative of Lieutenant Frank A. Haskell, which appears to be Endorsed by the MOLLUS Commandery of Massachusetts and the Wisconsin History Commission," box 2, doc. 41, p. 8, MOLLUS Collection, USAMHI.

81. Haines, *History of the Fifteenth Regiment New Jersey Volunteers,* 91.

82. Wilson, *Disaster, Struggle, Triumph,* 185.

83. Address of Colonel MacDougall, in *NY at Gbg,* 2:802.

84. William P. Seville, *History of the First Regiment, Delaware Volunteers* (Wilmington, Del.: The Historical Society of Delaware, 1885), 81.

85. William P. Haines, *History of the Men of Co. F, With Descriptions of the Marches and Battles of the 12th New Jersey Volunteers* (Camden, N.J.: C. S. McGrath, 1897), 42.

86. Wilson, *Disaster, Struggle, Triumph,* 187.

87. Simons, *A Regimental History,* 137–38.

88. One source for this often-told tale is Gilbert Adams Hays, comp., *Under the Red Patch: Story of the Sixty-Third Regiment Pennsylvania Volunteers, 1861–1865* (Pittsburgh: Market Review Publishers, 1908), 199. The 63rd Pennsylvania was Hays's first command.

89. Simons, *A Regimental History,* 144.

90. Theodore B. Gates, *The Ulster Guard [20th New York State Militia] and the War of the Rebellion* (New York: Benjamin H. Tyrrel, 1879), 473–74.

91. P. DeLacy, *143d Regiment Pennsylvania Volunteers, Second Brigade, Third Division, First Army Corps* (n.p., [ca. 1889]), 9.

92. Address by MacDougall in *NY at Gbg,* 2:802.

93. Oration of Capt. W. C. Dunton, in Benedict, *A Short History of the 14th Vermont Regiment,* 30.

94. "Fighting Them Over," *National Tribune*, May 3, 1894.

95. Albert Lawson, *War Anecdotes and Incidents of Army Life* (Cincinnati: E. H. Beasley, 1888), 125–26.

96. Seville, *History of the First Regiment, Delaware Volunteers*, 83.

97. Oration of Chaplain J. Hervey Beale, September 2, 1890, in *Pa at Gbg*, 2:789.

98. [Richard W. Musgrove], *Autobiography of Capt. Richard W. Musgrove* (n.p.: Mary D. Musgrove, 1921), 91; Bartlett, *History of the Twelfth Regiment, New Hampshire Volunteers*, 132.

99. Address of Rev. Gilbert Frederick, October 6, 1889, in *NY at Gbg*, 1:421.

100. Oration of General James Wood, October 16, 1888, in *NY at Gbg*, 2:923 (my italics).

101. Oration of Gen. L. S. Trowbridge, in *Michigan at Gettysburg, July 1st, 2nd and 3rd, 1863, June 12th, 1889* (Detroit: Winn & Hammond, 1889), 38.

102. "On to Gettysburg," *National Tribune*, June 10, 1886.

103. Address of James Tanner, July 2, 1888, in *NY at Gbg*, 1:290.

104. Address of Maj. Gen. Daniel E. Sickles, in *NY at Gbg*, 1:239.

105. See John L. Parker and Robert G. Carter, *History of the Twenty-Second Massachusetts Infantry, The Second Company Sharpshooters, and the Third Light Battery, in the War of the Rebellion* (Boston: Rand Avery Co., 1887), 342, and Carter, *Four Brothers in Blue*, 319–21.

106. Oration of Captain J. V. Pierce, July 1, 1888, in *NY at Gbg*, 3:993.

107. Edmund Randolph Brown, *The Twenty-Seventh Indiana Volunteer Infantry in the War of the Rebellion* (n.p., 1899), 391.

108. "Was Gettysburg a 'Decisive' Battle?" *National Tribune*, December 30, 1886.

109. "Merely a Specimen Battle," *National Tribune*, July 19, 1888.

110. Haines, *History of the Fifteenth Regiment New Jersey Volunteers*, 93.

111. Address of Col. Daniel B. Allen, July 1, 1890, in *NY at Gbg*, 3:1050.

112. "The Battle of Gettysburg," *National Tribune*, December 2, 1897.

113. "A Boy Spy in Dixie," *National Tribune*, May 31, 1888.

114. J. Watts DePeyster, *Andrew Atkinson Humphreys, of Pennsylvania, Brigadier General and Brevet Major General, USA, Major General, United States Volunteers . . .* (Lancaster, Pa.: Lancaster Intelligencer Press, 1886), 3; Joseph R. Orwig, *History of the 131st Penna. Volunteers, War of 1861–5* (Williamsport, Pa.: Sun Book and Job Printing House, 1902), 116; oration of Alexander K. McClure in *Dedication of the Monument Erected by Pennsylvania to Commemorate the Charge of General Humphreys' Division, Fifth Army Corps, Army of the Potomac, on Marye's Heights, Fredericksburg, Virginia, December 13th, 1862. Dedication Ceremonies, November 11th, 1908.* (n.p., 1908), 24.

115. For the prevalence of these themes in war literature see Rose, *Victorian America and the Civil War*, 235, 254–55, and George L. Mosse, *Fallen Soldiers: Reshaping the Memory of the World Wars* (New York: Oxford University Press, 1990), 32–33.

116. Simons, *A Regimental History*, 145.

117. Ibid., 146.

118. E. L. Godkin, "The Gettysburg Celebration," *Nation* 47 (July 12, 1888): 27.

119. Oration of E. H. Marston, in William Child, *A History of the Fifth Regiment New Hampshire Volunteers in the American Civil War, 1861–1865* (Bristol, N.H.: R. W. Musgrove, 1893), 228.

120. Haines, *History of the Fifteenth Regiment New Jersey Volunteers*, 94.

121. Address by Col. Edward L. Price, July 3, 1890, in *NY at Gbg*, 3:961.

122. Sellars, comp., *Souvenir, Survivors' Association*, 29.

123. Bartlett, *History of the Twelfth Regiment, New Hampshire Volunteers*, 134.

124. Oration of Col. John A. Danks, September 11, 1889, in *Pa at Gbg*, 1:359.

125. Address of Col. William Rickards, October 11, 1889, in *Pa at Gbg*, 1:201.

126. "Battle of Gettysburg and Personal Recollections of that Battle by Colonel Fred. Fuger (retired)," p. 1, copy in box 12, Robert L. Brake Collection, USAMHI.

127. Address of Capt. Porter Farley, September 17, 1889, in *NY at Gbg*, 3:958.

CHAPTER SIX

1. *National Tribune*, January 31, 1889.

2. Raleigh *Standard*, May 27, 1863.

3. [D. H. Hill], "The Haversack," *The Land We Love* 3 (June 1867): 159.

4. Peter Meekins, "The Virginia Fool," *The South-Atlantic* (1879): 178. Meekins added a postscript to his article: "I'll bet you $2.50 the Richmond papers ignore this article entirely."

5. "The Southern Rebellion," *New York Times*, August 20, 1875.

6. T. B. Kingsbury, "Another Witness—Gettysburg," *Our Living and Our Dead* 3 (October 1875): 457.

7. Letter printed in Michael W. Taylor, "North Carolina in the Pickett-Pettigrew-Trimble Charge at Gettysburg," *Gettysburg Magazine*, no. 8 (January 1993): 84.

8. "To North Carolinians Wherever They May Be," *Our Living and Our Dead* 1 (September 1874): 45–46.

9. Ibid.

10. Kingsbury, "Another Witness—Gettysburg," 457.

11. Isaac Trimble, "North Carolinians at Gettysburg," *Our Living and Our Dead* 4 (1876): 53–54.

12. James H. Lane to Editor, *Richmond Times*, April 11, 1867, reprinted in Kingsbury, "Another Witness—Gettysburg," 460–62.

13. Stories reprinted in T. B. Kingsbury, "North Carolina at Gettysburg," *Our Living and Our Dead* 1 (November 1874): 193–94; and Kingsbury, "Another Witness—Gettysburg," 459–62.

14. Randolph Shotwell, "Virginia and North Carolina in the Battle of Gettysburg," *Our Living and Our Dead* 4 (1876): 94.

15. "Thought and Movement. Recent Literature," *The South-Atlantic* (1879): 350.

16. The accounts in this and the following paragraphs can be found in full in Taylor, "North Carolina in the Pickett-Pettigrew-Trimble Charge at Gettysburg," 67–93.

17. A. M. Scales to John B. Bachelder, October 19, 1877, in John B. Bachelder Papers, Massachusetts Historical Society, Boston, Mass.

18. W. R. Bond, "Pickett's Men at Gettysburg," *Philadelphia Weekly Times*, October 28, 1882.

19. J. H. Moore, "Longstreet's Assault," *Philadelphia Weekly Times*, November 4, 1882; reprinted as "Heth's Division at Gettysburg," *Southern Bivouac* (May 1885): 383–95, and as "The Battle of Gettysburg," in John Berrien Lindsley, *Military*

Annals of Tennessee—Confederate (1886; Spartansburg, S.C.: Spartansburg Reprint Co., 1974), 244–53.

20. William H. Swallow, "The Third Day at Gettysburg," *Southern Bivouac* 4 (1886): 562–72.

21. William H. Swallow to John B. Bachelder, January 23, 1886, copy at GNMP.

22. James L. Kemper to W. H. Swallow, February 4, 1886, in James Lawson Kemper Papers, VHS.

23. Swallow, "The Third Day at Gettysburg," 562–72.

24. Ibid.

25. J. B. Smith, "The Charge at Gettysburg," *Southern Bivouac* 5 (1887): 646; printed as "The Charge of Pickett, Pettigrew, and Trimble," in *B&L*, 3:354–55.

26. William R. Bond, *Pickett or Pettigrew? An Historical Essay* (Weldon, N.C.: Hall & Sledge, 1888), title page.

27. Ibid., 6–7.

28. Ibid., 7.

29. Ibid., 10, 15.

30. Ibid., 9.

31. Ibid., 10–11.

32. Ibid., 11, 13, 15.

33. Ibid., 12, 16.

34. Ibid., 21–22.

35. Ibid., 29.

36. Ibid., 23–24.

37. Robert K. Krick, *The Gettysburg Death Roster: The Confederate Dead at Gettysburg*, 3rd ed. (Dayton, Ohio: Morningside Press, 1993), 7. The already small 9th Virginia lost twenty-four killed or mortally wounded, while the 38th Virginia lost fifty-five. These tallies are likely low, as some rosters are incomplete. One well-documented Virginian not on this list is Lt. P. F. Ford, whose sword was returned to Pickett's men at Gettysburg in 1887.

38. See T. J. Cureton to John R. Lane, June 15, 1890, John Randolph Lane Papers, SHC.

39. [S. A. Cunningham], "Impartial Between All Sections," *Confederate Veteran* 1 (1893): 197.

40. W. Gart Johnson, "Reminiscences of Lee and Gettysburg," *Confederate Veteran* 1 (1893): 246.

41. J. B. Turney, "The First Tennessee at Gettysburg," *Confederate Veteran* 8 (December 1900): 535–55.

42. "Heroism in the Battle of Gettysburg," *Confederate Veteran* 9 (1901): 15.

43. Untitled editorial comment by Captain F. S. Harris, 7th Tennessee, *Confederate Veteran* 9 (1901): 16.

44. [Dick Reid], "Incidents of Battle at Gettysburg," *Confederate Veteran* 11 (November 1903): 508. After the comments in praise of Archer's brigade, the editor noted that Reid was a Virginian.

45. Fergus S. Harris comment, *Confederate Veteran* 13 (April 1905): 177.

46. Captain June Kimble, "Tennesseans at Gettysburg—The Retreat," *Confederate Veteran* 18 (October 1910): 460–63.

47. Andrew J. Baker, "Confederates at Gettysburg," *Confederate Veteran* 4 (April 1896): 114–15.

48. W. D. Reid, "Peril by Rock Fence at Gettysburg," *Confederate Veteran* 19 (February 1911): 66.

49. B. F. Ward to ?, January 15, 1889, printed in John C. Rietti, ed., *Military Annals of Mississippi* (Jackson, Miss.: n.p., 1896; Spartanburg, S.C.: The Reprint Co., 1976), 149.

50. Address of Hon. W. M. Cox, December 1, 1905, in *Unveiling Confederate Monument (Carroll County, Mississippi), Carrolton, Miss., by P. F. Liddell Chapter, U.C.V.* (n.p., 1906), 42.

51. Rietti, ed., *Military Annals of Mississippi*, 148.

52. According to Krick, *Gettysburg Death Roster*, 14, the unit's casualties included 102 killed and mortally wounded, 168 wounded, and 42 missing.

53. Baxter McFarland, "The Eleventh Mississippi Regiment at Gettysburg," *Mississippi Historical Society Publications, Centenary Series* 2 (1918): 549–68.

54. See William A. Love, "Mississippi at Gettysburg," *Publications of the Mississippi Historical Society* 9 (1906): 25–51.

55. See Rietti, ed., *Military Annals of Mississippi*, 149.

56. J. Walter Coleman to Mrs. Calvin (Maud) Brown, February 29, 1941, copy in GNMP. This letter concludes a lengthy correspondence between Maud Morrow Brown, author of *The University Grays, Company A, Eleventh Mississippi Regiment, Army of Northern Virginia, 1861–1865* (Richmond: Garrett & Massie, 1940), and Gettysburg park officials over the placement in Ziegler's Grove of a marker to the 11th Mississippi.

57. "Veteran Defends Perry's Brigade," *Atlanta Journal*, March 30, 1901.

58. Francis P. Fleming, *Memoir of Capt. C. Seton Fleming of the Second Florida Infantry, C.S.A.* (Jacksonville, Fla.: Times-Union Publishing House, 1884), 79–88, and "Gettysburg. The Courageous Part Taken in the Desperate Conflict, July 2–3, 1863, by the Florida Brigade," *SHSP* 27 (1899): 192–205.

59. H. H. Herbert to E. Porter Alexander, August 8, 1869, copy in 8th Alabama file, GNMP; Herbert, "A Short History of the 8th Ala. Regiment," 30, copy in Lafayette McLaws Papers, SHC.

60. H. H. Herbert to E. Porter Alexander, August 18, 1903, Edward Porter Alexander Papers, SHC.

61. George Clark, *A Glance Backward, Or Some Events in the Past History of My Life* (Houston: Rein and Sons Company, 1914), 39–40. He also wrote a brief piece entitled "Wilcox's Alabama Brigade at Gettysburg," in *Confederate Veteran* 17 (1909): 229–30.

62. John H. Abbott, *Reminiscence of a Confederate*, copy in 8th Alabama file, GNMP.

63. *NC Regs*, 1:v–x.

64. Ibid., 315, 564; 2:90.

65. Ibid., 353; 2:24.

66. Ibid., 2:42, 674.

67. Ibid., 1:380, 590; 2:692; 3:108, 238.

68. Ibid., 2:43; 3:299–301.

69. Ibid., 43–44; 3:478, 661.

70. See Maj. W. M. Robbins, "Longstreet's Assault at Gettysburg," in *NC Regs*, 5:101–12.

71. S. A. Ashe, "The Pettigrew-Pickett Charge. Gettysburg, 3 July, 1863," in *NC Regs*, 5:137–59.

72. James S. Harris, *Historical Sketches, Seventh Regiment North Carolina Troops* (Mooresville, N.C.: Mooresville Printing Co., 1893), 36.

73. James I. Metts, *Longstreet's Charge at Gettysburg, Pa., Pickett's, Pettigrew's and Trimble's Divisions* (Wilmington, N.C.: Morning Star Press, 1899), 3.

74. D. H. Hill Jr., *North Carolina*, vol. 4 of *Confederate Military History*, edited by Clement A. Evans (Atlanta: Confederate Printing House, 1899), 186, 190.

75. Samuel A. Ashe, "The Charge at Gettysburg," *North Carolina Booklet* 1 (March 10, 1902).

76. Report of the Committee Appointed by the North Carolina Literary and Historical Society, *Five Points in the Record of North Carolina in the Great War of 1861–5* (Goldsboro, N.C.: Nash Brothers, 1904), 7, 10. See especially Judge W. A. Montgomery, "Farthest at Gettysburg," 21–34, and W. R. Bond, "Longstreet's Assault at Gettysburg," 35–46.

77. William R. Bond, "Pickett or Pettigrew?" *National Tribune*, October 10, 17, 24, 31, November 7, 1901.

78. "Address of J. R. Lane to N.C. Society of Baltimore," *Raleigh News and Observer*, July 5, 1903.

CHAPTER SEVEN

1. "Address of Col. Richard L. Maury, 24th Va. Infantry, Pickett's Division, A.N.V. to Geor[g]e E. Pickett Camp C.V., August 7, 1893. The Private Soldier of Pickett's Division," handwritten copy in Richard L. Maury Papers, DU.

2. James H. Walker, "The Charge of Pickett's Division," *Blue and Gray* 1 (March 1893): 221–23, and "A Survivor of Pickett's Division," *Blue and Gray* 2 (July 1893): 27.

3. "The Hero of Pickett's Division," *Confederate War Journal* 2 (June 1894): 47. A similar version may be found in [Miss M. C. Keeler], "The Hero of Pickett's Division," *Confederate Veteran* 1 (June 1893): 174.

4. Richmond *Times*, November 7, 1894.

5. Confederate States of America, *General Orders from the Adjutant General's Office, 1862–1863* (Richmond: n.p., 1864), 41–42.

6. Charles Pickett to Editor, Richmond *Times*, November 11, 1894, copy in Charles Pickett Papers, VHS.

7. Eppa Hunton to John W. Daniel, February 15, 1904, in John Warwick Daniel Papers, DU.

8. See Eppa Hunton, *Autobiography of Eppa Hunton* (Richmond: William Byrd Press, 1933), 98.

9. William T. Poague, *Gunner with Stonewall*. Edited by M. F. Cockrell. (Jackson, Tenn.: McCowat-Mercer Press.), 75.

10. Thomas Rosser to A. S. Parham, February 2, 1903, copy in box 4, Alexander Webb file, Robert L. Brake Collection, USAMHI.

11. John S. Wise, *The End of an Era* (Boston: Houghton Mifflin Co., 1899), 338–39.

12. The story is repeated in John Singleton Mosby, *The Memoirs of Colonel John S. Mosby*, ed. Charles W. Russell (Bloomington: Indiana University Press, 1959), 381–83.

13. Edmund Berkeley to John S. Mosby, March 20, 1913, in John Singleton Mosby Papers, Library of Congress, Washington, D.C.

14. John S. Mosby to Eppa Hunton [III], March 28, 1911, in John Singleton Mosby Papers, VHS.

15. James I. Metts, *Longstreet's Charge at Gettysburg, Pa., Pickett's, Pettigrew's and Trimble's Divisions* (Wilmington, N.C.: Morning Star Press, 1899), 10.

16. See Louis G. Young to J. Bryan Grimes, September 7, 1911, Bryan Grimes Papers, SHC.

17. Thomas R. Friend to Charles Pickett, December 10, 1894, in Charles Pickett Papers, VHS.

18. W. W. Wells to G. R. Harrison, December 13, 1894, copy in 14th Virginia file, GNMP.

19. Martin W. Hazlewood, "Gettysburg Charge. Paper as to Pickett's Men," *SHSP* 23 (1896): 229; originally published in *Richmond Daily Dispatch*, January 26, 1896.

20. Martin Hazlewood to Charles Pickett, December 6, 1894, in Charles Pickett Papers, VHS.

21. James Longstreet to Charles Pickett, October 5, 1892, in Charles Pickett Papers, VHS. For ongoing rumors of the report's existence, see Glenn Tucker, "What Became of Pickett's Report of His Assault at Gettysburg?" *Civil War Times Illustrated* 6 (October 1967): 37–39, and *Lee and Longstreet at Gettysburg* (Indianapolis, Ind.: Bobbs-Merrill, 1968), 148–58.

22. The loss of many of Pickett's family and military papers is explained briefly in Charles Pickett to James Longstreet, October 12, 1892, in James Longstreet Papers, SHC, and in Charles Pickett to Miss Lida Perry, March 24, 1896, in George E. Pickett Papers, DU.

23. See James H. Stine, *History of the Army of the Potomac* (Philadelphia: J. B. Rodgers Printing Co., 1892), 538–40, for the full text of letters from Col. Aylett, Charles Pickett, Bright, Symington, and J. F. Crocker of the 9th Virginia. See also Stine to Bright, June 9, 1892, in the Robert A. Bright Papers, Earl Gregg Swem Library, The College of William and Mary, Williamsburg, Va.

24. Charles Pickett to James Longstreet, October 12, 1892, in James Longstreet Papers, SHC.

25. James Longstreet to Major Nash, September 3, 1892, copy in Charles Pickett Papers, VHS.

26. W. Stuart Symington to Charles Pickett, October 17, 1892, and Symington to Charles Pickett, October 26, 1892, both in Charles Pickett Papers, VHS.

27. Robert A. Bright to Charles Pickett, October 15, 1892, in Charles Pickett Papers, VHS.

28. Edward R. Baird, "Gettysburg," an address delivered to the Essex chapter, United Daughters of the Confederacy, Tappahannock, Va., copy in Edward R. Baird Papers, Museum of the Confederacy, Richmond, Va.

29. W. Stuart Symington to Charles Pickett, October 17, 1892, and Symington to Charles Pickett, October 26, 1892, both in Charles Pickett Papers, VHS.

30. Robert A. Baird to Charles Pickett, October 15, 1892, in Charles Pickett Papers, VHS.

31. James Longstreet, *From Manassas to Appomattox* (Philadelphia: J. B. Lippincott & Co., 1895), 390–96.

32. LaSalle Corbell Pickett, "General George E. Pickett," *SHSP* 24 (1896): 151–54. This article originally appeared in the *Richmond Daily Dispatch*, May 3, 1896.

33. LaSalle Corbell Pickett, *Pickett and His Men* (Atlanta: Foote & Davies, 1899), dedication page.

34. Ibid., xi–xiii.

35. Ibid., 408.

36. Ibid., 425–29.

37. Ibid., 217–18.

38. Ibid., 302.

39. Ibid., 305, 310–13.

40. *New York Times*, September 23, 1899.

41. John Chase, "Ten Books of the Month," *Bookman* 37 (1913): 566.

42. Review of Pickett, *Pickett and His Men*, in *The Nation* (October 19, 1899): 303.

43. Among these writings are "In de Miz," *Arena* 8 (1893): 642–46; "Olive Branch of the Civil War," *Arena* 17 (1897): 694–704; "Old Time Virginia Christmas," *Harper's Bazaar* 41 (1907): 48–54; "In Memory of Old Virginia," *Lippincott's* 81 (1908): 236; and "Yule Log," *Country Life* 11 (October 1908): 191–92.

44. LaSalle Corbell Pickett, "My Soldier," *McClure's Magazine* 30 (1907): 563, 566.

45. N. E. Harris, *The Civil War; Its Results and Lessons. An Address Delivered at Louisville, Kentucky, to the Confederate Veterans in Reunion, July 15th, 1905* (Macon, Ga.: J. W. Burke, 1906), 27.

46. James Armstrong, *Grand Gathering of the Men Who Wore the Gray at the Capitol of the Confederacy* (Charleston, S.C., 1907), 5.

47. Edward A. Baird, "Gettysburg."

48. John Lamb, *Addresses Delivered at the Unveiling of the Monument to the Confederate Soldiers of Charles City County, Virginia [November 21, 1900]* (Richmond: Whitted & Shepperson, 1901), 24–25.

49. Fitzhugh Lee to "Editor *Times*," undated (but written after the publication of his *General Lee* in 1894), copy in box 5, Robert L. Brake Collection, USAMHI.

50. Charles T. Loehr, "The 'Old First' Virginia at Gettysburg," *SHSP* 32 (1904): 33. Loehr's article originally appeared in the Richmond *Times-Dispatch*, October 16, 1904.

51. Rawley Martin, "The Battle of Gettysburg, And the Charge of Pickett's Division," *SHSP* 32 (1904): 185. This article originally appeared in the Richmond *Times-Dispatch*, April 10, 1904.

52. James F. Crocker, "Gettysburg—Pickett's Charge," *SHSP* 33 (1905): 126. This lengthy article was reprinted in book form in Crocker, *Gettysburg—Pickett's Charge and Other War Addresses* (Portsmouth, Va.: W. A. Fiske, 1906), which was reprinted in 1915.

53. Crocker, "Gettysburg—Pickett's Charge," 126.

54. Joseph C. Mayo, "Pickett's Charge at Gettysburg," *SHSP* 34 (1906): 330–31.

55. William W. Wood, *Reminiscences of Big I*, ed. Bell Irvin Wiley (1909; Jackson, Tenn.: McCowat-Mercer Press, 1956), 45–49.

56. Clay's story is included in Winfield Peters, "The Lost Sword of Gen. Richard B. Garnett, Who Fell at Gettysburg," *SHSP* 33 (1905): 26–31.

57. Loehr, "The 'Old First' Virginia at Gettysburg," 37.

58. Crocker, "Gettysburg—Pickett's Charge," 131.

59. William H. Stewart, "Colonel John Bowie Magruder," *SHSP* 27 (1899): 209.

60. See James F. Crocker, "Colonel James Gregory Hodges. Address by Judge James F. Crocker, Before Stonewall Camp, Confederate Veterans, Portsmouth, Va., June 18th, 1909," *SHSP* 37 (1909): 194, and "Gettysburg—Pickett's Charge," 132–33.

61. Crocker, "Gettysburg—Pickett's Charge," 134.

62. Mayo, "Pickett's Charge at Gettysburg," 334.

63. In Peters, "The Lost Sword of Gen. R. B. Garnett," 30.

64. Mayo, "Pickett's Charge at Gettysburg," 328, 335.

65. Robert A. Bright, "Pickett's Charge," *SHSP* 31 (1903): 234. Bright's article first appeared in the Richmond *Times-Dispatch*, February 7, 1904. It was reprinted much later as "Pickett's Charge at Gettysburg," in *Confederate Veteran* 38 (January 1930): 263–66.

66. Loehr, "The 'Old First' Virginia at Gettysburg," 37.

67. "General Mahone on Gettysburg," in George Morely Vickers, *Under Both Flags: A Panorama of the Great Civil War* (Richmond: B. F. Johnson, 1896), 69. See also "Gettysburg Thirty Years After," *The Nation* 56 (May 4, 1893): 327.

68. Crocker, "Gettysburg—Pickett's Charge," 120–21.

69. Martin, "The Battle of Gettysburg, And the Charge of Pickett's Division," 189.

70. Crocker, "Gettysburg—Pickett's Charge," 123.

71. John H. Lewis, *Recollections from 1860 to 1865* (Washington, D.C.: Peake & Company, 1895), 85.

72. Loehr, "The 'Old First' Virginia at Gettysburg," 40.

73. Bright, "Pickett's Charge," 231.

74. Loehr, "The 'Old First' Virginia at Gettysburg," 35.

75. Bright, "Pickett's Charge," 232.

76. Crocker, "Colonel James Gregory Hodges," 194–96.

77. Peters, "The Lost Sword of Gen. R. B. Garnett," 26–31.

78. James E. Poindexter, "General Armistead's Portrait Presented. An Address Delivered Before R. E. Lee Camp No. 1, C.V., Richmond, Va., January 29, 1909," *SHSP* 37 (1909): 146, 148. Much of the speech reached a whole new audience as "Gen. Lewis Addison Armistead," *Confederate Veteran* 22 (November 1914): 502–4.

79. D. B. Easley, "With Armistead When He Was Killed," *Confederate Veteran* 20 (August 1912): 379.

80. Poindexter, "General Armistead's Portrait Presented," 151.

81. Martin, "The Battle of Gettysburg, And the Charge of Pickett's Division," 187–88.

82. Richmond *Times-Dispatch*, November 2, 1903.

83. Ibid., November 24, 1903.

84. Bright, "Pickett's Charge," 230.

85. Ibid., 229–30.

86. "Equine Heroes of Pickett's Charge," *Journal of the U.S. Cavalry* 24 (1913): 482–43.

87. John B. Gordon, "Gettysburg," *Scribner's Magazine* 34 (1903): 20; and *Reminiscences of the Civil War* (New York: Charles Scribner's Sons, 1904), 137–76.

88. E. P. Alexander, *Military Memoirs of a Confederate: A Critical Narrative* (New York: Charles Scribner's Sons, 1907; Bloomington: Indiana University Press, 1962), 422–32.

89. G. Moxley Sorrel, *Recollections of a Confederate Staff Officer* (New York: Neale Publishing Co., 1905), 163.

90. Helen Dortsch Longstreet, *Lee and Longstreet at High Tide: Gettysburg in the Light of the Official Records* (Philadelphia: J. B. Lippincott & Co., 1905), 50–53.

91. See Thomas T. Munford to R. E. Cowart, July 27, 1908, Munford to Cowart, October 24, 1908, and Munford to "My Dear Sirs," November 12, 1908, typescripts in Robert E. Cowart Papers, DU.

92. Bright, "Pickett's Charge," 235.

93. Robert W. Douthat, *Gettysburg; A Battle Ode Descriptive of the Grand Charge of the Third Day, July 3, 1863* (New York: Neale Publishing Co., 1905).

94. Bright, "Pickett's Charge," 229. Bright had trouble identifying the colorful Gordon, but he made an effort to find out about him. See R. M. Tuttle to "Mr. Bright," June 3, 1903, in which a former officer of the 26th North Carolina admitted that he did not know anything about Gordon and that his word could be believed because "I have been a *Presbyterian minister for nearly 30 years.*" Copy in John Warwick Daniel Papers, University of Virginia Library, Charlottesville, Va.

95. All of these arguments can be found in greater detail in [George L. Christian], "North Carolina and Virginia," *SHSP* 31 (1903): 340–64.

96. Martin, "The Battle of Gettysburg, And the Charge of Pickett's Division," 183.

97. Charles A. Patch, "Pickett's Division at Gettysburg," *Confederate Veteran* 6 (December 1898): 569.

98. John Clark Ridpath, *The New Complete History of the United States of America* (Chicago: Elliott-Madison Co., 1912), 10:5091.

99. Benson Lossing, comp., *Harper's Encyclopedia of United States History from 458 A.D. to 1902* (New York: Harper & Brothers, 1902), 4:72–73. The only other Southerners mentioned in connection with the charge were Wilcox's Alabamians, who were quickly dispatched by Stannard's Vermonters.

100. James Ford Rhodes, "The Battle of Gettysburg," *American Historical Review* 4 (1899): 675–76.

101. [Christian], "North Carolina and Virginia," 361–62.

102. Jonathan Leslie Hall, *Half-Hours in Southern History* (Richmond: B. F. Johnson, 1907), 247–50, and [Christian], "North Carolina and Virginia," 362.

103. [Christian], "North Carolina and Virginia," 363.

104. Thomas Nelson Page, "Run to Seed," in *The Burial of the Guns*, Plantation Edition, vol. 2 (New York: Charles Scribner's Sons, 1906), 137. This article was originally published in *Elsket and Other Stories* (New York: Charles Scribner's Sons, 1891).

105. Sheldon Van Auken, "The Southern Historical Novel in the Early Twentieth Century," *Journal of Southern History* 14 (1948): 158.

106. Mary Johnston, "Gettysburg," *Atlantic Monthly* 110 (July 1912): 1–9.

107. T. C. Harbaugh, "At Gettysburg," *National Tribune*, November 7, 1901. The same

author produced an equally partisan poem entitled "Pickett's Sword," *Confederate Veteran* 16 (1908): 147.

108. Elsie Singmaster, "The Battle of Gettysburg, July 1–3, 1863," *Outlook* 104 (June 21, 1913): 372–76. See also Singmaster, *Gettysburg; Stories of the Red Harvest and the Aftermath* (Boston: Houghton Mifflin Co., 1913).

109. Crocker, "Gettysburg—Pickett's Charge," 130–31.

CHAPTER EIGHT

1. "Gettysburg Vandalism," *National Tribune*, July 13, 1893.

2. David McConnaughy to John R. Ingersoll et al., August 18, 1863, copy in GNMP.

3. A good introduction to the work of the Gettysburg Battlefield Memorial Association may be found in John M. Vanderslice, *Gettysburg Then and Now: The Field of American Valor, Where and How the Regiments Fought and the Troops They Encountered.* Reprint ed. (New York: G. W. Dillingham Co., 1899; Dayton, Ohio: Morningside, 1983), 360–99.

4. "Anchor," "A Visit to Gettysburg," *Army and Navy Journal* 4 (June 8, 1867): 663.

5. *New York Herald*, July 9, 1863.

6. *New York Times*, July 4, 1913.

7. Winfield S. Hancock to John B. Bachelder, December 20, 1885, in John B. Bachelder Papers, Massachusetts Historical Society, Boston, Mass.

8. John B. Bachelder, *Gettysburg: What to See and How to See It* (Boston: John B. Bachelder, 1873), 20.

9. Ibid., 54–56.

10. G. G. Benedict to John B. Bachelder, December 24, 1863, in BP.

11. Theodore B. Gates to John B. Bachelder, October 26, 1865, in BP.

12. George N. Macy to John B. Bachelder, May 10, 1866, in BP.

13. James L. Kemper to Professor M. L. Stevens, November 24, 1865, in BP.

14. Walter Harrison, *Pickett's Men, A Fragment of War History* (New York: D. Van Nostrand, 1870), 177.

15. William W. Gordon to John B. Bachelder, June 8, 1886, in John B. Bachelder Papers, Massachusetts Historical Society, Boston, Mass.

16. J. L. Black to John B. Bachelder, April 18, 1886, in John B. Bachelder Papers, Massachusetts Historical Society, Boston, Mass.

17. George G. Meade to John B. Bachelder, December 4, 1869, in BP.

18. George Meade, Jr., to John B. Bachelder, May 6, 1882, in BP.

19. John B. Bachelder to Cols. Tate and Kenan, August 11, 1893, copy at GNMP.

20. At this time John M. Vanderslice took over this position, but Bachelder remained on the commission. See John M. Vanderslice, *Gettysburg Then and Now*, iii.

21. See "Marking the Battlefield of Gettysburg," *Grand Army Scout and Soldiers' Mail*, November 10, 1883; and Bachelder's reply to the article in ibid., November 24, 1883.

22. John Buckley, "A Stone From the Wall, reminiscence of Pickett's Charge," undated, in BP.

23. Thomas Galwey to John B. Bachelder, May 19, 1882, in BP.

24. David G. Martin, *Confederate Monuments at Gettysburg, The Gettysburg Battle Monuments*, vol. 1 (Hightstown, N.J.: Longstreet House, 1986), 210-13.

25. J. Irvin Gregg to John B. Bachelder, July 1, 1889, in John B. Bachelder Papers, Massachusetts Historical Society, Boston, Mass.

26. Daniel E. Sickles to John B. Bachelder, August 10, 1889, in John B. Bachelder Papers, Massachusetts Historical Society, Boston, Mass.

27. Joseph Wheeler to John B. Bachelder, August 26, 1889, in John B. Bachelder Papers, Massachusetts Historical Society, Boston, Mass.

28. Entry for June 12, 1901, William McKendree Robbins Diaries, SHC.

29. Entries for July 1 and August 28, 1901, William McKendree Robbins Diaries, SHC.

30. Entry for May 16, 1902, William McKendree Robbins Diaries, SHC.

31. Entry for September 25, 1903, William McKendree Robbins Diaries, SHC.

32. Entries for March 12 and 17, 1904, William McKendree Robbins Diaries, SHC.

33. W. M. Robbins to E. Porter Alexander, November 19, 1903, in Edward Porter Alexander Papers, SHC.

34. See Vanderslice, *Gettysburg Then and Now*, 259-63.

35. Philadelphia *North American*, September 16, 1906.

36. John W. Frazier, *Reunion of the Blue and Gray. Philadelphia Brigade and Pickett's Division, July 2, 3, 4, 1887 and Sept. 15, 16, 17, 1906* (Philadelphia: Ware Brothers, 1906), 33.

37. "Soldiers of Both Armies at Gettysburg," *Confederate Veteran* 15 (January 1907): 14.

38. *New York Tribune*, June 29, 1913.

39. Praise for Beitler's administrative effort can be found in "Gettysburg, Gettysburg," *Confederate Veteran* 21 (1913): 379.

40. *New York Times*, July 4, 1913.

41. C. Irvine Walker, "Conference of Gettysburg Commission," *Confederate Veteran* 21 (1913): 107.

42. "Gettysburg, Gettysburg," 379; Walker, "Conference of Gettysburg Commission," 107.

43. LaSalle Corbell Pickett, "Gloria Victis," *Confederate Veteran* 21 (1913): 359.

44. John Chase, "Ten Books of the Month," *Bookman* 37 (1913): 566.

45. LaSalle Corbell Pickett, *The Bugles of Gettysburg* (Chicago: F. G. Browne and Co., 1913), reviewed in Chase, "Ten Books of the Month," 566.

46. See advertisement in *Confederate Veteran* 21 (1913): 413.

47. See LaSalle Corbell Pickett, "The Wartime Story of General Pickett," *Cosmopolitan Magazine* 56 (1913): 611-22, for the Gettysburg installment of this series, which can be found irregularly in vols. 55 and 56.

48. Ibid.

49. For an advertisement of Sallie Pickett's *Heart of a Soldier*, which cost $1.30, see *Confederate Veteran* 21 (1913): 189.

50. "'The Heart of a Soldier,'" *Confederate Veteran* 21 (1913): 360.

51. LaSalle Corbell Pickett, *The Heart of a Soldier; as Revealed in the Intimate Letters of General George E. Pickett, C.S.A.* (New York: Seth Moyle, 1913), 92-97.

52. Pickett, *Heart of a Soldier*, 100. A similar suggestion appears in "General Pickett at Gettysburg," *Confederate Veteran* 21 (1913): 391, where the editor notes that

Pickett destroyed his full report of the charge, "but even the extracts [of his letter to Sallie] given below are filled with dramatic meaning."

53. Pickett, *Heart of a Soldier*, 102–9.

54. For the most detailed study of the issue, see Gary W. Gallagher, "A Widow and Her Soldier: LaSalle Corbell Pickett as Author of the George E. Pickett Letters," *Virginia Magazine of History and Biography* 94 (1986): 329–44. In all fairness, Sallie was not the only Southerner to fabricate or "improve upon" wartime and postwar writings for later publication. Even Rebel war clerk John Beauchamp Jones and diarist Mary Chesnut did this.

55. R. W. Douthat, "Opportunities of Veterans at Gettysburg," *Confederate Veteran* 21 (1913): 229.

56. J. Frank Hanly, *The Battle of Gettysburg* (Cincinnati: Jennings and Graham, 1912), 46–47, 54, 63.

57. Charleston *News and Courier*, July 1, 1913.

58. Portland, Maine, *Evening Express and Daily Advertiser*, July 9, 1913.

59. "Gettysburg, Gettysburg," 377.

60. Walter H. Blake, *Hand Grips: The Story of the Great Gettysburg Reunion, July 1913* (Vineland, N.J.: G. E. Smith, 1913), 184.

61. "Gettysburg, Gettysburg," 377, 381–82. See also, Francis Wiggins, "Fiftieth Anniversary of the Battle of Gettysburg," paper 6, box 3, MOLLUS Collection, USAMHI.

62. "At Gettysburg, 1913," *Outlook* 104 (July 12, 1913): 541.

63. Herbert Francis Sherwood, "Gettysburg Fifty Years Afterward," *Outlook* 104 (July 19, 1913): 612.

64. *New York Times*, July 4, 1913.

65. *Washington Post*, July 6, 1913.

66. "At Gettysburg, 1913," 541.

67. "Gettysburg, Gettysburg," 380.

68. Address of Speaker of the House Champ Clark, in *Fiftieth Anniversary of the Battle of Gettysburg, Report of the Pennsylvania Commission, December 31, 1913. Revised edition, April 1915.* (Harrisburg, Pa.: William Stanley Ray, 1915), 137.

69. Address of Rev. Newell Dwight Hillis, in *Fiftieth Anniversary of the Battle of Gettysburg*, 162–63.

70. "Gettysburg, Gettysburg," 378.

71. "Comment by Another Ohio Editor," *Confederate Veteran* 21 (1913): 385.

72. Walter H. Blake, *Hand Grips*, 112–13.

73. Sherwood, "Gettysburg Fifty Years Afterward," 611.

74. "What the 111th New York Regiment Heroes Say," *Confederate Veteran* 21 (1913): 385.

75. Robert McCulloch, "The 'High Tide at Gettysburg,'" *Confederate Veteran* 21 (1913): 475.

76. Walter H. Blake, *Hand Grips*, 44–45.

77. Ibid., 182–83.

78. Ibid., 22–23. The story is repeated in "Two Gettysburg Encounters," *Literary Digest* 47 (July 12, 1913): 75.

79. *New York Times*, July 4, 1913.

80. Walter H. Blake, *Hand Grips*, 77–78.

81. Sherwood, "Gettysburg Fifty Years Afterward," 611.

82. "About the Charge of Pickett's Division," *Confederate Veteran* 21 (1913): 475–76.

83. The actual numbers of participants is a matter of conjecture. In *Fiftieth Anniversary of the Battle of Gettysburg* (p. 168), a total of 180 Philadelphians faced 120 of Pickett's men. In the *New York Times*, July 4, 1913, 300 men served on each side.

84. Walter H. Blake, *Hand Grips*, 87–88.

85. Some disagreement exists over the leadership of the Union contingent at the wall. *Fiftieth Anniversary of the Battle of Gettysburg*, 168, cites Thomas Thompson as the commander. All sources agree on Frazier's appointment as adjutant.

86. *New York Times*, July 4, 1913.

87. Walter H. Blake, *Hand Grips*, 88.

88. *New York Times*, July 4, 1913.

89. Walter H. Blake, *Hand Grips*, 89–90. Herbert Francis Sherwood tells a similar story in "Gettysburg Fifty Years Afterward," 612.

90. *New York Times*, July 4, 1913.

91. Ibid.

92. "Gettysburg Fifty Years After," *Review of Reviews* 48 (1913): 182.

93. *New York Times*, July 4, 1913.

94. The American public could view a nice variety of such shots in "Gettysburg Fifty Years After."

95. Walter H. Blake, *Hand Grips*, 180–81.

96. "Gettysburg Fifty Years After," 177–78.

97. C. Irvine Walker to General J. M. Schoonmaker, August 15, 1913, in *Fiftieth Anniversary of the Battle of Gettysburg*, 224.

98. *San Francisco Examiner*, July 4, 1913.

99. John S. Henley comment, Aberdeen, Miss., *Aberdeen Examiner*, August 22, 1913.

100. "The Boston Journal on 'Pickett's Charge,'" *Confederate Veteran* 21 (1913): 384.

101. *Cincinnati Enquirer*, July 6, 1913. Not surprisingly, *Confederate Veteran* chose this single account—of all the many Northern reports of the reunion—for inclusion in "Gettysburg, Gettysburg," 382.

102. Sherwood, "Gettysburg Fifty Years Afterward," 610.

103. "Gov. Mann Doesn't Favor Gathering at Richmond in 1915," *Confederate Veteran* 21 (1913): 386.

104. Editorial note appended to "The Boston Journal on 'Pickett's Charge,'" 384.

105. Judge G. B. Gerald, "The Battle of Gettysburg," Waco, Tex., *Daily Times-Herald*, July 3, 1913, copy in box 7, Robert L. Brake Collection, USAMHI.

106. Andrew Cowan to ?, December 5, 1913, copy at GNMP.

107. Henry W. Newton to M. C. S. Noble, August 8, 1913, in Marcus Cicero Stephens Noble Papers, SHC.

108. "Committees Report of General Pickett, and His Command and Participation in the Battle of Gettysburg, July 3, 1863," copy in the Gregory Family Papers, VHS.

109. Wiggins, "Fiftieth Anniversary of the Battle of Gettysburg."

110. John C. McInnis to M. C. S. Noble, July 24, 1913, in Marcus Cicero Stephens Noble Papers, SHC.

1. Stephen Vincent Benet, *John Brown's Body* (New York: Holt, Rinehart and Winston, 1928), 276.
2. W. A. Johnson, "Gettysburg and the Battle," *Confederate Veteran* 25 (September 1917): 410.
3. "North Carolina at Gettysburg," *Confederate Veteran* 37 (August 1929): 286.
4. Address of Gov. Angus W. McLean in *Ceremonies Attending the Presentation and Unveiling of the North Carolina Memorial on the Battle Field at Gettysburg, July 3, 1929* (n.p., 1929).
5. "North Carolina at Gettysburg," 286.
6. See Frederick W. Hawthorne, *Gettysburg: Stories of Men and Monuments as Told by Battlefield Guides* (Hanover, Pa.: The Association of Licensed Battlefield Guides, 1988), 36–39, 41.
7. See Mrs. H. F. Lewis, "General Armistead at Gettysburg," *Confederate Veteran* 28 (November 1920): 406, and T. C. Holland, "With Armistead at Gettysburg," *Confederate Veteran* 29 (February 1921): 62, for this exchange.
8. See Walter Clark, "The Term 'Pickett's Charge' is a Misnomer," *North Carolina Booklet* 21 (1921–22): 21–27, and "North Carolina Troops at Gettysburg," *North Carolina Booklet* 22 (1922–23): 91–108.
9. Henry E. Shepherd, "Gettysburg—A Critical Review," *Confederate Veteran* 25 (May 1917): 216.
10. John Purifoy, "The Artillery at Gettysburg, July 3, 1863," *Confederate Veteran* 33 (January 1925): 13–14.
11. "Gettysburg Farewell: The Blue and the Gray Light an Eternal Flame," *Newsweek* 12 (July 11, 1938): 12–13.
12. Robert Littell, "Ghosts Speak at Gettysburg," *Readers' Digest* 33 (July 1938): 55.
13. Bernard DeVoto, "Gettysburg," *Harper's Magazine* 175 (August 1937): 333.
14. Littell, "Ghosts Speak at Gettysburg," 55.
15. See Gustav J. Fiebeger, *The Campaign and Battle of Gettysburg, from the Official Records of the Union and Confederate Armies* (West Point: U.S. Military Academy, 1915).
16. See Carol Reardon, *Soldiers and Scholars: The U.S. Army and the Uses of Military History, 1865–1920* (Lawrence, Kans.: University Press of Kansas, 1990), ch. 4.
17. Col. C. M. Bundel, "The Methods of War at Gettysburg," *Infantry Journal* 35 (1929): 124. Throughout his piece, Bundel managed to date the battle in 1864.
18. Capt. Victor A. Coulter, "Smoke at Gettysburg," *Infantry Journal* 44 (1937): 159–60.
19. See "Battle of the Generals; How Ike and Monty Would Have Fought at Gettysburg," *U.S. News and World Report* 42 (May 24, 1957): 60–63; and "Gettysburg Refought," *Time* 69 (May 27, 1957): 74.
20. An excellent summary of this reenactment can be found in Capt. John H. Craige, "The Marines at Gettysburg," *Marine Corps Gazette* 7 (September 1922): 249–52.
21. Ibid.
22. The fullest account of the Marines' visit to Gettysburg in 1922 can be found in "Gettysburg To-Day—and in '63," *Literary Digest* (July 22, 1922): 37–38. Also attending was Douglas Southall Freeman, a Virginia journalist.

23. E. D. Warfield, "The Repulse of Pickett's Charge at Gettysburg," *Chautauquan* 31 (1931): 340–42.

24. Benet, *John Brown's Body*, 274–78.

25. William Faulkner, *Intruder in the Dust*. Vintage Book ed. (New York: Vintage Press, 1972), 194–95.

26. For a fuller treatment of this subject, see Robert L. Bloom, "The Battle of Gettysburg in Fiction," *Pennsylvania History* 43 (1976): 309–27.

27. Ben Ames Williams, *House Divided* (Boston: Houghton Mifflin Company, 1947), 990–91, 1005.

28. Michael Shaara, *The Killer Angels* (New York: Ballentine Books, 1975).

29. Robert Skimin, *Gray Victory* (New York: St. Martin's Press, 1988).

30. Douglas Savage, *The Court Martial of Robert E. Lee: A Historical Novel* (Conshohocken, Pa.: Combined Books, 1993), 387.

31. Ted Jones, *Hard Road to Gettysburg* (Novato, Calif.: Lyford Books, 1993), 311–15.

32. Harold Coyle, *Look Away* (New York: Simon and Schuster, 1995).

33. Richard Armour, *It All Started with Columbus* (New York: McGraw-Hill, 1971), 74.

34. Douglas Southall Freeman, *Lee's Lieutenants: A Study in Command*, 3 vols. (New York: Charles Scribner's Sons, 1944), 3:148.

35. Ibid., 3:158.

36. See James I. Robertson Jr., "The Continuing Battle of Gettysburg: An Essay Review," *Georgia Historical Quarterly* 58 (1974): 278–82.

37. Glenn Tucker, *High Tide at Gettysburg: The Campaign in Pennsylvania* (Indianapolis, Ind.: Bobbs-Merrill, 1958), 267–70.

38. Longstreet always has had a few friends. An effort to build a monument to him at Gettysburg stalled in the depression years for lack of funds. A 1990s effort seems more likely to succeed; on July 3, 1998, an equestrian monument of Old Pete is scheduled to be unveiled on a site at Pitzer's Woods.

39. Alan M. Hollingsworth and James M. Cox, *The Third Day at Gettysburg: Pickett's Charge* (New York: Henry Holt, 1959).

40. See James E. Sefton, "Gettysburg: An Exercise in the Evaluation of Historical Evidence," *Military Affairs* 28 (1964): 64–72.

41. Capt. John H. Bassler to John B. Bachelder, ca. 1882, BP.

42. Allen Tate, "The Battle of Gettysburg: Why Was It Fought?" *Carleton Miscellany* 4 (1963): 34, 44.

43. See special program insert, including James Van Alen, "Pickett's Charge," in special issue of *Civil War Times Illustrated* 2 (July 1963): 1–16 [tucked in between journal pages 32–33]. Emphasis is mine.

44. Ibid.

45. "Task Remaining; Celebration of Centennial," *Newsweek* 62 (July 15, 1963): 18–19.

46. Jeff H. Stepp, undated letter to the editor, *Blue and Gray Magazine* 6 (October 1988): 6.

47. The evidence for the placement of the monument comes from the same Sergeant Olney of Arnold's battery who convinced a fellow Rhode Islander of the misplacement of the high water mark. See Chapter 8.

48. See Bruce A. Trinque, "Arnold's Battery and the 26th North Carolina," *Gettysburg Magazine*, no. 12 (January 1995): 61–67.

49. See, for example, Richard Pindell, "The True High-Water Mark of the Confederacy," *Blue and Gray Magazine* 1 (December/January 1983): 6–15.

50. Jay Luvaas and Harold W. Nelson, veteran staff ride leaders for the U.S. Army, draw special attention to Brig. Gen. Henry Benning's official report in which he wrote: "The part of it [the first line of the Confederate advance] in our front I took to be Law's brigade, and so I followed it. In truth, it was Robertson's, Law's being farther to the right. This I did not discover until late in the fight, a wood on the right concealing from me most of Law's brigade." Luvaas and Nelson have reprinted this report in their compilation, *The U.S. Army War College Guide to the Battle of Gettysburg* (Carlisle, Pa.: South Mountain Press, Inc., 1986), 98–99.

51. Tate, "The Battle of Gettysburg," 40–41,

52. See Barnum's advertising copy in *Blue and Gray Magazine* 6 (April 1989): 25.

53. See advertisement in *Civil War Times Illustrated* 32 (July/August 1993): 27. The alleged historical accuracy of the artistic renderings is not enhanced by a description of the second scene as "Stuart's Confederate Calvary [*sic*] charging headlong toward the enemy."

54. See Wolf Family, *A Simplified Tour of the Gettysburg Battlefield* (Gettysburg, Pa.: Audio-Tronics Tape Tours, n.d.). The 1st Minnesota's great loss occurred in the fighting of July 2.

55. "Historic Trees Becoming a U.S. Growth Industry," State College, Pa., *Centre Daily Times*, December 18, 1993.

56. Oscar Handlin, "The Civil War as Symbol and as Actuality," *Massachusetts Review* 3 (1961): 133.

57. George Will, "They're Watching Ga. Governor's Race from D.C.," State College, Pa., *Centre Daily Times*, September 22, 1994.

58. Harrisburg, Pa., *Patriot*, October 11, 1994.

59. "Pickett's Charge," *National Tribune*, January 29, 1914.

60. Frank Aretas Haskell, *The Battle of Gettysburg* (Madison, Wisc.: Wisconsin History Commission, 1908), 185.

BIBLIOGRAPHY

MANUSCRIPTS

Boston, Mass.
  Massachusetts Historical Society
    John B. Bachelder Papers
Carlisle Barracks, Pa.
  U.S. Army Military History Institute
    Robert L. Brake Collection
    Civil War Miscellaneous Collection
    Civil War Times Illustrated Collection
    D. B. Easley Papers
    Samuel A. Firebaugh Diary
    Harrisburg Civil War Round Table Collection
    Lewis Leigh Collection
    Military Order of the Loyal Legion of the United States Collection
    Save the Flags Collection
Chapel Hill, N.C.
  Southern Historical Collection, Wilson Library, University of North Carolina
    Edward Porter Alexander Papers
    Alexander-Hilhouse Papers
    Bryan Grimes Papers
    John Randolph Lane Papers
    Charles Edward Lippett Diary
    Benjamin F. Little Papers
    James Longstreet Papers
    Lafayette McLaws Papers
    Marcus Cicero Stephens Noble Papers
    Proffitt Family Papers
    Edward Payson Reeve Papers
    William McKendree Robbins Diaries
Charlottesville, Va.
  University of Virginia Library
    John Warwick Daniel Papers
    Dearing Family Papers
    Holladay Family Papers
    James Lawson Kemper Papers
Columbia, S.C.
  South Caroliniana Library
    Joseph B. Kershaw Papers
Concord, N.H.
  New Hampshire Historical Society
    John B. Bachelder Papers
Durham, N.C.
  Perkins Library, Duke University

Granville W. Belcher Papers
Rachel Susan Cheves Papers
Robert E. Cowart Papers
John Warwick Daniel Papers
George W. Jones Papers
William H. Jones Papers
Harry Lewis Papers
John Bowie Magruder Papers
Richard L. Maury Papers
George E. Pickett Papers
Stephens Calhoun Smith Papers
Tillinghast Family Papers
Samuel Hoey Walkup Papers
Fredericksburg, Va.
Fredericksburg and Spotsylvania National Military Park Library
William A. Miller Letter
Gettysburg, Pa.
Gettysburg National Military Park Library
Regimental Files
Richmond, Va.
Museum of the Confederacy
Edward R. Baird Papers
George K. Griggs Diary
Virginia Historical Society
Cabell Family Papers
Cocke Family Papers
Gregory Family Papers
James Lawson Kemper Papers
Josiah Staunton Moore Papers
John Singleton Mosby Papers
Charles Pickett Papers
Virginia State Library
Henry T. Owen Correspondence
Ross Family Correspondence
Washington, D.C.
Library of Congress
John Singleton Mosby Papers
Williamsburg, Va.
Earl Gregg Swem Library, The College of William and Mary
Robert A. Bright Papers

NEWSPAPERS

Aberdeen (Miss.) *Examiner*
Atlanta Constitution
Atlanta Journal
(Atlanta, Ga.) *Southern Confederacy*

(Augusta, Ga.) *Daily Constitutionalist*
Baltimore American
Baltimore Sun
Boston *Christian Science Monitor*
Boston Journal
Charleston Daily Courier
Charleston Mercury
Charleston *News and Courier*
Cincinnati Enquirer
(Columbia, S.C.) *Daily Southern Guardian*
Fayetteville (N.C.) *Observer*
Harrisburg Daily Telegraph
Mobile Daily Advertiser and Register
New Orleans *Picayune*
New York Herald
New York Times
New York Tribune
New York World
Norfolk *Landmark*
Philadelphia *Evening Telegraph*
Philadelphia Inquirer
Philadelphia *North American*
Philadelphia Public Ledger
Philadelphia *Times*
(Portland, Maine) *Evening Express and Daily Advertiser*
Raleigh News and Observer
Raleigh Observer
Raleigh Register
Raleigh *Standard*
Richmond Daily Dispatch
Richmond Enquirer
Richmond Examiner
Richmond *Sentinel*
Richmond *Southern Illustrated News*
Richmond *Times*
Richmond *Times-Dispatch*
Richmond Whig
San Francisco Examiner
Savannah Republican
(Sumter, S.C.) *Tri-Weekly Watchman*
Washington Post

ANTHOLOGIES, BIBLIOGRAPHIES, AND PERIODICALS

Annals of the War Written by Leading Participants, North and South. Dayton, Ohio: Morningside Press, 1988.
Army and Navy Journal

Buel, Clarence C., and Robert U. Johnson, eds. *Battles and Leaders of the Civil War*. 4 vols. New York: Century Printing Co., 1888.

Clark, Walter A., comp., *Histories of the Several Regiments and Battalions from North Carolina in the Great War, 1861–1865*. 5 vols. Raleigh, N.C.: E. M. Uzzell, 1901.

Confederate Veteran. 40 vols. 1893–1932.

The Land We Love, 1866–69.

Moore, Frank, ed. *The Rebellion Record: A Diary of American Events*. 12 vols. New York: D. Van Nostrand, 1862–65.

National Tribune, 1880–1940.

Our Living and Our Dead, 1873–76.

The South-Atlantic.

Southern Bivouac, 1882–87.

Southern Historical Society Papers. 52 vols. (1876–1927).

U.S. War Department. *The War of the Rebellion: A Compilation of the Official Records of the Union and Confederate Armies in the War of the Rebellion*. 127 vols. Washington, D.C.: Government Printing Office, 1880–1901.

GETTYSBURG NARRATIVES BY VIRGINIANS AND THEIR ALLIES

Alexander, Edward Porter. "The Great Charge and Artillery Fighting at Gettysburg." In *Battles and Leaders of the Civil War*, edited by Robert U. Johnson and Clarence C. Buel, 3:357–68.

———. *Military Memoirs of a Confederate: A Critical Narrative*. New York: Charles Scribner's Sons, 1907; Bloomington: Indiana University Press, 1962.

Blackford, Susan Leigh, comp. *Letters from Lee's Army*. New York: A. S. Barnes, 1947.

Bledsoe, Albert. "The Battle of Gettysburg." *Southern Review* 5 (April 1869): 433–45.

Bright, Robert A. "Pickett's Charge." *Southern Historical Society Papers* 31 (1903): 228–36.

———. "Pickett's Charge at Gettysburg." *Confederate Veteran* 38 (1930): 263–66.

[Christian, George L.]. "North Carolina and Virginia." *Southern Historical Society Papers* 31 (1903): 340–64.

Cooke, John Esten. *A Life of Gen. Robert E. Lee*. New York: D. Appleton & Company, 1871.

Crocker, James F. "Colonel James Gregory Hodges. Address by Judge James F. Crocker, Before Stonewall Camp, Confederate Veterans, Portsmouth, Va., June 18th, 1909." *Southern Historical Society Papers* 37 (1909): 184–97.

———. "Gettysburg—Pickett's Charge." *Southern Historical Society Papers* 33 (1905): 118–34.

Douthat, Robert W. *Gettysburg; A Battle Ode Descriptive of the Grand Charge of the Third Day, July 3, 1863*. New York: Neale Publishing Co., 1905.

Early, Jubal A. "Leading Confederates on the Battle of Gettysburg." *Southern Historical Society Papers* 4 (1877): 241–82.

———. "Letter From General J. A. Early." *Southern Historical Society Papers* 4 (1877): 50–66.

Easley, D. B. "With Armistead When He Was Killed." *Confederate Veteran* 20 (1912): 379.

Edwards, John E. *The Confederate Soldier, Being a Memorial Sketch of George N. and Bushrod W. Harrison*. New York: Blelock & Co., 1868.

Figg, Royall W. *"Where Men Only Dare Go!" or the Story of a Boy Company by an Ex-boy*. Richmond: Whittet & Shepperson, 1885.

Fremantle, Arthur James Lyon. "The Battle of Gettysburg and the Campaign in Pennsylvania." *Blackwood's Magazine* 94 (September 1863): 375–85.

———. *Three Months in the Southern States: April–June 1863*. Edinburgh and London: William Blackwood & Sons, 1863; New York: Bradburn, 1864; Mobile, Ala.: S. H. Goetzel, 1864.

Harrison, Walter. *Pickett's Men, A Fragment of War History*. New York: D. Van Nostrand, 1870.

Hazlewood, Martin W. "Gettysburg Charge. Paper as to Pickett's Men." *Southern Historical Society Papers* 23 (1896): 229–37.

"The Hero of Pickett's Division." *Confederate War Journal* 2 (June 1894): 47.

Heth, Henry. "Letter from Major-General Henry Heth." *Southern Historical Society Papers* 4 (1877): 151–60.

Holland, T. C. "With Armistead at Gettysburg." *Confederate Veteran* 29 (February 1921): 62.

Hotchkiss, Jedediah. *Make Me a Map of the Valley: The Civil War Journal of Stonewall Jackson's Topographer*. Edited by Archie P. McDonald. Dallas, Tex.: Southern Methodist University Press, 1973.

Hunton, Eppa. *Autobiography of Eppa Hunton*. Richmond: William Byrd Press, 1933.

Imboden, John D. "Lee at Gettysburg." *Galaxy* 11 (1871): 507–13.

Johnson, John Lipscomb. *The University Memorial: Biographical Sketches of Alumni of the University of Virginia Who Fell in the Confederate War*. Baltimore: Turnbull Bros., 1871.

Johnson, W. Gart. "Reminiscences of Lee and Gettysburg." *Confederate Veteran* 1 (1893): 246.

Johnston, David E. *Four Years a Soldier*. Princeton, W.Va.: n.p., 1887.

Jones, J. William. *Army of Northern Virginia Memorial Volume*. Richmond: J. W. Randolph & English, 1880.

[Keeler, M. C.] "The Hero of Pickett's Division." *Confederate Veteran* 1 (June 1893): 174.

Lamb, John. *Addresses Delivered at the Unveiling of the Monument to the Confederate Soldiers of Charles City County, Virginia [November 21, 1900]*. Richmond: Whitted & Shepperson, 1901.

Lewis, Mrs. H. F. "General Armistead at Gettysburg." *Confederate Veteran* 28 (November 1920): 406.

Lewis, John H. *Recollections from 1860 to 1865*. Washington, D.C.: Peake & Company, 1895.

Loehr, Charles T. "The 'Old First' Virginia at Gettysburg." *Southern Historical Society Papers* 32 (1904): 33–40.

Long, Armistead. "Letter from General A. L. Long." *Southern Historical Society Papers* 4 (1877): 118–23.

———. *Memoirs of Robert E. Lee; His Military and Personal History, Embracing a Large Amount of Information Hitherto Unpublished.* . . . New York: J. M. Stoddart & Co., 1886.

Longstreet, Helen Dortsch. *Lee and Longstreet at High Tide: Gettysburg in the Light of the Official Records.* Philadelphia: J. B. Lippincott & Co., 1905.

Longstreet, James. "The Campaign of Gettysburg." *Philadelphia Weekly Times,* November 3, 1877.

———. "Lee in Pennsylvania." In *Annals of the War,* 414–46.

———. "Lee's Invasion of Pennsylvania." In *Battles and Leaders of the Civil War,* edited by Robert U. Johnson and Clarence C. Buel, 3:244–51.

———. *From Manassas to Appomattox.* Philadelphia: J. B. Lippincott & Co., 1895.

McCabe, James Dabney. *Life and Campaigns of General Robert E. Lee.* Atlanta: National Publishing Co., 1866.

Martin, Rawley. "The Battle of Gettysburg, And the Charge of Pickett's Division." *Southern Historical Society Papers* 32 (1904): 183–95.

Mayo, Joseph C. "Pickett's Charge at Gettysburg." *Southern Historical Society Papers* 34 (1906): 327–35.

Mosby, John Singleton. *The Memoirs of Colonel John S. Mosby.* Edited by Charles W. Russell. Bloomington: Indiana University Press, 1959.

Pendleton, William Nelson. "Personal Recollections of Robert E. Lee." *Southern Magazine* 15 (1874): 603–36.

Peters, Winfield. "The Lost Sword of Gen. Richard B. Garnett, Who Fell at Gettysburg." *Southern Historical Society Papers* 33 (1905): 26–31.

Pickett, LaSalle Corbell. *The Bugles of Gettysburg.* Chicago: F. G. Browne and Co., 1913.

———. "General George E. Pickett." *Southern Historical Society Papers* 24 (1896): 151–54.

———. *The Heart of a Soldier as Revealed in the Intimate Letters of General George E. Pickett, C.S.A.* New York: Seth Moyle, 1913.

———. "My Soldier." *McClure's Magazine* 30 (1907): 563–71.

———. *Pickett and His Men.* Atlanta: Foote & Davis, 1899.

———. "The Wartime Story of General Pickett." *Cosmopolitan Magazine* 56 (1913): 611–22.

Poague, William T. *Gunner with Stonewall.* Edited by Monroe F. Cockrell. Jackson, Tenn.: McCowat-Mercer Press, 1957.

Poindexter, James E. "General Armistead's Portrait Presented. An Address Delivered Before R. E. Lee Camp No. 1, C.V., Richmond, Va., January 29, 1909." *Southern Historical Society Papers* 37 (1909): 144–51.

———. "Gen. Lewis Addison Armistead." *Confederate Veteran* 22 (November 1914): 502–4.

Pollard, Edward A. *The Early Life, Campaigns, and Public Services of Robert E. Lee.* New York: E. B. Treat, 1870.

———. *Lee and His Lieutenants.* New York: E. B. Treat, 1867.

———. *The Lost Cause: The Standard Southern History of the War of the Confederates.* New York: E. B. Treat, 1867.

———. *The Second Year of the War.* New York: Charles B. Richardson, 1864.

———. *The Third Year of the War.* New York: Charles B. Richardson, 1865.

Royall, William L. *Some Reminiscences*. New York: Neale Publishing Co., 1909.
Sorrel, G. Moxley. *Recollections of a Confederate Staff Officer*. New York: Neale Publishing Co., 1905.
Stewart, William H. "Colonel John Bowie Magruder." *Southern Historical Society Papers* 27 (1899): 205–10.
"A Story of Gettysburg." *Southern Magazine* 12 (1873): 654–61.
Taylor, Walter H. "The Campaign in Pennsylvania." In *Annals of the War*, 305–18.
———. *Four Years with General Lee*. New York: D. Appleton, 1878.
———. "Memorandum by Colonel Walter H. Taylor of General Lee's Staff." *Southern Historical Society Papers* 4 (1877): 84–85.
Walker, James H. "The Charge of Pickett's Division." *Blue and Gray* 1 (March 1893): 221–23.
———. "A Survivor of Pickett's Division." *Blue and Gray* 2 (July 1893): 27.
White, Henry Alexander. "The Battle of Gettysburg. Some Literary Facts Connected Therewith." *Southern Historical Society Papers* 27 (1899): 52–61.
Wise, John D. *The End of an Era*. Boston: Houghton Mifflin Co., 1899.
Wood, William N. *Reminiscences of Big I*. Edited by Bell Irvin Wiley, 1909; Jackson, Tenn.: McCowat-Mercer Press, 1956.

GETTYSBURG NARRATIVES BY SOUTHERNERS
OUTSIDE VIRGINIA

Ashe, Samuel A. "The Charge at Gettysburg." *North Carolina Booklet* 1 (March 10, 1902).
Baker, Andrew J. "Confederates at Gettysburg." *Confederate Veteran* 4 (April 1896): 114–15.
Bond, William R. "Pickett or Pettigrew?" *National Tribune*, October 10, 17, 24, 31, and November 7, 1901.
———. *Pickett or Pettigrew? An Historical Essay*. Weldon, N.C.: Hall & Sledge, 1888.
———. "Pickett's Men at Gettysburg." *Philadelphia Weekly Times*, October 28, 1882.
Clark, George. *A Glance Backward, Or Some Events in the Past History of My Life*. Houston: Rein & Sons Company, 1914.
Clark, Walter. *North Carolina at Gettysburg and Pickett's Charge a Misnomer*. Raleigh: n.p., 1921.
———. "North Carolina Troops at Gettysburg." *North Carolina Booklet* 22 (1922–23): 91–108.
———. "The Term 'Pickett's Charge' is a Misnomer." *North Carolina Booklet* 21 (1921–22): 21–27.
Five Points in the Record of North Carolina in the Great War of 1861–5. Goldsboro, N.C.: Nash Brothers, 1904.
Fleming, Francis P. "Gettysburg. The Courageous Part Taken in the Desperate Conflict, July 2–3, 1863, by the Florida Brigade." *Southern Historical Society Papers* 27 (1899): 192–205.
———. *Memoir of Capt. C. Seton Fleming of the Second Florida Infantry, C.S.A.* Jacksonville, Fla.: Times-Union Publishing House, 1884.
Fry, B. D. "Pettigrew's Charge at Gettysburg." *Southern Historical Society Papers* 7 (1879): 91–93.

Gordon, John B. "Gettysburg." *Scribner's Magazine* 34 (1903): 2–24.

———. *Reminiscences of the Civil War*. New York: Charles Scribner's Sons, 1904.

Graham, Joseph. "Gettysburg: Remembering Pickett's Charge, 'An Awful Affair.'" Max R. Williams, ed. *Civil War Times Illustrated* 23 (April 1984): 46–49.

Groene, Bertram, ed. "The Civil War Letters of Colonel David Lang." *Florida Historical Quarterly* 54 (1976): 340–66.

Harris, James S. *Historical Sketches, Seventh Regiment North Carolina Troops*. Mooresville, N.C.: Mooresville Printing Co., 1893.

"Heroism in the Battle of Gettysburg." *Confederate Veteran* 9 (1901): 15.

[Hill, D. H.] "The Haversack," *The Land We Love* 3 (June 1867): 157–60.

———. "Washington." *The Land We Love* 1 (1866): 92–93.

Hill, D. H., Jr. *North Carolina*. Vol. 4 of *Confederate Military History*, edited by Clement A. Evans. Atlanta: Confederate Printing House, 1899.

Kimble, June. "Tennesseans at Gettysburg—The Retreat." *Confederate Veteran* 18 (October 1910): 460–63.

Kingsbury, T. B. "Another Witness—Gettysburg." *Our Living and Our Dead* 3 (October 1875): 457–63.

———. "North Carolina at Gettysburg." *Our Living and Our Dead* 1 (November 1874): 193–97.

Lane, James H. "Letter from General James H. Lane." *Southern Historical Society Papers* 5 (1878): 91–93.

Love, William A. "Mississippi at Gettysburg." *Publications of the Mississippi Historical Society* 9 (1906): 25–51.

McFarland, Baxter. "The Eleventh Mississippi at Gettysburg." *Mississippi Historical Society Publications, Centenary Series* 2 (1918): 549–68.

MacPherson, Ernest. "Gettysburg and Its Effect upon the Fortunes of the Confederacy." *Confederate Veteran* 23 (February 1915): 75–77.

Metts, James I. *Longstreet's Charge at Gettysburg, Pa., Pickett's, Pettigrew's and Trimble's Divisions*. Wilmington, N.C.: Morning Star Press, 1899.

Moore, J. H. "Heroism in the Battle of Gettysburg." *Confederate Veteran* 9 (1901): 15–16.

———. "Heth's Division at Gettysburg." *Southern Bivouac* 3 (May 1885): 383–95.

Owen, William M. "Pickett's Charge." *Grand Army Scout and Soldiers' Mail*, December 17, 1885.

Purifoy, John. "The Artillery at Gettysburg, July 3, 1863." *Confederate Veteran* 33 (January 1925): 13–14.

[Reid, Dick.]. "Incidents of Battle at Gettysburg." *Confederate Veteran* 11 (November 1903): 508.

Reid, W. D. "Peril by Rock Fence at Gettysburg." *Confederate Veteran* 19 (February 1911): 66.

Rietti, John C. *Military Annals of Mississippi*. Jackson, Miss.: n.p., 1896; Spartanburg, S.C.: The Reprint Co., 1976.

Rozier, John, ed. *The Granite Farm Letters: The Civil War Correspondence of Edgeworth and Sallie Bird*. Athens: University of Georgia Press, 1988.

Shepherd, Henry E. "Gettysburg—A Critical Review." *Confederate Veteran* 25 (May 1917): 214–16.

Shotwell, Randolph. "Virginia and North Carolina in the Battle of Gettysburg." *Our Living and Our Dead* 4 (1876): 80–97.

Silver, James W., ed., *A Life for the Confederacy*. Jackson, Tenn.: McCowat-Mercer Press, 1959.

Smith, J. B. "The Charge at Gettysburg." *Southern Bivouac* 5 (1887): 646.

———. "The Charge of Pickett, Pettigrew, and Trimble." In *Battles and Leaders of the Civil War*, edited by Robert U. Johnson and Clarence C. Buel, 3:354–55.

Swallow, William H. "The Third Day at Gettysburg." *Southern Bivouac* 4 (1886): 562–72.

Taylor, Michael W. "North Carolina in the Pickett-Pettigrew-Trimble Charge at Gettysburg." *Gettysburg Magazine*, no. 8 (January 1993): 67–93.

———, ed. *The Cry is War, War, War: The Civil War Correspondence of Lts. Burwell Thomas Cotton and George Job Huntley, 34th Regiment North Carolina Troops*. Dayton, Ohio: Morningside Press, 1994.

"To North Carolinians Wherever They May Be." *Our Living and Our Dead* 1 (September 1874): 45–56.

Trescott, William Henry. *Memorial of the Life of J. Johnston Pettigrew, Brig. Gen. of the Confederate States Army*. Charleston, S.C.: John Russell, 1870.

Trimble, Isaac R. "History of Lane's North Carolina Brigade—The Gettysburg Campaign—Letter from General Trimble." *Southern Historical Society Papers* 9 (1881): 29–35.

———. "North Carolinians at Gettysburg." *Our Living and Our Dead* 4 (1876): 53–60.

Turney, J. B. "The First Tennessee at Gettysburg." *Confederate Veteran* 8 (December 1900): 535–37.

Wagstaff, H. M., ed. *The James A. Graham Papers, 1861–1884*. James Sprunt Historical Studies, vol. 20, no. 2. Chapel Hill: University of North Carolina Press, 1928.

Winschell, Terrence, ed. "The Gettysburg Diary of Lieutenant William Peel." *Gettysburg Magazine*, no. 9 (July 1993): 98–108.

Wright, Gilbert, ed. "Some Letters to his Parents by a Floridian in the Confederate Army." *Florida Historical Quarterly* 36 (April 1958): 353–72.

Young, Louis G. "Pettigrew's Brigade at Gettysburg." *Our Living and Our Dead* 1 (February 1875): 552–58.

GETTYSBURG NARRATIVES BY NORTHERNERS

Bachelder, John B. *Descriptive Key to the Painting of the Repulse of Longstreet's Assault at the Battle of Gettysburg*. New York: John B. Bachelder, 1870.

———. *Gettysburg Publications*. Boston: John B. Bachelder, n.d.

———. *Gettysburg: What to See and How to See It*. Boston: John B. Bachelder, 1873.

"The Battle of Gettysburg." *National Tribune*, December 2, 1897.

Benton, Charles E. *As Seen from the Ranks: A Boy in the Civil War*. New York: G. P. Putnam's Sons, 1902.

Bicknell, L. E. "Repulsing Lee's Last Blow at Gettysburg." In *Battles and Leaders of the Civil War*, edited by Robert U. Johnson and Clarence C. Buel, 3:391–92.

"A Boy Spy in Dixie." *National Tribune*, May 31, 1888.

Brown, H. E. "Cushing's United States Battery at Gettysburg." *Grand Army Scout and Soldiers' Mail*, December 19, 1885.

Carter, Robert G. *Four Brothers in Blue*. Washington, D.C.: Press of Gibson Brothers, 1913.

Coffin, Charles Carleton. *Four Years of Fighting*. Boston: Ticknor & Fields, 1866.

"Co. I, 13th VT., Three Days' Fighting." *National Tribune*, August 30, 1894.

Ditterline, Theodore. *Sketch of the Battles of Gettysburg, July 1st, 2d, and 3d, 1863.* . . . New York: C. A. Alvord, 1864.

Doubleday, Abner. *Chancellorsville and Gettysburg*. New York: Charles Scribner's Sons, 1882.

Emmell, Albert S. *"Now Is the Time for Buck and Ball": The Life and Civil War Experiences of Albert Stokes Emmell*. N.p., 1991.

"Fighting Them Over." *National Tribune*, August 20, 1885, and May 3, 1884.

[Fiske, Samuel]. *Mr. Dunn Browne's Experiences in the Army*. Boston: Nichols & Noyes, 1865.

Fleming, G. T., comp. *Life and Letters of Alexander Hays, Brevet Colonel United States Army, Brigadier General and Brevet Major General United States Volunteers*. Pittsburgh: Gilbert Adam Hays, 1919.

Foster, John Y. "Four Days at Gettysburg." *Harper's New Monthly Magazine* 28 (1864): 381–88.

Gerrish, Theodore. *Army Life: A Private's Reminiscences of the Civil War*. Portland, Maine: Hoyt, Fogg & Dunham, 1882.

Gibbon, John. *Personal Recollections of the Civil War*. New York: G. P. Putnam's Sons, 1928; Dayton, Ohio: Morningside Press, 1988.

Greeley, Horace. *The American Conflict*. 2 vols. Hartford, Conn.: O. D. Case & Co., 1866.

Gross, George J. *The Battle-field of Gettysburg*. Philadelphia: Collins, Printer, 1866.

Hall, Norman J. "Repelling Lee's Last Blow and Gettysburg: II." In *Battles and Leaders of the Civil War*, edited by Robert U. Johnson and Clarence C. Buel, 3:390–91.

Harbaugh, T. C. "At Gettysburg." *National Tribune*, November 7, 1901.

Haskell, Frank Aretas. *The Battle of Gettysburg*. Madison, Wisc.: Wisconsin History Commission, 1908.

Hunt, Henry J. "The Third Day at Gettysburg." In *Battles and Leaders of the Civil War*, edited by Robert U. Johnson and Clarence C. Buel, 3:369–84.

Jacobs, Michael. "Later Rambles over the Field of Gettysburg." *United States Service Magazine* 1 (January 1864): 66–76.

———. "Later Rambles over the Field of Gettysburg," *United States Service Magazine* 1 (February 1864): 158–68.

———. *Notes on the Rebel Invasion of Maryland and Pennsylvania and the Battle of Gettysburg, July 1st, 2d and 3d, 1863.* . . . Philadelphia: J. B. Lippincott & Co., 1864.

"John W. Plummer's Account." In *The Rebellion Record: A Diary of American Events*, edited by Frank Moore. Vol. 10. New York: Putnam, 1864.

Kettell, Thomas P. *History of the Great Rebellion*. Hartford, Conn.: L. Stebbins, 1865.

Lawson, Albert. *War Anecdotes and Incidents of Army Life*. Cincinnati: E. H. Beasley, 1888.

Lochren, William. "The First Minnesota at Gettysburg." In *The Gettysburg Papers*. Compiled by Ken Bandy and Florence Freeland. Vol. 2. Dayton, Ohio: Morningside Press, 1978.

McCoughtry, James C. "Not Particularly Game." *National Tribune*, August 4, 1892.

"Merely a Specimen Battle." *National Tribune*, July 19, 1888.

[Musgrove, Richard W.]. *Autobiography of Capt. Richard W. Musgrove*. N.p.: Mary D. Musgrove, 1921.

Nesbit, J. W. "Gettysburg." *National Tribune*, November 16, 1916.

Nickerson, Mark. *Recollections of the Civil War by a High Private in the Front Ranks*. N.p., 1991.

Patch, Charles A. "Pickett's Division at Gettysburg." *Confederate Veteran* 6 (December 1898): 569–70.

Patriot Daughters of Lancaster. *Hospital Scenes after the Battle of Gettysburg, July, 1863*. Philadelphia: Henry B. Ashmead, 1864.

"Pickett's Charge." *National Tribune*, January 29, 1914.

Quaife, Milo P., ed. *From the Cannon's Mouth*. Detroit, Mich.: Wayne State University Press, 1959.

Rice, Edmund. "Repelling Lee's Last Blow at Gettysburg." In *Battles and Leaders of the Civil War*, edited by Robert U. Johnson and Clarence C. Buel, 3:387–90.

"Saving the Nation." *National Tribune*, May 21, 1885.

Scott, Robert Garth, ed. *Fallen Leaves: The Civil War Letters of Major Henry Livermore Abbott*. Kent, Ohio: Kent State University Press, 1991.

Snow, William Parker. *Southern Generals, Who They Are, and What They Have Done*. New York: Charles B. Richardson, 1865.

Stine, James H. *History of the Army of the Potomac*. Philadelphia: J. B. Rodgers Printing Co., 1892.

Storrie, A. K. M. "Gettysburg." *Grand Army Scout and Soldiers' Mail*, March 6, 1886.

"Story of a Cannoneer." *National Tribune*, November 14, 1889.

Swinton, William. *Campaigns of the Army of the Potomac*. New York: Dick & Fitzgerald, 1866.

———. *The Twelve Decisive Battles of the War: A History of the Eastern and Western Campaigns, in Relation to the Actions that Decided Their Issue*. New York: Dick & Fitzgerald, 1867.

Wainwright, Charles S. *A Diary of Battle: The Personal Journals of Colonel Charles S. Wainwright, 1861–1865*. Edited by Allan Nevins. New York: Harcourt, Brace & World, 1962.

Walker, Francis A. "General Hancock and the Artillery at Gettysburg." In *Battles and Leaders of the Civil War*, edited by Robert U. Johnson and Clarence C. Buel, 3:385.

"Was Gettysburg a 'Decisive' Battle?" *National Tribune*, December 30, 1886.

UNIT HISTORIES

Banes, Charles H. *History of the Philadelphia Brigade*. Philadelphia: J. B. Lippincott & Co., 1876.

Bartlett, Asa W. *History of the Twelfth Regiment, New Hampshire Volunteers in the War of the Rebellion*. Concord, N.H.: Ira C. Evans, 1897.

Benedict, G. G. *A Short History of the 14th Vermont Regiment.* Bennington, Vt.: C. M. Pierce, 1887.

Blake, Henry N. *Three Years in the Army of the Potomac.* Boston: Lee and Shepard, 1865.

Brainard, Mary Geneve Green, comp. *Campaigns of the One Hundred and Forty-Sixth Regiment New York State Volunteers.* New York: G. P. Putnam's Sons, 1915.

Brown, Edmund Randolph. *The Twenty-Seventh Indiana Volunteer Infantry in the War of the Rebellion.* N.p., 1899.

Brown, Maud Morrow. *The University Greys: Company A, Eleventh Mississippi Regiment, Army of Northern Virginia, 1861–1865.* Richmond: Garrett & Massie, 1940.

Bryant, Edwin E. *History of the Third Regiment of Wisconsin Veteran Volunteer Infantry, 1861–1865.* Madison, Wisc.: Veterans Association of the Regiment, 1891.

Child, William. *A History of the Fifth Regiment New Hampshire Volunteers in the American Civil War, 1861–1865.* Bristol, N.H.: R. W. Musgrove, 1893.

Crotty, D. G. *Four Years Campaigning in the Army of the Potomac.* Grand Rapids, Mich.: Dygert Bros. & Co., 1874.

Cudworth, Warren H. *History of the First Regiment (Massachusetts Infantry). . . .* Boston: Walker, Fuller & Co., 1866.

Curtis, O. B. *History of the Twenty-Fourth Michigan of the Iron Brigade, Known as the Detroit and Wayne County Regiment.* Detroit, Mich.: Winn & Hammond, 1891; Gaithersburg, Md.: Olde Soldier Books, 1988.

DeLacy, P. *143d Regiment Pennsylvania Volunteers, Second Brigade, Third Division, First Army Corps.* N.p., [ca. 1889].

Gates, Theodore B. *The Ulster Guard [20th New York State Militia] and the War of the Rebellion.* New York: Benjamin H. Tyrrel, 1879.

Haines, Alanson A. *History of the Fifteenth Regiment New Jersey Volunteers.* New York: Jenkins & Thomas, 1883.

Haines, William P. *History of the Men of Co. F, With Descriptions of the Marches and Battles of the 12th New Jersey Volunteers.* Camden, N.J.: C. S. McGrath Printer, 1897.

Hays, Gilbert Adams. *Under the Red Patch: Story of the Sixty-Third Regiment Pennsylvania Volunteers, 1861–1865.* Pittsburgh: Market Review Publishers, 1908.

History of the Fifth Massachusetts Battery. Boston: Luther E. Cowles, 1902.

Holcombe, Return I. *History of the First Regiment Minnesota Volunteer Infantry 1861–64.* Stillwater, Minn.: Easton & Masterman, 1916.

Houghton, Edwin B. *The Campaigns of the Seventeenth Maine.* Portland, Maine: Short & Loring, 1866.

Hurst, Samuel H. *Journal-History of the Seventy-Third Ohio Volunteer Infantry.* Chillicothe, Ohio: n.p., 1866.

Irby, Richard. *Historical Sketch of the Nottaway Grays, Afterwards Company G, Eighteenth Virginia Regiment, Army of Northern Virginia Prepared at the Request of the Surviving Members of the Company at Their First Reunion at Bellefont Church, July 21, 1877.* Richmond: J. W. Furgusson & Son, 1878.

Loehr, Charles T. *War History of the Old First Virginia Infantry Regiment, Army of Northern Virginia.* Richmond: William Ellis Jones, 1884.

McDermott, Anthony W., and John E. Reilly. *A Brief History of the Sixty-ninth*

Regiment Pennsylvania Veteran Volunteers from Its Formation Until Final Muster Out
of United States Service. Also, an Account of the Reunion of the Survivors of the
Philadelphia Brigade and Pickett's Division of Confederate Soldiers, and the Dedication
of the Monument of the Sixty-ninth Regiment Pennsylvania Infantry at Gettysburg,
July 2d and 3d, 1887, by John E. Reilly. Philadelphia: D. J. Gallagher, 1889.

Nash, Eugene Arus. A History of the Forty-fourth Regiment New York Volunteer Infantry
in the Civil War, 1861–1865. Chicago: R. R. Donnelley and Sons Company;
Dayton, Ohio: Morningside Press, 1988.

Orwig, Joseph R. History of the 131st Penna. Volunteers, War of 1861–5. Williamsport,
Pa.: Sun Book and Job Printing House, 1902.

Osborn, Hartwell, et al. Trials and Triumphs: The Record of the Fifty-fifth Ohio
Volunteer Infantry. Chicago: A. C. McClurg & Co., 1904.

Page, Charles D. History of the Fourteenth Regiment, Connecticut Volunteer Infantry.
Meriden, Conn.: Horton Printing Co., 1906.

[Palmer, Edwin F.]. The Second Brigade; or, Camp Life, by a Volunteer. Montpelier, Vt.:
E. P. Walton, 1864.

Parker, John L., and Robert G. Carter. History of the Twenty-Second Massachusetts
Infantry, The Second Company Sharpshooters, and the Third Light Battery, in the War
of the Rebellion. Boston: Rand Avery Co., 1887.

Seville, William P. History of the First Regiment, Delaware Volunteers. Wilmington,
Del.: Historical Society of Delaware, 1885.

Sawyer, Franklin. A Military History of the 8th Regiment Ohio Volunteer Infantry; Its
Battles, Marches and Army Movements. Cleveland: Fairbanks & Co., 1881.

Simons, Ezra D. A Regimental History: The One Hundred and Twenty-fifth New York
State Volunteers. New York: Judson Printing Co., 1888.

Small, A. R. The Sixteenth Maine Regiment in the War of the Rebellion. Portland,
Maine: B. Thurston & Co., 1886.

Smith, John Day. The History of the Nineteenth Maine Regiment of Maine Volunteer
Infantry, 1862–1865. Minneapolis: Great Western Printing Co., 1909.

Sturtevant, Ralph Orson. Pictorial History, Thirteenth Vermont Volunteers, War of
1861–1865. N.p., [ca. 1910].

Survivors Association. History of the Corn Exchange Regiment, 118th Pennsylvania
Volunteers from Their First Engagement at Antietam to Appomattox. Philadelphia:
J. L. Smith, 1888.

Toombs, Samuel. Reminiscences of the War, Comprising a Detailed Account of the
Experiences of the Thirteenth Regiment New Jersey Volunteers in Camp, on the March,
and in Battle. Orange, N.J.: Journal Office, 1878.

Walker, Francis A. History of the Second Army Corps. New York: Charles Scribner's
Sons, 1886.

Ward, Joseph R. C. History of the One Hundred and Sixth Regiment Pennsylvania
Volunteers, 2d Brigade, 2d Division, 2d Corps, 1861–1865. Philadelphia:
F. McManus Jr. & Co., 1906.

Washburn, George H. A Complete Military History and Record of the 108th Regiment
New York Volunteers from 1862 to 1894. Rochester, N.Y.: E. R. Andrews, 1894.

Williams, John C. Life in Camp: A History of the Nine Months' Service of the Fourteenth
Vermont Regiment. Claremont, N.H.: Claremont Manufacturing Co., 1864.

Wilson, Mrs. Arabella M. Disaster, Struggle, Triumph: The Adventures of 1,000 "Boys in *Blue," from August, 1862, to June, 1865.* Albany, N.Y.: Argus Company, Printers, 1870.

REUNION LITERATURE

"About the Charge of Pickett's Division." *Confederate Veteran* 21 (1913): 475–76.

"Anchor," "A Visit to Gettysburg." *Army and Navy Journal* 4 (June 8, 1867): 663.

Armstrong, James. *Grand Gathering of the Men Who Wore the Gray at the Capitol of the Confederacy.* Charleston, S.C., 1907.

"At Gettysburg, 1913." *Outlook* 104 (July 12, 1913): 541.

"The Battle-Flag Flurry." *The Nation,* June 23, 1887.

"Battles and Leaders of the Civil War." *Century Magazine* 28 (October 1884): 943.

Bishop, Joseph. "Revisiting Gettysburg." *National Tribune,* November 28, 1889.

Blake, Walter H. *Hand Grips: The Story of the Great Gettysburg Reunion, July 1913.* Vineland, N.J.: G. E. Smith, 1913.

"The Blue and the Gray." *National Tribune,* April 22, 1882.

"The Boston Journal on 'Pickett's Charge.'" *Confederate Veteran* 21 (1913): 384.

"The Century War Series." *Century Magazine* 29 (1885): 788.

Ceremonies Attending the Presentation and Unveiling of the North Carolina Memorial on the Battle Field of Gettysburg, July 3, 1929. N.p., 1929.

"Comment by Another Ohio Editor." *Confederate Veteran* 21 (1913): 385.

Dedication of the Monument Erected by Pennsylvania to Commemorate the Charge of General Humphreys' Division, Fifth Army Corps, Army of the Potomac, on Marye's Heights, Fredericksburg, Virginia, December 13th, 1862. Dedication Ceremonies, November 11th, 1908. N.p., 1908.

DeVoto, Bernard. "Gettysburg." *Harper's Magazine* 175 (August 1937): 333–36.

"Dishonoring the Dead." *National Tribune,* April 29, 1882.

Douthat, R. W. "Opportunities of Veterans at Gettysburg." *Confederate Veteran* 21 (1913): 229.

Earle, David M. *History of the Excursion of the Fifteenth Massachusetts Regiment and Its Friends, to the Battlefields of Gettysburg, Pa, Antietam, Md, Ball's Bluff, Va, and Washington, D.C., May 31–June 12, 1886.* Worcester, Mass.: Charles Hamilton Press, 1886.

Fiftieth Anniversary of the Battle of Gettysburg, Report of the Pennsylvania Commission, December 31, 1913. Revised edition, April 1915. Harrisburg, Pa.: William Stanley Ray, 1915.

Frazier, John W. *Reunion of the Blue and Gray. Philadelphia Brigade and Pickett's Division, July 2, 3, 4, 1887, and Sept. 15, 16, 17, 1906.* Philadelphia: Ware Brothers, 1906.

"General Mahone on Gettysburg." In *Under Both Flags: A Panorama of the Great Civil War,* by George Morley Vickers. Richmond: B. F. Johnson, 1896.

"General Pickett at Gettysburg." *Confederate Veteran* 21 (1913): 391.

"Gettysburg: A Common Ideal." *Outlook* 104 (July 9, 1913): 554–55.

"Gettysburg Farewell: The Blue and the Gray Light an Eternal Flame." *Newsweek* 12 (July 11, 1938): 12–13.

"Gettysburg Fifty Years After." *Review of Reviews* 48 (1913): 177–83.

"Gettysburg, Gettysburg." *Confederate Veteran* 21 (1913): 377–86.

"Gettysburg Reunion." *Army and Navy Journal* 25 (June 30, 1888): 980.

"Gettysburg Thirty Years After." *The Nation* 56 (May 4, 1893).

"Gettysburg Vandalism." *National Tribune*, July 13, 1893.

Godkin, E. L. "The Gettysburg Celebration." *The Nation* 47 (July 12, 1888).

"Gov. Mann Doesn't Favor Gathering at Richmond in 1915." *Confederate Veteran* 21 (1913): 386.

"The Grand Army Encampment Upon the Battle Field of Gettysburg." *Grand Army Scout and Soldiers' Mail*, August 18, 1883.

Harris, N. E. *The Civil War; Its Results and Lessons. An Address Delivered at Louisville, Kentucky, to the Confederate Veterans in Reunion, July 15th, 1905*. Macon, Ga.: J. W. Burke, 1906.

Kensil, John C. "The Battlefield of Gettysburg, After Twenty Years." *Grand Army Scout and Soldiers' Mail*, September 8, 1883.

Littell, Robert. "Ghosts Speak at Gettysburg." *Readers' Digest* 33 (July 1938): 53–55.

McCulloch, Robert. "The 'High Tide at Gettysburg.'" *Confederate Veteran* 21 (1913): 473–76.

[Maine Commissioners]. *Maine at Gettysburg, Report of the Maine Commissioners Prepared by the Executive Committee*. Portland, Maine: Lakeside Press, 1899.

"Marking the Battlefield of Gettysburg." *Grand Army Scout and Soldiers' Mail*, November 10, 1883.

[Maryland Gettysburg Monument Commission]. *Report of the State of Maryland Gettysburg Monument Commission to His Excellency E. E. Jackson, Governor of Maryland, June 17th, 1891*. Baltimore: William K. Boyle & Sons, 1891.

Michigan at Gettysburg, July 1st, 2nd and 3rd, 1863, June 12th, 1889. Detroit: Winn & Hammond, 1889.

"More Rebel Impudence." *National Tribune*, October 11, 1888.

"Mrs. Pickett's Thanks." *Army and Navy Journal* 24 (July 16, 1887): 1011.

"A Nation United on the 100th Anniversary of the Battle of Gettysburg, July 1–3, 1963." Program insert in special issue of *Civil War Times Illustrated* 2 (July 1963): 1–16 [tucked in between journal pages 32–33].

New York Monuments Commission for the Battlefields of Gettysburg and Chattanooga. *Final Report on the Battlefield of Gettysburg*. 3 vols. Albany, N.Y.: J. B. Lyon Co., 1902.

Nicholson, John Page, comp. *Pennsylvania at Gettysburg. Ceremonies at the Dedication of the Monuments Erected by the Commonwealth of Pennsylvania to Mark the Positions of the Pennsylvania Commands Engaged in the Battle. . . .* 2 vols. Harrisburg: E. K. Meyers, 1893.

"The Nineteenth [Massachusetts]." *Bivouac* 3 (November 1885): 413–14.

"North Carolina at Gettysburg." *Confederate Veteran* 37 (August 1929): 286–88.

"On to Gettysburg." *National Tribune*, June 10, 1886.

Pickett, LaSalle Corbell. "Gloria Victis." *Confederate Veteran* 21 (1913): 359.

"The Picket[t] Memorial at Gettysburg." *National Tribune*, May 12, 1887.

Rafferty, Thomas. "Gettysburg." *National Tribune*, February 9, 1888.

Reunions of the Nineteenth Maine Regiment Association. Augusta, Maine: Sprague, Owen & Nash, 1878.

"Robert McCulloch at Gettysburg." *Confederate Veteran* 21 (1913): 424.

Rowland, Kate Mason. "High Tide at Gettysburg." *Confederate Veteran* 11 (1903): 365-66.

Sellars, A. J., comp. *Souvenir, Survivors' Association, Gettysburg, 1888-9*. Philadelphia: John W. Clark's Sons, [ca. 1889].

Sherwood, Herbert Francis. "Gettysburg Fifty Years Afterward." *Outlook* 104 (July 19, 1913): 610-12.

"Soldiers of Both Armies at Gettysburg." *Confederate Veteran* 15 (January 1907): 14.

"Task Remaining; Celebration of Centennial." *Newsweek* 62 (July 15, 1963): 18-19.

Tate, Allen, "The Battle of Gettysburg: Why Was It Fought?" *Carleton Miscellany* 4 (1963): 32-45.

"3d Corps Reunion—Monuments Dedicated." *Grand Army Scout and Soldiers' Mail*, July 10, 1886.

Thompson, Will Henry. "High Tide at Gettysburg." *Century Magazine* 86 (1913): 410-12.

Tregaskis, John. *Souvenir of the Re-Union of the Blue and the Gray on the Battlefield of Gettysburg, July 1, 2, 3, and 4, 1888 [sic; 1887]*. New York: American Graphic, 1888.

"25 Years Later." *National Tribune*, July 12, 1888.

"Two Gettysburg Encounters." *Literary Digest* 47 (July 12, 1913): 75.

Unveiling Confederate Monument (Carroll County, Mississippi), Carrollton, Miss., by P. F. Liddell Chapter, U.C.V. N.p., 1905.

"Unveiling of Lee's Monument." *National Tribune*, June 5, 1890.

"Valuable Historical Matter." *National Tribune*, June 12, 1890.

Vanderslice, John M. *Gettysburg, Then and Now: The Field of American Valor, Where and How the Regiments Fought and the Troops They Encountered*. New York: G. W. Dillingham Co., 1899; Dayton, Ohio: Morningside Press, 1983.

Walker, C. Irvine. "Conference of Gettysburg Commission." *Confederate Veteran* 21 (1913): 107.

Warren, Horatio N. *Two Reunions of the 142nd Regiment, Pa. Vols. . . .* Buffalo, N.Y.: Courier Co., 1890.

Webb, Alexander S. *An Address Delivered at Gettysburg, August 27, 1883, by Gen. Alexander S. Webb, at the Dedication of the 72d Pa. Vols. Monument. . . .* Philadelphia: Porter & Coates, 1883.

Wert, J. Howard. *A Complete Hand-Book of the Monuments and Indications and Guide to the Positions on the Gettysburg Battlefield*. Harrisburg: R. M. Sturgeon, 1886.

"What the 111th New York Regiment Heroes Say." *Confederate Veteran* 21 (1913): 385.

SECONDARY LITERATURE

Andrews, J. Cutler. "The Press Reports the Battle of Gettysburg." *Pennsylvania History* 31 (1964): 176-98.

———. *The South Reports the Civil War*. Princeton, N.J.: Princeton University Press, 1970.

Armour, Richard. *It All Started with Columbus*. New York: McGraw-Hill, 1971.

Bagby, George W. *The Old Virginia Gentleman and Other Sketches*. New York: Charles Scribner's Sons, 1910.

"Battle of the Generals; How Ike and Monty Would Have Fought at Gettysburg." *U.S. News and World Report* 42 (May 24, 1957): 60–63.

Benet, Stephen Vincent. *John Brown's Body*. New York: Holt, Rinehart and Winston, 1928.

Bloom, Robert L. "The Battle of Gettysburg in Fiction." *Pennsylvania History* 43 (1976): 309–27.

Bundel, Col. C. M. "The Methods of War at Gettysburg." *Infantry Journal* 35 (1929): 109–24.

Busey, John W. *These Honored Dead: The Union Casualties at Gettysburg*. Hightstown, N.J.: Longstreet House, 1988.

Busey, John W., and David G. Martin. *Regimental Strengths and Losses at Gettysburg*. Hightstown, N.J.: Longstreet House, 1986.

Carruth, Gorton, and Eugene Ehrlich. *American Quotations*. New York: Wings, 1988.

Chase, John. "Ten Books of the Month." *Bookman* 37 (1913): 564–68.

Coco, Gregory A. *Killed in Action: Eyewitness Accounts of the Last Moments of 100 Union Soldiers Who Died at Gettysburg*. Gettysburg, Pa.: Thomas Publications, 1992.

———. *A Strange and Blighted Land, Gettysburg: The Aftermath of a Battle*. Gettysburg, Pa.: Thomas Publications, 1995.

Coddington, Edwin B. *The Gettysburg Campaign: A Study in Command*. New York: Charles Scribner's Sons, 1968; Dayton, Ohio: Morningside Press, 1979.

———. "Rothermel's Paintings of the Battle of Gettysburg." *Pennsylvania History* 27 (1960): 1–27.

Confederate States of America. *General Orders from the Adjutant General's Office, 1862–1863*. Richmond: n.p., 1864.

Connelly, Thomas L. *The Marble Man: Robert E. Lee and His Image in American Society*. New York: A. A. Knopf, 1977.

Cooke, John Esten. *Hammer and Rapier*. New York: Carleton, 1870.

———. *Mohun*. New York: G. W. Dillingham, 1867.

———. *Surry of Eagle's Nest*. New York: G. W. Dillingham, 1866.

———. *The Wearing of the Gray, Being Personal Portraits, Scenes and Adventures of the War*. New York: E. B. Treat, 1867.

Coulter, Capt. Victor A. "Smoke at Gettysburg." *Infantry Journal* 44 (1937): 159–60.

Coyle, Harold. *Look Away*. New York: Simon & Schuster, 1995.

Craige, Capt. John H. "The Marines at Gettysburg." *Marine Corps Gazette* 7 (September 1922): 249–52.

Crozier, Emmet. *Yankee Reporters, 1861–65*. New York: Oxford University Press, 1956.

[Cunningham, S. A.]. "Impartial Between All Sections." *Confederate Veteran* 1 (1893): 197.

Dabney, Virginius. *Richmond: The Story of a City*. New York: Doubleday & Co., 1976.

DePeyster, J. Watts. *Andrew Atkinson Humphreys, of Pennsylvania, Brigadier General and Brevet Major General, USA, Major General, United States Volunteers. . . .* Lancaster, Pa.: Lancaster Intelligencer Press, 1886.

Eggleston, George Cary. *A Rebel's Recollections*. New York: Riverside Press, 1875.

"Equine Heroes of Pickett's Charge." *Journal of the U.S. Cavalry* 24 (1913): 482–83.

Faulkner, William. *Intruder in the Dust*. Vintage Book ed. New York: Vintage Press, 1972.

Fiebeger, Gustav J. *The Campaign and Battle of Gettysburg, from the Official Records of the Union and Confederate Armies*. West Point: U.S. Military Academy, 1915.

Foster, Gaines M. *Ghosts of the Confederacy: Defeat, the Lost Cause, and the Emergence of the New South*. New York: Oxford University Press, 1987.

Frank, Joseph Allan, and George A. Reaves. *"Seeing the Elephant": Raw Recruits at the Battle of Shiloh*. New York: Greenwood Press, 1989.

Freeman, Douglas Southall. *Lee's Lieutenants: A Study in Command*. 3 vols. New York: Charles Scribner's Sons, 1944.

Fussell, Paul. *The Great War and Modern Memory*. New York: Oxford University Press, 1975.

Gallagher, Gary W. "A Widow and Her Soldier: LaSalle Corbell Pickett as Author of the George E. Pickett Letters." *Virginia Magazine of History and Biography* 94 (1986): 329–44.

———, ed. *Third Day at Gettysburg and Beyond*. Chapel Hill: University of North Carolina Press, 1994.

"Gettysburg Refought." *Time* 69 (May 27, 1957): 74.

"Gettysburg To-Day—and in '63." *Literary Digest* 74 (July 22, 1922): 37–38.

Hall, Jonathan Leslie. *Half-Hours in Southern History*. Richmond: B. F. Johnson, 1907.

Hamblen, Charles P. *Connecticut Yankees at Gettysburg*. Kent, Ohio: Kent State University Press, 1993.

Handlin, Oscar. "The Civil War as Symbol and as Actuality." *Massachusetts Review* 3 (1961): 133–43.

Hanly, J. Frank. *The Battle of Gettysburg*. Cincinatti: Jennings and Graham, 1912.

Harrison, Kathy Georg, and John W. Busey. *Nothing But Glory: Pickett's Division at Gettysburg*. Hightstown, N.J.: Longstreet House, 1987.

Hawthorne, Frederick W. *Gettysburg: Stories of Men and Monuments as Told by Battlefield Guides*. Hanover, Pa.: Association of Licensed Battlefield Guides, 1988.

Hollingsworth, Alan M., and James M. Cox. *The Third Day at Gettysburg: Pickett's Charge*. New York: Henry Holt, 1959.

Holmes, Richard. *Acts of War: The Behavior of Men in Battle*. New York: Free Press, 1985.

Jenkins, Philip. *Intimate Enemies: Moral Panics in Contemporary Great Britain*. New York: Aldine De Gruyter, 1992.

Johnson, W. A. "Gettysburg and the Battle." *Confederate Veteran* 25 (September 1917): 410.

Johnston, Mary. "Gettysburg." *Atlantic Monthly* 110 (July 1912): 1–9.

Jones, Ted. *Hard Road to Gettysburg*. Novato, Calif.: Lyford Books, 1993.

Kammen, Michael. *Mystic Chords of Memory: The Transformation of Tradition in American Culture*. New York: Vintage Press, 1993.

Krick, Robert K. *The Gettysburg Death Roster: The Confederate Dead at Gettysburg*. 3rd ed. Dayton, Ohio: Morningside Press, 1993.

Latimer, Miss E. *Idyls of Gettysburg*. Philadelphia: George Maclean, 1872.

Linderman, Gerald. *Embattled Courage: The Experience of Combat in the American Civil War*. New York: Free Press, 1987.

Lossing, Benson, comp. *Harper's Encyclopedia of United States History from 458 A.D. to 1902.* 10 vols. New York: Harper & Brothers, 1902.

Luvaas, Jay, and Harold W. Nelson. *U.S. Army War College Guide to the Battle of Gettysburg.* Carlisle, Pa.: South Mountain Press, Inc., 1986.

McRandle, James H. *The Antique Drums of War.* College Station, Tex.: Texas A&M Press, 1994.

Maddex, Jack P., Jr. *The Virginia Conservatives, 1867–1879.* Chapel Hill: University of North Carolina Press, 1970.

Martin, David G. *Confederate Monuments at Gettysburg, The Gettysburg Battle Monuments.* Vol. 1. Hightstown, N.J.: Longstreet House, 1986.

Meekins, Peter. "The Virginia Fool." *South-Atlantic* (1879): 173–81.

Mitchell, Mary H. *Hollywood Cemetery: The History of a Southern Shrine.* Richmond: Virginia State Library, 1985.

Mosse, George L. *Fallen Soldiers: Reshaping the Memory of the World Wars.* New York: Oxford University Press, 1990.

Page, Thomas Nelson. *The Burial of the Guns.* Plantation Edition, Vol. 2. New York: Charles Scribner's Sons, 1906.

Pfanz, Harry W. "The Development of the Gettysburg National Military Park." *Civil War Times Illustrated* 2 (July 1963): 45–48.

Pindell, Richard. "The True High-Water Mark of the Confederacy." *Blue and Gray Magazine* 1 (December/January 1983): 6–15.

Piston, William Garrett. *Lee's Tarnished Lieutenant: James Longstreet and His Place in Southern History.* Athens: University of Georgia Press, 1987.

Reardon, Carol. *Soldiers and Scholars: The U.S. Army and the Uses of Military History, 1865–1920.* Lawrence: University Press of Kansas, 1990.

Rhodes, James Ford. "The Battle of Gettysburg." *American Historical Review* 4 (1899): 665–77.

Ridpath, John Clark. *The New Complete History of the United States of America.* 12 vols. Chicago: Elliott-Madison Co., 1912.

Robertson, James I., Jr. "The Continuing Battle of Gettysburg: An Essay Review." *Georgia Historical Quarterly* 58 (1974): 278–82.

Rollins, Richard, comp. *Pickett's Charge: Eyewitness Accounts.* Redondo Beach, Calif.: Rank and File Publishers, 1994.

Ropes, John Codman, and W. R. Livermore. *The Story of the Civil War.* 3 parts. New York: G. P. Putnam's Sons, 1913.

Rose, Anne C. *Victorian America and the Civil War.* New York: Cambridge University Press, 1992.

Sauers, Richard A. *The Gettysburg Campaign, June 3–August 1, 1863: A Comprehensive, Selectively Annotated Bibliography.* Westport, Conn.: Greenwood Press, 1982.

Savage, Douglas. *The Court Martial of Robert E. Lee: A Historical Novel.* Conshohocken, Pa.: Combined Books, 1993.

"School Histories of the United States." *Southern Review* 3 (1868): 154–79.

Sefton, James E. "Gettysburg: An Exercise in the Evaluation of Historical Evidence." *Military Affairs* 28 (1964): 64–72.

Shaara, Michael. *The Killer Angels.* New York: Ballantine Books, 1975.

Shay, Jonathan. *Achilles in Vietnam: Combat Trauma and the Undoing of Character.* New York: Athanaeum, 1994.

Singmaster, Elsie. "The Battle of Gettysburg, July 1–3, 1863." *Outlook* 104 (June 21, 1913): 372–76.

———. *Gettysburg; Stories of the Red Harvest and the Aftermath.* Boston: Houghton Mifflin Co., 1913.

Skimin, Robert. *Gray Victory.* New York: St. Martin's Press, 1988.

Stedman, Edmund C. "Gettysburg." *Army and Navy Journal* 9 (May 11, 1872): 623.

Stewart, George R. *Pickett's Charge: A Microhistory of the Final Confederate Attack at Gettysburg, July 3, 1863.* Boston: Houghton Mifflin Co., 1959; Premier Civil War Classic edition. Greenwich, Conn.: Fawcett Publication, 1963.

Thelen, David. "Memory and American History." *Journal of American History* 75 (March 1989): 1117–29.

Tourgee, Albion W. "The South as a Field for Fiction." *Forum* 6 (1888–89): 404–12.

Trinque, Bruce A. "Arnold's Battery and the 26th North Carolina." *Gettysburg Magazine*, no. 12 (January 1995): 61–67.

Tucker, Glenn. *High Tide at Gettysburg: The Campaign in Pennsylvania.* Indianapolis, Ind.: Bobbs-Merrill, 1958.

———. *Lee and Longstreet at Gettysburg.* Indianapolis, Ind.: Bobbs-Merrill, 1968.

———. "What Became of Pickett's Report on His Assault at Gettysburg?" *Civil War Times Illustrated* 6 (October 1967): 37–39.

———. *Zebulon Vance: Champion of Personal Freedom.* Indianapolis, Ind.: Bobbs-Merrill, 1965.

Van Auken, Sheldon. "The Southern Historical Novel in the Early Twentieth Century." *Journal of Southern History* 14 (1948): 157–91.

Warfield, E. D. "The Repulse of Pickett's Charge at Gettysburg." *Chautauquan* 31 (1931): 340–42.

Wecter, Dixon. *The Hero in America: A Chronicle of Hero Worship.* New York: Charles Scribner's Sons, 1941.

Wert, Jeffry D. *General James Longstreet: The Confederacy's Most Controversial Soldier—A Biography.* New York: Simon & Schuster, 1993.

Williams, Ben Ames. *House Divided.* Boston: Houghton Mifflin Co., 1947.

Wolf Family. *A Simplified Tour of the Gettysburg Battlefield.* Gettysburg, Pa.: Audio-Tronics Tape Tours, n.d.

INDEX

Abbott, Capt. Henry L., 13

Abbott, John, 148

Aiken, David Wyatt, 92

Alabama: views on Pickett's Charge, 4,
147–48, 201–2

Alabama troops: 4th Infantry, 150, 182;
5th Infantry Battalion, 7, 31, 35, 144;
8th Infantry, 8, 147, 148; 9th Infantry,
8; 10th Infantry, 8; 11th Infantry, 8,
148; 13th Infantry, 7, 48, 59, 77, 140,
144; 14th Infantry, 8

Albertson, Jonathan, 54–56, 60, 66

Alexander, Lt. Col. Edward Porter, 34,
36, 91, 153

Alexander, Peter W., 57–58, 59, 170

Allen, Col. Daniel B., 127

Allen, Col. Robert C., 208

Anderson, Maj. Gen. Richard H., 8, 10,
56, 179, 186

"Annals of the War" series, 89–90,
137–38

Antietam, battle of, 13, 52, 116

Archer, Brig. Gen. James J., 7

Archer's brigade, 7, 58–59, 138–40,
144–45

Armistead, Brig. Gen. Lewis A., 6,
24–25, 26, 129, 144–45, 156, 199,
208, 211, 212; in press accounts, 48,
53, 55–56; in artwork, 71, 72, 168,
201; controversy about, 88, 201; monuments at Gettysburg to, 95, 193,
201; captured sword returned, 183

Armistead's brigade, 6, 46, 160, 164,
167, 190

Armour, Richard, 205

Army of Northern Virginia: First Corps,
5, 7, 33, 84; Second Corps, 5; Third
Corps, 7, 8, 33, 51, 140; deals with
defeat at Gettysburg, 31–38, 54–60,
63. See also individual divisions,
brigades, and regiments

Army of the Potomac, 2, 5; I Corps,
9–10, 47, 112, 120, 124; II Corps,
8–9, 29, 46–47, 67, 69, 101, 116,
120, 121; III Corps, 47, 112, 126;
V Corps, 47, 126, 209; VI Corps, 128;
XI Corps, 10, 46; XII Corps, 5, 112,
127; deals with victory at Gettysburg,
28–31, 110; history of, 160. See also
individual divisions, brigades, and
regiments

Arnold, Lt. William A., 9, 23

Ashe, Samuel A., 151, 152, 169

Austerlitz, battle of, 42, 65

Aylett, Col. William R., 98, 101, 102,
104, 105, 211

Bachelder, John B., 69–70; and Pickett's
division memorial, 92, 94; at 1887 reunion, 101, 102, 232 (n. 75); as battlefield historian, 137, 145, 178–83, 207

Bagby, George W., 75

Baird, Capt. Edward R., 160, 164

Baker, Andrew J., 145

Baker, Maj. William J., 64

Balaklava, battle of, 17, 53–54, 119, 128,
196

Banes, Col. Charles H., 97–98

Barnum, Francis J., 210

Barrineau, Lt. Isaac, 36

Bartlett, Capt. Asa W., 129

Battlefield of Gettysburg Commission,
184

"Battles and Leaders of the Civil War"
series (Century Magazine), 90–91, 121,
140

Beall, Col. Lloyd J., 82

Bechtel, Pvt. J. L., 13, 17, 18

Beitler, Lt. Col. Lewis E., 184–85

Belcher, Pvt. Granville, 18, 31

Belknap, Pvt. Charles, 20

Benedict, G. G., 179

Benet, Stephen Vincent, 200, 204

Benning, Brig. Gen. Henry L., brigade
of, 209, 253 (n. 50)

Bentley, Capt. William W., 21, 192–93

Berenger, Tom, 211

Berkeley, Maj. Edmund, 158

Bicknell, Lt. L. E., 91
Bingham, Henry H., 88, 201
Bird, Edgeworth, 31
Blackford, Charles Minor, 31–32, 34
Blanton, Sgt. Leigh M., 53
Bledsoe, Albert, 76
Blenheim, battle of, 119
Bloch, Marc, 63
Bond, William R., 138–39, 140–42, 152, 153, 182
Boone, Mark, 193
Bowen, Capt. George, 23
Boy Scouts, 184, 189
Bright, Capt. Robert A., 160, 167, 168, 169, 171, 180, 182–83, 246 (n. 94)
Brockenbrough's brigade, 8, 59, 205, 212; as target of criticism, 133, 136–37, 145, 150
Brown, Maud, 147, 209, 241 (n. 56)
Brown, Lt. T. Fred, 9
Bruce, Philip A., 173
Bryan barn, 23, 146–47, 150, 176
Buckley, Pvt. John, 181
Buford, Brig. Gen. John, 7
Bugles of Gettysburg, The (Sallie Pickett), 185, 204
Bull, Lt. Col. James, 23
Bunker Hill, battle of, 155
Burns, John, 71
Burns, Pvt. William J., 25
Burns, Gen. William W., 101
Burtchaell, W. D., 147
Burton, Capt. John E., 121
Butler, Maj. Gen. Benjamin F., 96
Butterfield, Brig. Gen. Daniel, 112

Cabell, Col. H. C., 102
Caisan, John, 192
Calder, Lt. William, 32
Carlton, Lt. P. C., 136
Carpenter, Judge B. F., 136
Carter, Capt. Robert G., 119
Cemetery Hill, 10, 125, 177
Cemetery Ridge: monuments on, 93–95, 99–103, 112, 181; as proposed site of Pickett marker, 94–97; preservation of, 177–78

Chancellorsville, battle of, 36, 42, 60, 92, 132, 202
Chancellorsville and Gettysburg (Double-day), 88
Chapultepec, battle of, 162
Charleston, S.C., seige of, 41
Chase, John, 163
Chickamauga, battle of, 202
Chippewa, battle of, 50
Christian, George L., 171–72, 182
Clare, Lt. Henry P., 17, 44
Clark, Champ, 189–90
Clark, George, 148, 241 (n. 61)
Clark, Judge Walter, 148–49, 182, 201
Clay, Pvt. John W., 166
Clopton, Judge William G., 95
Coates, Capt. Henry, 25
Cocke, William Fauntleroy, 78–79
Cocke, William H., 32, 35
Coddington, Edwin B., 207
Coffin, Charles C., 31, 67, 116, 126
Confederate Veteran (magazine), 143, 145, 188, 196, 201
Connecticut troops: 14th Infantry, 9, 13, 19, 20, 28, 29, 30, 115, 120
Conservatives, Virginia, 87, 164
Cook, T. M., 49
Cooke, Charles M., 150
Cooke, John Esten, 75, 133, 141, 142
Corley, Col. James, 80
Corse, Brig. Gen. Montgomery, 94, 105
Cosmopolitan Magazine, 185–86
Cotton, Lt. Burwell T., 15, 16
Cowan, Capt. Andrew, 101, 105, 139, 185, 197
Cox, James M., 207
Coyle, Harold, 205
Crocker, Maj. James F., 101, 165, 166, 167, 175
Crotty, Col. Sgt. Daniel G., 69
Crounse, L. L., 43
Cuddy, Sgt. Michael, 29
Culp's Hill, 5, 12, 16, 177
Cunningham, S. A., 143
Cureton, T. J., 142
Cushing, Lt. Alonzo H., 9, 43, 47

Daniel, John W., 157, 168
Danks, Col. John A., 130
Davis, Jefferson, 8, 96–97, 163
Davis, Capt. Joseph J., 133, 135
Davis, Brig. Gen. Joseph R., 8, 18, 199, 218 (n. 45)
Davis, Capt. William, 24, 25
Davis's brigade, 12–13, 23, 24, 59, 145–46, 150
Davy, John M., 120
Deacon, Pvt. Garrett, 28
Dearing, Maj. James, 33, 160
Deering, C. P., 192
DeLacy, Sgt. Patrick, 124
Delaware troops: 1st Infantry, 9, 20, 29, 122
Dent, Lt. John, 20
"Deo Vindice" (correspondent), 58–59
Devereux, Col. Arthur, 25, 30
Devil's Den, 126, 144, 195, 209
DeVoto, Bernard, 202
Ditterline, Theodore, 65
Doubleday, Maj. Gen. Abner, 47, 88, 118, 195
Douthat, Robert W., 171, 187, 194
Dowdey, Clifford, 206
Downey, Fairfax, 206
Dudley, Bishop, 82
Dunton, W. C., 124

Early, Maj. Gen. Jubal A., 84, 85, 157, 164, 204, 205, 206
Easley, Sgt. D. B., 11, 12, 13, 168
Eggleston, George Cary, 89
Eisenhower, Dwight D., 203
Ellis, Lt. Col. John T., 18, 34
Ellis, Maj. Theodore, 19, 29
Ellyson, J. Taylor, 104–5
Emerson, Ralph Waldo, 140
Emmell, Pvt. Albert, 29
Eshelman, Maj. Benjamin, 18
Ewell, Lt. Gen. Richard S., 5, 85

Fairchild, Lucius, 94–95, 98
Faulkner, William, 204–5
Featherstone, Lt. Daniel, 18
Figg, Royal, 88

Firebaugh, Pvt. Samuel A., 12
First Virginia Infantry Association, 91, 93, 94
Fish, Franklin W., 102
Fiske, Capt. Samuel, 30, 221 (n. 136)
Fitzgerald, William, 35
Five Forks, battle of, 74, 77, 80, 86, 158, 162, 170
Flags, 29, 30, 92, 96–97, 186
Fleming, Capt. C. Seton, 147
Florida: views on Pickett's Charge, 4, 147
Florida troops: 2nd Infantry, 8, 27, 29, 31, 36, 59–60; 5th Infantry, 8; 8th Infantry, 8, 36
Foraker, Gov. Joseph B., 95
Ford, Lt. P. Fletcher, 107, 240 (n. 37)
Ford, Thomas H., 105–7
Fort Delaware, 192
Franklin, Tenn., battle of, 63
Frayser's Farm, battle of, 57
Frazier, John W., 95–97, 193
Fredericksburg, battle of, 13, 52, 63, 92, 128
Freeley, Edward G., 191
Freeman, Douglas Southall, 36–37, 205–6, 251 (n. 22)
Fremantle, Lt. Col. Arthur James Lyon, 63–64, 211
Friend, Thomas, 159, 169
From Manassas to Appomattox (Longstreet), 161
Fry, Col. Burkett D., 7, 48, 87, 148
Fuger, Sgt. Frederick, 130
Fulton, W. F., 35
Fussell, Paul, 15–16, 17

Gage, Sgt. Jere, 147
Gaines Mill, battle of, 57, 63, 149
Gallon, Dale, 210
Galwey, Thomas, 181
Gardner, Gov. O. Max, 200
Garnett, Brig. Gen. Richard B., 6, 24, 156, 157, 169; in news accounts, 48, 56; eulogized, 168, 199
Garnett's brigade, 6, 18, 116, 139, 144, 157, 160, 182

Gates, Col. Theodore, 9, 21, 124, 179
Geiger, Capt. George H., 78
Gerald, G. B., 196–97
Gerrish, Theodore, 88, 115
Gettysburg, Pa.: terrain of, 13, 176–78;
    as tourist attraction, 65–66, 92–93,
    199–200, 211–12. *See also* Reenact-
    ments; Reunions
"Gettysburg" (movie), 211
Gettysburg Battlefield Memorial Associ-
    ation, 93–95, 101, 110, 177
Gettysburg Hill, 79–80, 83, 105
Gettysburg Lutheran Theological Semi-
    nary, 188–89
Gettysburg National Military Cemetery,
    201
Gettysburg National Military Park, 182,
    200–201, 209
Gibbon, Brig. Gen. John, 5, 8–9, 30, 48,
    71, 199
Gomer, Lt. A. P., 165
Goodrich, Pvt. Loren, 28
Gordon, Lt. Col George T., 171
Gordon, John B., 96, 169–70
Graham, Capt. Joseph, 13, 17
Graham, Joseph A. (27th N.C.), 50
Grand Army of the Republic (GAR), 90,
    92, 104, 110–11, 114, 177, 184
Grant, Brig. Gen. Lewis A., 188
Grant, Lt. Gen. Ulysses S., 162, 163
Graydon, Ross E., 191
Greeley, Horace, 66
Gregg, J. Irvin, 182
Griggs, Capt. George S., 34
Gross, George J., 65–66

Hall, Col. Norman J., 9, 18, 20, 21, 25,
    30, 45, 91, 199
Hamilton, Albert H., 191–92
Hancock, Maj. Gen. Winfield S., 88,
    178; during the battle, 8, 19, 26;
    argues with Hunt, 18, 21, 121; hon-
    ored, 30, 46–47, 176, 199
Handlin, Oscar, 211–12
Hanly, J. Frank, 187
Harbaugh, T. C., 174–75
Harris, Fergus S., 145

Harris, Capt. J. G., 135
Harris, James S., 152
Harrison, Joseph, 71
Harrison, Walter, 76–78, 79, 180, 187
Harrow, Brig. Gen. William, 9, 21, 26,
    30, 45, 199
Haskell, Lt. Frank A.: on history, 1–2,
    122, 213, 237 (n. 79); at Gettysburg,
    12, 15, 16, 21, 24, 25, 27, 30
Hastings, battle of, 119
Hatchett, Pvt. William, 15, 34–35
Hayden, Cpl. (1st Minn.), 47
Haynes, Capt. A. S., 136–37
Hays, Brig. Gen. Alexander, 9, 19, 23,
    123–24, 199
Hays's division, 21, 23, 117–18, 122–24
Hazlewood, Martin, 159
Heart of a Soldier, The (Sallie Pickett),
    186–87
Heath, Col. Francis E., 26
Hedges, Ira M., 118
Herbert, Col. Hilary, 147–48
Heth, Brig. Gen. Henry, 7, 51, 80, 87,
    145, 186, 230 (n. 18)
"High Tide at Gettysburg" (poem),
    113
High water mark of the Rebellion, 3,
    24; Pickett's Charge first described as,
    62–63, 66–68, 70, 77, 83; critics of
    Pickett's Charge on, 126, 146–47, 199,
    208; memorials to, 170, 176, 179, 181,
    232 (n. 75)
Hill, Lt. Gen. Ambrose P., 7, 8, 143; in
    news reports, 42, 45, 49
Hill, Lt. Gen. Daniel H., 76
Hill, Daniel H., Jr., 152
Hodges, Col. James Gregory, 166, 168
Hoitt, Pvt. William B., 18, 29, 30
Holden, W. W., 60
Holladay, H. T., 32
Holland, Capt. T. C., 193
Hollingsworth, Alan M., 207
Hollywood Cemetery, 79–80, 82–83,
    105, 157
Holmes, Richard, 11–12, 15, 27
Holt, Surgeon Joseph, 147
Hotchkiss, Jedediah, 32

Houston, Thomas D., 90
Howard, Maj. Gen. Oliver O., 46
Humphreys, Maj. Gen. Andrew A., 128
Hunt, Brig. Gen. Henry J., 10, 18, 21, 121
Hunton, Brig. Gen. Eppa, 104, 157, 158, 162–63, 180
Hunton, Eppa III (son), 157–58
Hutchins, Thomas A., 111

Imboden, Brig. Gen. John D., 79
Indiana troops: 27th Infantry, 127
Irby, Richard, 88

Jackson, Lt. Gen. Thomas J. ("Stonewall"), 163, 164, 174, 229 (n. 87)
Jacobs, Prof. Michael, 64–65
James, Lt. John, 90
Jeffress, Capt. Thomas D., 183
Jenkins, Col. David T., 69–70
Jenkins, Lt. John, 35
Johnson, Brig. Gen. Bradley T., 82, 225 (n. 94)
Johnston, David E., 88, 230 (n. 23)
Johnston, Mary, 174
Jones, Capt. A. N., 26
Jones, Lt. George W., 35
Jones, Lt. Col. John, 136
Jones, Ted, 205
Jones, Pvt. William H., 4, 20–21, 34
Jordan, Richard, 211
Joslin, Lt. Col. George C., 26

Kamman, Michael, 62, 68
Kemper, Brig. Gen. James L., 4, 24, 139, 156, 164, 169, 179–80, 199; in news accounts, 53, 55, 56; at Pickett's funeral, 81–83; as governor, 87; and monument dedications, 94, 104
Kemper's brigade, 160
Kensil, John C., 68–69
Kettell, Thomas P., 66
Killer Angels, The (Shaara), 205
Kimble, June, 145
Kingsbury, T. B., 133
Kinney, Lt. D. F., 136

Kirkpatrick, Sgt. James, 32
Kunstler, Mort, 210

Lakeman, Col. Moses B., 12
Lamb, Capt. John, 164
Lancaster, James, 211
The Land We Love (regional journal), 76
Lane, Brig. Gen. James H., 8, 79, 87, 134, 150, 199
Lane, Col. John R., 153
Lane's brigade, 8, 24, 36, 117, 140, 152, 196
Lang, Col. David A., 8, 147
Lang, Stephen, 211
Lang's (David) brigade, 27, 36, 56, 59–60, 136, 142, 168, 179; ignored, 64, 65, 117, 196
Latimer, Miss E., 69
Law, Brig. Gen. E. M., 188, 209
Lee, Fitzhugh, 96, 104, 165, 170, 233–34 (n. 111)
Lee, Gen. Robert E., 5, 8, 153; in news reports, 43, 44, 46, 50–51, 64; biographies of, 73–74, 209– 10; on history, 76; on Pickett's men, 77–78, 167; postwar image of, 84–88, 166–67; monuments to, 114
Lee, Lt. Gen. Stephen D., 182
Letterman, David, 199–200
Lewis, John H., 167
Lewis, John S., 31
Liggett, Brig. Gen. Hunter, 184
Lincoln, Abraham, 37, 50, 114, 162, 163, 177, 191, 201, 204
Linderman, Gerald, 16
Lippett, Surgeon Charles E., 34
Littell, Robert, 202
Little, Capt. B. F., 35, 39, 136
Little Round Top, 21, 119, 126, 178, 209
Lochren, Lt. William, 116
Loehr, Charles T., 88, 93, 95–96, 165, 166, 167, 168
Long, Brig. Gen. Armistead, 85
Longstreet, Helen Dortsch, 170, 189, 203
Longstreet, Lt. Gen. James, 5, 6, 8, 180;

in news reports, 42, 43, 45, 46, 49, 52;
assists Northern historians, 70, 85,
180; blamed for defeat at Gettysburg,
85–88, 135, 146, 153, 169, 173–74;
replies to critics, 86, 90–91, 161;
Pickett's men support, 88–90, 167;
praises Pickett and his men, 112, 153,
162; seeks help from Pickett's staff,
160–61; modern views of, 205–7, 252
(n. 38)
Lossing, Benson, 173
Lost Cause, 8, 63, 72–88, 113, 157, 164,
165; Southern opponents of, 86–87,
89, 162; Northern opponents of,
108–9, 114–15
Louisiana troops: Washington Artillery,
10, 18; Louisiana Tigers, 69, 223
(n. 23)
Love, William A., 146–47
Lowrance, Col. W. Lee, 8, 209

McCabe, James Dabney, 73, 133, 134,
141, 142
McCarroll, Joseph, 183
McClellan, Maj. Gen. George B., 69,
162
McClure, A. K., 98
McConnaughy, David, 177
McCrae, Lt. Tully, 121
McCulloch, Robert, 191
McDermott, A. W., 99, 101
McDougall, Col. Clinton, 119, 122, 124
McFarland, Baxter, 146
McGowan's brigade, 117, 179
McInnis, John C., 198
McIntyre, Adj. D. M., 135
McLaurin, William, 149
McLaws, Maj. Gen. Lafayette, 10, 90,
155
McMichael, Col. William, 71
McMillan farm, 8, 64
McNeil, Sgt. Alexander, 13, 20
McPherson's Ridge, 9, 56
McRandle, James H., 8
Macy, Col. George N., 179
Magruder, Col. John B., 35, 166
Magruder, Capt. William T., 146

Mahone, Brig. Gen. William, 80, 167
Mahone's brigade, 66, 117
Maine troops: 3rd Infantry, 12; 16th
Infantry, 115, 117; 17th Infantry, 69;
19th Infantry, 9, 26, 28–29, 116; 20th
Infantry, 88, 115, 209
Mallon, Col. James, 18, 29
Malloy, Lt. Thomas, 135–36
Malvern Hill, Va., battle of, 13, 42, 165
Mann, Gov. William H., 196
Marathon, battle of, 110, 119, 155
Marengo, battle of, 65
Marshall, Col. Charles, 159, 167
Marshall, Col. James K., 8, 168, 199
Marshall, Gen. S. L. A., 11
Marshall, Vice President Thomas Riley,
189
Martin, Col. Rawley, 165, 167, 168–69,
173
Marye's Heights, 128
Massachusetts troops: 5th Battery,
17; 1st Infantry, 69; 10th Infantry,
118–19; 15th Infantry, 9, 92; 19th
Infantry, 9, 10, 18, 25, 29, 91, 121;
20th Infantry, 9, 25, 179; 22nd
Infantry, 119, 126; 1st Sharpshooters,
91
Maury, Brig. Gen. Dabney H., 82, 87
Maury, Richard L., 95, 154–55
Maxwell, David, 27, 31
Mayo, Col. Joseph C., 26–27, 165, 166
Mead, Cpl. Christopher, 22
Meade, Maj. Gen. George G., 5, 30, 45,
71, 180
Meade, Capt. George G., Jr., 180–81
Meekins, Peter, 239 (n. 4)
Memory: links with history, 1–4, 10; in
and after combat, 11–13, 15–16, 20,
24, 27; and postwar amnesia, 62–63,
68–69; colors history, 108–9, 130,
131, 176–81, 199–202, 212–13
Metts, James I., 152, 159
Mexican War, 86, 162
Meyer, Sgt. Thomas, 28
Michigan troops: 3rd Infantry, 69; 7th
Infantry, 9, 25
Military Order of the Loyal Legion, 122

Miller, Lt. William A., 36
Minnesota troops: 1st Infantry, 9, 17, 25, 47, 116, 120, 190, 209–11, 253 (n. 54)
Minnigerode, Rev. Charles, 83
Missionary Ridge, battle of, 63
Mississippi: views on Pickett's Charge, 4, 145–46
Mississippi State Historical Society, 146–47
Mississippi troops: 2nd Infantry, 7, 140, 142, 147; 11th Infantry, 8, 18, 145–46, 147; 16th Infantry, 32; 18th Infantry, 32; 42nd Infantry, 7, 142; Jeff Davis Legion, 180
Montgomery, Bernard, 203
Moore, J. H., 138
Moore, Congressman J. Hampton, 194
Moore, Brig. Gen. Patrick T., 79, 82
Moore, Sgt. Robert A., 32
Morris, Col. W. G., 136
Mosby, Col. John S., 158–59
Munford, Col. Thomas T., 170
Murray, Orderly Sergeant, 166

Napoleon Bonaparte, 50, 119, 173
Nash, Capt. Charles E., 28–29
National Tribune (journal), 131, 153, 201
Nesbit, J. W., 117
New Hampshire troops: 5th Infantry, 129; 12th Infantry, 116, 125, 129
New Jersey troops: 12th Infantry, 9, 10, 20, 23, 28, 29, 122–23, 205; 13th Infantry, 115; 15th Infantry, 116, 129
New York City draft riots, 41
New York troops: B, 1st Artillery, 9; 1st Battery, 101, 119; 11th Battery, 121; 39th Infantry, 9; 40th Infantry, 126; 42nd Infantry, 9, 18, 29; 44th Infantry, 119; 57th Infantry, 125; 59th Infantry, 9, 13, 17, 217 (n. 12); 80th Infantry, 9, 124, 179; 82nd Infantry, 9, 26; 83rd Infantry, 17; 95th Infantry, 118; 108th Infantry, 9, 17, 19, 120; 111th Infantry, 9, 118, 120, 122, 190; 125th Infantry, 9, 20, 116, 123, 129; 126th Infantry, 9, 23, 115, 120–21, 122, 123; 136th Infantry, 125; 145th

Infantry, 129; 146th Infantry, 69–70; 147th Infantry, 127; 154th Infantry, 127
Nickerson, Pvt. Mark, 118–19
North Carolina: views on Pickett's Charge, 4, 60, 76, 132–38, 172, 196–98, 200
North Carolina Historical and Literary Society, 152, 171
North Carolina troops: Charlotte Artillery, 17; 2nd Infantry, 32; 7th Infantry, 8, 135–36, 149; 11th Infantry, 8, 19, 35, 60, 149–50, 160; 13th Infantry, 8; 16th Infantry, 8, 29; 18th Infantry, 8, 149, 150; 22nd Infantry, 8; 26th Infantry, 8, 13, 60, 136, 142, 153, 200, 209, 210, 246 (n. 94); 27th Infantry, 50; 28th Infantry, 8, 150; 33rd Infantry, 8, 149; 34th Infantry, 8, 15, 60, 136, 171; 37th Infantry, 8, 136, 149, 150; 38th Infantry, 8, 150; 47th Infantry, 8, 60, 133, 135, 149, 150; 52nd Infantry, 8, 35, 136, 168; 55th Infantry, 7, 150, 172
Norwood, Lt. Thomas, 136

O'Brien, Thomas, 193
Ohio troops: 8th Infantry, 9, 19, 23–24, 91, 120, 123, 181; 55th Infantry, 116; 73rd Infantry, 115
Olney, Sergeant, 197, 252 (n. 47)
Otey, Maj. Kirkwood, 53–54, 155–57, 159, 161, 163
Our Living and Our Dead (journal), 133, 134
Owen, Capt. Henry T., 35, 37, 89–90, 211
Owen, Brig. Gen. Joshua T., 99–101
Owen, William M., 90

Page, Thomas Nelson, 89, 174
Patch, Charles A., 173
Payne, Serano, 119
Peach Orchard, 5, 12, 143
Peel, Lt. William, 18, 23
Pender, Maj. Gen. W. Dorsey, 8

Pendleton, Brig. Gen. William N., 85

Pennsylvania National Guard, 112, 184, 202

Pennsylvania troops: 1st Cavalry, 125; 63rd Infantry, 130; 69th Infantry, 8, 13, 24, 25, 93, 99–101, 120, 181, 210; 71st Infantry, 8, 27–28, 93, 99, 101, 125, 192; 72nd Infantry, 8, 13, 26, 191; 90th Infantry, 119, 129; 106th Infantry, 8, 116, 193; 118th Infantry, 115; 131st Infantry, 128; 143rd Infantry, 9, 124; 148th Infantry, 28; 149th Infantry, 9, 117; 150th Infantry, 9; 151st Infantry, 9, 124, 179

Pettigrew, Brig. Gen. James Johnston, 7, 8, 60, 199

Pettigrew's brigade, 8, 59, 60, 64, 76, 133, 135, 142

Pettigrew's division: attack of, 18–19, 21, 23–24; accused of failure to support Pickett, 33–34, 54–57, 63–65, 66–67, 69; after the battle, 35–36, 147; ignored, 65, 66, 69, 117–18, 196, 208, 211; Bachelder on, 70, 179; Lee's friends on, 87; postwar views of Pickett's men on, 88–90, 160, 167–68, 171; Longstreet on, 91; postwar praise for, 131–53, 159, 163; Sallie Pickett on, 163, 186; Union veterans on, 197; modern historians on, 206

Petty, H. S., 102

Peyton, Maj. Charles S., 18, 20, 27, 157

Philadelphia Brigade, 8, 13, 48, 93, 95, 121–22, 190

Philadelphia Brigade Association, 93–103, 105–7, 183, 193

Phillippoteaux, Paul, 72, 202, 210

Phillips, Capt. C. A., 17

Phillips, James J., 32–33

Pickett, Maj. Charles, 90, 93, 157, 159, 160

Pickett, Maj. Gen. George E.: at Gettysburg, 6, 8; in news accounts, 53, 54, 56, 57, 58; postwar descriptions of, 66, 69, 74, 114, 115; postwar activities of, 79, 86, 87; death and funeral of, 80–83; and Longstreet, 86, 90, 112,

162; and alleged drinking problem, 86, 155–59, 163, 230 (n. 11); debate over July 3 location of, 155–56, 160, 168–69, 197; postwar Virginia critics of, 155–59; missing report of, 159–60, 186, 248–39 (n. 52); postwar praise for, 160–64, 168–69, 195; wife's description of, 161–63, 186; in popular memory, 200, 204, 205, 210

Pickett, George (general's son), 97, 98, 102, 183

Pickett, LaSalle Corbell: and Gettysburg reunions, 97, 98, 101, 102, 103, 111, 183, 185–86; writings of, 160, 161–64, 185–86

Pickett and His Men (Sallie Pickett), 162–63, 185

Pickett Camp of the UCV, 154–55, 159, 197

Pickett or Pettigrew? (Bond), 140–42, 182

Pickett's Charge: bombardment before, 6, 17–18, 115–16; numbers in, 6, 65, 67, 116–17; attack formations in, 19–21, 24, 70; newspaper coverage of, 41–59; first postwar images of, 62–83; in artwork, 70–72, 200; Longstreet's enemies on, 85–88; as symbol of national reunion, 84–107, 188–98; Pickett's veterans on, 88–91, 161–71; in literature, 89, 174, 175, 204–5; as symbol for opponents of reunion, 108–30; as name for entire charge, 117, 165, 171, 208; as a misnomer, 118, 138–39, 141–42, 181, 183; religious symbolism of, 128–29; opposition to Virginia's version of, 131–53; souvenirs of, 200, 209, 211

Pickett's division: composition of, 6, 8, 34, 77; in 1863 news coverage, 49, 51–59, 63–64; in immediate postwar accounts, 66–69, 72–74, 76–81; Virginia veterans' views of, 88–91, 164–70; Northern praise for, 99–101, 113, 118–19; Northern critics of, 119; Southern critics of, 131, 133–53 passim

Pickett's Division Association, 93–98, 111, 157, 183

Pickett's Men, A Fragment of War History (Harrison), 76–78, 187

Pierce, Capt. J. V., 157

Plummer, Sgt. John, 7, 25–26

Poague, Col. William T., 158

Pollard, Edward A., 64, 73, 133, 141, 142, 226 (n. 7)

Pollock, Capt. Thomas G., 78

Posey's brigade, 65, 117

Price, Col. Edward, 129

"Private, A" (correspondent), 59–60

Proffitt, Pvt. W. H., 31

Purifoy, John, 201–2

Railroad Cut, 8, 127, 146

Rea, J. S., 49

Reams Station, battle of, 152

Reenactments, 192–94, 203, 208–9

Reeve, Edward Payson, 95, 98, 104

Reid, Dick, 144–45, 240 (n. 44)

Reid, Raymond J., 36

Reid, W. D., 145–46

Reid, Whitelaw, 40, 42, 43, 46–47, 49, 67

"Repulse of Longstreet's Assault, The" (painting), 70

Reunions, 91–92, 164, 183; in 1887, at Gettysburg, 97–103, 108, 109, 110, 156, 208; in 1888, at Gettysburg, 99, 108, 109–13; in 1888, at Richmond, 103–7, 113–14; in 1913, at Gettysburg, 4, 184–85, 188–98; in 1938, at Gettysburg, 202; in 1963, at Gettysburg, 207–9; in 1988, at Gettysburg, 209

Reynolds, Maj. Gen. John F., 127

Rhode Island troops: A, 1st Artillery, 9, 23, 252 (n. 47); B, 1st Artillery, 9

Rhodes, James Ford, 173

Rice, Col. Edmund, 91

Richardson, Major, 123

Ridpath, John Clark, 173

Rietti, J. C., 146

Robbins, Maj. William McK., 150–51, 182–83

Robertson, Brig. Gen. Felix H., 188

Robinson, Lt. S. S., 10

Rocco, Keith, 210

Rockwell, J. L., 193

Rorty, Capt. James McK., 9, 43

Ross, FitzGerald, 226 (n. 5)

Ross, Pvt. James Eastin, 35

Ross, Pvt. William Daniel, 35

Rosser, Brig. Gen. Thomas, 158, 170

Rothermel, Peter F., 70–71, 210

Royster, Lt. Iowa M., 149

St. Nicholas (children's magazine), 140–41, 149

San Juan Island, 58, 162, 171

Satterfield, Capt. E. Fletcher, 150, 172

Savage, Douglas, 205

Sawyer, Lt. Col. Franklin, 19

Scales, Brig. Gen. Alfred M., 8, 137

Scales's brigade, 117, 135, 140, 209

Scheibert, Justus, 226 (n. 5)

Scott, Col. R. Taylor, 104

Scott, Gen. Winfield, 50, 118

Second Manassas, battle of, 42, 57

Sefton, James, 207

Seven Days Battles, 48, 60, 225 (n. 94)

Shaara, Michael, 205, 211

Sheen, Martin, 211

Shepard, Lt. Col. S. J., 172

Shepherd, Henry E., 201

Sherman, Gen. William T., 71

Sherrill, Col. Eliakim, 9, 91, 199

Sherwood, Herbert Francis, 196

Shiloh, battle of, 202

Shotwell, Randolph, 134–35

Sickles, Maj. Gen. Daniel A., 108–9, 112, 126, 182, 189, 209

Singmaster, Elsie, 175

Skimin, Robert, 205

Smith, A. C., 191–92

Smith, J. B., 139–40

Smith, Stephens C., 32

Smith, Lt. William, 29

Smith, Maj. Gen. William F., 101

Smyth, Col. Thomas A., 9, 23, 139, 199

Snow, William Parker, 66

Society of the Army of the Potomac, 96

Sorrel, Col. G. Moxley, 170
Southern Guards, 164
Southern Historical Society, 84–88, 132–33, 135, 143
Southern Historical Society Papers (journal), 201, 206; shut out Pickett's men, 85, 87–88, 89; reopened to Pickett's men, 147, 148, 159, 165, 166
Spangler farm, 20, 70, 102
Spangler Spring and Meadow, 6, 16, 115
Stackpole, E. J., 208
Stannard, Brig. Gen. George J., 9–10, 20, 21, 70. *See also* Vermont troops: Second Vermont Brigade
Steele, Lt. Col. Amos, 25
Stephens, Alexander, 74
Steuart, Brig. Gen. George H., 168
Stewart, George R., 4, 207
Stiles, Robert, 81–82
Stine, J. H., 160, 161
Stokes, Maj. Robert, 193
Stone, Col. Roy, 9
Stonewall Brigade, 78, 199
Stuart, Maj. Gen. J. E. B., 75, 85, 164, 167, 253 (n. 53)
Suffolk, seige of, 157
Swallow, William H., 138–39
Swinton, William, 67, 85, 133
Symington, Capt. W. Stuart, 160

"T" (correspondent), 56–57
Tacitus, 119
Taft, William H., 184
Tanner, "Corporal" James, 96, 99
Tate, Allen, 208, 209–10
Taylor, Lt. W. B., 19, 35
Taylor, Col. Walter H., 80, 85, 135, 136
Tener, Gov. John, 184
Tennessee: views on Pickett's Charge, 4, 138–40, 143–45
Tennessee troops: 1st Infantry, 7, 29, 143–44; 7th Infantry, 7, 144, 145; 14th Infantry, 7, 29, 140, 145, 206
Terry, Col. William R., 93
Texas Brigade, 155, 188
Thelen, David, 2

Thermopylae, battle of, 46, 98, 110, 141, 155
Thomas's brigade, 117, 150, 179
Thompson, Will Henry, 113
Tibbin, I. E., 192
Toombs's brigade, 144
"T. P." (correspondent), 54
Trimble, Maj. Gen. Isaac R., 8, 87, 117, 133–34, 199
Trimble's division: attack of, 19, 23–24; after the charge, 35–36; ignored, 60, 65, 66, 69, 117–18, 196, 208, 211; Longstreet on, 91; praise for, 131–53, 163; Bachelder on, 179; Sallie Pickett on, 186; modern historians on, 206
Troiani, Don, 210
Trowbridge, L. S., 126
Tucker, Glenn, 206–7
Turner, Ted, 211
Turney, Capt. J. B., 143–44
Turpin, William H., 192
Tuttle, R. M., 246 (n. 94)

United Confederate Veterans, 143, 146, 168, 185
United States Army War College, 202, 209
United States Marine Corps, 203
United States Military Academy. *See* West Point
United States Regulars: I, 1st U.S. Artillery (Woodruff), 9, 121; A, 4th U.S. Artillery (Cushing), 9, 25, 130, 166; at reunions, 112, 184, 188
United States War Department, 96–97, 181–82
"Unus" (correspondent), 54

Van Alen, James, 208
Van Auken, Sheldon, 174
Vance, Gov. Zebulon, 60, 132
VandeGraff, Lt. Col. A. S., 31
Vanderslice, John M., 247 (n. 20)
Venable, Lt. Col. Charles, 159, 167
Vermont troops: 13th Infantry, 9, 20, 21, 27; 14th Infantry, 9, 21, 27; 16th Infantry, 10, 20, 27, 29; Second Ver-

mont Brigade, 9–10, 20–21, 27, 47, 65, 92, 115, 116, 124, 142, 158, 168, 167

Vick, Capt. J. W., 136

Vicksburg, Miss., seige of, 41

Virginia: views of Pickett's Charge, 4, 53–58, 73–80, 88–89, 161–71, 200

Virginia Historical Committee, 173–74

Virginia Military Institute, 78, 83, 205

Virginia troops: 1st Infantry, 6, 53, 82–83, 88, 165, 166, 169; 3rd Infantry, 6, 165; 7th Infantry, 6, 26, 88; 8th Infantry, 6, 157, 158; 9th Infantry, 6, 32, 101, 155, 165, 240 (n. 37); 10th Infantry, 12; 11th Infantry, 6, 27, 53, 90, 155–56, 171, 187; 14th Infantry, 6, 11, 111, 159, 166; 18th Infantry, 6, 35, 36, 80, 88, 89, 166; 19th Infantry, 4, 6, 18, 20–21, 34, 78; 22nd Infantry Bn, 8, 15; 24th Infantry, 6, 21, 27, 93, 192; 28th Infantry, 6, 190, 192, 193, 208; 38th Infantry, 6, 34, 240 (n. 37); 40th Infantry, 8; 47th Infantry, 8; 53rd Infantry, 6, 165, 192; 55th Infantry, 8; 56th Infantry, 6, 183, 191; 57th Infantry, 6, 18, 31, 34, 35, 166, 193; Dearing's battalion, 93–94, 105; Parker's battery, 88; Pegram's Artillery Battalion, 104; Richmond Howitzers, 82–83, 104; Richmond Light Infantry Blues, 104

Wagram, battle of, 50, 65, 119

Walker, C. Irvine, 185, 195

Walker, Francis A., 121, 237 (n. 74)

Walker, James (painter), 70, 71, 141

Walker, Sgt. James H., 155

Ward, Surgeon B. F., 146

Warfield, E. D., 203–4

Waterloo, battle of, 40, 46, 65, 115, 130, 155, 196

Webb, Brig. Gen. Alexander S., 199; in 1863, 3, 24, 25, 26, 30, 45; after the war, 70, 71, 103, 123

Wells, Sgt. W. W., 159

Weston, Maj. J. A., 149

West Point, 58, 81, 202

Wheatfield, the, 125, 129

Wheeler, Joseph, 182

White, Pvt. R. P., 35

Wiggins, Octavius, 149, 150

Wilcox, Brig. Gen. Cadmus M., 142, 148, 163

Wilcox's brigade, 8, 27, 36, 54, 56, 59, 65, 142, 157, 168, 179, 186, 246 (n. 99); ignored, 64, 196

Wilderness, battle of the, 70, 92, 123, 202

Wilkeson, Samuel, 42, 44–46, 48–49, 195

Will, George, 212

Willard, Col. George L., 9

Williams, Brig. Gen. Alpheus S., 16

Williams, Ben Ames, 205

Williams, Col. Lewis B., 169

Wilson, Woodrow, 190

Wingfield, Pvt. "Monk," 167–68

Wisconsin Historical Commission, 122

Wisconsin troops: 3rd Infantry, 118

Wise, Capt. George D., 81, 82

Wise, John S., 158

Wood, Gen. James, 125

Wood, Lt. W. W., 90, 166

Woodruff, Lt. George A., 9, 43, 121

Woodward, C. Vann, 12

Wright, Brig. Gen. Ambrose R., 5, 8, 54

Wright's brigade, 56, 57, 65, 117

Young, Capt. J. J., 13

Young, Capt. Louis G., 64

Ziegler's Grove, 122, 147, 150, 209